WHATEVER HAPPENED TO THE G⦿⦿D SISTERS?

WHATEVER HAPPENED
TO THE **G∞D**

SISTERS?

A Collection
of Real Life
Stories

Edited by:
KATHLEEN W. FITZGERALD, PH.D
CLAIRE BREAULT, MA.

WHALES' TALE
P · R · E · S · S

160 Wildwood
Lake Forest, Illinois 60045

Published by Whales' Tale Press
160 Wildwood, Lake Forest, Illinois 60045, (708) 295-2350

Printed in the United States of America.

Library of Congress Catalogue Number: 92-096880

ISBN 1-882195-00-0

The publisher gratefully acknowledges the use of "Spirit Journey: Ebb and Flow" by Rita Bresnahan from *A Time to Weep, A Time to Sing* edited by Mary Jo Meadow and Carole A. Rayburn, 1985. Reprinted by permission of Harper-Collins Publishers, Inc.

Photographs used in this book are taken from family albums and frequently show age and wearing. It was the decision of the editor to use these photographs as opposed to using current professional poses to better capture the flavor of the stories.

10% of the profits from *Whatever Happened to the Good Sisters?* will be donat-ed to the Retirement Fund for Religious.

Cover Illustration by Kathleen Plunkett Katz

This book is dedicated to our beloved brother,
Angelo, who opened our windows

Acknowledgments

From Claire:

For all my friends who have patiently listened to me babble endlessly about this book throughout the process.

For those who have helped in the close-reading process.

For Kathleen, for endless patience with my perceptions and philosophies, and for her spirit of delight.

For the gift of sharing in the lives of the women who have written this book.

For all the "Good Sisters" in my life who have helped me shape it to the joyous reality that it is.

From Kathleen:

To Claire who midwifed our Love Child.

To Mary Gene Kinney, B.V.M. and Lettie Close, B.V.M., InterCongregational Addictions Program, Oak Park, Illinois.

To Cynthia Percak Infantino, M.S., Research Librarian, Lake Forest Public Library.

To Eleanore Kilcoyne for her careful and loving proof-reading of the manuscript.

To Chris Harnesk who professionally and caringly put it all together.

To Joan Hall who kept us organized and non-crazy.

Editor's Caveat

A caveat is, by definition, a caution or warning. It is not an apology but can frequently be understood as an explanation or clarification. It is in this sense that these words are written.

First, *Whatever Happened to the Good Sisters*, is not a "Kiss and Tell" book. Readers looking for the sensational, the exploitative will be terribly disappointed. Nor is it a sort of verbal pablum, glossing over reality. It is simply truth. All lives, religious or secular, have times of happiness, times of sadness, times of anger, times of healing. These women have told the truth of their lives.

We have made a few editorial decisions. They were not made out of ignorance or cowardice, but out of sensitivity to the highly unique philosophies of our writers. We have had enough of conformity in our lives. Therefore, the reader may become aware of a few inconsistencies. For example, we have respected the individual's choice of a pronoun referent for God, and the capitalization or non-capitalization of that pronoun. We have also respected that individual's choice of inclusive or non-inclusive language.

An obvious deviation from standard editorial policy is the size of the book. Prudence would have dictated a volume one-half the size, but every word in these stories needs to be there. The book, therefore, is almost as big as the hearts of the women who wrote it.

We already participate the need for a second volume. We therefore invite all women who have shared this very unique journey to contribute their own stories. Editorial guidelines are available from Whales' Tale Press for the small investment of a self-addressed, stamped envelope.

God's blessings on us all.

Contents

Introduction

Whatever Happened
To The Good Sisters?

According to the Tri-Conference Retirement Office there are 603 women's congregations in the United States. Membership in these congregations totals 92,857. The median age is sixty-six for active sisters, and sixty-four for contemplatives. Only eight of these communities have a membership of over a thousand; 342 communities have less than a hundred members.

There was a time, in the 40's and 50's, when bumper crops of young women entered religious life each year. That phenomenon no longer happens. A combination of factors, including the post-Vatican II exodus, normal attrition, and different concepts of dedication and service have cut memberships in women's congregations by far more than half. Huge novitiate buildings stand empty; young — and not so young — women seeking vowed religious life spend a time in the field, and then frequently go to a common novitiate.

Why did — and do — women seek religious life? Why, having lived that life for years, did and do some of them leave?

In the United States, during those prime decades and during even earlier times, young women sought religious life for a variety of reasons. Some of these reasons were overt and simple: a pull towards God; a desire to serve; a desire to be holy. Other reasons, frequently not conscious, stemmed from a need to belong, a need to feel safe, a need to run away from complexities not dreamed of, nor understood. In our fairly free society there was no need to use religious life as a means of societal avoidance described by Marta Danylewycz in *Taking the Veil: An Alternative to Marriage, Motherhood, and Spinsterhood in Quebec, 1840 - 1920.* More often than not the motive for "entering the convent" was pure and uncomplicated, just as the young women themselves were products of a more innocent and uncomplicated time.

And so enter they did. And these girls, young women, have contributed thousands of years of dedicated service to our society. The Good Sisters have been educators, role models, stand-by mothers, nurses, visible signs of Christ's own charity among our poor: the economically poor, the emotionally poor, the valueless poor, all the poor which we have with us always.

Somewhere along the way the misjudgments, the personal problems of some of the hundreds of thousands of good sisters became the focal point of memory. The memories of the kindnesses and love given by these women religious were overshadowed, and soon the good sister was forgotten; tales of the tyrant took her place in our church lore. Rita Bresnahan, in a side piece to the story which appears in this book, states that one of the difficulties in revealing her history as a sister was that it often "sparked an angry tirade about Catholic schools or about mistreatment experienced at the hands of nuns." She had to struggle with the processing of that anger, and often felt "personally attacked," not knowing how to reconcile the "not-always-the-perfect-nun memories in myself that were triggered at those times."

Father John Banahan of Chicago, in describing the anger he feels when people tell horror stories about being abused by nuns in elementary school, says:

> My defense of my teachers does not mean that the system did not break down every so often. Certain people become teachers who don't know how to teach or control a class. Sometimes they turn mean. Sometimes they are nuns! They are the exception and often (not always) they can be checked by the safeguards within the system. This I know! Torquemada was never a Mistress of Novices. Nuns were never trained to be mean.

Undoubtedly, and this is easily seen in the reading of the stories in this book, many women were drawn to religious life only to discover at some point that this way of life was wrong for them. That discovery might have stemmed from hurt and disillusionment; it might just as easily come from self-revelation and personal development. Whatever the cause, the result was the massive exodus mentioned before. However, that massive departure can never be treated as a sign in itself.

Each departure was the decision of one unique person, in one unique set of circumstances. One can judge neither the individual nor the system.

Father Banahan states in a letter:

> Certainly people will grouse about "vocation" no longer being a life long commitment. But I think we have a broader vocation to use the life we have to its best advantage. If switching our dedication to various causes or people serves that end, then we should be free to switch. Life is too valuable not to be used by us.

The women who have told their stories here are remarkable examples of using life to its best advantage. Some have chosen to live out their lives in a recognized, vowed way of serving God by service to others. Some have chosen another way to serve. Each woman has her own charism. And, as Kristin Neufeld noted in her story, the answer to "Whatever Happened to the Good Sisters?" is best answered with the simple statement: "They got better."

Over thirty religious communities are represented in this book. Fifty-six women have contributed over 1600 years of vowed service. That fact alone is stunning. It is even more stunning to add the continued years of ministry given by the women who chose to live their lives in another way than that of the recognized religious sister. Hundreds of thousands of lives have been touched, changed by all these women.

Rarely does material edited so profoundly touch the heart of an editor as these stories have touched me.

For a few short months I have been intimately involved with the lives of over fifty great women. I have rejoiced with them, praised with them, laughed with them, wept with them. I have experienced great pain with them, and great healing. In reading what they have had to say, in corresponding with them, talking with them, I have been taught new lessons about God and God's presence in our lives.

Thank you, good sisters.

Claire
August 1992

Prologue

"A people without history is like wind on the buffalo grass".
—*Sioux proverb*

There is an ancient tradition in monastic life, wherein a bell would ring at the appointed time and the world within the monastery became instantly silent. *Silentium Magnum*: the grand, holy, and profound silence. To break this silence was a major infraction of the Holy Rule and in some instances, we risked being sent home if we broke silence.

Silence allowed us the luxury of not having to talk, but of turning our thoughts and attention to that world within, that very temple of the Holy Spirit that inhabited our deepest selves and there we could dwell, freed from the worries and obligations of our external tasks.

We eased back into the world of words and work in the morning after mass as we prepared for the day's tasks. Sometimes it was jarring to come out of the silence; sometimes it was a relief. During our retreats when silence was maintained for twenty-four hours for eight straight days, to come out of the silence was almost frightening and we would begin to experience our voices in squeaks and rasps, almost like the thirteen-year-old boy who wakes one morning with the voice of a man.

Morning has broken and the retreat has been long over, but still our lips form no words. Daily we prayed, "Thou, O Lord, shall open my lips, and my mouth shall declare Thy praise." But our lips have remained tightly closed and our mouths have shared no history. Perhaps the Sioux would hear wind through the buffalo grass.

Or perhaps we have not been ready to speak. Or that we thought we had nothing to say. A Mercy nun, celebrating her diamond jubilee, wrote, "My life history is much too simple, only four to five pages of double-space typing ... there have not been any extraordinary events ... I have had a rich religious experience which helped me to persevere". Her widowed sister had seen her nun-sister's life as full and wonderful and worthy of telling; the nun had seen it as "too simple".

1

Perhaps we thought it wasn't right for us to speak. Our idle words would be used against us.

Or that we would be disloyal. What happens within these four walls stays here, we had heard at home. Many of us had come from homes that held deep and painful secrets that we never shared with our closest friends. We knew well how to keep secrets. Our secrets made us sick.

Or that the less said the better. Were we confused and even shamed by the strange life we led? We kept the details from our parents and brothers and sisters and only showed them the good parts. So many women said to us, "I'd love to write my story and I need to write my story, but no one here knows that I was a nun. I can't tell them." If we had been in the Peace Corps., would we be so private? Would we not be proud? Why the silence? Why the shame? What did we do wrong?

Or that as women, we just didn't know how or that it was somehow unladylike to speak out for ourselves, that we ought to let men tell our stories because they did it so much better. The bishops presently have been engaged in doing a pastoral letter on us. We'll just let them tell us who we are because we've always let men tell us who we are.

Men have told our stories and they have come up with such caricatures as: *Nunsense; Do Patent Leather Shoes Reflect Up?; Agnes of God; Sister Act; Sister Mary Ignatia Explains It all To You; Handy Dandy; Bicicletta.* And we smile and nod and do our teaberry shuffle and inside we die a little bit more as the wind howls through the buffalo grass.

It is a terrible thing to be storyless. It is to be without nouns and verbs, without sentences and paragraphs, without chapters and volumes. It is to be without history, without heroes or heroines, without spirit, without images or narrative or myth. It is to have left a path of breadcrumbs in the forest.

So we allow bishops and playwrights and comics to tell our story, as if all our mirrors are cracked or it is indecent for us to give a mighty roar across the great divide and wait with ecstasy for our voices to come hurling back at us.

Swallowing our stories makes us sick and opens the doors for lies. The order Claire and I were in had as its motto: Truth. That means to stand up and be counted, not to let others speak for us when we must open our own lips and declare the truth of our lives. Bishops and comics do not have that right.

2

One of the greatest spiritual phenomena that the world has ever seen is the Twelve Step recovery programs. Day after day, year after year, in church basements and kitchens, in meeting rooms and halls throughout the land, wounded people tell their story.

And in the telling, comes the healing; in the telling, goes the shame; in the telling, community is born.

The Big Book, as it is affectionately known in recovery groups, has given us the model for telling our stories. Recovering people have written down what it was like, what happened, and what it is like today. The unvarnished beauty of Truth.

This is simply what the fifty-six women in this book have done: we have shared the unvarnished truth of what it meant to live a hidden, mysterious, misunderstood life that the world will never again see.

This book is not about artistry, although the stories are beautifully written. Nor is it about revenge nor justification nor sensationalism. It is simply about the beauty of Truth as a group of women have found voice to articulate their lives and are no longer content to hide these most precious stories under the musty, murky bushel of fear and secrecy.

In Washington, D.C., at the end of the Mall is the breath-taking, glistening white Lincoln Memorial. And at its feet lies the arched, black-marble memorial to the Vietnam veterans with gifts of wilted roses, books, love letters, baby shoes, and mothers' prayers lying at its base. This memorial is about the shame and secrets of a nasty war that our country knows only too well. It is also about healing and reconciliation and a forgiveness that we are only now learning about.

Perhaps one day we shall have a beautiful memorial in white and gold and green with the names of the thousands and thousands of women who generously, perhaps impulsively, but always silently gave their lives to God's holy church and to God's holy people.

Today as the old brick convents grow ever-more empty and long-dressed women no longer pull their black shawls tightly across their shoulders and make their way across the icy playgrounds to the sixty-five squirmy kids waiting for Sister to teach them about spelling and math and God, let us take time to remember, for we may forget a most precious treasure that the church and the world will never again see.

Kathleen
August 1992

MATINS

"Thou, O Lord,
Shall open my lips.
And my tongue shall
Announce Thy Praise.
And the words of my mouth
Shall be such as may please;
And the meditation of my heart
Always in Thy sight."
—*Psalm 18*

Marlene Halpin
Dominican

Director, Ministry Formation, Nine County Diocesan Program

Associate Director, Permanent Diaconate Program, Kalamazoo

Author

Bachelor of Arts, English, St. John's University, New York

Master of Arts, Philosophy/Ethics, The Catholic University of America, Washington, D.C.

Doctor of Philosophy, Metaphysics, The Catholic University of America, Washington, D.C.

Marlene lives in an apartment far from her official convent assignment, but maintains close contact with her community by spending a summer month "at home," attending workshops and retreats, and having "one vote in *everything* votable, reading *everything* sent, responding to *everything* requested." She has a special interest in photography, and kids, with an exclamation point. Beyond the now? "I don't think much about it — things always happen."

Marlene Halpin

The Good Sisters:
What Happened?

Forty-some years ago, when first I entered my community, I was so sure about what it was like, and what it would be like, for the rest of my life. I would be a Dominican Sister and I would teach elementary school, on Long Island, for the rest of my life. That was just fine with me. More than content with it, I was thrilled and grateful to be part of it.

There was a certain mind-set, an attitude, about religious life that pervaded the parish and school and neighborhood. Being a priest or nun was the "which of which there was no whicher." Fortunate the parent whose child was "called". Honor was due: God surely smiled on such a family with a great smile. Mystery and faith, humility and gladness, swirled together at the notion of having a priest or a nun in the family. (Maybe some relief, too. A good neighbor lady said to my mother: "You're so lucky with your daughter! Now you don't have to tell her the facts of life!")

Priests and nuns were held in unquestioned high esteem. "Father said ... " lent authority to a statement. And prestige, too, for the speaker had been spoken to by Father. When a child reported, "Sister said ..." that was the living end to any discussion. On the other hand, if "Sister said ... " were quoted by a parent, the child had no recourse.

Such was the attitude. At that time, in that place, it was unquestioned and for the most part served us well. We respected and esteemed our priests, generally not knowing them well in our large city parishes, but absorbing their idiosyncrasies peaceably. We loved our Sisters, I still think, with good reason. They were good to us.

Recently my elementary school class had a reunion. More than forty of us were gathered that evening. Much of the talk centered on fond memories of the Sisters. Fourteen of our sixteen teachers were Sisters - we took that for granted then.

9

The now gray-haired choir boys remember playing tag among the laundry lines in the convent basement, being chased by the Sisters who were giggling as much as they. What surprised me was how aware my former class-mates were of how much the Sisters helped each other help the children. It was common knowledge that when a Sister got "promoted" to another grade, the one who had it previously mentored her. We watched that in operation and loved it.

That was from the outside. Then I entered the community and began to know it from the inside. Some of the mysteries began to become clear. The first involved the habit. Dominican habits are white. Washable. Good smelling. As a child I always loved the ways the Sisters smelled. As a postulant I learned what made the smell: Fels Naphtha brown soap, an entire bar of which was required to scrub clean the white, floor-length hems and the long sleeves.

The mind-set, the attitude which pervaded parish and school and neighborhood, had its twin in the novitiate. Unspoken was the assumption: "They know what it takes to be a nun. They will teach us to be holy. They know God's will and will show us how to know it, too. If this is what it takes, we'll do it." We bought the package. There were the rules, the *horarium*, the close control of every waking moment and how it was to be lived.

Much of it seemed peculiar, but that was God's will. So we learned to walk quietly; to be "convent clean" at all times; to have no access to phone or radio; to be quite restricted with mail and visits (or any contact with the *world*); to say the rosary aloud while peeling vegetables (and praying faster when there were funeral guests expected and more vegetables than usual needing peeling); never to miss a community exercise — or even to be late; to attend to the ubiquitous permissions and penances. And for me, after several disastrous episodes, to keep my questions unasked.

If there was fear in the novitiate, it was fear of "being sent home", of not being accepted by the community to be a living part of it. And the joy was the joy of the day of being clothed in the habit, with all that that meant, and the joy of *vowing* to God all that one is or could be, and of having one's vows accepted by the Church through a loved community. It was called, then, being "the Bride of Christ," "the Spouse of Christ." Behind the terminology is the reality: here is expressed the life-long

10

commitment of being called and of answering; of covenant and of consecration; of something awesome and holy and utterly beyond one's own personal self, but one's personal and whole self being utterly and always immersed in it.

Life is lived, simultaneously, on a multitude of levels.

With the awe and wonder and delight of brand new vows we were sent forth to a mission. Virtually all of us were sent to teach. It was enough that the superior said so. It was up to us to make good on it. Did I know how to teach? No. Out of some consideration of my being new, I was given the smallest class in the school, some sixty fourth graders in a neighborhood on the Brooklyn-Queens border in New York City. Did I make a mess of it? I sure did. .

Even then, at the age of nineteen, I knew I had not been prepared to handle those children. But even then I had no fear that the resources would be there - principally, the other Sisters. The older (they had to have been in their twenties, some even in their thirties!) Sisters were *there*, every day after school, to listen and coach and help. We didn't use the word "mentor," but mentors they were. There was no question of giving up. We learned. Even now I correspond with the mother of one of my first students. She played the piano for school events. Today, at age eighty-one she writes: "You were so very young ... we were happy at St. Thomas..."

Sputnik.
For want of another peg, Sputnik will do.
Russia was ahead of us!
Our math and science were not on a par.
We had to gear up curriculum. Teachers had to go back to school and learn new math, more science.

Teacher (and other professional) certification became something a once-immigrant church could no longer ignore. The community, poor as we were (and are), had been somewhat casual about higher education; that could no longer be permitted.

In teaching we moved from heavily deductive (this is the rule — now apply it) to heavily inductive (gather information and *think*). In math and science that was praiseworthy. In *religion?* I remember well the utter horror and consternation when students began to gather information, experience and to *think* and to *question* matters of *religion*. What fun! Some of us laughed a lot, too. And got wonderfully excited! It was exhilarating and distressing.

Korea and Vietnam. In a real way they were a watershed for our country. For the first time in our history our people, as a people, said: "This is not right." No longer was it: "My country right or wrong." There was just too much wrong. These conflicts forced us into growing up, into thinking and being critical in a way new for us.

When the people of a country become more mature, more responsible in thinking, when the people of a country think more and more independently for themselves, attitudes and mind-sets change. But thinking hardly is isolated. It affected family life, social and sexual mores, religious life. It was inevitable. New members of the community brought these attitudes and mind-sets with them. They made a difference.

And then there was that wonderful, grace-filled man named John, who went about opening windows. Our Pope John XXIII was beloved of many people. When he died I was in Washington, D. C. A woman stopped me on the street and said, "I'm not a Catholic. But I want to tell you that I'm sorry your Father died." Well, our "Father John" plays a large part in "what happened to the Good Sisters." Maybe he never thought of it that way. My guess is, if he did, he would chuckle that chuckle of his.

Things were happening in the educational world of which I was a part. The changes were not just curriculum and methods of teaching. Professional standards for certification and accreditation were required and the requirement enforced.

Things were happening in the church world of which I was a part. Not just Vatican II in general, but that part of it - *Perfectae Caritas* - which required us to look at our Rules and Constitutions in the light of Scripture and the spirit of our founder. It was as if our great good religious life ship had acquired a large load of barnacles. We hadn't noticed. It was time to scrape them off.

"Any rule which does not add to the holiness of the community in its members is a nail in the coffin of the community." That's what was said to us by the President of the Canon Law Society, Father Paul Boyle. That was a really practical guide to reviewing our Constitutions. Put together with a re-studying of our founder, attending more to original sources rather than to some of the pious but perhaps not too authentic biographies, Scripture, the other Vatican II documents (particularly the one which urged us to attend to the "signs of the times"), we re-wrote the documents which governed our lives. And they were approved: first by our community members, then by our larger Church.

That was the exciting and easy part.

Now we had to find out how to live it.

In living memory there were no precedents for much of what we had come to see was needed. We had no living role models. What we did have was a great deal of disagreement. Bursts of energy. Some chaos. Strong opinions. Sporadic forays into "now permitted" areas. *Experimentation* was the word. There was some foolishness. There was a dawning consciousness that we women in our 30's and 40's and 50's really didn't know much about some very ordinary and practical things such as appropriate personal grooming and dress if not wearing that very concealing habit, or managing money well in a quite changed economy.

There are the courageous among us. Courage takes many roads. Some are courageous in venturing out into the new and as yet unseen ways. Some are courageous in holding the fort against newly prevailing opinion. We have plenty of both among us.

Perhaps one of the most woeful murmurs was: "This is not the community I entered." Well, was it? Whichever way the question was answered, the heart-ache, the doubts and maybe the despairs behind it, were real. Much of what we had been taught, which we had heartily embraced and internalized, which we thought to be eternal and unchanging, we found going or gone. How were we to think? What were we to think? Some among us were not accustomed even to thinking in these categories. Not only had it not been encouraged, it had been utterly unacceptable before. Now it became almost a matter of survival.

Such critical thinking about our lives, about the way we were to live our lives, naturally moved further. Unasked questions could no longer lie dormant. Some once unacceptable behaviors now were expected and seen to be good. Some hitherto unfaced doubts burst into consciousness. Some underdeveloped areas of adult life could no longer be ignored.

For the most part, I think, our sisters loved God and God's people more than ever. For many (if not most among us) there was a serious question: Is this the way God is calling me, now, to love and to serve?

For some among us, the integrity at the core of our being, said: "No." Our sisters, many of them, left the community remaining our sisters, remaining faithful in love and in service to our much-loved God.

For some among us, the integrity at the core of our being, said: "Yes." We remain sisters vowed in community, remaining faithful in love and in service to our much-loved God. And many of our communities are learning to include and embrace other women as sisters, as part of our community. These women do not share our vowed commitment, but do share our commitment of love and service

Attending to Scripture, attending to the spirit of our founder, attending to the signs of the times, leaves us, in many practical ways, in ambiguity. These ambiguities are far from resolution. We cope in practical ways with the living out of our vows. But how changed that is!

It used to be that we had, in personal possession, absolutely no money. At travel time we were given the exact amount needed. When things were needed, we asked the superior, who (eventually, more or less, it all depended) supplied them. "A religious with a cent isn't worth a cent," was the prevailing opinion. If one forgot and kept mission money, or milk money, or candy money, in her possession overnight — ah, that was not a good thing.

Today, in many communities, Sisters are budgeted a certain amount of money for personal needs: clothing, toiletries, vacation, gifts, cultural events. How does this fit in with the vow of poverty? How is this income supplemented when inadequate? How does that supplementing fit in with the vow of poverty?

Friendships and relationships with people of both sexes, both in and out of the community, are common now. For decades — well, within living memory — that was not the ordinary way for the ordinary sister. A visit in the parlor (with the door open and the time restricted); perhaps a letter (censored by the superior in some communities); a phone call

14

(reported and perhaps questioned) did not permit the exercise of friendship as is far more common today.

We had to learn to do this well and appropriately. We learned unevenly. So our vow of chastity (celibacy) is lived differently. From my point of view, it is far more difficult, far more loving, and far better for and in ministry, and far more dangerous. But it seems to me that Jesus never said much about being safe. He did have something to say about " ... life, and life to the fullest."

Obedience? It used to be made manifest in a letter from the motherhouse for big things; in the words of the local superior for every-day things; in the Rule for all things. ("You keep the Rule and the Rule will keep you.") Generally we were assigned to a house and to a work without discussion. The order came. We went.

Consultation and discernment are more the order of these days. We get to ask, to talk it over, to discuss, to speak and to listen and to be listened to. It's more human; it's more sensible; it's more difficult; it's more truthful. It certainly is more demanding, holding in awareness both one's personal good and the common good, and discerning God's will. It lacks the sort of security one enjoyed. It brings us closer to Paul's fear and trembling in working out salvation.

On an everyday, practical level, the uncertainty includes such things even as housing (as assignments are no longer made by letter from the motherhouse), and ministry (job security is no longer a guarantee). These new freedoms carry responsibilities which, in turn, engender worries once unthought of. Is it good, in the sense of better? Probably. But the ways of coping and working it through are far from finished.

Perhaps one of the most telling changes among the things which happened affects community.

When "the good sisters" was a commonly used phrase for us, one thing which happened was that every head was in chapel at the appointed times. Every body was in the refectory for every meal. Every chair was occupied during the set recreation period every evening unless permission had been explicitly granted for an absence. Often, too, every community member had the same work schedule.

With attending to "the signs of the times" with more voice about professional, ministerial choices, the work schedules of local community members are quite different. So much is affected by this! Cooking and serving community meals, companionship at meals, gathering for community prayer time, offering each other companionship as an ordinary part of each day — each of these things becomes more and more difficult to manage.

Sisters have more communities than before: not just the local house, but the work community, social groups, and more opportunity to attend to birth family (including helping to care for elderly parents). What has happened to community life is drastic. And we aren't much different from what is happening in family life: single parent families, two income families, the host of varied commitments of family members. Families, too, find difficulty in being together regularly

What about prayer?

Community prayer was frequent, regular, expected. Private prayer was just that — private. Now community prayer is, for most active good sisters, very difficult to manage. Some of us work days; others, nights; some work week-days; others, week-ends. Our ministries require our being available when the people we serve are available. So community prayer becomes more an exception than a rule. Being "deregulated", being very busy and on-call, the ways (times and even places) for private prayer need more attention than ever. It's a challenge! Like all challenges, it is unevenly met.

Being "a good sister" today is — externally — quite different from The Good Sisters known in other decades. For one thing, we wouldn't even use the term! Its endearing quality is no longer with us; its controlling quality is not accepted. Internally, this might not be so.

As time went on, it became evident to me that I was not going to teach elementary school on Long Island for life.

Initially the difference came from my community. I was assigned to high school teaching, to college teaching, to college administration. Then the day came when they told me, in just about as many words, I was over-qualified for anything the community had and they (the descendants of the *they* who knew God's will for us and assured our being good sisters) confessed not knowing what to do with me. Fortunately that coincided with the evolving and acceptable ways of finding one's own ministry, one's own job.

So instead of teaching in community schools on Long Island, I taught in a seminary in Iowa; in universities in Illinois, Indiana and Colorado; in workshops in more than half of these United States and in several other countries; in diocesan programs far, far from home. Instead of living in community in convents, I've lived in community in rented houses, and alone in an apartment.

Community is as precious as ever, perhaps even more so, because it shaped and shapes me, because it is so very present in its physical absence. Community no longer means "every car in the garage and every head in chapel at 5.30 a.m. and p.m."; it does mean a group of like-committed women with whom I am dedicated to living out my life in a vowed commitment to God and God's people. The way we share our goods and services, our presence, is different. The reality is no different.

We found out, over and over, that those who taught us in those early days did what they knew best. Now we do as best we know how. We have changed the way of forming young, would-be members, not the reality of formation. We have changed the way we think we might discover God's will; the reality of knowing God and God's unconditional love for us, the reality of wanting, of longing, to do God's will has not changed. The way we understand and practice the vows has changed; the reality of wanting, of longing, to respond to God's call as fully, as completely as best we can, has not changed.

Probably all serious Christians today would be saying much the same thing about wanting, about longing, to live the Gospel values as fully as is each one's human possibility. And that is right.

For me that wanting, that longing, has to take the living form of a perpetually vowed commitment as a Dominican Sister. Many things have, in the course of our recent history, changed. Factors in society, in the world community, in the church, in the professional world, in ourselves, required change. Externally. But the deepest reality has not changed. The life-long commitment of being called and of answering, of covenant and of consecration, of something awesome and holy and utterly beyond one's own personal self, but one's personal and whole self being utterly and always immersed in it, remains. For me — and I say this with the same great gladness and awe and wonder that I did forty-some years ago — there is no other way.

May everyone be so blessed in the way of each life.

Virginia Unverzagt
Former Sister of Providence

Married, two children, one with special needs

High school teacher: Religious studies, math

Bachelor of Arts, Psychology and Math, St. Mary of the Woods

Master of Arts, Pastoral Theology, St. Mary of the Woods

Parish Ministries: Council, Archdiocesan delegate, Minister of Care, Providence

Virginia is enrolled in a Doctorate of Ministries program, and dreams of someday operating "a retreat center in Appalachia." In addition to tending to the needs of her two children and her "big rig" truck driver husband, she spends time as a volunteer for the Special Olympics, and in clogging!

Virginia Unverzagt

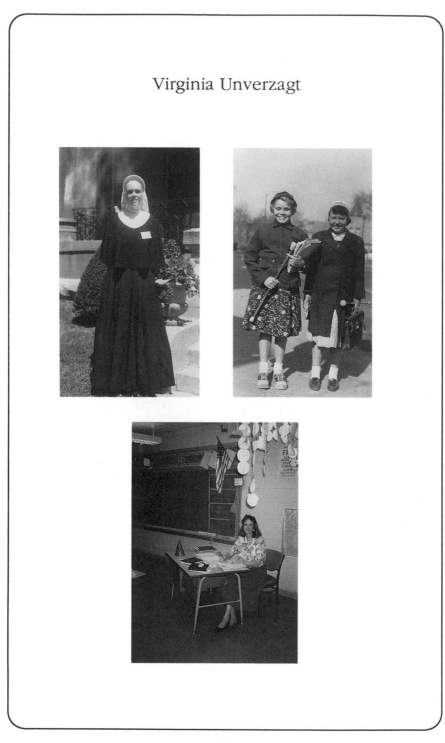

Well-Worn Shoes

There it is, still sewn into the corner of this sturdy, blue towel: *136*— my novitiate laundry number. As I stand folding linen in the laundry room of our home, my thoughts take me back- can it be over thirty years! Some people define their lives by the "hats" they wear. I'm definitely a product of my shoes.

My sweet enchantment with the life of a nun began in the 50's while I daily wore uniform-code saddle shoes to school. Those always-tied, black and white shoes symbolized my compliance and attachment to a home and Church of structure, dependability and constraint. With the obvious exception of my family, from age four to eighteen the constant presence in my life was nuns. Sister was there not only to teach me, but unknowingly and most powerfully as a role mode for my saddle shoe years. During grade school I never thought it odd that math problems involved the sum of the six precepts of the Church and the twelve fruits of the Holy Spirit. I never took exception to the fact that every social unit included David, Ann and Sister Mary. "See David. See Ann. Sister Mary sees David and Ann." Of course every child went to daily Mass, offered up pain for the pagan babies and made a May Altar for her house. Mine was a foil-covered saltine box with a statue of Mary and lilacs from the bush next door. I can still recall the smell of soap, coffee, bacon and toast coming through the convent doors at school. I can still feel the breeze of Sister passing me in an aisle, her serge habit brushing my cheek.

In high school Sister taught me to conjugate Latin verbs, to use the SQ3R method of study and to know the details of Church History. During these latter saddle shoe days the smells, sounds and classroom techniques of the nuns was not enough. I wanted to see behind the convent doors. I wanted to know for myself how to be holy. I wanted to see my hand coming through a serge sleeve.

21

I began to make scrap books of anything having to do with nuns. I hid the books under my mattress lest anyone in my family discover my collection. I had pictures from the newspaper of nuns at Riverview or at Wrigley Field. I gathered pamphlets from a vocation awareness expo at McCormick Place into my scrapbooks. I began to write letters to the vocation director at the motherhouse. Her replies went into the books, too. Almost daily I took them out and looked through them delightedly. My own sister had to pass through my room to hers and as she recalls, each time she interrupted my reverie I yelled at her, "Shut up, leave me alone." Her room was covered floor to ceiling with Beatle paraphernalia. Surely I was entitled to my few dog-eared treasured collections of nun-obelia.

The day I left home to enter the convent was then, and still is, one of the most thrilling of my life. I wore an old dress since it would never be seen again. My mom (who was then my age now, so I understand why) cried and cried and cried. When a woman entered the convent in the early 60's it was "forever". So like that dress I, too, was never to return. My sister, the Beatle-maniac, wouldn't wake up to say good-bye. My brothers didn't seem to care. My dad drove me the four and a half hours to central Indiana. When I said good-bye to him, I couldn't be sad— I was so excited. The novice assigned to my care directed me upstairs to my room where I changed into my postulant dress, black-boxy nun shoes and all.

It only took two weeks for me to severely sprain my ankle on those nun shoes. All I wanted to do was make it to Compline on time and it seemed like such an easy jump down the short flight of stairs. Even with the sprain I began to walk a path many faith-filled, brave women had set on before me. Led by scholarly, insightful women I was directed to Vatican II soil. In my nun shoes I walked miles to classes at the college, to serve food trays at the Infirmary, and to pray at the chapel. For seven years, known as Sister Roch, I wore my nun shoes. They never hurt my feet, caused a blister or led me astray. I cannot recall a single time that I didn't love being in the convent. After seven years' wearing my shoes became foot-formed. Almost too comfortable. Contemporaries of mine were wading through jungles in a place called Viet Nam. Others my age were marching in picket lines to protest at the Democratic Convention. My peers in college were being shot for taking a stand to control government involvement in the war. It was not a time for shoes that were overly comfortable — my shoes began to pinch my feet.

I liked the freedom of my sandals! In the 70's I walked into my adolescence and my rebellious years finally began. While other twenty-four-year-old women had gone through gradual stages of making mistakes with boys/men/life, I was studying in a library or teaching CCD to the rural poor. While young girls passed through adolescence to young adulthood by going to movies, to malls, to dances, I washed marble staircases, chanted the Divine Office and took vows of poverty, chastity and obedience. My sandals led me to a whirlwind of far-out 70's happenings: rock concerts, sit-ins, walk outs. I knew people who had been to Woodstock, were hippies and had betrayed the establishment. As a modern-nun I was featured in the Chicago Sun Times Sunday Magazine and was the "truth" on *To Tell the Truth*. Near the expiration of my temporary vows, I met a man, fell in love and left the convent. In that order.

"Enjoy the comfort of a slip-on sandal, with the support and protection of a shoe. It stretches to 'give' with every step and offers secure footing." I bought the spiel, the shoes and the marriage proposal. I was betrayed by the lot. For the next seven years I tried marriage to the man I met in the 70's. During the sixth year of our marriage, my son was born, the greatest gift I had ever received. Within a year of his birth, my son and I were abandoned by my husband who joined a Far-Eastern cult. He was never to be heard from again. I threw the sandals out.

Today I wear Rockport shoes for their all-day comfort, superior shock absorption and pleasant style. I am middle-aged, happily married and have been blessed with a second child who has special needs. Interestingly, I had kept my name from the convent until my Rockport years. Soon after I married again, a wise deacon friend encouraged me to consider my Baptismal promises and privileges, and I resumed the name Virginia. With the passage of time I began to realize what the evangelical counsels truly implied. I have known more poverty of money, spirit and time in the past thirteen years than ever in the convent. I have experienced more obedience to life, God and community than I dreamed possible in the convent. To remain chaste in mind and faithful in body to one man required more of the vow than I was taught in postulant formation.

I remain involved with the Catholic Church as a religious studies teacher in a Catholic school, a Minister of Care, a Eucharistic Minister, and a member of the parish Pastoral Council. Four years ago I earned a Master's Degree in Pastoral Theology.

I maintain contact with the motherhouse. Recently at the sesquicentennial of the community's founding, all present and former Sisters were invited to the festivities. Each one was embraced and celebrated as a vital contributor to the community's history.

Sometimes the pull to be back in the convent is overwhelming. It comes at times when I long for quiet or for conversation with learned women of similar interests as mine. I admire the community's ability to empower each member to discern and facilitate her gifts within the community's charisms. I envy the community's power and support in risking to live out Scriptural values in its daily tasks. The assurance of loving care in sickness and old age is alluring. Yes, I feel a loss at times. Yet daily I am sustained and nourished by family, friends and ministry.

The single most convincing truth in my life is that even though I left the convent, I have not left a religious life. My shoes may have changed styles, but my feet are still drawn to stand on holy ground.

Helen E. Gourlay
Sisters of Charity of the Blessed Virgin Mary

Secretary, Receptionist, Havern Center

Bachelor of Science in Education, University of Nebraska

Master of Arts in Religious Education, Mundelein College

Chaplaincy Certificate

Campus Ministry

For the present Helen lives alone in an apartment, but maintains her relationship with her community by attending area meetings, and by letters and phone calls. In the Fall of 1992 she and another sister will live and work in inner-city Milwaukee where she hopes to teach ESL and/or literacy. She is vitally concerned with peace and justice issues, creation-centered and women's spirituality. She is also concerned with "developing play and humor in my life."

Helen E. Gourlay

God, Close and Real

Growing up in Lincoln, Nebraska was idyllic for me. I lived with my parents, two brothers and two sisters in a five-bedroom, white frame house. I loved it. Hot summers meant lots of leisure time and swimming; fall days brought the fun of being in school again and the smell of fall leaves; snowy winter days gave time to be in a warm house and play with my brothers and sisters; and springtime meant we could play outdoors again. Looking back, I seemed a very normal child growing up in an ordinary town—where the biggest event in those days was the Nebraska State Fair held every fall.

My parents were Geraldine and Jack Gourlay. Dad had come to Nebraska from Ontario, Canada when he was twenty-one; my mother came from a small town about twenty miles south of Lincoln—Princeton. When Dad was thirty-two and my mother twenty-eight, they married. To them were born: Madeline, John, myself (Helen), Frances, and Jim. I was born July 13, 1936. Only six years separated the oldest of us from the youngest which probably accounts for the closeness I felt with my brothers and sisters. As children, we had our share of teasing and arguments, but those times were outnumbered by the good times of playing in the backyard, ice-skating in winter at the neighborhood lake, getting to know each other's friends, and sharing the small talk of children about what was happening at home, school, and in the neighborhood.

When I was a child, religion was very important to me. For ten years I attended Blessed Sacrament School, five blocks from home, where the Sisters of Mercy from Omaha were the teachers. Being a conscientious and good student, I tried to please the sisters. Their lives held interest and mystery for me. They seemed happy and joyful. Their clothes showed me they lived differently from other people—that they gave themselves totally to God. Their home was a small house near school where we got to go for music lessons or for special times of adoration in their chapel once or twice a year.

My Catholic faith was part of who I was; God seemed close and real. Daily Mass was part of my life from grade school through high school. I was immersed in an environment where God and religion were at the center.

For me, entering the convent was not a hasty decision. In a way it was a natural outgrowth of my life and upbringing. Believing I had been blessed with a happy home and family and with the Catholic faith, I wanted to return my life to God.

Early in life I was attracted to the life of the Sisters because their lives were totally given to God. I wanted to love God as they did. Giving myself to God seemed the best way, too, to save my soul, which the catechism said was the goal of life—"to know, love, and serve God in this world and to be happy with Him forever in the next." I wanted to live so as to be ready for death. And to live a life of service to God, for me, meant to teach others about who God was. I felt called to do this in religious life. To have a family of my own was appealing, but God's call to religious life was stronger.

So at age twenty-two, after four years at the University of Nebraska, I entered the Sisters of Charity of the Blessed Virgin Mary (BVMs). These Sisters had taught me in high school. It was a difficult decision the last four months or so before I decided on the BVMs. Should I be with the Mercy's and live 60 miles away in Omaha, or move 400 miles to be a BVM? After a visit to both places and weighing the pros and cons of each, I decided on the BVMs.

Late afternoon August 2, 1958, I walked up the front steps of St. Joseph's Convent. A new and different life awaited me across the threshold. I was scared, excited, giggly, nervous, eager. Seventy-two others entered with me; seventeen of us are still in the Order.

I had nuns on pedestals. When I tried to be one myself, my life came shattering down. Before the six months of postulancy were over, I began to sense an unreality about myself and about my environment. The quietness seemed unreal, and I felt cut off from the rest of the world. My world view seemed no bigger than the grounds as I gazed over the river to the mysterious, unknown city and scenery in the distance. It would be two years later when I was a senior novice, during the presidential campaigns of John F. Kennedy and Richard Nixon, that the novitiate got television and brought the world a little closer. Shortly before that, we had begun semi-regular discussions based on *Time* and *Newsweek*; these discussions also helped broaden my horizons.

During a two years' novitiate, I felt a stranger to myself. Laughter and talk in recreation times were overshadowed by the regimentation of the schedule and the demands of rules and regulations. I stuffed my feelings and sank into depression. By masking feelings and a hurting self I managed to keep up with the daily routine. Finally, scared by suicidal thoughts, I sought out the novice directress and poured out my feelings. I risked being sent home. However, sharing honestly turned the tide for me. Progress in moving out of negative feelings was slow, but my life and feelings began a turnaround — a turnaround that took years, even with the eventual help of psychotherapy.

Although my feelings were shaky, I went forward with first vows. Shortly thereafter I went to Chicago for six months of theology at Mundelein College. In a more stimulating atmosphere, and returning to a more normal life, I began slowly to feel comfortable in religious life.

What happened to me in the novitiate — near mental collapse, depression, crisis of faith — colored my life for years to come. Only in recent years have I accepted the feelings and experience of those days without hurt, anger, pain, resentment, confusion, and the question why. Hadn't I given myself to God? If I couldn't find God in the convent, it obviously was my fault, not God's. I own the weaknesses I had at that time. However, in retrospect, I know I was caught in the oppressive system which religious life had become in the days before Vatican II. It was in the last throes of death, and in less than ten years, it was engulfed in upheaval and transformation. Stages of grief had not yet been identified nor had an understanding of how to express anger been developed. Virtually no individual attention was given in the way of spiritual direction, counseling, or support groups - all of which have come about since that time, and have helped me.

Soon, however, the Spirit began to stir and shake the church. During most of Vatican II I was in Chicago teaching at a large high school for girls, and living with forty or more of our Sisters in a convent attached to the school. Sometimes I would cry as I heard other Sisters laughing during a TV program while I struggled in my room trying to get lessons prepared by 10 p.m. curfew. I had three preparations at three levels of English, as well as religion and journalism classes to prepare. In addition, I had a senior homeroom, and was moderator of the school newspaper and memory book. Feeling overwhelmed with work, without the assertiveness I needed to state my limits, I simply felt sorry for myself and cried.

I now look upon my experiences of those early years as treasures that were and are waiting to be mined. Over the years I have begun to discover the gems as I unearth the treasures in myself that once were hidden. Painful experiences have become the mulch to fertilize growth in dealing with memories and hangups that have taken years to heal.

Until those unpleasant novitiate experiences, I was unacquainted with any depth of suffering. Their lessons provide insights to draw upon when I encounter hurting and suffering people. As I accept and integrate my shadow side, I grow in awareness of the richness of even painful experiences.

Through a transactional analysis workshop in the seventies, I learned of the inner child. I needed to relearn and experience play. Unlike others with less happy childhoods, I had a lot of good memories and experiences from childhood on which to draw. Being a serious, responsible person, however, I have found that releasing the inner child in play has come slowly.

Religious life has provided many growth and healing opportunities that I might not have taken advantage of were I raising a family. As breakthroughs came about in religious education, teaching religion became more interesting. In teaching others I grew more open to a future freed from the tight boundaries I had previously known. Teilhard de Chardin's vision opened a new view of the world.

Why have I stayed in religious life? I put a lot of discernment and energy into my original decision. Even though things did not go well for me in the novitiate, I remembered the closeness I had felt with God and the consistency of the call I had heard. I didn't feel free to leave. In the novitiate we were told we had a vocation unless we were asked to leave. What sustained me were memories of God from my childhood, adolescence, and young adulthood. I toughed out the novitiate and early religious life, hiding my real feelings even from myself, pretending all was well when I was hurting so much inside from the confusion as to what religious life was about, and what I was about. I eventually felt free to stay or leave. I made first vows in February 1961 and temporary vows each year after that till 1966 when I made final vows. Each year I had enough reasons to say yes again.

I welcomed changes in religious life and in the church, although friends and acquaintances began to leave. Each time someone left I reevaluated my own vocational choice and stayed with it. Gradually, as choices in dress, lifestyle, and ministry became possible for individuals to make, I began to shape the direction of my life. I enjoyed high school teaching and, later, parish work. Opportunities for personal growth became available within the congregation. Fortunately, in our congregation we were involved in changes at the grass roots level. As an active participant in what was going on, I began to experience a say-so in the direction, not only of my personal life, but also of the congregation, and, to some extent, the broader church.

I was one of the first to change into secular dress, and to move to an apartment. In the school year of 1968-69, while teaching at our local high school in Chicago, I lived with two other BVMs about two miles from school among Southern white people in a very poor housing area. It was my first experience of small group living and contact with the poor, as well as having Eucharist in a living room environment.

I see myself as quite a bit different than I was earlier in religious life. Now I have a voice and make choices about every aspect of my life and ministry: where I will live—alone or with others; how I use my free time; where I will minister. Earlier, I was passive and did not seem to have much say-so in the direction of my life. I felt depersonalized by the cutting of my hair and the wearing of unusual dress. I seemed older than my years. Critical thinking and personal decision-making were not encouraged. I suffered from low self-esteem that manifested itself often in feelings of depression, stomach distress, low energy.

Parish work in the 70's in Boulder, Colorado allowed me, for what seemed like the first time, to enter the world of adults. People were open, enthusiastic, eager to participate in those early days after Vatican II. Ministry was wonderfully varied and fun. Colorado's beauty healed my spirit. As adult education coordinator, I worked with others to help develop a family religious education program—a new concept in those years. I was in my 30's and my life had begun to blossom.

Although life was clouded by earlier unpleasant religious life experiences I continued my commitment. I went through another soul-searching time when I developed a close relationship with a priest. Since entrance I had buried or disregarded sexual feelings, but in this relationship I had to deal with them. The joy and closeness I felt in the relationship was equaled by the burden of guilt I felt. Working through the feelings in this relationship was difficult, but led to growth, especially in prayer. These feelings affected my satisfaction in ministry, so when an opportunity came to take a job in another locale, I did so.

During a phase of the relationship, I agonized over whether to stay or leave religious life. A turning point came when I was home one time. While I was reading, thinking about what to do, my reflection centered on the fidelity I witnessed in my parents' marriage and on the dimension of love which comes with fidelity. Religious life had brought me into a unique relationship with God; only by being faithful to the relationship as I knew it through religious life, could I ever know the fidelity dimension of love. With those thoughts, my choice to remain in religious life deepened.

I reevaluate my choice annually and each time have recommitted myself. One of my most healthful, fun, and life-giving experiences was living in a Catholic Worker house for four years. At this time I lived under the same roof with lay people and religious, with men, women, and children in need from diverse backgrounds. This experience challenged me to grow in understanding and living the social Gospel and, in the carrying forth of the ministry there, called on all my gifts of personality and training. Other ministries have been teaching high school, adult education and youth ministry work in parishes, working in the ministry resource office of our congregation, and campus ministry.

My experience at the Catholic Worker led me more deeply into the peace movement, and I have grown in my understanding of civil disobedience and non-violent direct action. I have been involved in two protest actions at the SAC Base near Omaha, one of which involved detainment, and a ban-and-bar letter, an arrest at Lowry Air Force Base in Denver, and an arrest at the Nevada Test Site. These actions are a living out of the Gospel and have been done with the knowledge and support of my congregation. Through these actions I have taken a stand for what I believe.

As a direct result of my interest and involvement in peace issues, I took a two-week trip to the Soviet Union in the summer of '87. The focus of the trip was citizen diplomacy: people talking to people. My understanding of life in the Soviet Union was greatly enhanced by the trip.

After a period of burn-out and uncertainty as to what ministry to take next in my life, I chose to be part of an holistic growth program for Sisters. In a nine-month program with twenty-seven other Sisters, I got more in touch with my own femininity and experienced healing of earlier pain in religious life. Upon leaving the program, my choice was to work with children, as I had never done so, except incidentally. For five months I worked in a day care center with children five years old and under. After five months I had the experience I desired.

Over the past couple of years ministry has been a difficult exploration for me. I have made deliberate efforts to cut down on stress in my life; thus I have tried to eliminate applying for jobs that encompass too extensive a job description. I have not been inclined to look for a job in a parish, or with the institutional Church; most of the jobs advertised for these have either seemed like more that I would want, or they were not geographically convenient to my family or congregation members. Many church jobs seem too confining, involving me in too narrow a focus on life. Currently, I am a secretary/receptionist in a school for children with learning disabilities.

Since the early 80's I have worshipped primarily with intentional Eucharistic communities where I have found nourishment and involvement. For several months, on first moving to Denver where I now live, I attended a large parish and loved the liturgies. However, after eight months or so I felt I had no relationships in the parish, and could not find anything to which I wanted to be plugged in. So I began attending an alternate Eucharistic community and have found my niche there. Previous to this time I participated in alternate Eucharistic communities in Dubuque, Iowa and Winona, Minnesota (campus liturgy).

I consider myself an active Catholic, but need to find my own niche within the church. Ministerially, I am much less involved with the institutional church than previously and am, therefore, less concerned about what comes from the diocesan office regarding guidelines, etc. I expect the Church to take stands on issues and to be a presence and help for people in need. I am disappointed that the institutional Church has found so few ways to use my gifts as a woman and as a woman religious. There seem to be minimal aids to furthering one's interests or pursuits or avenues by which one can find ministry positions. Collaboration and reconciliation are needed with regard to the institutional Church so that all people can find an equality within the structures.

Feeling comfortable in religious life has been an ongoing challenge as I strive for the ideal and try to respond to new challenges of meeting the needs of society as well as my own search for the balance. Through the years I have regularly participated in small prayer or discussion groups. Right now I participate in a weekly base Christian community with three other BVMs. With a few others from my Eucharistic community I am part of a small faithsharing group that began as prayer and discussion. My ideas about where religious life is headed for the future have been influenced by the writings and talks of Joan Chittester, Mary Jo Leddy, and Sandra Schneiders.

Currently I live in an apartment by myself. This is my first experience of living alone and I enjoy it. It gives me a chance to know myself better and I welcome time for solitude and discernment, especially as I consider moving to a new locale and ministry next year.

Outside of a few men with whom I interact casually at church or in a discussion group, I have currently no significant relationship with a male. My past experience includes two close relationships with priests, both of whom, at different times, were "significant others" for me. Through my ministries, I have developed friendships with a few males who make me feel valued and appreciated for who I am. I would welcome a relationship with a male, especially in a community-ministry endeavor, but I choose that it be inclusive of others, rather than exclusive.

Financially, I am earning just enough to meet expenses. I am being subsidized by my congregation for insurance and for annual assessments to the congregation. It has been very painful for me not to be able to contribute a full salary to the congregation and to have money to spend as freely as I would like, but I have come to accept where I am and to accept my financial situation as it is. My congregation is supportive and understanding of my present choices. I feel consistently called to a simple lifestyle and to identify with the materially poor.

I have known many persons, in my order and in other orders who left religious life. I felt sad at their leaving, particularly when large numbers left in the late 60's and early 70's. Each departure prompts my own soul-searching. Although I did not know people's gut-level reasons for leaving, I respect their decisions. Few, if any, make the choice lightly or without apprehension regarding the future. What I wish is that there could be more openness regarding their struggles and decision before their departure. Ultimately, however, I feel most decisions are made in the intimacy of individual hearts, hopefully with input of trusted friends, counselors, or confidants. One of the blessings of the past ten years or more is that the women who have left have been welcomed to congregation gatherings. They are friends, co-ministers and people who have a wealth of insight and experience to share with the rest of us, with society, and with the church.

Coping with stress has been a consistent health consideration for me. In recent years, I have received help through participation in Codependents Anonymous (CODA) and Recovery, Inc. Books such as *Women Who Do Too Much, The Language of Letting Go,* and *Daily Affirmations* place my issues in the broader contest of women and society. Quieting my mind and listening to the wisdom of my body are daily challenges. I try to make choices that will not lead me into doing more than I can realistically handle. Staying healthy is a day by day call as I try to balance my life and grow in a relationship with the Lord that integrates centering prayer, contemplation, and action.

The Gospel call I hear today is articulated in the ministry priorities of our congregation, as stated by our 1991 Senate: "implementation of the transformational model of ministry; response to unmet needs; service with the poor, and works of education, peace and justice." The world, church, and religious life are radically different from what they were in the 40's and 50's, but, fundamentally, the call is the same.

Belonging to a community of women with a history of shared experiences and memories and with a vision and commitment to living out the Gospel enriches my life and invites me into a future filled with hope. Those of us who have stayed in religious life have carried this form of community living into a new era. We are fewer in number; our congregations may eventually die out. For the foreseeable future, however, we have the challenge of becoming prophetic communities. As I move into this future, I do so with gratitude to family, friends, and all who have been part of the unique journey which has been mine in religious life.

Judith I. Kubish
Former Sister of Saint Joseph

Married

Transition: Archdiocesan consultant to "free-lancing" in areas of interest.

Master of Arts in Theology, University of Pittsburgh

Master of Theology, Notre Dame University

Special Areas of Training: Organizational Development

Human Relations and Multicultural Diversity

Dances of Universal Peace

Searching for an inclusive community

Judith is intensely involved in recovery and earth-based spiritualities, women's issues and spirituality, the environment, poetry and coupleship. The latter is related to her search for an inclusive community. She hopes to continue in her personal healing and expressiveness, "bearing fruit in renewed or reformed community involvements that support healing and transformation of social structures for the good of the planet."

Judith I. Kubish

Earthsister, Moonsister, Me

Leading the newly forming group toward trust and intimacy, the therapist asks, "Are there any secrets that you would like to share; anything that you would like to reveal that you are holding on to?" I breathe deeply, feeling blood rush into my face, stomach tightening, heart pounding — "Why that?," an inner voice questions. "Why not", wisdom prods, "Go for it. That's why you're here."

"I was a member of a religious community of women for twenty-five years", I softly announce. I don't look around. I have told my "secret"; I am content to rest for the moment. But Dave's voice, from the other end of the circle, gently probes: "You were a nun?" I hesitate, my mind racing with the Catholic distinction between a sister and a nun; I opt for the gut: "Yes." "Oh," is his response; its tone, "Why didn't you say that?" Then, another response, from Cynthia, sitting next to him, diagonally across the circle from me: "Why is that a secret?" "I don't know," I demur, "it feels like a secret to me - that's why I shared it- something I'm afraid to share-something you wouldn't know if I didn't tell you- 'something', I'm sure, that's related to why I'm here." "Oh," again, this time perplexed.

I feel relieved. I've taken a step. I'm going to deal with this veil that still covers me, eight years after I left, eighteen years after I actually removed a material veil from my head. I wonder what I will find.

And what I find is rage. I come to know the "secret" feeling as shame and I exercise it with rage, an incredibly powerful outpouring of anger at the black cloth enveloping my young womanhood, at the messages that swathe and stifle my natural sensuality and unfolding sexuality, at my own youthful idealism that drives me to headstrong wilfulness, then to teeth- gritting will power against myself. I am angry at those who presented such an option to a fifteen-year-old. I have excused them for years, knowing that if they had been harsher or more repressed people,

39

I would have been damaged much more severely. My gratitude for their kindness has kept me from hearing the strong "no" that also longed to be said.

I am angry at the losses: the young adult woman's developmental processes of self-knowledge, identity, intimacy, choice-making. I am angry for handing them over to "religious formation". And when the dust settles and my anger turns to laughter at the forcefulness of my power, another storm arises: more rage at the binding shame, shame for having been a sister, shame for no longer being one. It is the Catholic Church's brilliant Catch-22 of upholding religious life as a higher way. It separates me from my peers, and makes it seem impossible ever to become peer again. Just tell the secret aloud and you will arouse curiosity, animosity, devotion, anger, reverence, fear, revenge, anything but indifference.

Under the veil, the veil lifted, removed, buried, grieved, left behind, I find a woman staring into a void, nearly paralyzed by the realizations that she is facing. "I am forty-six years old and I don't have any idea how I'm going to provide for myself economically. I am forty-six years old and I don't know what I want to do with my energies in this wide world that has called me to it."

I am forty-six years old and at fifteen I stopped asking myself "What do I want?" I gave up my wants to the community response: "But, we need you to....". Or, when I was engaged in the process of listening to my inner wisdom, I submitted to the intervention: "This is what we want you to do right now; there isn't time to keep discerning." And, with the twisted assurance of a vow of obedience, I bent my will to give the very best I had to what was asked of me, and nurtured myself on the reassurance, "You've done what we've asked you to do, and you've done it so well."

But now I'm not asking any more. I don't need anyone to tell me. I don't have a formal faith community to discern with. In the desert of a world of competing value systems and eroding social security, at forty-six years of age, I am asking myself, "What do you want to do?" And the feelings of vulnerability threaten to drown me.

I do have a job. I still work for the church. I am a consultant to parishes. I receive a substantial salary. It's tempting to imagine getting vested in my pension plan and living out the next thirty years as a loyal employee.

However, the Spirit has been working hard in me to follow the way of Jesus: new wine, new wineskin; wisdom made flesh; loving the world enough to send a beloved daughter into it. And this Spirit is hovering over the void mirage of my fear and keeps whispering: "Let go. There is little life for you here any more right now. There is little joy. There is precious time invested and valuable energy that is yielding a paycheck and little else. Quality of life is more important than income." "Yes," I sigh with relief; "Yes; it is lifeless and ineffective for me." Why?

My husband is a former Jesuit, an ordained priest. We could not be married in the Roman Catholic Church; another former Jesuit, now an Episcopal priest, witnessed our marriage with the faith community who supported us. Although my Catholic bishop is willing to take the risk of having me continue to work for him, an important part of my identity is in exile and grief. I do not readily speak of my marriage in Catholic communities. My job and the Bishop's credibility are in jeopardy with some members if I do. I do not belong to a parish, partly for the same reasons. I do not belong, also, because I find liturgy too exclusive and parish life too demanding. The energy which I would have to expend in taking on a leadership role to help create what reflects my under-standing of faith community would be exhausting, another full time job. I would also have to deal with the consistently frustrating dynamics that I deal with on my job: the clerical, hierarchical, paternalistic authority system.

My friend, Nancy, is a minister in the Disciples Church. She witnesses to me what it would be like to have my leadership recognized, to facilitate the sharing of faith from among the faithful. Her worship services engage the rich faith witness of her parishioners. At the same time she is, undeniably, the minister they have chosen to work for them and with them, to be accountable to them and to provide the atmosphere for growth in the community. The gift of experiencing this contrast enables me to affirm that I no longer want to face the day-to-day minimizing of my talents and diminishment of my energies that occurs in subordinating myself to the Catholic Church structure. There is more to me than either my job description or the opportunities for service available in the structure allow. I am a creative, spiritually dynamic person without an outlet in the Roman Catholic Church for sharing that to the fullest. Therefore, I choose not to continue to stunt myself in full-time church work. I also do not choose to continue the tortuous mental activity of attempting to make it all make some kind of sense to me. I will look at myself and what I need to change.

"I have to detox from the church," I announce to my therapy group as a part of our aftercare planning. They applaud warmly. I have realized that I am carrying around heavy baggage of wanting to fix the church, of feeling responsible for making it change. Deep wisdom affirms that I am not responsible for anyone else, that I can choose to be responsible to it, but I do not need to carry the weight of trying to fix it. This pattern that I learned early in life needs to change; I want to change. Deep inside me there is a seed of hope. I have been trying to come to this choice for the past six years. I now know that I will do it. I feel terror about the economic conditions of our society. I feel terror about the lack of a financial safety net under me. I feel terror at the void in myself: how do I do this? But what I know is that I can and I will, and that I'll ask for help and help will be there. I will trust the process.

When I look back the process teases: "Whatever happened to you?" I grew up; I leapt over the walls of security and safety and pleasing others; I was transformed. I chose an ocean instead of a swimming pool, I chose to float and be carried on waves instead of straining so hard to swim laps. I was guided. I was led. I saw visions of a dance. I wanted to dance. I joined millions of women and men struggling for life in our secular culture.

Whatever happened to me? Whatever happened to the good sister, who, for me, was often an idealistic, workaholic, community-dependent, perfectionist, controlling, precocious, obedient, rebellious, out- on- the edge experimenter? The bubble burst, the seed germinated, the shell broke open. There was no where else to go but out, no where else to live the charism of hiddenness and oneness and unity which my community espoused except hidden and one and unified with every-one else in the world, on the planet. I had to stop being different, terminally serious, terminally responsible, and, at the same time, inef-fective. I had to stop disregarding the still small voice of sexuality and sensuality and intimacy, the closeted mistress's progression of secret emotional affairs. I had to stop the duplicity and agony over creating the perfect life. I had to be me: so trite, it's nauseous; so true, it is yet profound. I saw sisters and brothers being themselves in celibate

42

lifestyle: content, fruitful, full-grown, at home. Yet I was lost and losing ground even more as I got older. I needed to make choices. I needed to make love. I needed badly (goodly!) to be myself.

And I need to affirm my awareness that this choice was more than personal, or, as women's consciousness so aptly affirms, that the personal is also political. Not wanting to be celibate was not only an admission of personal preference and a discernment of the path of personal wholeness. I also knew that it meant that I didn't want to be governed by a male-conceived structure of power that splits genitality from sexuality, that connotes a negation of marriage, that dictates external regulations that stifle one's "energies for being and making" (a wonderful Teilhardian statement about chastity!), regulations that imply that religious power means no touching or being touched, no attraction or attractiveness, no passion. During my time of commitment to religious life I would discourse on how all of those characterizations are not what celibacy is. But my gut was not convinced. That was part of the political package and I no longer wanted it. I no longer wanted to be defined within it. I no longer wanted to try to be reconciled with it.

I went back to my fifteen-year-old inner self and told her: "You don't have to do this. You don't have to lock up your vitality, habit it, cloister it, silence it, communize it, Church it, to sanctify yourself. You are holy. You shall be confirmed in holiness, in body and blood, wholeness and truth, by a faithful life. You shall be sanctified by grace, not by a lifestyle." I was more convinced of God's love for me that day than I had ever been. Truth had broken through layers of repression. I started the process of leaving.

What did I leave? I left security. I left friendships, which I hoped to maintain and find increasingly difficult to do so. I left Church protection and identity. I left fear of my own choices and of the hostility of the world. I left one of the best kept secrets about the possibility of generating creative options for economic, political, and social change in the world-community. I left separatism from the incredibly difficult task of faithful, intimate male-female commitment. I left the community's aspiration for me to be Superior General. I left my father's ticket to heaven: "I'm the daddy of a nun." I left the mask of a socially formed and recognized, institutionally guaranteed judgement of goodness.

I am probably only now being more completely faithful to that call of eight years ago. I have been bargaining for that paycheck, for a resume that looks impressive within the Church, for some way to stay connected, to belong. I have no doubt that I will find a new way to belong if I take this one last leap. To affirm myself so strongly, however, flies in the face of all of the years of self-putdown that I have practiced. The Great Mystery's promise to me to be the Sanctifier, and my consistent inner wisdom's invitation to let go of judging and negating myself, prods and stirs me.

And I find a very grey world and a suffering world and a rather desolate world in terms of the safety and support it provides for me. I find a hard row to hoe to advance the dreams I have for living more creatively. I find a very difficult work to be with myself, with the necessary weeding out of old and planting of new patterns of self-care and relating to others. I find that looking back at the road behind is every bit as important as looking ahead; that telling my story is appropriating myself in deeper truth and wisdom. I find that grace and faith are both more tangible and less tangible than I had ever imagined. Every genuine message or feeling of devotion has a concrete action or consequence in daily interaction. I find that "The ocean refuses no river."

The image of floating in the ocean instead of swimming laps in the pool still delights and sustains me. The ocean of my experience keeps expanding and revealing incredible contents: cultures, religions, lifestyles, personal dimensions —the ocean refuses no river. And, within the very terror and struggle of letting go of external definitions of myself, I discover that I am the ocean, both more uniquely defined and more boundless.

Sufi wisdom capsulizes the person, process, and end as one: "God is lover, loved and beloved." For me, there is only that dance and no other, going on with each breath, carrying me with each movement. I have learned to sing and to dance my prayer, alone and with others. I have learned to listen to the spirituality of Twelve-Steppers and to study the mystics of Buddhism and Islam as intently as I ever listened to any sermon. I have learned to kneel on the earth and to kiss the awakening spring blades of grass, to cry into her soil, "Bless me, mother, who am your child". I have learned to celebrate earth's seasons and to watch each night for stars and for the changing moon.

The ocean in which I float is life, is the Divine, is me — an impressively powerful woman when I listen to myself, an obviously vulnerable human being when I surrender control, capable of and made for the great mystery of connection with every other aspect of life in the universe: a moonsister, earthsister. I have rivers that originate way back before my Judeo-Christian flowage, rivers bedded in a working class Polish confluence that conserves and recycles and plants and prunes and builds with vigor and rigor. I float on this ocean, "breathe this water and I am at home. The more I welcome and express this truth of myself, the clearer the vision arises and the more steadfastly action follows. And the vision is carrying me — even further away from the institutional church, yes, but, surely, into the arms of the Divine.

The new array of choices that beckon me are exciting and energizing. Once I step through my fear, I enthusiastically name my desires. I want a home, first and foremost, and time to spend in my home, foster-parenting and sustainable gardening and being involved in my community. I want to share the vision of universal spirituality that calls to me and others for expression and exploration. I want to improve my singing and dance-leading skills for the Dances of Universal Peace. I want to write poetry and write essays and, simply, write. I want to share with other couples the incredibly challenging work it is to be married and to stay married. I want to find more ways to play with and celebrate marriage, too, as well as work at it.

I want to look out every day and see and hear and touch and taste and smell the earth and its other inhabitants and to be grateful and to be aware of how my life and the lives of other humans are impacting on this life support system. I wouldn't mind teaching about any of the above, also, and speaking, and sharing a vision of freer, simpler living for the end of this century and the beginning of the next. About fifteen year ago, I was gifted with spending a retreat time in Appalachia, and I realize that the vision expressed in the Appalachian bishops' pastoral is the seed that unfolds in me: "A life, free and simple, with time for one another and for peoples' needs, based on the dignity of the human person, at one with nature's beauty, crowned by poetry." I will continue to connect more with that vision, within and without, and my heart will know it's home.

A lot has changed in my spirit since I left a celibate women's community eight years ago. Yet much remains the same. I recognize the same hunger and thirst for integrity, within and without, in myself. I know that there is the same desire for union with God, for making God known, for living in fidelity as a loyal, devoted, loving co-creator. I know that I probably will always be most vulnerable to myself, needing recovery from dysfunctional ways of living. But, the miracle and the challenge is that I do make progress and my life does become more uniquely my own and more common with others.

"I like to look good. I like to sound good. I wasn't feeling very good inside, though," I share in my good-bye statement to my therapy group. "I've learned that it feels better to connect with you in the moment than to plan what I'm going to say. I've learned that it's O.K. to ask for help. And...I am who I am; I know what I know; I can do what I can do." There are tears on my cheeks and in my throat. There are smiles and wet eyes and hands clapping before me.

I am surrounded in my journey by a diverse array of people seeking to change their own lives and relationships. It is my hope that we will grow in numbers and expand in dimension so that social structures will also change. The process may have different roots and play itself out under different guises throughout the world, but we humans are in a life and death struggle for community and for life on the planet. Life in a religious congregation and in the Church nurtured such a perspective in me. For this, I will always be extremely grateful. I have come to know, however, that this reality was conceived in me at birth. Furthermore,, the present and future actions of this one person, embodied in this particular historical time and context, in community with other persons, will add to or diminish the realization of a whole world. At the age of twenty-five I wrote the following words of Rilke at the front of my Bible. Little did I know the process it would be for them to be enfleshed in my life!

> This is my strife: dedicated to desire through all days to roam.
> Then, strong and wide, with a thousand root-fibers deep into
> life to grip-and through pain far beyond life to ripen, far
> beyond time!

Madeleine Perkins
Sisters of Mercy of America

Activities Director (Certified), McAuley Manor

Bachelor of Arts, Music Education, St. Xavier University, Chicago

Master of Arts, Business Education, Northern Illinois University

Master of Arts, Religious Education, Fordham University

American Red Cross Water Safety Instructor

Madeleine lives in a community house with four other sisters. She receives a monthly newsletter, attends the yearly Assembly, and belongs to the Meanings of Membership Committee, which meets monthly. One of her delights and interests is swimming, and until this year she taught this life-time sport at the YWCA. Beyond the now? "Indefinite!" She sees a change, but does not know to what. "I am in the process of discerning."

Madeleine Perkins

A Need to Grow

From birth until after high school I had lived in the same house in Bridgeport, Connecticut. Our family consisted of my father and mother, and a sister and brother both older than I. Our close family relationship nurtured all my talents and taught me an appreciation for nature, sports, music, arts and crafts; most of all, it allowed the gift of Faith to grow. I can remember as a child that it was the example of my mother that made early-morning Mass during Advent and Lent a joy.

Many times my mother recounted the fact that my father was a convert to Catholicism and that he received his First Communion on their wedding day. He, too, was a source of edification to me when he would kneel with us on the floor to pray, and I could tell how tired he was after a long day's work. I sincerely believe that he knew his Bible far better than I ever will.

I completed eight grades at St. Patrick's, ninth grade at Congress Junior High, and three at Central High across the street where I continued my interest in sports, poetry, music and the rifle team until I graduated in 1942.

I worked as a typist until my mother and I moved to Fond du Lac, Wisconsin in 1943 to join my father who had been sent there to open a corset factory. We helped him in any way we could once he had interviewed, hired, and trained the women. But I was aware of how close the three of us were becoming, doing everything together from work to recreation. Friends did not happen overnight. Because I feared the loss of one or both parents through death, I decided to make the break first.

I joined the women's branch of the Navy, the WAVES, in December of 1944. My boot camp was at Hunter College, New York; Yeoman Training at Oklahoma A & M, Stillwater, Oklahoma; my first and only tour of duty at the Main Navy Department in Washington, D.C. I stayed there until the end of the war in 1946 when I was honorably discharged. But it was while I was in the Navy that the thought occurred: "If I can serve my country in this way, why can't I serve my God?"

However, the idea lay dormant while I was secretary at the Fond du Lac School Board and most of the time I was working in the office at the tractor factory. Finally I asked our parish priest about how you can tell if you have a vocation. This happened during the summer of 1948. We had a long talk and he gave me four suggestions regarding orders. After an exchange of letters and an interview, I entered the Chicago Province of the Sisters of Mercy in February of 1949 at the age of twenty-four.

My first profession was in 1951 and my final profession in August of 1954. It was during the remote retreat preceding final profession that my father died, in July of 1954.

From 1951 until 1961 I taught in high school in Milwaukee, Wisconsin and DesPlaines, Illinois, teaching in the areas of religion, music and business, and forming and teaching the drum corps. While in Milwaukee the need for accredited business teachers was expressed to me, so I began work on my Masters in Business Education in DeKalb, Illinois. While teaching in DesPlaines (one year I was Assistant Principal) I applied for and received the Cardinal Meyer Scholarship to earn a Master's in Religious Education. I chose to study at Fordham University in New York, starting the summer if 1969 and completing it the summer of 1970. Sadly, my mother had died in the fall of 1968.

Then I returned to Chicago to teach in Mercy High School in the areas of religion and music. During the summers of 1973-1975 I was waterfront director at our former camp in Eagle River, Wisconsin.

In 1973 Mercy merged with Loretto Academy to become Unity High. Then Unity merged with Visitation and St. Thomas in 1980 to become Unity Catholic. During all these years I taught various courses in religion, swimming, accounting, chorus and introduction to music. Extra-curricular activities have included yearly musicals, talent shows, and a drill team.

After leaving teaching in high school I took a sabbatical which included a four month Ministry to Ministers program in San Antonio, Texas. It was exceptional. I still am motivated by things I learned there. That was from September into December of 1981.

Then I spent the month of April in an Ashram in Summit Station, Pennsylvania, experiencing "Body, Mind and Beyond."

From there I went to Washington, D.C. where I spent a year working as a secretary at the Sisters of Mercy Generalate. I found this, and the subsequent two years at the United States Catholic Mission Association a truly enlightening few years. In Washington I felt like I was at the hub — where things happen. When stones are dropped into the water, there is action. But here in Aurora we are hardly aware of the ripples!

During the last few years I have taken part in the Intensive Journal Workshops as well as a workshop in Sadhana.

I am becoming more and more aware of God's workings in my life and a greater need for time alone for quiet contemplation. I have done a lot of soul searching and am willing now to wait.

At present I am the Activities Director at McAuley Manor and Convent in Aurora, Illinois. I am responsible for scheduling the daily program which will encourage the residents' involvement. There needs to be variety in order to touch each person at some time: spiritual, physical, sensual, mental and social and an opportunity to assist with community service as well.

Part of my growth in the Church is to admit that the Church needs to grow, too! God is unchanging, but the Church needs to change. Change is a sign of growth. To continue to grow means to change often. The Catholic Faith is *my* path to eternal life, but I don't believe it is the only path.

My prayer and meditation, next to the Mass, are a vital part of my daily life. I live in a house with four other Sisters of Mercy. It might not be called a convent by old standards, but it is for me — a home for religious. We pray together after our evening meal and share our concerns about our work and the people whose lives we touch.

I follow the vows I made of poverty, chastity and obedience and service to the poor, sick and ignorant. In truth, my understanding of them today is different from when we first studied their meaning in the novitiate.

Poverty is still to live with less and chastity is to be committed to Jesus Christ as my one love. Obedience is to follow the command to love God with my whole self and my neighbor as myself. Whatever I may choose to do must be within the framework of these chosen obligations.

Naturally I grieved for those who left; I still do not understand why some did. I do not feel betrayed or angry. We each have to follow the spirit we know.

I've had minimal health problems, one of which is the heart that almost kept me from entering in the first place.

I am concerned about ecology. I try to help through letter writing to senators and representatives about issues like oil drilling, rain forests, huge net fishing, water conservation, atomic energy plants.

Peace! If only we could close down all armament plants and make peace instead of war.

We could feed the poor of the world with what the government tells farmers to throw away or store.

Some companies are raising cattle in Central and South America on what was once rich forest land before the cutting down of the trees. They fatten the cattle on precious grain. The rich companies raise beef for the rich while the hungry all over the world are starving.

Injustices, especially among our politicians, are also a great concern to me.

There is need for our married clergy to be able to return to their ministry; there is need, as well, for the ordination of women who are called.

I believe that the AIDS victims of today are the lepers of Jesus' time, and they are crying out for evidence of the compassionate love of God. It cannot happen unless we show it.

It has been forty-three years this February! I taught in the elementary grades for ten years and in high school for twenty years. I've earned a Bachelor of Arts degree with a major in Music Education, a Masters in Business Education, and a Masters in Religious Education. I've always said I should have been given a C.D. — Doctor of Campuses — because of all the different colleges where I have studied. I've been challenged to use my God-given talents and to grow into a more questioning believer who is recognizing each day the on-going mystery of life and Love! I really think I am quite different from the person I remember in the 1960's.

Lyndal-Marie Armstrong
Former Sister of the Sacred Heart

Married, two children

Staff Nurse

Registered Nurse

Eucharistic minister

Lector

Sister Parish committee secretary

Lyndal-Marie has an Arabian horse whom she enjoys. "He has taught me a great deal about the care of the equine." She likes trail riding and riding lessons, and loves music and singing. Some walking and hiking are part of her life. "I particularly love it in the mountains and at the ocean." She intends to continue nursing studies and "will continue my journey for wholeness and reaching out to others."

Lyndal-Marie Armstrong

Lyndal-Marie's Story

Why did I go into the convent in the first place? That is a question I thought I knew the answer to through all the years. I saw myself as so full of love to give that the possibility of marriage and children was not enough for me. I wanted to give my life and love to Our Lord, and in so doing share my life with all people. When I would care for them, share their joys and struggles, share in their learning and growing, their pain and their healings I would be sharing in the life and love of Our Lord. So I sought to be the "bride of Christ".

Today I'm not so sure. What was really behind such grandiose dreams and images? What was it I needed? Was it that no one man could love me enough? Was I so in need of love that only the cosmic Christ could possibly fill the deep void and "hole" in myself or whole of myself?

What is the journey I've taken? How did I get from there to here? Perhaps if I mark that path I will be able to get some idea of where I am going.

I entered the convent in the same month that I graduated from high school. I had six months as a postulant and two years as a novice; following that I made my first profession of vows. We renewed our temporary vows every year for six years. I spent the six months after my first vows assisting in an elementary class room. At my request, and repeated urging, I then went to nursing school; it was a hospital diploma program for three years. After graduation I requested to go to the British Isles to work. Since I was the only nurse in the United States in my order, I thought I would like to get the feel of the life of my sisters who were nurses. I also was experiencing a feeling of being out of place, of not really belonging to the community because I was the sole nurse among the teaching sisters I knew as community.

While I was in the motherhouse in England I found my novice mistress from the U.S. now serving as novice mistress in England. Her presence helped ease my own adjustment to this larger, old world community. I stayed in the motherhouse for four weeks. From there I went to Cardiff, Wales. I worked in surgery for a year in one of the community's small, private hospitals. There was a lot to see and learn from just living and working there. I was wide-eyed as I took in the skills of surgical nursing, the contrast of social medicine and private medicine within the British Isles, the history and its people.

I experienced some of the Church life in this old world. One December evening we walked from the hospital to the Cathedral to hear Fr. Clifford Howell speak. I had been influenced in high school by him; my class had used his book to study the Mass. The understanding and love I had inherited from him before was enhanced that evening for me and remains with me today. Our journey to and from this event was also special, as it was one of those fun sisterly times of chatter, and giggling as we walked, exploring the streets and closed shops of this new land.

It was also a stimulating break from the routine of rising at 5:30 and going to chapel for Matins and Lauds, Meditation, Mass, breakfast, surgery, lunch and Tierce, Sext and None, surgery, Vespers and rosary, supper, clean surgery and prepare for the next day, recreation hour, Compline, up late with spiritual reading, a bath and bed only to be up again at 5:30 to begin the routine again, and again and again!

I found the convent life and the hospital extremely integrated. The two structures were part of each other. It seemed the Sisters worked seven days a week, with only a half day off for themselves. On that half day, individually scheduled each week, one usually went to her room and spent the day alone, frequently having dinner there. It seemed that that was all the interest or energy that remained. I judged I was lucky as I worked Monday to Friday and Saturday mornings, and was on call for emergencies. Each day we had one community hour of recreation together in the evening. Some knitted, some played cards; all visited. Sometimes there was something on "teley" which we watched together.

While I was in England, I tried to apply to an English nursing school for Midwifery studies. I began a process of applying to the school, which referred me to the General Nursing Council to get my American license recognized in the UK. After several letters to the Council I became frustrated, and I was overwhelmed with the kinds of materials they were asking for, along with their statement "...it would appear...that you will be required to undergo a further period of training..." This meant I was going to have to go back to nursing school to get my RN in England before being admitted to study midwifery. I knew school had not come easily for me, and I dreaded going back to a level through which I had previously struggled.

I wish I had found someone with whom to share my dilemma. I did not confide with anyone, and there were some wonderful women with experience and knowledge who could have encouraged or advised me. I liked the women I worked with; I liked my superior. But I did not experience a relationship of close sharing. My superior did call me in one day to ask me what I had heard and how it was progressing. I told her I had received a letter from the Council asking for more information, and that it seemed I would have to go back to school to get my RN for England. I told her I really did not want to do that, but I did not show her the letters, nor did I ask her opinion. I wish now that I could have consulted more with her, and not have made my decision in isolation, because that was the end of my dream and I did not have another one to replace it. So I lived each day and waited for what life would bring.

A few months later I was called into my superior's office. She said there was a job in a rural community clinic in a California town where the Sisters had a school. She asked me if I would be interested in doing that. I was elated. I would be going home and would have a new focus.

I arrived at the clinic in the fall. The season was beautiful; the leaves on the trees and grapevines took on such vibrant colors in their process through life to death. I found the work just as vibrant and exciting. I was moving into a stage of new life, looking for a home where I would belong and have roots. I was an independent person on a daily basis within the community again. We had morning prayer, meditation, and Mass together, followed by breakfast in silence. I went off to work and returned home for lunch. After that I returned to work until closing at 5:00 p.m. My evenings were made up of more hours of prayer, supper and dishes, spiritual reading, community hour, and night prayer.

At work there was a great variety of patients and patient needs, physicians, specialists, medical students, office help, administrators, and nurses. All were dealing with a great variety of emergencies as well as prenatal care, plastic surgery, minor surgery, orthopedic clinics, colds and flu, skin rashes, general surgery, pediatrics and more. There was a Portuguese community, an Italian community, the larger Catholic community; there was a striking Mennonite community. There were farmers, farm labors, agricultural factory workers, large land owners, merchants, young mothers, babies, children; there were the school football team, grandmothers, teachers, fathers, grandfathers. I learned a great deal from all those with whom I worked and from this rural community for whom I cared.

A couple of years after working there my provincial gave me an opportunity to go back to school for my degree. She stated that our mother general thought it would be good for me at this time. I replied that she just did not understand how much I was learning here. It was such an unusual situation, very stimulating, and I really didn't want to go. I also felt like I belonged and I had a longing for some roots. My provincial asked me to write to the University for an unofficial evaluation of what credits I had and what I needed. I did this and when it was returned, I shared this with her. I acknowledged my fear or dread of school, how unsure I was of my ability to succeed. She listened to me and did not push me.

Since I was back in the states, I was wearing the slightly modified "American" habit with the small tuft of hair peeking out from my veil. It seemed a small testimony to my humanity. I did have a longing to be "off duty" from the role of being a nun. Occasionally we would go out to a movie without our habit. This was not approved by superiors, but many of us did this on our own. I was surprised at the number of us who were doing this, young and old alike. It was almost like an unofficial approval. I found it relaxing to be in public for some recreation without having to be conspicuous. I had freedom to be in a public place for the sole purpose of refreshing and recreating myself. However, I was never totally comfortable with this. I felt like I was betraying something or somebody. This led to my giving myself permission to go with my sister friend and a couple of priests on some day trips for sight seeing, visiting, driving, dinner and home. We had permission for our visits and excursions, but we made a little detour after leaving to change into lay clothes; of course the priests already were out of the collar. These three or four times were some of my most wonderfully relaxing, refreshing times.

One day I went to my mother superior to tell her that a number of us from the clinic staff were going over on Saturday to the house of the new doctor. He was single and was renting a disastrously dirty and unkept house. We wanted to help him clean it up. She told me she didn't think it was a good idea. I stated I thought it was. She restated her opinion, but I left, assuming we just had a difference of opinion. A month or more later I heard through another sister that our mother superior said I had been deliberately disobedient to her. I was horrified at this suggestion. I explained to my friend the way I had understood it. My friend seemed to understand. As for myself, I was filled with shame, guilt and horror as I embraced the accusation of my disobedience and the violation of my vow.

On another occasion one of the families of the parish had invited me to go horse-back riding with them. Our provincial said, "No, that is not a good thing for a nun to do." I was quite surprised with her response, and I could not find the words to plead my case.

I had been reading and studying de Chardin in those years. I never was, nor am I today, a master in understanding him, but he had a great impact on my life. I was seeing that all of creation, the world, life, and our humanity was created by God; and God saw it was all good. I heard the challenge to see this goodness, and know this goodness, experience it, and proclaim it even as I proclaim God and my love of Him. So it seemed to me that my body was good and the horse was good. I could not comprehend her refusal.

I began to slip into a depression. It went on for months and I remembered I had felt this depression in the British Isles before my return to the U.S.. This one did not seem to shake off. I wanted very much to stay where I was with my community and my work. In the British Isles I had seen how slow things were to change there. It seemed as though the amount that our life style had to change to meet my needs was far too much to be realistically expected. I was in conflict within myself.

In order to find some peace within myself, I needed to step back and submit to the strict observance of the rules. Yet I did not like the kind of person I would become if I did that. The person I was would die if I did. But it also caused me great distress to be secretive.

While I struggled with this, my mother's stepfather died. My mother was extremely distraught by this. My father was with her, but she had relied on our relationship for support. She seemed to have a great need for me at this time. So I asked for a leave to be there for her. I had delayed my final vows for a year, so I was still under temporary vows. I was not able to obtain a leave; so I chose to withdraw from the community. I was told I would be welcomed back at anytime, and they would see what they could do about adapting my novitiate. I remember the terror that filled me as I was driving away and the isolation I felt as I gave up my ring.

I have always been grateful for my years in the convent. I believe they made me, for the large part, the person that I am today. My love for the Living Body of Christ and the Living Church is a gift to me from these years. The development of prayer and meditation in my life, my awareness of the poor, and an openness to bigger questions of the world and universe are my inheritance.

I was extremely overwhelmed making the adjustment to being a single lay person. There was the opening of a bank account, writing checks, buying clothes, getting a job, having dates, and setting up my life. I was embarrassed many times by my lack of everyday life skills. I found I was feeling lost and alone. I was like a foreigner in my homeland. I seemed to have no sense of identity. At the same time I found it was exciting and freeing as I learned each of those skills, as I began to make new friends, discovered a new side of myself and acquired a new sense of identity and belonging.

I got a job in a small community hospital. I had worked there several years when I began to date a man I particularly enjoyed. I felt comfortable with him, we had some good adventures, and we seemed to be able to talk so easily about our goals and values in our lives. We then lost contact for a while. One day, much to my surprise, I came home from work to find a note wedged in the door, "Where are you? Bill". Later I learned he had been out of town for an extended time. I, too, had been out of town for a time, and then I had made a job change. He had been unsuccessful in reaching me, so he had driven to where I lived, leaving the note as his last desperate attempt to get in contact with me. After this we found every opportunity to get to know and enjoy each other.

We exchanged vows during the Nuptial Mass, surrounded by our families and friends. I had said "yes" with a great fear that it would not work. But Bill pointed out that nothing ventured was nothing gained. I knew that the joy I felt in being with him and loving him could not grow or always be there for me if that step out in the unknown wasn't taken. The day of our wedding my heart was full of hope and promise as we took that step together.

Our journey in life together up to the present still continues to be a source of support and challenge in our growing faith and relationship with God and the Living Body of Christ whom I see in His people.

We had looked forward to having children, but that did not work out in the Divine Plan. I was unable to conceive. We grieved our loss. The Lord, however, opened another door even as this one was closed. We were able to adopt an infant girl, our Anne-Marie; and 4 years later we were blessed again with an infant boy, our David. They have been such a gift of joy, watching them unfold, watching them perceive the wonder of life. It has also been painful to watch such little ones take on the pain of failures in society. Both our children have learning disabilities; one has dyslexia and the other has Attention Deficit Disorder. Some of what I learned while living with the community of teachers has given a starting place to build parenting skills.

We became members of a small rural parish community. We have now spent all of our seventeen married years in this parish. Over the years we have had struggles and happiness. More than anything it is the people, a sense of belonging to them, imperfect as they might be, that keeps me going and involved there. Perhaps it is because I have been involved with them that I have a sense of belonging to them.

About five years after we were married Bill and I made a Worldwide Marriage Encounter weekend. We hadn't been having any particular stress or difficulties in our marriage, but some friends had made one and recommended it to us. They said it had been a very special time for them, and that during that time they had learned a communication tool for their relationship that they could take home and use. It took us a few months to make time for it, but eventually we did.

Until that weekend I hadn't admitted what a rut I had gotten into in our marriage, how I lacked the deeper communication that should have been in our marriage. This process did just what they said: we came to a new appreciation and knowledge of each other, and we were resolved to continue the process at home.

As a result of this experience we were asked to be a presenting couple for Marriage Encounter. That took a whole different process to decide. I found it quite a scary idea. After much discussion we decided we had gained so much from other couples' generosity and that we did not want to be takers only. We would just take it one step at a time until we reached the limits of what we could do.

We ended up serving for ten years. We wrote a few talks at a time. Gradually we wrote more, and rewrote. We served different terms in various leadership roles. Ultimately we served a term as Executive Couple. We were privileged to be part of an Ecclesial Team, serving with a priest who gave these weekends. This had an immense impact on our growth as persons, as a couple and in our faith and relationship with God and His People.

From the beginning of our step into this area of service I felt like I had found a new community. I had a mission again to grow in my giving of love and enabling others to live in an environment, world and life of love. I seemed to be on fire with this, and that fire appears to have been built on all I had learned about knowing and loving while in the convent. For me this was a fuller gospel life.

I liked sharing with others the mission of the gospel call and lifestyle. I found that by opening and sharing my own pain, my own failures, my own struggles and successes others took heart and could believe in themselves because they weren't alone. As we worked to renew the Sacrament of Matrimony I often thought of how my life in the convent had enhanced greatly my appreciation of marriage as a sacrament. It was there that I came to appreciate married life and religious life as two different sacred life styles that were equal.

While doing this ministry I had grown in awareness of how difficult it is to live the gospel call in United States culture. We often talked with priests who were home from serving in the missions in Third World countries. We heard how the faith is strong in those areas, and how there is great enthusiasm for that faith. They told us how much more difficult it was here. People seemed more cynical and were engrossed in consumerism. Within my own life I struggle with the seduction of wanting more things and better things. I struggle with the lack of involvement with families we meet at our church, with the suppression of the people by the clergy who seem to find it so hard to work with the adult laity who are capable and willing. I heard and felt a kinship with the clergy from the missions who said the U.S. is more like missionary work because a conversion of heart was not forthcoming. I became aware of issues of social sin where our government, in our name, support dictators and death squads. I heard the clergy who have worked in the mission lands, now ministering here, got their strength from the powerful faith of the so called "missions".

At a Parish Council meeting I explored the openness within our parish to having a sister parish relationship with some parish in the Third World. Within a year this took off. Our sister parish is San Padro Carcha in Guatemala. Within this parish a group of Indian women are being gathered together in religious life for the first time in church history. Pope John Paul has been to visit them; they are recognized as a sisterhood. It is interesting that I find myself involved with woman religious. I also find it possibly more than coincidental that they are Indian women, for my name in religious life was Kateri, for Kateri Techawetha the North American Indian woman who is now called Blessed.

Recently my husband, our children, and I went down there to visit. It has had an immense impact on all of us. We have shared our visit often since our return. In this way we raise our own awareness, as well as that of others, of our brothers and sisters who live in a world full of poverty, but also vibrantly full of hope and promise, generosity and faith.

In the last couple of years that my husband and I were in Marriage Encounter I came to see a great deal of frustration and anger that would explode from me out of proportion to the situations. I began to see how verbally abusive I was to my husband and my children. It grieved me to see the pain I was inflicting on my daughter as she withdrew from me. I was shocked to see how angry I was at my husband for using the wrong word (in my opinion) in a sentence. I was also overweight and couldn't seem to get anywhere, even though I was on Weight Watchers for an extended time. My husband had been considering making a job change.

63

It had been a risky transition. But in the end the decision was good and it took some pressure off Bill so he could enjoy life and his family more.

It seemed as though we were entering a new stage in our life together. Yet my unhappiness and frustration seemed to be more apparent. I decided to get some counseling as a needed investment in the rest of our lives together.

I have been doing this now for four years. I see how much energy I have put into making the world a better place, helping others have happier lives. And yet I did not seem to know who I was, and what I wanted, even in simple situations. I have read several books, attended seminars, group therapy, couple and family counseling. I have come to see many of my issues are those of codependency. In addition I have had to break silence on the sexual abuse I was a victim of in my childhood. I participate in the Twelve Step programs of Survivors of Incest Anonymous and Codependence Anonymous.

I have done a reentry program and preceptorship for nursing a couple years ago. I have gone back to work part time at the local hospital as a Medical-Surgical Nurse. This is one of the hardest things I have done. At first I was so afraid of making a mistake. Now I am feeling comfortable with the work. The nurses have voted for the California Nurses Association (CNA) to represent them in collective bargaining for a first labor contract. I am part of the negotiating team. This is a further growth and learning process for me.

Six months ago we had a reunion gathering of the women who are, or have been, a part of the religious community with whom I lived. Over the years I had kept in touch with a couple of the sisters and had a couple of visits. For the most part I felt like I had been dropped by the community. Even though I asked to leave, that leaving did not change or remove some kind of tie I continue to feel for my community. They were and are my sisters in a greater sense, one that could never be changed, even as blood ties in a family can never be negated or rendered nonexistent. It seemed to me I was closer to them in spirit than to my own blood family. That did not change the fact that I did not wish to live my life according to the structure and rules that governed their lives. I was never sorry to have left the convent, but I was eager to see them and to know how they were doing. I wanted to be there to ease the loneliness and loss felt by any of my sisters who may have left. I wished I could have had them as friends when I made the most difficult adjustment of my new life.

I had been so excited about getting together again, and seeing women whom I hadn't seen in years. However, as I got nearer to the location I was surprised to see how anxious I was getting. I was feeling tense. I couldn't take a long deep breath. I got lost. I made wrong turns. I even lost the card that had the address, so that when I finally got to the right street I wasn't sure which house it was. I drove the length of the street and nothing looked like a school or convent. I was darned if I was going to just go away after all this. So I started looking for a gathering of cars, possibly with out of the area tags. I found something along this line, but I couldn't tell which house. I went to ask at one house, and I lucked out. As I was approaching the house one of the Sisters came out to meet me. I experienced the joy of finding my long lost sisters in more than one way.

It was fantastic to see my sisters. We had a large group in which we shared who and where we were. Some shared what they had done since leaving, and others in the community shared what work they were doing. It was interesting to see how the community and its work and some aspects of the life style had changed. We then had a meal together and some time to just visit, which I found to be the most valuable. I heard more here about what people were thinking and feeling in their lives. My regret was that the time was so short and that I was not able to visit enough with everyone. It did seem like a beginning. I hoped for more.

In the time that followed I felt confused once again as to what all this meant for me. I had this longing to be in closer contact with my sisters for myself as well as to be available to those still struggling to make the adjustment. I know I could make that happen, yet I felt very over-whelmed by my life as it was. I seemed to have too much on my plate of daily life already.

As I pondered this I also found that I did not relate to our daughter in her normal adolescent rebellious and frivolous actions. I noticed that my friends of today often had childhood friends or college friends with whom they shared experiences. That seemed to give them some level of understanding or sympathy for their daughters. I never had those college parties, roommates, or the sharing of clothes, the experimenting with makeup, and the comparing of notes about dates. Some of the women at our reunion said they felt the same thing. We discussed how we felt lost, out of it, abnormal when in these situations.

My choice to go to the convent for my maturation as a woman was nice and safe for me; it was a great life that met my needs at the time, but by going there I deprived myself of those skills, events, encounters, experiences and behaviors of searching for myself, and being an independent individual. Because of that I am not able to understand our daughter. Resentment, anger, hostility, suspicion are often the facets of our interactions. I hate having this kind of relationship with her. I am finding that for the first time in my life I am resentful that I ever went into the convent.

So now I am not so sure why I went into the convent. Did I go because of a selfless quality of wanting to love God and His people? Or did I go because I needed such a great deal of love myself? Was I mixed up and confused about my sexuality, which seemed a very dangerous and betraying aspect of life? Was it a place to go to avoid feelings of abandonment, separation, anger, resentment, failure, imperfection, betrayal, intimacy, untrustworthiness, isolation, and loneliness?

Perhaps that is too simplistic a contrast. Perhaps things are not so black or white. Perhaps there are a lot of shades of gray, and it was a little of both sides. I am beginning to break free of some of my addiction to perfection so that I can start to put these two sides of myself together. I can say, "There are shades of gray and that's ok".

Roberta Allen
Former Ursuline

Single

Retired

Bachelor of Arts, Mount St. Scholastica

Master of Fine Arts, Notre Dame University

Master of Arts, The Catholic University of America

Biology, Stanford University

Art, Art Institutes of Chicago, Kansas City, Madison

Special Linguistics, Georgetown

Eucharistic minister

Robbie might be officially retired, but she stays more active than most of us. She has just recently moved, so she is not yet known in her new parish. She loves proclaiming the Word, visits with her many friends and former students, and wants "to be a small cap saint." Although working with Mother Teresa's group would match her former training and work, she feels that the age of eighty "is a good age to start *being* for all."

Roberta Allen

It's Still Fun

"Happy Birthday! Happy Birthday!" I saw the sea of faces. But where is Janet? We're late. It's her birthday. Yet everyone keeps chanting, "Happy Birthday!" Then I heard "Aunt Robbie."

My niece Janet came forward; my sister Stasia, gracious at ninety, swept me into her arms. "But it's a whole month yet.' Why make me eighty before my time?" We laughed.

Only by anticipating the date could the party be a surprise and a real surprise it was!

Immediately I was seated. No looking back, please, for "This is Your Life" began, with my friend of fifty years, Pat Felton, officiating. Pat and my three nieces had planned everything.

That was November 1991. What a cross section of my life!

There were students from high school classes, men and women, grandparents now, recalling fun shows, debates, biology, English and art classes. My first kindergarten child who enrolled at age four and who finished junior college with me was there. My acting buddy of these last twenty years flew in from Ohio. Nuns from the convent, nieces and nephews from Washington, D.C. and Chicago came. It was an evening recalling the thirty-nine years spent as an Ursuline nun as well as the last twenty years teaching in the ghetto, selling insurance, painting, acting. Over a hundred friends came to celebrate my eighty years. They love Sister Roberta, Bernice, Miss Allen, Madre, Robbie — under any name I am the same.

Why, at age eighteen, on July 29, 1930, did I enter the small Ursuline Order in Paola, Kansas? Because I loved God, loved the Sisters who prepared me for First Holy Communion at age seven and taught me again in my junior year. Because I admired their lives, I wanted to serve God in their way.

During a retreat I felt a pull , a need to say "Yes" to God. But I had scores to settle first: boy friends to whom explanations were due, a tennis tournament to be played or a substitute found.

I returned to St. Teresa's Academy in Kansas City, Missouri for my senior year. Three of those classmates made it to this party!

After the Sisters let me enter, I sometimes felt they were just being nice to let me stay. There could be many reasons to say, "You gave your all, but, Bernice, it really isn't for you! We don't need a tap dancer, a cheerleader, a kid who loves the stage. You really need more growing up to do." I didn't want that to happen. I feared it might. If it did then I'd know God had other plans. He didn't. I stayed. I loved every day of my thirty-nine years.

Like all nuns, study played a large but not major part of my life. Daily prayer, Mass, meditation and all the "little way" practices were much a part of the spirituality of that time.

We all had assigned home jobs. For years I got up at five o'clock, a half hour early to run a three-foot wide mop up and down the main hall in the convent's four corridors. I finished in time to ring the Angelus. Then we prayed until 7:30. Classes began at 8:15.

I love teaching. God gave me an extra gene for creativity. No one ever stymied it. I was given full play in drama, dance, athletics, art and camp work.

In the summer after our degrees were earned, universities opened their male dorms to Sisters. We flooded into St. Louis U. for speech, Catholic U. for drama, Notre Dame for art.

Summer school was a strenuous but joyous time where many of us met Sisters from various orders. Lifelong friendships were forged. We danced together at Notre Dame. We sat on scaffolds and dripped paint from frescoes one delightful summer under Jean Charlot. We interviewed people in the street for a radio workshop at St. Louis U. We climbed mountains, painting watercolors in Colorado with the Lorentine's prisoner of war instructor.

We spent long hours talking, praying, studying with nuns from other orders who thought as we thought, taught as we taught. We were becoming unified, large orders, small congregations. We were spiritually being prepared for change.

Then came Vatican II.

Each convent., no matter how small, should send someone to the missions. I read it. I had always wanted to be a missionary. I prayed. I hoped. I said nothing.

Then a former principal, Father Ramon Carlin, for whom I had taught in Oklahoma City at McGuinness High, asked if I could come to Guatemala one summer to teach a drama for the celebration of his village, St. James, Santiago Atitlan, high in the mountains.

I spent a charismatic summer directing, costuming, and lighting a pageant given on the circular steps of their ancient church. How medieval could we get!

I spoke English; they spoke Tzutuhil; no one spoke much Spanish. We communicated in signs of love — eyes, hands, body language. We taped the story in Tzutuhil. We pantomimed with music the story of St. James. The story was taped again in Spanish for the *Ladino* population of the village.

That summer I fell in love again. I fell in love with the Mayan Indians. I truly felt God wanted me there, dirt and all. That summer my long black habit swept the fleas and dirt of the ancient village with every step. I counted seventy-seven flea bites one night on one leg and knee. A change of habit was needed if I were to return.

The next year our superior, Sister Charles McGrath, innovative and foreseeing, chose to let the Ursulines experiment with a short habit. Two beautiful Sisters in Oklahoma City began the school year 1964 in a sensible jumper, blazer, straight skirt combination.

Sisters Stephen Miller and Immaculata Elmer were well received.

Many die-hard "we-want-our-nuns-nuns" wrote to the convent, complaining. Letters were kept. Pros and cons were tabulated. The summer bulletin board at the motherhouse told the whole story. Nothing was held back from the community.

But the starched hats once off would never go on again. An ava-lanche of reform beginning as a quiet experiment in little Paola, Kansas under Mother Charles tumbled down mountain heights, sweeping the habit into oblivion.

The starched headband folded just so, the under cap to hold the hair (no, we didn't shave our heads!), the voluminous black petticoats with great pockets, the pencil holder, the long, rattling rosaries and big flat shoes with cotton stockings soon became memories to smile about.

It wasn't all easy. Many of us had to learn to sew. Why did I constantly make everything two sizes too big?

Experts were brought in to share pattern construction, fabric and design. We learned the hard way. We sewed. I thought being out of habit would be easier. It really wasn't.

Many times now I wish all I had to do was don a habit or put another hole in a cincture as my waist expands. Our black and white was appropriate for classroom, Mass, the dentist, a banquet., a speaking engagement, a wedding or a funeral. We could meet the mother of a child, the governor, the bishop or even the Holy Father and be in perfect attire.

I can't say the same for my slacks, sweatshirt, and Reeboks. It's a constant nothing-to-wear battle. Of course I miss the habit!

The following year after my summer in Santiago, Father Carlin asked for me to join his team. Two Sisters could be the answer to the Holy Father's directive.

When Sister Elizabeth Nick and I flew out of Kansas City for Guatemala, I thought it was for the rest of my life. I never expected to return. This was it.

I loved Santiago Atitlan. The little village, the Indian girls, men, boys would be my life. I set up a workshop for art classes in a long shed. Girls and women came daily. When tourists arrived via boat at 11:30 I met them on the steps of the church. How delighted they were to hear English from this white-haired woman.

A tour of the *bodega* ended in a pocket full of money to hand out the next day in class. Almost every painting, true primitives of village subjects, sold.

The men weavers were generally working. I took orders for shawls because two weavers could not produce enough for the demand.

Afternoons were spent in Tzutuhil with Antonio, a native with rudimentary Spanish and less English. I taught him English as I learned Tzutuhil. I know he learned faster than I. It is sad commentary to realize during the past revolution his dear life was taken—wise man, a true Christian, a person of culture and grace, *killed* because of political strife.

Evenings were given to teaching sculpture, the one art I know is still practiced since the men restored the carved pieces of the altar. From 7 to 9 o'clock any men who applied were taught. One of the twenty men walked fifteen miles twice a week for class. When I learned that, I gave him a set of tools, C-clamp, wood and enough instruction to let him work at home. His first piece was a twelve-inch statue of Jesus, beard colored in with pencil. It is one of my treasures.

I loved the mission, "Micatokla", named for the mission of Oklahoma. The diocese supported us. There were four priests: Father Carlin, an organizer; Father Robert Westerman, a builder; Fathers Tom Stafford and Jude Pansuri, entrepreneurs. A nurse, Marcella Faudree, ran a medical clinic, a well-baby instruction center and developed plans for a hospital. Marcella was a convert to Catholicism, a navy nurse, a salty woman of God loved by the whole village.

Two young women, Penny Gerbich and Rita Well, gave three years to set up and run a Montessori school. It was glorious to turn an old abandoned chicken coop into a colorful, delightful school room.

Sister Elizabeth Ann worked on translation and organization of Tzutuhil into written form. With Father Carlin and Juan Diego, a young Indian man, they constituted the office force.

Here truly great things happened. The unwritten language took written form. Juan, a brilliant Mayan, could easily be Ph.D material, or president of a University if he were born in our country, had our opportunities. His life, too, was lost to marauding soldiers in the '70's.

But the greatest loss came after the revolution worsened. We were all gone. Only Father Stanley Rother, a replacement for all of us, remained to offer Mass, hold the spiritual life of the village in his great capable hands. One night, July 28, 1981, three men entered his room, tortured him, shot him, left him bleeding to die. The villagers sent his body back to the States, but kept his great heart. They wanted his strength, his love never to leave.

The efforts of the men of the village established a small chapel, a shrine for his heart. It was dedicated on July 28, 1989. My companion Pat and I were there. My joy was to walk the cobblestone lanes, be remembered as Madre Roberta, or simply Madre. I shed more tears on that joyous trip than I care to tell.

Twenty-plus years ago when I was called home to Ursuline, I suffered re-entry culture shock. That was a turning point in my religious life. I remember standing on the front steps of the convent and looking over a manicured lawn; my Indians had no such space. I watched pampered girls eating candy bars, and complaining about the nutritious meals served in the dining room on white tablecloths. The Indians never starved, but they seldom had sweets, tablecloths never. I was vowed to poverty; my Indians lived it. I felt a great loss. I didn't fit in anymore. I was restless, critical, and even in a crowd, lonely.

One night I awakened at 11:30 and couldn't get lack to sleep. I decided to dress, go to chapel, and talk with Jesus. The rotunda clock showed ten minutes to midnight.

I loved the darkness, the open chapel windows, the June night air. Kneeling at the altar rail (we still have a marble one) I looked at my Friend and He at me. I don't remember what He said. I do know when I finally left to go back to bed I felt joyous and relaxed. The clock in the rotunda read 5:15!

In the breaking morning light I walked to the cemetery to tell all my friends there, "I have decided to leave Ursuline. There must be other work to do. It's not because I don't love you. I do. I love every brick here, but this is what I'll do now." Then I walked all over the campus. I skipped down the driveway to the grotto. I threw a kiss to the pergola. I danced before the Sacred Heart Shrine. The Angelus caught me off guard. I was late for morning prayer. We still kissed the floor when tardiness was our fault. I would.

The hall cleaning job had long ago been assigned to younger legs. I remember thinking, "Mmm — no one has cleaned yet, but who cares!" I kissed the floor and determined joyously to hold my secret for a while.

Our community was building Lakemary School for Exceptional Children. That summer a friend and former pupil, Pat Felton, had come to assist the Sisters in setting up office forms, files, purchasing supplies and in general overseeing and guiding an inexperienced staff through the initial stages of setting up the office for the new school.

Over thirty years Pat and I had kept in touch. I offered her support and companionship. For her I felt protective, and breaking the news of leaving bothered me. Imagine my surprise when her reaction was, "Great! Will you come live with me?" That would be impossible. She lived in an apartment in the small town. People have such imaginations; I'd never do anything to cast a shadow on the Sisters.

So she moved to Kansas City. I then accepted her invitation until I'd know my plans. That was twenty-two years ago. We still share a home.

74

God provided me the stability, guidance and love that every soul needs. I got all that from Pat. We seem to be opposites, but time has proven our compatibility. I pray God bless her and give her continued good health, humor and patience. For me, Pat made re-entry easy and joyous.

Two weeks later my job opportunity came as I washed windows in our little rented house. Novitiate training never leaves one; we all scrub diligently. The phone call was in answer to my letter to the Kansas City, Kansas school board. Could I attend a meeting at 2 o'clock? I was needed to teach English in a junior high. I was sorry, but my little VW would not be delivered until the following day. Never mind. A gentleman would pick me up. Could I be ready in a half hour? I was.

Enroute to the meeting I realized the gentlemen was from the main office, a man in charge of hiring, firing and evaluating. He was rushing me to a meeting he was to chair.

When I asked what was expected of seventh grade English students, the answer seemed ludicrous. "Miss Allen, just get them to write one good paragraph of five sentences by the end of the year and you'll be fine.

Five sentenccs! In a year! Not this gal. True, I had taught seventh grade for one year; senior English was one of my favorite classes to teach. But five sentences! He was not too far wrong.

No master's degrees were necessary. Doctorates that were unfinished could wait. I never got one. Now I saw God's plan. A Ph.D would have priced me right out of the ghetto junior high market. Here is where the Holy Spirit placed me.

My classes were almost solidly black. Every little face looked the same that first week. But I decided to treat each one like the prince and princess each never was! We got along famously.

There were exceptions: the sixteen-year old in the back seat who wrote "zwgny" twenty times for the spelling words; the pretty, belligerent twelve-year old I found crying because someone called her a "Toastie". "My daddy is white," she sobbed. Then there was the brilliant ten-year-old who read at high school level. He would be bored if I didn't do something fast. I did.

I asked the principal, a wonderful black educator, if he'd let me arrange the classes according to ability. For truly all men are not created equal in seventh grade English.

It was necessary to get all the teachers handling seventh grades to sign a consent. They signed. We reorganized. The five sentence paragraph seemed a nearer possibility. By year's end, autobiographies of several pages, illustrated and bound, were on display.

The "zwgny-kid" had met an untimely end. Over Christmas vacation he had killed his mother, chopped her body, bagged it and deposited it behind a grocery store. I often wonder if he hadn't such plans for "Mizzz Zallen"! I still pray for him. I found my Indians again.

After a few years I found I was not being paid for either master's degree. I called on Mr. Robert Burns, the head man, presented my case and walked out with a new job and more money — traveling art teacher to demonstrate for the classroom teachers, using their children. This was the life of a gypsy. Even Mr. Burns knew that.

When the new Schlagle High School was erected, he asked me to take over ordering and arranging the two teacher department. It became a showplace. Mr. Paul Shein, a talented black man, and I delighted in space for photography, silver work, clay wheels, individual storage and desk space and beauty. We made the rooms beautiful!

But the years were climbing, and retirement would soon be on me. I studied the Insurance business. Kansas City Life sent a young man to sell me life insurance. I knew everyone should have what he offered. In fact, he sponsored me, and I passed for my license. At that time there were only two women in sales. The men spoiled us. Like a sponge I absorbed all the hints. Being a lover of people and a ham, I sold well and easily. At the close of the school year I resigned with forty-three years' experience. Now it was fun climbing the business ladder to the President's Club. I found selling insurance was still teaching. My classes were smaller, families and businessmen. In this business one is rewarded with golf clubs and trips. Acapulco was a highlight.

A move to Tulsa, Oklahoma put an end to insurance sales. Instead I joined an acting group. The local Gaslight Theatre paid; the local Tulsa Theatre was volunteer. What fun to be Miss Marple, a Madame, a crazy artist, character types naturally. It was delightful. The list of credits grew and grew. I was no longer directing, I was being directed and loved it. But dinner theater six nights a week for three months can grow tiresome.

It began when Pat's grandmother came to live with us. Pat was a convert and her grandmother, a non-church goer, asked one day to go to church with us. We offered to take her to any church of her choice. She wanted ours. Finally she asked to be a Catholic. We had prayed together daily and answered her questions. She believed.

A priest friend, Father Donal Schwalm, was coming for Christmas. He offered Mass, baptized, confirmed, and gave our dear wheelchair patient her first Holy Communion and anointed her in our home! Pat's grandmother, my good friend, lived to become a great source of joyful prayer.

During the final months when she needed care we could no longer give, we had to put her in a nursing home. Here I took her Communion. It was shocking to learn other Catholics were envious. No one brought Jesus to them. I did.

Taking care of every person, Catholic and non-Catholic alike, became my job. It took two full days a week. Some days I carried twenty-seven hosts to the two homes.

Danny, a child-like octogenarian, asked if he couldn't have Jesus, too. I gave him Jesus. That night he died in his sleep.

Gramps, a wheelchair darling who always met me at the door, smiled his crooked, paralyzed smile one day and said to me, "Not bap— Not bap". "You're, not baptized, Gramps? You want to be?" Oh, the smile, the nods. In the corner of a sitting room using a towel and glass of water from the beauty parlor, I baptized him. Then Gramps and I received Jesus, loved Him and talked to Him together for one far too short hour. When I returned the next Wednesday Gramps was not at the door to greet me. His room was empty. Gramps was in heaven.

But there was the Italian man who made a fist and covered his face and yelled curses at me as I entered his room. I used the Eucharist to bless the room and him. His roommate was a gentle soul who should be spared such scenes. He decided, though, that Rizzio needed Jesus to come to the room. We'd put up with the outbursts. One day I stopped praying to say, "Rizzio, for God's sake, shut up." Silence. "Thank you, Rizzio. Now Jesus can hear our prayers." That toothless old fellow smiled. It was a first. We all laughed together.

I ruffled his hair and said, "You old geezer, you, Rizzo. I think all you want is to tell Jesus you are sorry for being such ani old ogre. He smiled again. I wondered if he had a mind at all. Then he looked me straight in the eye. "I need a priest," he said. "I'll get you one," I said. I got him the most gentle priest I knew. Each week for months Rizzo's room was the first and last I visited. It took a long hard cancer to get him into heaven, but he made it. I was with him when he died. These are the works of mercy, the ministries of the modern nuns.

We all pray as much as ever, not in the same way, but as ardently. We all have Dannys and Rizzios to help. We must keep our souls filled to overflow to all God's little oldies.

God was good when He directed President Roosevelt to establish Social Security. Without it. I would be a bag lady. With it I am quite comfortable, thank you God! Although I am dispensed of my vows I still practice poverty, keep chastity and observe obedience everytime I prepare dinner, stop at a red light or go shopping for groceries.

My prayer life, judging from changes in poetic writings, has deepened. I'm an avid reader. Sometimes I admit being too critical. Then I relax, love God, myself and my neighbor.

All these years I've been saying, "Here I am, God. Use me." He does. I find joy in letting Him move me around.

One year in Washington, D.C., I found a notation in a book attributed to St. Thomas More: "God, I am your chessman. Move me, Move me if you can, but move me like a man." I made this my prayer. For twenty-five years I taught at Ursuline junior college and academy. After making this prayer my own, I was moved often. I am grateful.

Many good things happen to let me know "God's in His heaven. All's right with the world." A student sends a plane ticket for a two week visit to Florida. Another student sends a ticket for an over-Easter visit so we can have Holy Week together. For these joys, I thank Thee, Lord.

But people, even those who know me, still are filled with questions. "Have you been sorry you never had a family?"

Of course, I'd love a family, I'd like a family of ten. I'm number eight in ours. I knew the extent of my offering on vow day. I held up to Him all the babies He could have given me. I prayed never to disappoint one soul. Many are happier husbands with someone else. Some are bright children of other mothers. But yes. Aren't most women nesters by nature? That was my father's only worry. "Are you sure you can live a life alone? You are so much like your mother!" Bless him. He knew Mama; he knew his daughter.

"Did you mind being moved around from school to school?"

Not really. God takes us at our word. I say, "Yes, Lord. Use me, Lord. Move me like a man. I am yours no matter the place nor time nor name. The soul, the essence is the same."

So one is used. Moved from a cultured girl's boarding school to dusty but cultured Indian girls, from the brown skins to black. Who cares if they cannot read nor write. That's my job to break the mold. What if it's to the elderly who are crotchety, the weak. I still go. Use me.

Then some ask, "Are you still a Catholic?" Of course. I serve on the liturgical committee, am a lector and a Eucharistic minister. Yes, I'm active in a variety of ways, a regular Catholic. It isn't what one does that is important, it is what one is. Yes, I'm still a Catholic.

Another question, "Would your order take you back?" Of course I never asked. I don't know canon law on this question, but I do know the Ursuline's love for every nun and student who passed through her doors. I'd not want to add another responsibility to the young superior. I'd only go back if all my work here were finished and if I had something to offer my sisters. But the answer is "Yes." I trust the love of the Ursuline.

Often I'm asked, "How does it happen you have such diverse fields of teaching?" I'm not cut according to the usual pattern. Before I started work on a master's degree, my superior mother complimented me on my work in science. She asked my choice for graduate study.

I had hoped she would ask. "I think we need a medical doctor. I'd like to go into medicine," I replied.

"Kansas University has an excellent program," she replied thoughtfully "We'll see."

The, next summer I spent immersed in formaldehyde and cadavers. When Mother Jerome learned I was the only woman in the program, she felt guided to ask me to transfer to another field "Why not drama or art?" So my teaching field changed direction, branching out from biology, anatomy and physiology to art and drama. I have not been sorry.

But the most frequent of all: "Why did you leave?" Do you have a couple of days? But I can put the answer in one sentence. God moved me.

Next question, please. On and on they go.

Even for these questions, I thank Thee, Lord.

The litany of thanks grows longer with each passing year. The Sisters at Ursuline invite us to lunch when we stop to visit. For this joy, thank You, Lord. A letter comes from a student taught forty years ago. I thank You, Lord. The sun floods my room with a rosy dawn. For this beauty, I thank Thee, Lord. My art show is well accepted. I paint a fresco and it's still there in the chapel. For this gift I thank Thee, Lord. For giving me eighty long, joyous vibrant years, I thank Thee, Lord. Yes, I'm still Sister Roberta Allen with a little "s" to my family, students and friends. For this, and all the joy of celebrating eighty years, "Happy Birthday to me!", I thank Thee, Lord.

2
LAUDS

O God, my God,
To Thee do
I watch at break of day.
Thus will I bless Thee
All my life long,
And in Thy name
I will lift up my hands.

Doris Althoff Kozlowski
Former Sister of Charity

Married, four children

Day care provider; homemaker and mother

Bachelor of Arts, Clarke College, Iowa

Doris is especially interested in curriculum development in elementary education. Her concern for children's issues is a natural outgrowth, or perhaps cause, of that interest. She enjoys gardening and music, and not only hopes to raise her family, but also wishes to "improve elementary education to meet the needs of special children."

Doris Althoff Kozlowski

Small Worlds and Large

Most people think of convents as closed places, institutions which narrow the lives of the people who enter them. That was not the case for me. Joining the Sisters of Charity brought me into a new larger world. I have met people and acquired values which have expanded my life and continue to do so over the more than twenty hears which I have passed since I left the order.

I grew up on an Iowa farm. For the first eighteen years of my life I was sheltered, cloistered indeed. My father and mother, two brothers and sister and I worked the farm together. The daily chores plus the plantings and harvestings made all our lives a constant round of hard physical labor. We had no holidays. Before and after the brief respite which school provided, there were dozens of chores which just had to get done.

My sister was the only member of the family that I could share my thoughts and feelings with. We were not just biological sisters, but soul sisters as well. She was three years older than I and we had long heart to hearts as we sweated away at the chores.

Both my Mom and Dad came from large families. We had, quite literally, hundreds of first cousins who provided our main social contacts. Every Sunday mobs of aunts, uncles and cousins would come over to our house. My mother, who seemed to relish masses of visitors, always prepared ample meals of simple, heavy, but tasty food. Those Sunday dinners, along with our T. V. set—a rarity among our relations — were a big draw. While the adults gabbed, we would play softball in the pasture or take part in some other team sport. Since we never traveled farther than the nearest town, these Sunday gatherings were just about our only glimpse at the world outside our farm.

Most of the older people in my family had barely finished grade school. A few of the younger ones went to high school, but nobody ever went to college. By contrast, I was a good student; I liked school work. In my heart I knew that I wanted more than a high school diploma, farmer husband and a bunch of kids. Yet these ambitions were vague dreams. I had very little idea of how I could carry them out. I did know that I like and respected my teachers. Most of them were nuns. By the time I got to high school I began thinking of entering the convent. My teachers encouraged me and I was accepted as a postulant by the BVMS.

My parents' reactions to this were not very positive. I first told my dad as he lay on the couch resting. He did not say anything, but his eyes slowly welled up with tears. After a while, he got off the couch. He went into the bedroom and stayed there a long time. He never said a word about it. My mother put up a stiffer fight. To get ready for the convent I had to gather a wardrobe which met a strict set of guidelines. My postulant's habit was a most demanding garment which had to be made to order. Although my Mom was a whiz with the sewing machine, she refused to help. I had to get one of my aunts to sew it for me.

On the last day of July in 1964, I set off for the motherhouse. My parents had not warmed up to the idea. When my brothers carried my big, black trunk out to the car, my mother looked at me and said, "Well, there goes your coffin!" It was social death as far as she was concerned. Her attitude was not improved by the way things went once we got to the motherhouse. We were ushered into a room. A couple of novices more or less snatched me and I did not have the chance to say a proper good-bye to my family.

For the first few weeks I was lonely. I had never been away from home before. I missed my sister and the fields and the familiar daily routine. I cried a lot without really knowing why I was crying.

The motherhouse itself was set on a high bluff overlooking the Mississippi River. It was surrounded by trees and other scenery. It was a huge place full of people; almost all of them seemed happy to be there. The other young women in my set of sixty came from all over the U.S., from places I had only heard of: New York, New Jersey, Chicago. I began to realize that this was what I had been looking for. I stopped crying.

86

Our first visiting day came in October. I could not wait to see my family and find out whether or not they had started to understand why I had come to this place. My sister came with her husband and brand new baby. He was a big hit with the other girls who lived too far away to have their families visit. My Dad found that he was able to joke with some of my classmates. My parents were building a new barn and so they had something to talk about. Of course I still cared about them and the farm, but I wanted to tell them all about what I was doing. They were not too curious about that. Before they left, my Mom managed to ask, "So, when are you coming home?" That was enough to make me all the more determined to stick it out. Throughout the next three years as postulant and novice, their visits came every six months. During each visit my Mom asked, "So, when are you coming home?" That question always kept me going for the next six months.

I stayed for four years. Now I am forty-six years old. Those four years represent only a small portion of my lifetime, but they had a tremendous impact on me. During those years I made many friends who came from backgrounds very different from my own; four of them are still my closest friends to this day. All of us eventually left, but even now they are there when I need them. When my mother died in 1984 and my father passed on in 1989, three of them left their own husbands and children to stand by me in my grief.

Beyond those personal attachments I learned about the larger world which I could only imagine as a farm girl. I became concerned about issues of social justice, not only in the U.S.A., but also in places like Latin America. In the 1960s the convent was an exciting place to be. Everybody seemed to have some new insight, some passionate cause which was always contagious. We talked about everything and anything. Also, the many hours we had for study and reflection gave us the chance to examine our souls in a way that few people can do. Even today I need my time to meditate on my self and the world. If I do not have the opportunity for quiet reflection, I feel cheated somehow.

Throughout the four years, my only struggle was with the notion of living a chaste life forever. Poverty and obedience were not problems when compared to that. I finally decided that I really wanted to marry and have children. I left in 1968 and became a public school teacher. I met a man who was an ex-seminarian. We shared so much because both of us appreciated what life on the inside was like. Similar ideas and values brought us together. My husband became a college professor specializing in the study of Muslims in India and Pakistan, so, I got to see a larger chunk of the world than even I had imagined. I have lived in India, Pakistan and England. If I had not stepped off the farm and into the cloister, I would not have had those experiences.

My convent days also helped me with family life. We have four children; two of them are adopted. In 1990 we adopted a little biracial baby, something that would have been unthinkable if I had not had the kind of moral education I got in the convent. Raising four children, two of them teenage girls, in a big city, can be a tense activity. Still, I have some pretty clear ideas about the values I want them to have. Convents can help to create independent-minded, caring women. I would like my daughters to be that way.

Apart from all the serious stuff, the thing I remember most about being in the convent is the laughter. We always had something to howl about. So many things happened that struck us as hilarious.

As novices, three of us were assigned to clean the chapel used by the retired sisters. Only the old nuns used it, so there was not a whole lot of dirt. However, a retired novice-mistress was assigned to oversee our work and she seemed to think that cleaning this chapel was one of Holy Mother Church's most important apostolates. Even though there was no dirt, every day she made us take the mops and do the floors. When we complained that it was hard to tell where we had mopped and where we had not, she suggested that we "make an imaginary line," and go on from there. In order to prevent our getting bored by this, she would sometimes pull out a stop watch. She would walk beside us as we mopped, repeating in an anxious whisper, "Faster, sisters, faster!"

Once a month we not only mopped the floor, but we had to clean imaginary cobwebs (at least on the farm the dirt was real) off the chapel ceiling. Our taskmistress devoted considerable ingenuity to inventing a way to clean the corners of a twenty-five foot high ceiling. She got three long bamboo fishing poles. We lashed these together and tied a rag to the end of them. The three of us who did this work were advantageously different in terms of height. At 5' 8", I was the tallest. One of my good friends stood 5' 5". Our other partner was only 5'2". She was also, by the way, short on a sense of humor.

We would line up in order of height with me in the lead. I would attempt to aim these bending, swaying poles in the general direction of the ceiling. The other two, in order of size, would attempt to steady this contraption. What gave my friend and me fits was the way the poles would dip. There were always a few elderly nuns praying in the chapel and the poles would sometimes hover precariously close to their heads. My friend and I, much to the horror of our serious partner, would begin speculating under our breath about what would happen if we accidently brained one of the old dears. "She'd never know what hit her!" It would certainly have put an end to the quest for imaginary spider webs on the ceiling of the retired nuns' chapel.

The main chapel was a favorite roosting place for a colony of bats. Occasionally during Compline the bats would decide to have some fun by dive-bombing the assembled nuns. From the rear pews it was quite a show. Suddenly a hundred veiled heads would lean to the right or lean to the left in unison depending on which way the bats were making their runs. Some of us got the bright idea of trying to drive the bats out of the chapel. We grabbed a bunch of tennis balls and entered the chapel. We tried to aim at them as they hung in the dark corners. All we did was carom tennis balls off the statues. Unfortunately, we did not scare off the bats.

Working in the kitchen had its disadvantages and advantages. The old heavy habits and restrictive veils were sheer hell in the summer time. When assigned to fry hundreds of pieces of bacon and dozens after dozens eggs in the middle of July, we tended to leave puddles of sweat anywhere we had been standing for more than a couple of minutes. When it was possible, we would sneak into the walk-in freezers and try to cool off.

One of the advantages of kitchen duty was being able to dish out a few extra helpings when some real goodies were on the menu. One of my good friends had a great fight in those circumstances. She was working with one of our really serious colleagues, a person who took everything too seriously for her own good and ours. One day they were supposed to dish out ice cream for dessert. This was a rare treat. My friend was wielding the scoop with wild liberality. Sister Serious was doling it out one dab at a time. The serious nun finally said to my friend that she did not think that such large portions of ice cream were in keeping with holy poverty. My friend simply answered by saying, "You are nuts!" and handing out even bigger portions. Eventually, Sister Serious threw down her spoon and ran out of the kitchen, crying with vexation. These small victories still make us laugh.

By the time I had reached the scholasticate things had really begun to change. We got permission to go back to our family names and to adopt a modified habit, one that did not contain eighteen feet of heavy serge. A couple of us, none very good tailors, did the work in record time. We found that we were getting a small cash allowance every month. We also discovered that the old habit had advantages over the new one. We ended up blowing most of our money on panty hose.

It was while I was in the scholasticate that I decided to leave. Before I knew it, I found myself temporarily back on the farm. Mom was delighted to see me. "Oh! there wasn't an ocean big enough to hold my tears when you left," she told me later. I do not think I ever did find a way to tell her that my journey to the cloister had taken me out of her world forever and brought me into a bigger world that I may not understand, but which is filled with possibilities.

Terri MacKenzie
Society of the Holy Child of Jesus

Free-lance ministry

Bachelor of Arts, Mundelein College

Master of Arts, Notre Dame University

Terri, who is temporarily sharing an apartment with her brother, continues her involvement with community through Eucharist, prayer, social and business meetings, mail and telephone. "I hope to grow in my appreciation of and ability to enhance the gift of life," states Terri. This profound interest in the great mystery of God and the human mystery are part of Terri's interest in community, science, mythology, creating a better future, and all the connections "between and among" the above.

Terri MacKenzie

Boundaries

When I was a little girl, I always colored within the lines. I liked to try new colors and ever-more-difficult patterns, but I never veered from the given outline. It was the forties and I, like my Roman Catholic contemporaries, was used to firm boundaries. We accepted many lines which crisply divided, for example, Roman Catholics (who went to heaven) from others (who did not); mortal sins from venials; perfect contrition from imperfect; when we could eat meat from when we could not.

Entering the convent was definitely a break from the normal pattern of college, marriage, children. It was a step I tried hard to avoid. However, something within assured me that if I didn't follow my call, I'd regret it. I pictured myself about thirty, drinking coffee some morning, knowing I had made the wrong choice. I entered the convent in 1952.

Once within the new set of boundaries, I felt at home. The spirit, the values, the purpose, the people — and, I'm sure, the fifties — helped me feel comfortable with the very rigid rules and regulations. It was, indeed, the right choice for me, and I looked forward to spending the rest of my life following the same daily, weekly, monthly, yearly schedules. I vividly remember realizing that I would probably teach the same junior high grades for the rest of my life, and I was suffused with joy. Living within the lines was as easy for me as coloring within them.

In the sixties our high schools needed art teachers. Although my artistic development had not progressed much beyond the coloring book stage, I began summer studies for a masters in art at Notre Dame University. One of the sharpest memories I have of my many summers there is of the first time I took my brush and deliberately broke through one color boundary to blend that color with its partner. Then I broke another line and another, until I was looking at my first abstract painting. I was surprised and pleased to find it harmonious and pleasing.

I'm not sure why I broke those line-barriers, or why it took me so long to do so. Perhaps there was some connection with the fact that Catholic rules, rules in religious life, and thus, my life, were beginning to change.

Since that time I have taught, administered schools, served in community leadership, and worked with teachers, parents and parishioners. By the eighties we religious were exercising our ministry in many ways. I worked with/for an international organization for global change (Global Education Associates); represented non-governmental groups at the United Nations; gave talks and workshops throughout the United States and England; spent time in Mexico; visited Eastern Europe six times; produced a TV series and video materials; published articles....

Like many religious groups, mine learned to live without authoritarian government, rigid rules, certainties. We learned, and are learning, to respect our experiences, feelings and intuitions, and to trust them as we search together for answers that are not final. Not without growing pains, we shifted from reliance on outside forces (superiors and rules) and learned to take greater responsibility for our own, and our corporate, actions.

These and other influences helped me to break out of the boundaries with which I grew up: boundaries separating various religious communities, religions, gender characteristics, nations, cultures, etc. By the Nineties my journey had taken me outside the once-clear separation of humans from the rest of Earth, and I identified with the living unity of all creation. What my either-or mentality had once viewed as absolute and isolated categories, (e.g., secular and sacred, heaven and earth, good or evil), I now see as interrelated parts of a whole.

I realize that many people facilitated my move beyond boundaries, some known to me and some of whom I was never aware. My own religious sisters provided both catalyzing directives and loving support. Religious from other communities helped me, too, as did ex-nuns and men and women from other life choices. I treasure them all.

The religious life I entered is gone. Outside the boundaries we once knew, we now face many uncertainties. No longer are we secure about numbers, finances, our relationship with the official church, our prayer styles, living arrangements, government, new modes of membership — even our role and ministry in a church and world that have also changed. Our future is no longer clear. I'm nearly twice-thirty now, and I drink herb tea in the morning. When I think about my life, I regret neither the lines that bound me nor the boundaries that I've broken. My future is a mystery; because of my past, I feel prepared to live it "out of bounds."

Kathleen Grace Burke
Former Dominican

Divorced, annulled, one son, 19.

Director of Communications, Regina Dominican High School

Senior Lecturer, Loyola University, Department of English

Bachelor of Arts, Loyola University, Chicago

Master of Arts, DePaul University

Doctor of Philosophy, Loyola University, Chicago

Active parishioner

Former member of Cardinal's Conference of the Laity

Centering Prayer Group

In April of 1991 Kathleen celebrated five years of survival by running the Boston Marathon. Her long distance running for the past fourteen years has "kept me sane throughout dissertation writing, my divorce, and cancer therapy." In the summer 1992 she hopes to complete a triathalon, but "since my warranty ran out in 1986 I cannot assume that I'll live too far beyond the now." She is searching for a publisher for her survival story.

Kathleeen G. Burke

Unforgetting the Convent

Alethea, Greek for truth, literally means "unforgetting." For twenty years, I worked hard to forget my brief time in the religious life. When my fourteen-year marriage ended in 1984, the convent memories came rushing through the cracks in my armor. I knew I had to resolve all of that unfinished business before I could get on with life. I had made a small dent in that process when, in 1986, I was diagnosed with advanced Hodgkins' Disease. Despite my strong will to survive, I knew that given the extent and concentration of tumors, total cure was unlikely. During that summer my life passed before me in slow motion.

Sometimes I would just sit and savor the blessings I had received. By then I realized that my decision to enter and then leave the convent had profoundly affected my life. My brief time in religious life strengthened me to face future challenges as I recalled one summer morning, just after undergoing my third round of chemotherapy.

Unable to sleep more than two or three hours a night, I would try to calm myself by reading the day's Lectionary. Hours before dawn I found Paul's words to the Corinthians:

> We possess a treasure in earthen vessels to make it clear that its surpassing power comes from God and not from us. We are afflicted in every way possible, but we are not crushed; full of doubts, we never despair. We are persecuted, but never abandoned; we are struck down but never destroyed. Continually we carry about in our bodies the dying of Jesus, so that in our bodies the life of Jesus may also be revealed. While we live we are constantly being delivered to death for Jesus' sake, so that the life of Jesus may be revealed in our mortal flesh. Death is at work in us, but life in you. . . .

Everything is ordered to your benefit, so that the grace bestowed in abundance may bring greater glory to God because they who give thanks are many.

—2 Corinthians: 7-12, 15

For the first time I had a sense of what Paul was talking about in that evocative passage. I was grateful, for abundant grace had ensured that I, also an earthen vessel, had survived so far, that I had been "struck down but never destroyed." Maybe this illness had come to remind me that I was not invincible. Carrying the death of Jesus in my body, with the wounds in my feet from surgical scars, and the wounds in my heart, where the largest tumor was concentrated, I was more aware of the brevity and fragility of life.

Now that I was staring death in the face, once fearsome memories no longer threatened me. I did a lot of truth-seeking, a lot of courageous unforgetting that summer. If I could not turn back the clock to relive my life, I could at least try to understand the decisions that had shaped it. I recalled the first day of spring, 1965, the day I came home from the convent.

"That was a real death in life, the way you were cut off from us, even from your family," one of my friends observed at the time. But for me, the death in life was not the restricted contact with secular friends and family. It was the hairsplitting regulation of every aspect of our lives, right down to what we could read and think. It was over the thinking issue that to be true to my self, I finally had to leave. I could keep silent for twenty-three hours a day, but I could not turn my mind off. It teemed with far too many questions about the quality of life in that pre-Vatican II novitiate.

I paid a heavy price for my return to the world. My freedom to think was restored to me, but I felt like an android with implanted tapes. Before leaving I had been sworn to secrecy about convent life. I could process what happened only in very strained conversations with my confessor.

"If it were such a beautiful experience, why do you look so sad?" asked the young parish priest.

"I'm not supposed to say."

100

"You have to get it out somehow," he said. "If you can't talk, then write about it."

For a few days I hesitated to follow his advice. The formation director had warned me not to write about the convent for a few years. Claiming divine inspiration, she told me I was "an intellectual monster" and would be "of no use to society." Nearly twenty years later I found out this was a standard exit line in many communities, but what nice girl still in her late teens, is going to question, much less repeat that curse?

If entering the convent involved a death to the world, leaving the convent involved another death, a total loss of identity. Not only had I changed spiritually and psychologically in the convent, but physically as well. Pleasingly plump when I had entered in the autumn of 1964, I was a wraith-like shadow of my old self when I emerged the following spring. This shrunken stature reflected my shattered self-esteem.

After many years I came to realize that I entered the convent to satisfy my need for stability and for power. I thought that as a religious I could remain passive, and give over the right to make all choices to my superiors. In addition, I'd gain the recognition of being the Bride of Christ. It had taken less than a year for me to realize that to save my soul, I had to leave the convent. Trading my Sleeping Beauty dream for what I imagined was autonomy, my impressionable adolescent psyche was nevertheless deeply scarred by the effects of pre-Vatican formation methods.

I was free, but not free of that past. I had to wall up my soul, which for decades would remain buried in the convent. I couldn't stand to be in remote country places. The sound of classical church music would break my heart. I threw myself into urban university life, into activism, into dating. Grades were a secondary consideration—I was determined not to be an intellectual monster.

After college I married a handsome Jewish medical student. Aggressive as I was retiring, confident as I was full of self-doubt, he offered stability, the promise of a pleasure-filled life, and vicarious power. Women couldn't become doctors back then, but we could marry them. If I couldn't marry Christ, I'd marry the next thing to God! My spouse was not intimidated by my intellectual interests. Best of all, there was nothing about him to remind me of my buried convent self. Yet for all fourteen years of our marriage, "a Godshaped blank" yawned in my heart.

My ties with the church became increasingly tenuous after the awful spring of 1968, when assassinations of Dr. Martin Luther King Junior and Robert Kennedy cast a pall over a graduation otherwise full of hope and promise. "How can a God who is good cause this to happen?" I raged. But I continued to attend church, and even to bow, initially, to the wisdom of *Humanae Vitae* on the dubious grounds that if I hadn't quit the Church over the brutal end of my dream of religious life, I sure wouldn't leave it over an encyclical.

I did take a sabbatical of sorts from the Church after witnessing my father's harrowing death of kidney cancer just before my first wedding anniversary. The day after his funeral, I found a new god in literature. As I started my lesson plans for the week's unit on *Romeo and Juliet*, I found in Shakespeare the friend who would never die or leave me. For the next few years my only remaining contacts with the Church were occasional weddings and funerals. The loss of my father, a wonderful, giving, loving man of faith, was more than my immaturity could bear at that stage. I went into hiding from God.

The hound of heaven chased me down the years and up three stories to a Victorian three-flat in Lincoln Park where, late in 1973, 1 was watching a PBS version of *Catholics*, Brian Moore's novella. Although I still avoided triggering the associations evoked by country scenes or traditional church music, I did not expect a movie about monks in Ireland in the twenty-first century to unleash any dangerous memories. The same art that I had used to flee from God provided the vehicle for the return trip. At the end of *Catholics*, when the faithless abbot had struggled to say the "Our Father," I inadvertently began, then deliberately continued to speak the words. Watching his agony, I finally appreciated the gift long hidden in my heart.

The next day I participated in an Advent reconciliation at the school where I was teaching. Though restored to institutional membership in the Church, I was only marginally involved for the first few years. I was too consumed by my dry, soul-less quest for academic achievement for myself and material success through my spouse. We moved to the North Shore, Chicago's symbol of "making it." I worked on my dissertation.

During those years I had occasional nightmares about the convent. Usually it was a funeral procession down the aisle of the motherhouse chapel. I'd get to the casket and see my old self. I would awaken, not terrified about the sight of myself in the coffin, but filled with deep longing to return to the chapel.

With more time on my hands I became politically active in archdiocesan politics and in Call to Action. I became an expert on the Church. Music no longer bothered me as much. In 1980 I quit smoking (which I'd started when I left the convent) and joined the choir at St. Clement's. I hadn't sung a note in fifteen years, but my voice came back. Yet I'd feel terribly lonely when I'd have to go home after the rehearsal or the mass or the concert. A part of my self still lived in that music, but I couldn't bring her home.

Once I finished my doctorate, activism and running compensated for the dull suburban split-level trap I had bought into. My husband was busy starting his internal medicine practice, then rising through the ranks of the staff at his hospital. I was intellectually and emotionally exhausted from the much too rapid writing of my dissertation on the grotesque in the fiction of Joyce Carol Oates. I finished my first draft the day they discovered the first bodies in serial killer John Wayne Gacy's basement. That and the Jonestown Massacre too closely mirrored the shadow of contemporary American life which I had been exploring through Oates' fiction. I declared a TV news blackout for several months.

I found in running a new connection with nature. I rediscovered the connection with my body that had been neglected for nearly twenty years, since the conservative social mores of the early 1960s had prohibited the possibility of athletic activity for young women. Now that I wasn't using running to compose dissertation chapters, or to unwind from writing them, I used it to push back limits in a life I saw as otherwise limited. Physically in my prime, I ran better times at increasingly longer distances.

I was powerful. I was carefree. But I was passively dependent on an unloving spouse who announced late in the summer of 1982 that he was leaving me for a younger woman. In shock and utter disbelief, I told no one for weeks. I prayed that it was hormones, that it was male menopause, and that he'd come to his senses. I prayed that I would find a better-paying job. I prayed that we would sell the house. It was good to have so many things to juggle; no one issue could weigh me down. Prayer and running kept me sane. Effortlessly, I set personal records at every distance from the mile to the marathon.

When the house was sold my son and I moved back to Lincoln Park. I was still willing to salvage the marriage, but had to file for divorce when the ex offered to give me half the proceeds from the sale if he could "divorce me quietly," with no future obligations to me or to our son. Awakening again, kissing Sleeping Beauty good-bye forever this time, I ransomed myself and reclaimed my very spirit, a spirit that had gone into hiding, if it had not died altogether during that marriage.

"You seem to have this situation under control," my therapist said. "But you still have to resolve those issues about leaving the convent."

"I have enough to deal with without drudging up that stuff! That was more than half my life ago! " I argued.

Thanks to some of the "abundant grace" St. Paul wrote about, I eventually made the trip east to face down the convent ghosts. My first trip back, in the fall of 1984, came at the end of a long day's journey. I had run a IO K that morning, then a mile and then a quarter-mile around the college track. A marathon through the Michigan hills concluded the day-long Ultimate Runner. After the awards banquet that night I drove down to the motherhouse with Kathy Schubert. For close to twenty years I had avoided going anywhere near the place, but now that we were so close, I had to go back and take a look.

We circled the town a few times before zeroing in on the campus. "How can you not find a place where you went to school?" Kathy asked in exasperation.

"Well, we didn't go out at night," I explained.

My role as Kathy's tour guide and my ultramarathon-induced endorphin high insulated me from the reality of where I was. I was flying so high on how far I had run that I did not realize how far I had come. When I awakened Sunday morning, facing the blazing hillside of a Michigan woods, I knew I had come home. I was more myself, more at peace, than I had been in years. The soul I'd left amid those trees in the novitiate garden so many years ago breathed itself back into me. With the spirit I had reclaimed after the divorce I was reassembling myself.

104

I ritualized this return to life the following April when I attended the first weekend for former sisters of that community. My divorce had been final for a year, and the ink on the annulment papers was not yet dry. I had decided go back to face and finally heal that shattered childhood dream of becoming a nun. But at some level, I did not want to go. About a week before the retreat, I started having back pains for the first time in my life. I assumed that it had more to do with the trip to the convent than any physiological cause. How could I, who had run so many long races, who had carried a large baby boy to full term, suddenly develop paralyzing back pain? I would be unable to sit still for the six-hour drive, so I flew. With women I had not seen in twenty years, I drove to the motherhouse.

I was immediately appalled by the barrenness of the place.

Once crowded with hundreds of postulants and novices, the convent was now occupied by a handful of middle-aged and elderly women, and for this one brief weekend, by the fifty-some of the women who had once lived there, too.

During our opening session one of the sisters read Luke's story of how the disciples met Jesus on the road to Emmaus, of how they probed his wounds. It spoke to all of us as we met once again on the road to heal one another's wounds. And it spoke most profoundly to the women who had left the convent before the effects of Vatican II had filtered down. These women were cut off when they departed. Like the undead, they walked around for decades without ever saying good-bye or finishing their business.

"You can't really look forward until you look back," Bishop Timothy Lyne had told a group of divorced and separated people the year before, and now I knew what he had been talking about. Former nuns also had to look back and close that chapter of their lives. Those who left before the examined life became the norm may have carried unresolved guilt and grief down years of days, walling themselves up in tombs with no rear view and spending undue energy keeping memories of the convent at bay, all the while trying to prove they were really okay.

Drawing on her experience with the dying, our former prioress spoke of our need to take the time to grieve and say good-bye in the very place where we had all been together, where we could finally name our collective sorrow and by naming it, begin to heal. We gave our sorrow words that weekend. We walked through our pain. We absolved and were absolved. And many of us finally resolved all of our unfinished business. We realized that we were in the same game after all. As teachers and mothers, as lawyers and writers, as musicians and businesswomen, we were still bringing Christ's presence into the world, re-creating it, and moving towards the wholeness we sought when we were drawn to the community forty, thirty, or twenty years before.

Everything that rises does converge and that weekend we all met people from that other part of our fragmented lives. That, too, made us whole. John Shea has written that "the pain of the second coming is in the second leaving." For many of us who had been forced to depart in silence in the dead of night, this was the first time we could say goodbye. And this was the first time we could cry. But this time we could really move on. We had spent three days daring to look back, facing down those fears of turning to stone and finding, ironically, that it was the not looking back that had been so hard, so hardening. During those three days we became more real, more accepting of our total selves, including that sometimes undead nun component we had been so busy walling off. All of us had come together in faith to acknowledge our losses. And by coming together for another moment on the road, we had all gained more to share on our journey towards wholeness.

We closed that reunion weekend with a Sunday mass in the motherhouse chapel. Like every woman there I had prayed through dawns and noons and dusks and nights in the miniature Gothic chapel. I felt it was especially fitting that we say our final farewell in the same place where my odyssey had started when, on a bleak predawn March morning, just before the first day of spring, I had decided to leave. Not until the sunny morning twenty years later, surrounded by women I had known back then, could I let go of the past and at last embrace the future. In an hour we would all leave again to continue about the business of the reign of God. Now we were getting food for the journey. When I went up to communion, I took the cup of wine from a sister I had known in graduate school, who had been at my wedding. That last memory tapped the well of tears I had kept tightly sealed for twenty years. The choir was singing "We hold the death of the Lord deep in our hearts. Living now we remain with Jesus the Christ." All of us, in and out, had held that death in our hearts as we died many of our own.

I cried most of the way home, but I had reached a critical decision. I would accept the teaching position at a community school. I had gone back to the convent to let go of my youthful dream, only to catch another and emerge whole.

"It sounds like they've awakened Jairus's daughter," my spiritual director said later when I told him about the weekend. "That young idealist was only sleeping all those years."

"And to think of all the energy I wasted keeping her locked in the tomb! "

The following spring I decided not to go to the next reunion. I couldn't weather such a storm of emotions again. Maybe I already knew how fragile my hard-bought wholeness had become. I spent reunion weekend running through the night, facing down other losses, and providing other memories that would fuel my struggle to reclaim my body from the next battle. In the early hours of April 27, 1986, I ran a forty-five mile ultramarathon. The run was both an exorcism and a victory dance. Since the divorce I had never ventured beyond thirty miles. Despite a track record that included one 62.2-mile and three 50-mile races, I did not believe I could stand to be "alone in my head" for so long ever again. There were just too many awful memories of the marriage's end, memories best left alone, undisturbed.

But this warm spring night, some two years after the divorce had become final, I at last had the courage to run through the land I had left. If it's true that the real dark night of the soul comes at four o'clock in the morning, I had a sense of it at just that time. I ran the length of Lake County, Illinois and back, feeling alone despite the company of three men. I let myself admit to myself for the first time that it is not always easier to be alone. For the last three years all the effort I had invested in material survival bracketed the loss of my former spouse who, for better or for worse, had been a partner of sorts for fourteen years.

On that night journey, in the middle of a suburban landscape I had seldom passed through since the marriage ended, I gazed at the full moon and felt the loss of the better parts of the marriage. I had to admit the reality of those better parts before I could let it go. One mark of a true survivor is the full knowledge and acceptance of the magnitude of what she has lost. I finally reached that point that night on the road.

With the dawn came rejoicing, excitement that we were almost halfway home. I tuned my walkman to a talk show about the apostles on the road to Emmaus. The speaker remarked on how Jesus' first followers so often pretended everything was all right when it wasn't. During the next few hours, I did my share of pretending. I ran the last thirteen miles with my youngest sister, Sharon. I attributed my nausea and fatigue to the heat and the distance I had already covered. In the last mile through Fort Sheridan, where our father had started his army career just weeks after he married Mom late in 1941, I told Sharon to run on.

"You're still running strong—go for it!" I gasped as I wound up at a slower pace. I was feeling more than a runner's high. I had not felt so victorious, so whole, since my first ultramarathon. Now, seven years later, I had recaptured the distance, rebuilt my life and, finally, let go of the past.

But, as it turns out, my journey was only beginning.

For a few brief shining weeks, I imagined I was in charge. I could do anything! I had conquered my past and the hills of Lake County. Secure in spirit and in soul, I did not dream that the body that had served me so well was about to betray me. Now I know I was already ill then, if not the year before when I had the strange back pains before going to the convent. But not until a large tumor appeared overnight on my collarbone did I think there was anything wrong with me.

On the morning after receiving the news of a probable malignancy, I moved my car to a safer parking spot for the duration of my hospital stay. The surgeon had warned it could be a long one, several weeks or even months. As I pulled into the parking lot at St. Clement's, where I had gone to church since the late sixties, Frank Sinatra crooned: "And now, the end is near, and as I face the final curtain. . . ."

I went into the church which had continued to be my spiritual home through two decades of moves to three different suburbs. If today I faced the dying of the light, it was only common sense to stop in for the early morning mass and fuel up for the latest challenge. I was a bit late, creeping down a side aisle and trying to erase Sinatra's lugubrious line

108

from my mind's ear. My neighbor, Maria Leonard, was reading the day's passage from St. Paul:

> I put no value on my life if only I can finish my race and complete the service to which I have been assigned by the Lord Jesus, bearing witness to the gospel of God's grace. I know as I speak these words that none of you among whom I went about preaching the kingdom will ever see my face again.
>
> —*cts 20: 24-25*

How strange that my two passions, running and teaching, would be entwined in the same passage on this very day! Since scriptural selections are based on the church calendar, this verse was about as coincidental as a horoscope. To my mind and soul, though, it was far more inspired.

I stood as our pastor read Jesus' last farewell to his followers from John's gospel. Good-bye after good-bye, I reflected, and again thought of my son and my students. I, too, entrusted to them the message and wanted nothing more than to return to work, to business as usual. But maybe not, I thought as the pastor read the conclusion: "I am in the world no more, but these are in the world as I come close to you."

Within an hour I was in Northwestern Memorial Hospital. The years of trials in the deserts of the convent and my marriage had strengthened me for this battle. I had girded myself as if for a race and was comforted when, in the intake area, I was ushered to a locker room. If I could treat the day's adventures as another race, I would survive. I was determined to cling to the last vestiges of my real, running, healthy self.

During the admissions interview, I corrected the married name and suburban address that had been logged into the hospital computer years before. Exhilarated by that reassertion of my identity and again conscious of the great price I had paid to reclaim Kathleen Burke, I tackled the next hurdle with a fighting stance. I decided to view pre-admissions testing as the first event in a pentathalon. It seemed less annoying, less intrusive, and less frightening that way. I treated it like The Ultimate Runner, the series of races I had completed on my way back to the convent. As I shed my running T-shirt for a hospital gown,

I recalled that grueling day. I would pace myself today, too. I was determined not to burn out early by investing too much emotional energy on the trivia of pre-admission testing when all the big events were yet to come. The EKG and the chest X-ray were uneventful, so I passed from one testing area to another in the same relaxed, hypnotic daze in which I cover the early miles of an ultramarathon. I roused for a moment when the technician had trouble finding a vein for a blood sample and calmly offered her my other arm.

Moments later an attendant was carrying my gym bags across the overpass to Passavant Pavilion, where Abe had been born. I looked east towards the forsythia waving in the wind on Olive Park Promontory. Was I really running there just Saturday? When we reached my room, my world constricted even more to the size of a narrow bed and night table on the door side of the room, closed off from the window side by a curtain. From across the years, a Shakespearean refrain replayed itself: "Fear no more the heat o' the sun. " It's dark enough in here, I thought. I hadn't been brought out of that desert of the marriage just to die, not when I had just started living.

By evening I had completed my triathalon of a neck-node biopsy, a bone marrow biopsy, and a CAT scan. I hadn't been back in my room for an hour when the surgeon came in with the results, standing as close to the door and as far from me as possible. I read "malignant" before I heard the word.

On the last day of summer, 1986, I once again went back to the convent with my son, for what I thought could be the last time. The chemotherapy had not succeeded, and the next morning I was sched-uled to begin radiation therapy. I had taken one last long day's running into night at The Ultimate Runner, once again covering a marathon, a 10k, and assorted shorter distances. "I ran just about this far yesterday," I explained as we drove into the sleepy town, passed the Victorian County Courthouse, then drove out to the motherhouse.

"It looks just like you said!" he exclaimed.

"There are a few differences. There were more people then," I explained as I took him around the deserted complex. Twenty-two years ago, it had been swarming with over 200 postulants and novices. Today, hardly a soul could be seen. We looked at the historical exhibit on the lower level of the motherhouse. "We used to keep our trunks down here," I said.

From a panel lettered in the familiar convent calligraphy, I read T.S. Eliot's lines from "Little Gadding:"

> We will not cease for Exploration
> And the end of our exploring
> Will be to arrive at where we started
> And know the place for the first time.

Not yet ready to "cease from exploration" either, I stood in silence in the convent where I had started as I came to "know the place for the first time." Like Ulysses I had wandered long enough to find that my only home was on the road and in the memories I replayed on the journey.

Former selves passed before me as I knelt upstairs in the chapel. I recalled the frightened teenager I had been nearly twenty-two years before, when I had knelt there before dawn one cold March morning and had decided to seek the Lord on the more open road of the world. I recalled the healing reunion weekend when I had finally faced my convent memories and reclaimed my self. Now, the late September evening light poured through the stained glass window of the Agony in the Garden. I thought of how many of my sisters had gone to assorted missions to face challenge, failure, and sometimes even death. My memories of those women empowered me with the hope that I still had many reasons to live. I had made my peace with the place, with the people who remained. The brief visit to the convent was like going to a healing pool, a well from which I gathered strength.

"I'll be back," I promised as Abe and I went out to the car. Facing the setting sun all the way, we drove west through Ohio and Indiana to reach Chicago at dusk. A paler sun rose the next morning, the first of autumn. Without the warmth and light of memories I had embraced the day before, I doubt that I could have survived the long journey into darkness that lay ahead.

Ruth H.
Sisters of St. Joseph

Sister Visitor, Pastoral Care Department Discharge Planning, Social Services Department

Graduate Diploma, School of Nursing, St. Joseph's Memorial Hospital

Operating Room Nursing, Supervision

Job-related Ministry

Sister Ruth is closely tied to her community, not only attending the ordinary meetings and assembly days, but acting as a contact person through whom all requests are made. Community sponsored Days of Recollection, picnics and outings with other Sisters help keep this relationship lively. Sister Ruth, although living in an apartment with another sister, acts in a support group at the motherhouse. Her primary interest is working with other alcoholics through A.A.. She takes daily walks, and is an avid reader. Her desire for the future? She would like "to be a support person in a half-way house for recovering women."

Ruth H.

Good Times, Hard Times

My name is Sister Ruth. I will have been a member of the Sisters of St. Joseph for fifty years as of September 1, 1992.

I have gone through some good times and some hard times during those fifty years.

As I was raised in a strict religious German home, the oldest of five girls, I could not wait to leave home. When my parents sent me to St. Joseph's Academy for girls for my sophomore year because I was such a "bad kid," I had the opportunity to see the postulants and novices attending classes because it was on the motherhouse grounds. I thought, "Here is my chance to get away from home." After three weeks I wrote home telling my parents I was entering the convent. Naturally they freaked out. With such a quick decision, both my parents and the religious community felt I should wait a year and that if I still wished to enter at that time, they would approve. I was just fifteen years old.

I entered the convent of the Sisters of St. Joseph at the start of my junior year, September 1, 1942, just four days after my sixteenth birthday.

My reasons for entering? First, to get away from home. Second, God might like me if I was a nun. Third, maybe it wouldn't be so bad to work for God if I could be a nurse. And, after graduating from high school, I entered St. Joseph Memorial Hospital School of Nursing and became a registered nurse.

Most of my nursing career has been in the operating room as a surgical nurse and/or supervisor of surgery.

During all the following forty-one years, in the novitiate and in nursing, I was working for Ruth and not for God. I did all the things necessary to appear as a good nun. It was all on the outside; all prayers were mechanical and I was great putting on a good front; I appeared happy. In nursing I worked hard to be the super nurse, to receive affirmations, compliments and pats on the back, all the while feeling guilty for I knew I was working for the wrong reasons. I hated myself on the inside, for I carried with me my negativism and the brainwashing that I had received daily in my childhood when I was told that I was dumb and stupid, that I did not know anything and was an "asshole".

In 1973, at the age of forty-seven, after a severe head injury in a bicycle accident, a deep depression set in because I felt I could not cope with trying to be this "super" nurse; I had short periods of amnesia, and started drinking to feel better.

My drinking continued very gradually and secretively, of course, and as it increased, so did my depression to the point that I felt suicide was my only answer.

Because of my erratic behavior I was admitted to a psychiatric hospital for six weeks and during the next three years, I had numerous admissions to various hospitals for acute depression and possible suicide. At no time was I ever questioned about my drinking. Who would ask a nun if she had a drinking problem?

From 1976 to 1983 my alcoholism advanced, secretively, of course. I changed jobs and geographic locations, all in an effort of not getting caught, and finally after another bout of threatening suicide, was sent to the House of Affirmation in Montara, California. After evaluation they turned me down. They felt I needed an alcohol evaluation which they did not do, for it was not that type of Center. They told me their program would be too threatening, and that they might have a suicide on their hands. How true they were, for the ocean was just two blocks from the Center and the urge was strong to walk straight west and not look back. Their recommendation was for me to contact St. Luke Institute in Suitland, Maryland, a chemical dependency treatment center for men and women religious, which I did.

Ten days later I was only 100 miles from the Atlantic Ocean, and admitted to St. Luke. After evaluation the diagnosis was: 1) Alcoholism, 2) Acute Depression and 3) Brain Damage. This was rock bottom for me.

My stay was just over six months, from September 15, 1983 to April 1, 1984. It was the hardest thing I have ever done, and yet it was the best thing that ever happened to me. At the start I thought my world had come to an end, and that God had really done me in as I had felt He would some day.

Yes, St. Luke's was a turning point in my life. God changed for me. For the first time in fifty-seven years I realized that God was a loving God, that he really did love me, and that I was OK. Also, I realized I was not "dumb, stupid, and did not know anything" as I had been told by my mother since I was old enough to remember. Yes, I found God. He moved from my head to my heart during those six and a half months so everything changed for me. I was introduced to Alcoholics Anonymous, and was freed from my craving for alcohol. This was a miracle; I was a daily drinker.

My prayer life changed as I worked the third and eleventh steps and it is still exciting for me today. No longer are there hours in prayer, pleading and begging God to heal me of my drinking problem as in the past. Now there is a simple asking for knowledge of His will for me, and the power to carry it out and, of course, the grace not to drink today. All prayer requests from others I simply place in God's hands and ask Him to care for them and accept whatever His will is for them.

I attend the liturgy regularly at our local church and serve as Lector on weekends at the church and as Eucharistic Minister at the hospital. I am actively involved in the Renew Program in our parish. I consider church attendance a supplement to my twelve step program, and not a substitute. Now I attend because I want to and not because I have to.

I have never regretted my decision to be a religious. I know God had to have called me for I would never had persevered solely on the motives I had on entering the convent.

I live in an apartment with another sister of my community; we are the only two sisters working at the hospital here, which is owned and operated by our religious order. I work in the Pastoral Care Department, and feel my ministry serves as a vital link between the Sisters and the local community, as well as being a witness of God's love and compassion for the sick and dying. We also hear the question many times: "What ever happened to the good sisters?" At one time our hospitals were staffed entirely by sisters.

Sr. L.A. and I pray the "Liturgy of the Hours" together each morning before leaving for work. My personal prayer life today consists of one hour of quiet time each morning — a few moments of doing what is asked in the eleventh step — endeavoring to improve my conscious contact with God and praying for knowledge of His will for me and the power to carry it out throughout the day. The remainder of time is spent in listening. That time I spend with my Higher Power (God) is the most important time of the day for me and is the difference between my day being one of serenity or one of frustration.

I meet monthly with a Spiritual Director, a diocesan priest, and also have an "Emmaus Partner" who is a sister of my community. We meet monthly also, mainly for sharing and support. We share our prayer life and the struggles and successes of daily living, which I find most helpful.

At the hospital, apart from working in Pastoral Care, I have the opportunity of working with alcoholics who are admitted, often at the referral of the attending physician.

Outside my hospital duties, I am active in Alcoholics Anonymous. In fact, I feel today it is my primary ministry. I attend five to six meetings weekly and have a sponsor whom I use on a regular basis. I also sponsor six girls at the present time and am active in my home group. I have been speaker (told my story) over 150 times throughout Indiana, and on one occasion in Washington D.C. and at another in Cleveland, Ohio during the eight and a half years I have been sober. I have never been able to tell my story without being overcome with gratitude and awe, and filling up with tears when I am again reminded of the hell I lived in for ten years, and what God has done for me.

Until this past year I was the only sister in our community in a twelve step program. The sisters have been very supportive, and the community finances any conferences or workshops I choose to attend.

I have many friends today, both lay and religious, but find most of my friends are members of Alcoholics Anonymous.

I close by saying my heart is filled with gratitude and unity with Mary in the words she uttered: "My being proclaims the greatness of the Lord...for He has looked upon His servant in her lowliness...God who is mighty has done great things for me. Holy is His name."

Barbara Joan Tandy
Former Benedictine

Divorced

Director of seminars/workshops Therapist

Bachelor of Science in Education, Loyola University, Chicago

Parish ministries Minister of Care at local hospital

Counseling staff at Franciscan Retreat Center

Barbara's interests are reflected in her work She would like to write books on several different topics, and at present is working on the development of her new business, *Living*, which is centered in developmental stages for personal wellness and integration and enlightenment for spiritual living. She would like to travel throughout the United States, doing workshops and giving retreats.

Barbara Joan Tandy

Alone Together

I was born, the third daughter of Irish Catholic parents, and baptized Barbara Joan Tandy. Today that single sentence speaks volumes. "I was born..." God lovingly created me, a perfect (meaning whole) baby.

"...The third daughter...", in time I became the classic "third child", namely the lost child. During early childhood I learned that it was not good to do wrong things. I withdrew from arguments and fights and instead focused on pleasing people. This behavior has caused me great losses and much pain during my life. I was encouraged and rewarded for pleasing others by family, friends and most certainly during my convent life. The big problem was that I wasn't taught to take care of myself, nor did I realize that I needed to do that and set some boundaries when pleasing people conflicted with my own well-being.

"...of Irish Catholic parents...", and of the Irish heritage that my mother spoke about. I can still hear her saying. "The land of saints and scholars." For as long as I can remember, I was always going to the convent . I knew this before I even started school in my parish. I just accepted it like I accepted all other basic information for daily living that was taught and modeled in my home. I can remember not thinking of my own personal choice when Sister asked me in the primary grades, "Barbara, what do you want to be when you grow up?" The thought of entering the convent became as automatic as breathing.

"...and baptized Barbara Joan Tandy." The Godly characteristic for Barbara is "coming what Joy" and for Joan is "God's Gracious Gift". Today because I feel I have only begun to fully live my own life, I am becoming what it means to be Barbara Joan.

Today I feel this knowing that I was always going to the convent stemmed from an unhealthy enmeshment between my mother and me. It seems to me that she lived her life through me. This relationship started so early that it was all I ever knew. One of the saddest effects of this is that I feel I never had an intimate relationship with my sisters, because I always knew that I would be living in the convent.

Another loss was not experiencing a typical adolescence. I dated very little, had friends, but none that were really close. As I look back, I know I felt alone and rather different in my home and school. Even then I somehow knew I was alone, by myself, yet together with God. There are so many things or times that I never experienced; they are gone forever.

The only decision I am consciously aware of making regarding entering the convent was the date. I insisted on entering just a few days after high school graduation. Several times my father had urged me to wait for at least one year and then decide. The years of knowing that this was what I was born for propelled me straight forward without looking right or left, not even a glimpse. I know now that I had no idea what or how much I was giving up. That pattern was to be repeated again and again in my life. Today I no longer have to do that. Reality is clearer; I have choices.

The convent I entered had been founded by sisters from Europe. I found it to be strict, and of course, strictly religious. I was familiar with that because of my home life and my mother's absolute devotion to the church. I immediately loved the Gregorian chant and the sisters' dedication to the liturgy in the Mass and the Divine Office. I still retain that love today. The sisters' full habit was both beautiful and simple to me. The centuries-old customs held newness and interest. I'm not sure I always understood why things were done a certain way; explanations were not frequently given, nor did I tend to question. To this day I don't know why we walked around in a circle while meditating. I remember being distracted because I had to be careful not to walk into the nun in front of me.

The focus of prayer and its frequency was something I loved very much and still do. During this time I learned memorable lessons on the process, value and appreciation of prayer life. I have been able to keep what I had learned and build on that foundation. The outward manifestation of public penance, e.g., kneeling and begging for prayers and/or forgiveness, appeared extreme to me. I was surprised that regular dental checkups were not routine, that you went only when something was wrong. During my ten and one-half years in the convent I came to feel that my community had placed either a slow and/or low priority on our education. During all those years I had not even completed half of my undergraduate degree.

Shortly before taking perpetual vows, I became ill. I had some kind of blood deficiency, and my body wasn't producing what was needed. I remember being sent from the doctor's office directly to the hospital for a blood transfusion. I feel today that my pre-conditioned mind would not allow any doubt of or consideration for living my entire life in the convent. It simply just shut down; after all, wasn't I born for this? It was all that I ever knew. I felt my body was trying to tell me to take a look at what I was doing. I paid no attention, for I had learned my lesson early and well — too well. I went ahead and took perpetual vows, again repeating the pattern of not knowing what or how much I was giving up.

My life in the convent was extremely busy, too busy. Between my religious prayer life, teaching duties, taking college courses, there was very little self-nuturing. Today I feel that I was not treated as an individual, nor developed for the person I could have been.

Instead, I think that I was molded to fit the needs of the convent. The thought that I had never lived my own life and that I was living the life which was my mother's choice for me was buried deep within, not to be realized for many more years. My daily schedule was so demanding and filled with so many activities that there was little time for reflection. There were no vacations, either. Sisters who had out-of-state families were allowed to go home periodically. Since my family lived with the area, they visited me during prescribed times at the convent. During those ten and a half years, I was allowed to return to my home twice: once for two to three hours for my brother's First Communion, and then the day that my father was buried.

The combination of a growing uneasiness and increasing burnout from a hectic schedule set me to wondering about my life. Still being the people pleaser, I too quickly buried these thoughts, much to my personal detriment, and determined to try more and to work harder. Now it is obvious to me that that was a poor choice. For each poor choice there is a natural consequence. At that time I labeled them punishments. I kept wondering what I was doing wrong, yet I continued the same behavior.

Concurrently, there was a change in administration. The previous, highly spiritual Reverend Mother was replaced by another nun, whom I came to realize in time was vastly different. I sensed strong and negative feelings emanating from her. Before long I became the target for the outward expression of these feelings. My life became unpleasant and painful. I was watched, reported on, lectured to, and given the most difficult assignments. I was very unhappy and confused. What had I done wrong? Why was I being treated in this manner? All during my life, adult-modeled behavior taught me that the older person or the person in authority was always right. In my eyes that meant that I must be at fault in some way and needed to try harder. Today, I no longer believe this to be true. Then that was all that I knew.

I began to question seriously my life in the convent. Over a period of two painful years filled with plaintive prayer, increasing difficulties, and demeaning treatment, I came to grips with the problem. I felt my back was to the wall and again I felt alone, yet together with God. Somehow, finally, I became aware that I did have value and capabilities and that God did want me to live. I knew I would die if I stayed. The years of difficulty had taken their toll. My weight was down to eighty-nine pounds and I was experiencing physical problems. I still did not know that I never should have been in the convent in the first place. That realization would come more than twenty years later.

I did decide to ask for a leave of absence and a dispensation. As I expected, a most trying series of events followed. This was before Vatican II. I was requested to leave my classroom, taken unknowingly to a hospital, given various physical tests against my will, was ostracized from the Community by virtue of the fact the nuns were told not to speak to me unless in the community room in the company of others. I was deprived of the use of a breviary for Divine Office.

Surprisingly, after a week, I was told that I was being allowed to leave. My mother and sister were on their way to pick me up. In the presence of my former novice mistress I gave up my habit, donned secular clothes and prepared to go down the stairway and out the front door. Sister stopped me. I was not to be allowed to leave by the front door. I was in complete shock! The ten and a half years flashed before my eyes. Strong feelings of dehumanizing treatment that I had endured rushed through my entire being. What purpose or value did those ten and a half years serve? We went outside onto the porch. Sister called down to my mother to put the headlights on so we could see our way down the fire escape stairs. It was February 2, the feast of the Purification. Again I felt alone yet together with God. My total being knew that I would cease to live if I remained. I chose life.

Returning to home life was not an easy task. My family was most comforting; they wanted to help me. They talked to me to help soothe my injured feelings. My mother told me everything would be fine, and that we now had happy hour. There was no regular drinking in the convent and the only drink I remember was on my eighteenth birthday at a special lunch with my father before I entered the convent. Now as I took the drink, it tasted very strong, too strong, but it felt good.

As I continued with what I thought was adjustment, I tended to talk little about the convent. Counseling was not discussed nor considered in my family; consequently, I continued to enjoy happy hour. Outside of my immediate and extended family, I never shared my convent experience. I kept that a secret for twenty years, which now I know was unhealthy. Then, of course, I continued to enjoy happy hour. Habits (no pun intended) and things we do frequently do have a way of catching up with us; the happy hour did.

After years of drinking and denying that I had a problem, I admitted that I was an alcoholic. That day is even more memorable than the day I left the convent. I felt even greater pain. Again I felt alone, yet together with God. My choice was again life. But this time there was a big difference. Upon this day I was born anew, and started to live my own life for the very first time. It was both exciting and fearful. By using a twelve step program, I didn't have to feel alone in my attempt to stop drinking. I had God, a support program and group for all the help I wanted. Believe me, I not only needed it and wanted it—I used it! I still do to this day. I have nine years of continuous sobriety.

During these nine years I have learned invaluable truths about myself, and I have survived many losses. I know that I am forever God's child and that alone gives me unlimited value. I no longer need to be a people pleaser, nor to keep trying harder and harder in order to make others happy. Each of us is responsible for his/her own happiness. It is a gift that we give to ourselves. Others can certainly add to my happiness, but they are not the source.

I learned to begin to live my own life by allowing myself to leave my mother. Physical separation was necessary in order for me to become aware, and to be able to live my own life on a mental, emotional and spiritual level. As a result my religious beliefs have blossomed into spiritual living. During therapy I came to learn of the generous gift of faith in God that he bestowed upon me early in my life. My therapist told me that, surprisingly, I had never experienced a nervous breakdown upon leaving the convent, and that this was because of my faith in God. I agreed, and said, "It was not God who did those things to me, but people who were only human like me".

The last several years in my life have been marked by many losses: my sister died unexpectedly; my marriage was dissolved (I had married in 1986); I was in a serious automobile accident; my first and second sponsors in my support group died; two different jobs ended because of a loss of funding and financial company problems; my mother died. During this painful time in my life there were many issues for me to examine. I chose to deal with them through therapy, which included family of origin and inner child work. I came to know that whatever I do is about me and me, and God and me. From that union flows all living. That was a powerful awakening. Realization that I am a human being and not a human doing was another big awareness.

Today, more than ever before, I feel I am living my own life together with God. I continue to be a member of the Catholic Church by choice. I volunteer in my church as a Minister of Care, which entails visiting the sick and administering the Holy Eucharist at a local hospital. At a religious retreat center I volunteer as a facilitator for various groups. Currently I have a part time job at a University, and have started my own business. The name for my business is an appropriate choice. It is called *Living*. I enjoy living in my own life and living in my own business. My business consists of presenting living workshops, recovery seminars and spiritual living retreats .

My process has been long, and not easy. But it has been real, and at last I have become real. The past no longer exists. My religious beliefs which blossomed into spirituality continue to grow as they are meant to. I stand before the world, a completely revitalized woman. Today, I know who I am. My identity statement is as follows:

126

I am Barbara Joan Tandy, a loving, whole, healthy, joyous, prosperous, responsible, multi-talented, intelligent and human woman!

I am Barbara Joan Tandy, seeking to follow God's Divine Will, participating fully, living in the present moment and enjoying the benefits of the giving/receiving cycle of life.

I am who I am, not what I do.

If you looked at me right now, I might appear to be standing Alone but now you know that I am Together with God!

Penelope Pope
Former Sister of Charity

Single

Insurance Consultant Administrator

Bachelor of Arts, Mundelein College

Special Training, Life Management Association

Master Practitioner, Neuro Linguistic Programming

Recently Coordinator, Adult Education Program

Teacher, Rites of Christian Initiation for Adults

"We have a big house surrounded by a perennial garden." In addition to collecting hand-made pottery and fine arts prints and painting, she works with macrame, fancy knot-tying, rope constructions and weaving. As a certified practitioner of NLP she sees a small select number of clients, teaching these skills to small groups and in workshops. "I plan this to be my retirement career, and will continue NLP training."

Penelope Pope

First an Image...
Then Explanations

I am conscious again
Slowly my attention comes back to me
And my memory of time I can't account for.

They are standing before
The girl kneeling next to me.
An archbishop with a small sharp scissors
And a novice holding a tray
Piled with locks of hair.
They add Sue's token strand of harvest gold
And next to it my tight black ringlet.
My scalp tingles. We stand and turn in pairs.
A tall sister drapes new clothes over my arm.

I am conscious slowly.
My attention comes back to me.
And my memory.

We are seated before small mirrors.
I am ready in my starched white hood and veil.
Sue is tying up her long hair.
The tall sister, standing behind her,
Is helping with the pins.

My attention comes back to me.
We are reflected in the glass
of classroom doors that pass
Like slides changing scenes.
I am featured,

My white veil fluttering behind me.
Scenes about a time I can't account for
Are blank places between the frames.

I am conscious with all the explanations.

I have assumed my own identity.
I am using my own name again.
In my mother's childhood home,
My grandmother is cooking
Pasta-and-peas and someone
Is asking me questions
That I answer easily.

Slowly my attention comes back to me
And my memory and the dark shapes
Of time I can't account for.

I spent just less than one year in the novitiate between August 1960 and July 1961. I am not sure that even qualifies me to participate.

As I look back to the time when I was deciding to enter Mt. Carmel, and at the time I was deciding to leave, the first thing that strikes me is that no one actually asked me why I was going or why I was leaving. In fact, with one exception, no one had ever asked me until this anthology.

My parents had heard me talk about the convent from the time I was nine years old. They were surprised when I was eighteen that I didn't tell them before I applied. My mother still says that the first she heard of it was when I was showing off my acceptance letter and buying black stockings.

When I wanted to leave, the novice mistress asked if I were sure, and when I said yes, she made the arrangements for me. No discussion. I must admit that it did not seem strange to me at the time. In my family silence was an institution. Even recently there was nothing so serious, so important, peculiar or so fine that it could not be handled with silence. Fortunately that has changed a little since the middle 80's when my sister's divorce led us all into the exploration of our family's three generation history of codependence.

The exception occurred in my own home about five years ago. Sister Betty, a friend, was coming to visit. We had invited our new pastor, who had gone to graduate school with her, and she brought along Sister Mary Lou, whom we had never met. At dinner Fr. Jim asked when I had been in the community, and Sister Mary Lou, without even a pause, asked why I left. I was surprised that no one had ever asked and that no one had ever been that direct. I answered something like " I was one of the ones who was called, but I wasn't chosen."

Later that night when our guests had gone, Irene commented that she was shocked that Sister Mary Lou had asked so personal a question. During twenty-five years of close friendship, Irene had wondered, but did not think she had the right to ask me that question. That night we talked long into the night and I told her everything I thought and felt during that time in my life. It isn't that it had been a secret; many of my friends had heard my stories.

I told stories all the time, stories about the people, the place, some funny anecdotes. I did not talk about the factors that motivated me to go and the criteria I used to decide to leave.

The time I spent with those women is part of the fabric of my subsequent life. It seems more like a turning point, a hub around which my life revolves. A marker — the stories of my life are sorted pre-and post-convent. To be clear about it, there are other pivotal events around which stories cluster but none around which time is sorted.

Part of the sorting phenomenon, I think, has to do with identity and naming.

The formation programs in those years seemed to be a three-phase process. During the first phase the community, particularly the novitiate staff, got to know you and determined if you met specific criteria for admittance.

The second phase seemed to be a process through which you were taught (encouraged, led) to shed many or most of your individualizing characteristics. You gave up your name, never referred to your past, family or nationality. Hobbies were out; special talents were obscured deliberately, either by denying them or by turning them to mundane service.

Then there was the old detachment, as if loneliness were next to godliness. All old connections were disconnected.

The ideal novice was like a clone of every other ideal novice. Three hundred or more eighteen, nineteen and twenty-year-olds keeping their eyes lowered and listening to the inner voice of the Spirit. For me the inner voice was that of an inexperienced spirit who usually said things like, What is it I'm supposed to be saying to you?"

We weren't miserable, the spirit and I. We were bewildered.

Bewildered was an emotion new to me. I had been a confident and bright little girl. Except for a short while in my preteens, I was social, popular, assured. I lived in Chicago, knew how to go anywhere on a bus, knew where to find anything in the Loop, knew that I had leadership qualities and knew when and how to use them. And I was in a place, for the first time, that required that I obscure the confidence and make a virtue of following without asking questions.

To be honest, the women who had been my teachers were not women devoid of individual characteristics. They were wonderful in their diversity and variety. They were wonderful role models for young girls in grade school and high school in the 1950's.

I was a girl who knew her own mind in a place where, from one week to the next, the most complex decision was when to wash my hair. I left because the day-to day living of religious life was too easy. I also left because my other-than-conscious mind resisted this disorganization of my personality. It felt dangerous. I just was not able to turn over my will to the process. It seemed there was no personal bond with the person who was leading. I couldn't put myself in her safe hands. It was too perilous a journey. I did not have the maturity or the insight to know that individuality would be restored. At least, I had lost confidence that mine would.

The third phase seemed to be the re-building of the personality, filtered through the rule and customs so that there was a community attitude, walk, mannerism, posture. Individualizing characteristics returned later to most, but in some of my sisters, even thirty years later, there is no trace of some delightful original traits. There are only the disconnected connections which never got turned on. Friendships were shunned as sinful. Even common interests seemed grounds for rebuke, for the silent separations.

Through it all was the keeping of silence. I do not mean the not uttering words during some parts of the day. I mean the taboo about talking about what was on your mind, never apologizing when you did an idiotic something, never resolving a misunderstanding, and never knowing if you were getting it right. Just like at home, only different. I had indeed lost confidence.

I must have left just as the rebuilding phase started. I got home to my family and I was a stranger. They felt the changes, but could not name them because there was nothing new in place of what was missing. My sister said later that I seemed vague.

The transition into cloister was handled gradually; coming out was "cold turkey".

I had spent a year without looking at a newspaper, seeing a movie, reading anything other than text books. I had not been alone even for a few minutes, except in the silence. I found going out by myself terrifying. My former friends had said good-bye forever and they did not have the experience to introduce me into their new lives. I felt as if they had passed me by. They felt that I was a stranger, or at least strange.

A few weeks after my return, my father died suddenly. I added grief and depression to the reintegration process.

It did not take long for me to make new friends. I started college, met new people, enjoyed dating, got a job, fell in love, selected a partner for life, made a home, established a career, wrote a book.

Despite the fact that individual friendships were discouraged, a tremendous comradeship grew among our set. The bonds grew, despite the rule and custom against them, and have lasted to this day.

A few years ago I received an invitation from the Community to attend a party, a reunion to which they invited all of their current members, affiliates and former members, their spouses, children or significant others.

I went with Irene, the woman with whom I have lived for more than twenty-five years, and Helen, neighbor, a woman in her 70's who left the community around the time I entered. She had been part of the Community for many years then. So, we went with Helen and her husband and three of her "Sister" sisters. She encouraged me to go; on my own I would not have gone. We met Sister Betty and Sister Mary Lou there.

After the dinner the speaker announced that instead of a speech she was going to read a list of the former members in attendance so that their friends and classmates might find them.

Classmates, former teachers from grade school, high school, college, and the novitiate came to see me.

Meanwhile, having heard my name read, and assuming that Irene would be there with me, Irene's classmates, teachers and community friends flocked to see her. It never crossed our minds that she would receive a welcome in her own right or that the fact of our long relationship had been such a matter-of-fact thing with them. No one ever said anything to either of us about our lifestyle.

My set dragged me off to the tables where they were sitting together. We talked for hours. Every so often someone would come by and ask if Irene were with me, and I would point her out to them, among the five or six-hundred women. My classmates had no idea who Irene was. I had not seen most of these women in more than 25 years. I was impressed by the matter-of-fact way that they learned and accepted the information.

It was a transforming experience to talk candidly about my alternative lifestyle, the people who are my comrades now, my work, my art, my place in the church and society, my family; to drop the euphemisms about relationships, identity, preferences, dreams.

Try to appreciate the sense of delight in many women all laughing and talking at once; the rare sense of mutual goodwill that happens only among small groups of intimate friends, occasionally in families, never in business, never in any kind of public context.

The result of having been affirmed in that context and in that way, prompted me to go back to look at the building, and see some of the people who had the greatest influence and with whom I had the closest friendships.

I went specifically to see the elderly sisters, who would have known, I thought, how influential they had been, what extraordinary role models they were.

What I found was that some knew. Some had a full appreciation of their influence, the potency of the modeling, and had achieved a sense of person and professional satisfaction in the reports they heard of us.

But as late as 1991, there were others who lived in a state of frustration because of the changes since Vatican II. They were still faithfully living the rule as they were taught it, in spite of the mandates that changed the clothes they wore, the kind and size and style of community they live in, the presuppositions about their relationships with one another in community, and with us who had abandoned them.

I had not thought that these women, who had been so strong and assured, needed my affirmation, but I found that being affirmed was as powerful an experience for them as being acknowledged had been for me. I was amazed at the numbers of sisters who remembered me specifically.

Today I write to six or seven of my classmates and see a few of my teachers. I send gifts and letters (condolences mostly) to some of the old ones. My neighborhood friend has developed the serious memory loss of old age, so I have lost my day-to-day link.

My partner has custody of her nephew, so I have the experience of being a parent to look forward to. Teaching and modeling spirituality to a child is an entirely different experience from teaching religion to adults.

In the process of writing this I have discovered how different are my beliefs from those I was taught. I think the effect of the difference is a tolerance I have evolved for diverse beliefs and different forms of religious practice.

I have one friend who is a witch. She says she practices a pagan religion. She dances on the solstice. Her ritual greeting is "blessed be".

Another close friend has recently converted to Buddhism. She chants accompanied by bells and drums and meditates before a mandala. She burns incense, pours water into silver cups, as water is the spirit of life. She has traveled to Tibet to prostrate herself before the enlightened ones.

I have the same profound sense of the personal holiness of these women as I had of the good Sisters of my childhood.

The whole notion of religious life had been that the life of the spirit was somehow better than the life of the world. You went outside, out of the world, you turned over your will as a means of attaining personal holiness, you engaged the world only as much as was necessary in order to be a channel of God's grace and by doing this you achieved sanctity and earn an eternal reward. Somehow the world could not get grace in any other way and you could not attain real holiness or personal salvation any other way.

I view holiness as a human rather than a divine state of being. Because all of life is holy by virtue of divine creation and because the holiness of all of human life is reaffirmed in Christ's humanity, there is a lot of room for all kinds of practices and for those whose spirituality is not linked to traditional, formal religious institutions.

Now I believe that holiness is the starting place, the base state from which all living begins and having been given free will, virtue lies in exercising choices consistent to your values.

Imelda Byron
Sisters of Mercy of the Americas

Prison Ministry

Bachelor of Philosophy, Cardinal Stritch College

Advanced studies in art: The Art Institute of Chicago, Mount Mary College, University of Wisconsin

Sister Imelda lives in a community convent and belongs to a regional assembly. She enjoys doing crafts and engages in two seemingly diverse activities: her jail ministry and telling stories to the second grade children in a local parish school. Sister Imelda looks forward to "trips to visit family and friends."

Imelda Byron

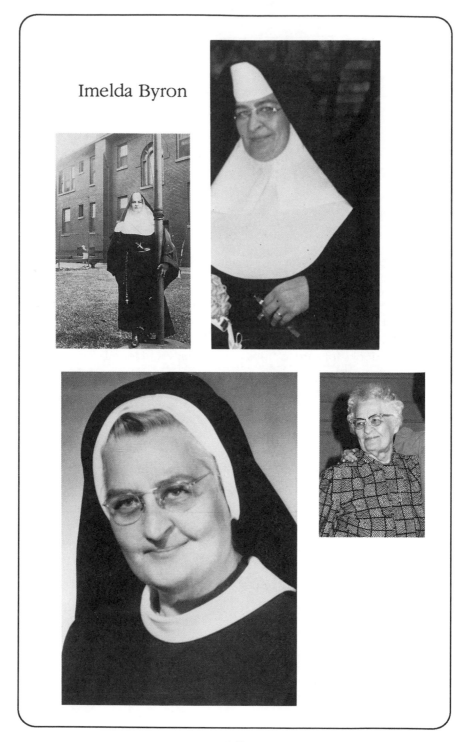

Three Circles of Life: My Story

At midnight on April 21, 1912, a baby girl made her appearance in a small cottage on the south side of Milwaukee, Wisconsin. Because of a disfiguring hare-lip, the disappointed parents made arrangements at the hospital for a surgical repairment. To play it safe, they stopped at the parish church to have Mary Ann baptized. When they left her room, my mother looked up at the pictures of Mary and Jesus above her bed and said, "You give her to me today, and I'll give her back to you someday." She never told me that until fifteen years later, when I told her I wanted to be a nun.

My second surgery took place when I was seven, and I shall never forget the feeling of utter helplessness in that hospital bed until, somehow, I knew the Lord was there with me. A feeling of great trust and bonding came over me, and I felt that we were in this together, as it were. All my life, through fourteen surgeries, the feeling of its being His doing, His will that I be different from others, has made me accept my disfigurement. Whenever my parents would ask me to have another surgery, I'd say "If God made me this way, He must have wanted me this way." Whereupon my mother would answer, "But God has put into doctor's heads how to make it better." She always won, of course, but I know I would not have wanted to be without that special something from Him. At fourteen, after my third surgery, my mother came to take me home, but was told I'd had a serious hemorrhage the night before and couldn't be moved. Each operation, however, did bring about an improvement in my face.

At fifteen, I decided to enter the convent, and in my naivete, imagined the Sisters of St. Dominic would welcome me, just as I was, with open arms. They did welcome me, and I enjoyed six months there, but in what I know now was a premature try at religious life.

One day the novice mistress told me that the major superiors had decided that it was unfair to me to ask a girl of sixteen to make a decision to be a lay sister for the rest of her life. They asked me to go home, have another surgery, and if it were successful, to come back. I went home, had the surgery, which was quite successful, and which made quite a change. However, when I made plans to return, Dad asked me not to go so far from home again. I've always felt, though, that standing at that dormitory window, overlooking the pines at the Mound, crying inwardly with a terrible lonesomeness, yet giving myself totally to God, that was the beginning of my marriage to the Lord, and that because of it I have had sixty-four years of the hundred-fold.

Soon after the surgery I began teaching Christian Doctrine in my parish, and it was with the teachers of that group that I made a retreat at Mercy High School in Milwaukee that Thanksgiving.

As soon as I entered that chapel, I knew that was where I had to be for always. I went out into the hall and asked the first Sister I saw about an appointment with the superior. I entered there on February 2, 1929. I was the last novice to be received as a bride, and while all my aunts and my mother were in coolest voile on July 17, I was supremely happy and cool in storm serge, about six layers of it, counting my church cloak! The senior Sisters were rather sad, because there would be no more "white-veils" in that convent. Our order had joined together to form a Union, and we were soon down at St. Xavier College, in Chicago, where we joined novices from many cities. Eventually we moved again, this time to St. Patrick Academy, in DesPlaines, Illinois.

There, novices were expected to prepare the meals for the professed Sisters as well as the novices. When all others had been pressed into service, my turn came. The potatoes were usually peeled in a centrifugal machine, in which potatoes, water, in small amounts, were placed, and the electricity turned on. I dutifully put in the potatoes, added some water, turned on the electricity, and blithely went up to Sunday lecture. As time passed, with no sign of our assistant provincial ending her talk, I became increasingly nervous; I was so nervous that, when the talk ended, I dashed to the kitchen, and, without turning off the machine, opened the door. Potatoes, like marbles, flew out and around the walls and ceiling, while the floor became a gooey grey ooze. Needless to say, the nearest I ever got to the kitchen again was peeling onions outside the kitchen door.

Another memorable fiasco occurred one laundry day, when I sauntered down the hall, swinging my arms as usual. Rounding the corner, I "biffed" my little novice-mistress in the stomach. She folded up like a jack-knife, and just managed to gasp, "Now you know why I don't want you to swing your arms." My penance was to walk up and down behind Sister Luccetti, trying to learn to walk like a lady.

My first mission was to teach second grade at St. Patrick's School in South Chicago. On the first day, as sixty little ones emerged from the coat-room, I became amazed that there were that many that age in that town, much less that room. Somehow we managed to keep busy, and I must have taught them something because sixty years later I still get letters from one of those little ones who lives in Boulder, Colorado.

One event each year was the class play each class had to give to close the year. Since the eighth graders had to change into caps and gowns later, they went on first. Our little first and second graders had to be awakened when it was their turn to perform. Our play was about Mother Goose Nursery Rhymes. Old King Cole and Mother Goose sat on the stage intoning in turn, "Here comes Little Miss Muffet," or "Here is Little Jack Horner." The problem arose when, as I reached the top of the stairs leading to the stage, the script fell to the floor, and fanned out at my feet. Having no notion of who should go on, Sister Luke and I pushed a little character out through the palms as soon as one or the other spoke. The effect was hilarious: when Mother Goose announced "Here comes Little Bo-Peep," Jack-be-nimble was likely to appear. The people screamed and yelled, and laughed 'till they cried. They told us later we should have charged twice as much for that performance. Unhappily, our superior was not amused.

I was sent next to North Chicago; our school was very close to the Great Lakes Naval Training Station. On Sunday mornings a car would pick up two of us and deliver us to a huge hall where thousands of men in white were, at the sound of the bugle, assembled to attend mass. On one side of an immense curtain, mass was going on; on the other side ten little officers' children and I held a class in Christian Doctrine.

Several years later I did an oil painting of Salmon's "Head of Christ." It hung in our front room when our Novice Mistress (who had her share of grief from me) came to visit. When she said, very seriously, "I'm not asking you, I'm *telling* you, to paint one of those for our new novitiate building, I knew better than to argue. I lugged easel, paints, original painting, and new canvas up to the roof of our convent, where the light was best. Hanging the original on the side of the easel, I made the Sign of the Cross over the new canvas, and began. The picture came out well (the Sign of the Cross usually works for me), and years later a novice told me that the best spot she knew for meditation was in front of that picture. When the building was dismantled, a sister's mother bought the picture, and when she died, the sister sent it back to me. I sent it to my bachelor nephew in California, to be his friend.

It so happened that in North Chicago my bedroom was next to the wall separating me from the school hall, where, every Friday night a jukebox provided music for the dances until about 1:00 a.m. I'm afraid I knew the words to Beer Barrel Polka at least as well as my prayers when I left to go to Janesville, Wisconsin, my next assignment.

After several years in Janesville, I was sent to St. Patrick School in Milwaukee, where every member of my family except my mother had gone to school. It was while teaching there that I received my degree from Cardinal Stritch College. From St. Pat's I went to Immaculate Conception School, and began to tell my students the mystery stories which, in that school, I became rather famous for. Whenever my pupils couldn't go out for recess, I would tell them a chapter of a story I made up as I went along. Each time, I managed to end the chapter at the most exciting part, and of course, the children always wanted more. That became a bit of a problem, when, after I left that school in the middle of the year, a mother wrote asking if I could please write and tell her the ending of the story and get her son "off her back"! As for the transfer: on Friday I was called and asked if I would be willing to go to a new school in a different city so that another sister could take my place. I replied, "Please, Mother, will you repeat all that very slowly?" She did, and I was willing, and at 10:00 p.m. that night my bedroom was bare, my trunk packed. It was no small miracle that my classroom happened to be in perfect order, with all the desks washed and waxed. I was never known for punctuality, but for once in my life every graph, report card, and test score was up to date and ready to distribute.

My life at the new school was fulfilling, and it was there that I celebrated my twenty-fifth anniversary as a sister. The summer was spent at the Art Institute of Chicago, and the following year saw me at Mercy High School, an all-girls high school on the south side of Chicago. I was to teach English, art, religion, and have the yearbook. Having never even held a yearbook, it was with a great deal of trepidation that I took on that assignment. However, I had a most helpful adviser in Mr. Koenig, head of King Publishing Co., who was my absolute salvation that year. We didn't do too badly, and, though we didn't win the fabulous awards my predecessor did, my staff and I did produce a yearbook.

My work with the yearbook staff began when the rest of the school had left for the day. We therefore became closer than my other students and I were. The staff, mostly seniors, were more my age, it seemed, than the older Sisters with whom I lived. The staff admitted me to their "club", and when we went on a skiing holiday to Sunset Point, a lodge we operated near Rhinelander, Wisconsin, we really had a great time.

I had always loved skating. In fact I had often boasted that I could Charleston on ice before I entered the convent. Now, though I hadn't skated in twenty-five years, I took to it like a "duck to water". It was glorious, skating to the "Skaters' Waltz" at 11:00 p.m. when it was -15 degrees! All would have been well if I hadn't tried to go down the toboggan slide on a "flying saucer". I'm still carrying the scars from that!

Before we went to the Point I was called to the phone while I was trying on a girl's skates in my classroom. I imagine I'm the only nun in history who, while wearing the long black habit who answered the phone wearing Johnson's Racers!

Whenever I was at the Point, even though it was a magnificent Tudor home, there was always something vaguely disquieting about it. Years later, I figured out what it was: there was no chapel and I missed it.

Near the end of the school year, girls began coming to talk about their vocations. Because my vocation had always meant marriage to me, that was the way I presented it to the girls who came to me. After they entered the novitiate we were permitted to visit them frequently. One week one of the novices asked me to talk with another instead of her. When we were together I asked the other how she pictured herself ten years in the future. She answered, "As a mother with a baby". I told her to go to her novice-mistress immediately and tell her what she had answered me. She was back in her parents' home the next day. Several years later I attended her wedding, and her joy at seeing me was beautiful to see. She soon became a mother with a baby.

As for art, English, and religion, in the beginning I'd open my mouth and was the most surprised person at what came out. The Holy Spirit really worked overtime that first year.

From Mercy High School I went to Siena High School, another all-girls school, this time on Chicago's west side. I think I can truthfully say I did my best teaching there. The sister with whom I worked taught the music and dance for our Fine Arts department, and she had the gift of bringing forth my best art teaching. We both enjoyed our work, and the results showed it. We often took our pupils to the Saturday morning sessions of the "Opera for Students." We were privileged to hear and enjoy full-dress rehearsals of many famous operas. It was fascinating to see the way stages were elevated or lowered to form mountains and valleys, and to see the huge racks, each containing the costumes for a single opera.

It was at Siena that our change came for me, from the long black habit to the short navy blue one, and from the long thin veil to the short heavier one. Because I would be at Mount Mary College in Milwaukee that summer, I took my new habit and veil with me, but couldn't wear it because the tri-fold, without which the veil was incomplete, was missing. All summer the Notre Dame Sisters kept after me to put it on, and finally one day the Dean met me to tell me my "package" had come, and I should hurry up and change. I went down and had a cooling swim in the pool; then, with the picture propped against the mirror, I proceeded to try to make myself look something like it. When I was dressed I stepped outside my door and was mobbed. I had to fasten and unfasten the scapular and belt, put together with velcro, over and over, and then I descended to the large dining room, where I was greeted by a standing ovation. Later, I went to visit Mom, who was in a nursing

146

home across town. I went and stood at the foot of her bed where she could get a good look. Her comment, "Oh, how beautiful!" was all I needed. She liked it. I didn't care too much about anyone else. For the first time a little of my hair was showing and felt a little undressed around the ankles. When I began to pull it apart, her eyes got bigger and bigger. She, who all her life had sewn on buttons and hooks, just couldn't believe how simple it all was. What was encouraging to me was the fact that all the little children whom I passed on the way addressed me as Sister, though they probably had never seen one so chic!

On the third finger of her left hand, every Sister of Mercy wears a silver ring, the sign of her marriage to the Lord. The ring is engraved with the Sister's motto, the talisman which leads her through the years. My motto, "All for Jesus through Mary," was given to me by my mother before I became a nun.

During the summer of 1971 Sister Marie, our language teacher, and I took a group of fifteen students to Europe for a five week study tour. We traveled on a plane so huge that one couldn't see the front seats while standing in the rear, and the young people seemed to think the greatest thrill on earth consisted in going to the rest-room 30,000 feet above the ocean! Our entire tour: meals, lodging, and transportation (even to and from New York) cost $1000, including passport and photo. While in London it was rather coincidental that we saw the film *Ann of a Thousand Days* the night before we visited the Tower of London, where Anne had awaited death. We enjoyed the tourist sights; the students haunted Picadilly Circus. One trip took us to Stratford-on-Avon to see a Shakespearean play, but what was really memorable to me was riding back to London, late at night, through the dark cobbled lanes, between shuttered Tudor houses and shops, so close one could almost have touched them. This was really old England to me.

From London, we crossed into Belgium, and thence to Paris and the rest of France. The Sorbonne, where we stayed, reeked of history, and it was a curious feeling, living in the rooms where so many famous characters had lived and studied. Because I had set aside a whole day to visit the Louvre, I was most disappointed when I found the guards were on strike; hence, the building was closed. I did manage, another day, to see a few specials: the Mona Lisa, Winged Victory, and a Raphael.

It was an education in itself to enter the immense dining hall attached to the University of Paris. Every nationality and culture was represented by an array of truly stunning clothing. Colorful turbans, saris, African headdresses, and Arab robes were everywhere. Each day a new display of exotic clothing and jewelry was offered for sale.

Our trip to the chateaus along the Loire valley was also educational: one hundred and twenty-four rooms and not a single bathroom!

One of our greatest thrills came when, on August 15th, Sister Marie and I attended Mass at Notre Dame Cathedral. When the Archbishop extended his arms and intoned the *Gloria,* almost 2000 worshippers chanted it to a glorious end.

St. Peter's Basilica was the high point of our trip; I literally drank in the magnificent *Pieta* of Michelangelo, and was suitably stunned by the hugeness of everything in the building. The high altar seemed to have a kind of insect crawling around until I realized it was a priest walking around lighting the candles, themselves at least eight feet tall.

The Sistine Chapel was awe-inspiring, and the statue of David impressive. The only thing I missed was in Venice —a gondola ride in the moonlight. One of the students later informed me I didn't really miss anything; the water smelled, the gondolier had no voice, and there wasn't any moon.

As an art teacher I was, of course, most anxious to see all the famous works of art I could; for the students it seemed far more important that their parents see the statues with them standing near-by. They took hundreds of pictures and bought souvenirs of all kinds. I'm sure our bus alone accounted for thousands of dollars worth of watches in Switzerland. And this was in 1971!

Switzerland was gloriously clean and beautiful, and we enjoyed a lively snowball fight on the top of the Alps on the 4th of July. Because ours was an almost entirely Catholic bus, our driver gave us an extra little side visit to Assisi on our way to Paris, where we were to take the plane for home. It was unbearably sad to see this cradle of the mighty Franciscan order so dirty and dilapidated.

Because my knees were becoming too painful I decided to have surgery on one of them during the summer of 1974 at Mercy Hospital,

Aurora. The surgery was successful, but a massive lung embolism afterwards brought me close to death. One of our nursing sisters told me later that I was clinically dead for four days and four nights. Just before I "woke up" I knew I had to say, "Thy will be done," that I was willing to get better, if that is what God wanted - I surely didn't. I wanted to go to heaven.

As soon as I said, "Thy will be done," a beautiful thing happened. Call it a dream, an illusion, an hallucination. All I know is that Our Lady of Mercy, on her throne, the Little King on her lap, each wearing a crown and dressed in beautiful robes, was there. She put her arm around my shoulder and said, "Don't worry. You're going to be all right. I'm going to take care of you." Just those three sentences, but I could never forget them.

When I opened my eyes I said, "You can all go home now. I'm going to be all right". The sister at my bedside said, "You're not out of the woods yet, Imelda." "I know," I said, "but you can all go home now. I'm going to be all right." My niece, my god-child, was there from Ohio. The sisters were writing my obituary, the family was planning my funeral service. Recuperation took an entire year; I had to learn to walk again; therapy continued even after I went home.

In 1975 I became the permanent substitute teacher at Unity High School, formerly Mercy High School. Most of the subjects I could teach; some, like chemistry, I baby-sat. The teachers all had work planned, and the girls were usually very cooperative. It always amused me though, to listen to the teachers planning which days they would be "sick". I guess it was quite convenient, having a substitute teacher.

In 1979, while at Unity High I answered an ad asking for volunteers to assist the Bishop of British Columbia, Canada. By return mail I received my assignment: to help a little priest in a camp for Cree Indian children in Chetwyd, British Columbia. I traveled by Greyhound to Prince George, where I was welcomed by the Irish Sisters of Mercy, who staffed many schools in the Alberta and British Columbia districts. My strongest memory of that visit was the constant invitation, "Will ye have a cup o' tea?" After a few days I boarded a train to Chetwyd, and was greeted there by Father Jungblut, a dear man who lived in an abandoned caboose left behind by the defunct railroad which no longer continued north to Dawson Creek. Father drove me to Moberly

Lake, where the camp was actually situated, and on the shore of which I found the little log cabin church where Father said Mass each day.

At the lodge I found a small clean room ready for me. Since the nights were cold, my covering was an opened sleeping bag. Without indoor plumbing, I soon asked for lye to drop down the "hole", and was amused to hear from one of the boys that the little priest had remarked that Sr. Imelda certainly was no pioneer! Our little children were very good. After a morning of lessons in Christian Doctrine, we allowed them to go swimming. Only the Cree children went in the lake. It was too cold for the white children, because the lake is fed by a glacier. It was so clear that we could see the rocks below the water many feet from shore.

When the Bishop was scheduled to come for Confirmation the older girls and I scrubbed the little log church and renovated the drawers in the sacristy. Every once in a while a scream told me that a spider had been found under the rough pews. After washing the altars I tried to find something to replace the coarse blue drapes on each side of the altar; they had been chewed along the bottom by chipmunks. I looked everywhere, and finally found some gold drapes which had been used as drop cloths. After a good soapy wash and a good pressing, the satin drapes were just beautiful and looked splendid. Now the only flaw was a spot on the front of the altar where the paint had chipped off. A large vase of wild flowers strategically placed took care of that.

The Bishop appeared in a doe-skin miter, made for him by some of his parishioners.

From the Moberly Lake we went, that same day, to Kelley Lake, Alberta, where the Bishop was to confirm another group of Cree Indians. Here, there were many young people in long mail-order dresses and Sunday suits, along with dozens of babies of all ages running around between the benches while their mothers gossiped and chatted. Between that noise and the Cree ladies singing hymns in their native tongue, it was such bedlam that every few minutes Father Jungblut had to go up to the altar, ring a bell, and plead, "Mothers, gather your children; keep them quiet, so the Bishop can hear."

After the Confirmation we were invited to the school hall for supper; I decided that moose sandwiches tasted much like beef.

When we arrived at Beaver Lodge, where I was to live for the next two weeks, I was shown to a lovely little room in the basement, complete with private bath. The Catholic couple, the wife of whom was part Cree, had asked Fr. Jungblut if they could "borrow" me for a few weeks. Each day we went by truck out across the fields to a Bingo Hall, where we taught Christian Doctrine to the little Cree Indians on that reservation. Little boys are the same everywhere: I can still see the beautiful little black beady eyes, dancing with mischief, in those reddish brown faces. Afterward, while walking around the area, I saw moose antlers, and I had some very interesting talks with the older Cree women whose job it was to clean the skins of fur, using the same bone instruments their ancestors had used for centuries. When the skin was completely bare, the hides would be smoked and then made into moccasins by the same women, to be sold in the shops.

Two years later I returned to Canada, this time going north through Banff, Lake Louise, and Jasper. This wealthy man's playground was overwhelmingly beautiful and overwhelmingly crowded. Not one room was to be had, but finally a kindly inn-keeper let me have a room, hardly more than a closet, right next to the hotel's ballroom.

Father Jungblut again met me, and took me to the little log church for Mass. When I returned to Prince George I intended to board the elite train to Spokane, Washington. I was told at the ticket counter that today was the day the train came north. Yesterday was the day the train went south!

That summer I must have traveled about 11,000 miles by Greyhound, to visit relatives all over the "lower 49". My amazement was constant as I met people all over the continent of all cultures, all so willing to share their life stories with me. Cattle ranchers, bikers, even a lady rodeo rider, made my journey most interesting and enjoyable.

One interesting encounter was with a young girl returning to her home in Medicine Hat, Alberta. She was most interested in the object of my trip, and asked many questions about religion. It so happened that I had brought with me two copies of our Sister Gloriana's book *Listening for the Lord.* Why, I hadn't known. As she continued to ask questions, I knew why.

By the time my grand-nieces and grand-`nephews were ready for marriage we were permitted to go to weddings, and attend them I did. From New Jersey to California, and as far north as Minnesota I traveled. I usually got in one good polka and one good waltz. Usually I ended up teaching the groom how to polka; it seemed slightly sinful for a member of a Milwaukee family not to know how to polka Because I am the matriarch of the clan, my presence is always welcome at weddings, or, for that matter, just for a visit. Because most of my people have large families, I have made it a practice of visiting them, rather than asking them to bring a number to visit me. It is a big bonus that I love to travel. And because I so enjoy it, I thank God every day that I am able to do it. With two false knees, one eye almost blind, and almost as much metal in me as in the Bionic Woman, my thanks for each day can no longer be just a *Deo Gratias*, or even an *Alleluia*, but a sincere and heartfelt *Gaudete*.

Twelve years ago, while living at Mercy Manor, Aurora, I gave an art appreciation class at our Golden Ages Meeting. The next day some of the ladies attended a meeting at the local county jail, where the warden asked if they knew anyone who could volunteer to teach art to the prisoners, and they volunteered me! When the warden called, I told him I'd be happy to teach the art, but I didn't drive, so that if he could get me there it would be great. He did, and I taught art at the jail about four years. We even had an Art Exhibit at a local church.

Then, about five years ago, I started teaching Bible classes to the medium security men while my good friend, a big Baptist minister taught the maximum security men. Mr. Johnson was my chauffeur to and from the jail for several years, and for part of that time we both ate with the guards at noon. Last year I was fortunate to find a lovely lady who teaches the girls, and who was willing to take me along each time she goes to the jail.

This is my tenth year there, and I cannot praise the prison personnel nor the men who come to my classes enough for their cooperation and good spirit. I have always experienced respect and courtesy from all. People are always praising me for my work at the Kane County jail, but I tell them I deserve no praise because I enjoy it so much. Each time I go we first sing a lot, then have a Bible lesson, questions and discussion. Afterward we form a circle, holding hands, and say the Lord's Prayer aloud. Then I pray for them and their families and friends, asking God to go with them when they leave, and help them wherever they are. We become pretty good friends, week after week. My boss, Mr. Tevis, has

152

been incredibly kind in making my time at the jail easy and pleasant, so much so that it seems incredible that I've been going there nearly ten years.

In September 1989, I finally got to visit Ireland, where my great-great-great-grandmother, Nancy O'Neill, was supposed to have been born. I found no traces of Nancy, but I visited what was to me of far greater importance, our foundress's grave and the beautiful motherhouse Mother Catherine McAuley founded in Baggot Street, Dublin, in 1831. I spent several hours in the garden, and more in the small chapel erected over her grave. Many more were spent in the large chapel she had built. Because this was my sixtieth anniversary as a Sister of Mercy, these were memorable moments for me.

The people on the trip with me made it even more memorable by doing something so beautiful that I found it hard to believe. When I returned to the bus that evening, they sat me down and presented me with a lovely gold Gaelic cross on a chain and a beautiful card signed by everyone on the bus. When we arrived at our hotel, they insisted that I join them in the pub below for a drink. I chose Irish coffee and tried to be jovial, but my day had been too emotionally draining, and I finally had to say good night. Not, however, before a last picture was taken of our bus driver and our tour guide giving me a goodnight kiss, one on each cheek, simultaneously.

Some of the highlights of that trip were seeing Windsor Castle, Stonehenge, and castles and manor homes in each of the British Isles. The scenery in each was very beautiful. Because I am somewhat of a coward, I walked up one hundred and twenty steps in Blarney Castle, but didn't kiss the Blarney Stone. I wasn't swinging from my heels for anyone.

Several months after I returned I fell and really smashed my left femur. After a successful surgery, I again developed a massive lung embolism, and again they had to operate to save my life. This time it took even longer to recuperate, so I found myself at our Mercy-run McAuley Manor. Now, at McAuley Convent, connected with McAuley Manor, I spend my days making rosaries, making and decorating ceramics, and assisting at switchboard. I've always been able to do a lot of crafts, and here I can. One of the most fun things I do is make earrings for pierced ears. A priest friend likes to tease me by saying "What would Mother McAuley say?" I answer, "I think she would say, "Go for it, Imelda.""

I have never considered myself an artist. I wasn't creative as an artist should be creative. I wasn't even a very creative art teacher. While studying in art classes through the years, I'm sure the young people in my classes looked with some measure of contempt at my timid offerings, and I looked with amazement at their bold nudes and flamboyant colors. Through the years I did many portraits of the Lord and Our Lady, copying them in oils, pastels, or water colors. Whenever a priest had an anniversary, the superior would ask me to do a picture, and often, in the beginning, I thought I did. Soon I came to realize I couldn't have done them. They were too good. Of course I always knew God was working through me, but I never realized it. Every bit was His. Now, painting roses on ceramics or on a piece of calligraphy, I'm much more aware of where the credit belongs. I know now that without His help, our hands cannot produce, our thoughts are stymied, and our voices are mute.

Here, then, are my three cycles of life, for I have been brought back three times to new life.

First, I was given blood when I was one day old, to stop the hemorrhage which was depriving me of life. Why? Probably because the Lord had a vocation to religious life in mind for me.

Second, when I was clinically dead for four days, and Our Lady interceded for me. Why? Probably because the prison ministry awaited me.

Third, when an "umbrella," a procedure for stopping blood clots, was given me when I was really dying, and saved my life. Why? Maybe to be the "Story Lady", telling fairy tales to second graders, maybe to go back to the jail, and maybe, just maybe, it's because the Lord wants another old nun around who loves Him an awful lot!

3

PRIME

I rejoiced at the things
That were said to me;
We shall go into
The house of the Lord.
From the beginning,
And before the world,
Was I created,
And unto the world to come
I shall not cease to be;
And in the holy dwelling place
I ministered before Him.

Sally Butler
Dominican Religious

Director, Social Service Agency

Bachelor of Science, Education, St. John's

Master of Arts, English, College of St. Rose, Albany

Master of Social Work, Hunter School of Social Work

Job-related ministries

Sally shares an apartment with Georgianna, who teaches social work to minority students, and has "a breath-taking view of the towers of lower Manhattan." Friends keep her in touch with community; she is blessed with a prioress who "is genuinely concerned about all of us." Sally and several of her sister have opened a house of hospitality for African-American women who want to be religious. She is an opera buff, a player of an upright piano, and a frequent attender of architectural lectures and art galleries. Sally is the "Carol" in her story, and therefore looks forward to seeing the grandchildren grow up, and prays for a "happier day for our Church, one in which each of us is valued."

Sally Butler

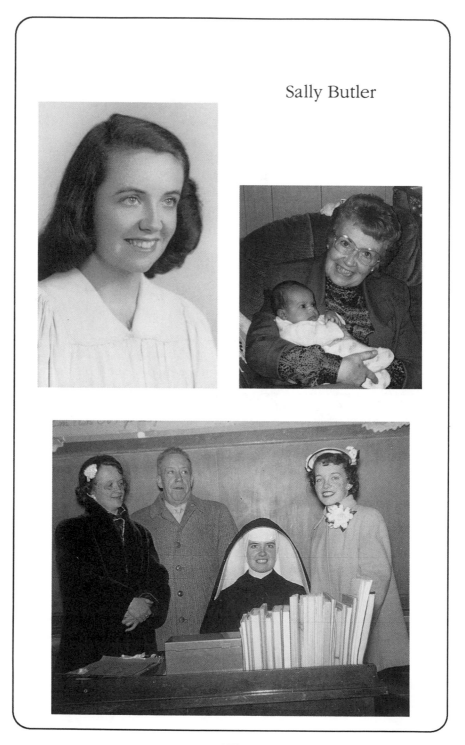

Thanks for Asking

At one gathering of nuns here in New York, we settled on an acronym for our informal group: VOCO (Victims of Clerical Oppression) or The Poor Banished Children of Eve. All of us had been made homeless at least once by a pastor bent on contracting with Social Services for hostels for retarded adults.

"Maybe," offered Marianne (thrice evicted), "if we act retarded they'll let us stay."

We bickered about our logo. A hand outstretched, thought some. "That docility is what got us into this fix!" Right.

A fist raised in protest? Too war-like, warned the doves. Finally, a Picasso-like fist holding flowers. A few still murmured.

We needed a slogan: "A time-clock in every rectory!" "Make policy, not altar bread!"

And so went another evening shared by a group of today's good sisters.

All of us have taught school in the Catholic system and most of us loved it. And now, most of us love a new kind of service. We are less visible because the medieval wimple, the one needing hours of starching and ironing, has been discarded. But we are, most of us, still thrashing about trying to make things better.

Eileen is responsible for a rather large group of mentally ill, homeless people, the kind who won't ever fully recover, who won't settle into a group home, who resist most attempts to help them. She follows them to the notorious Port Authority building in Manhattan, or to crack-infested abandoned buildings and coaxes them back. A friend asked if this was a new experience. "To tell you the truth, most of the guests at my jubilee mass sat with their backs to the altar. I guess I've always liked these folks."

Karen thought, at age sixty-two, that her productive years were over. But, through a series of unplanned meetings, she became the manager of a Single-Room Occupancy Shelter in Brooklyn. Suddenly she was godmother to two hundred formerly homeless single people who learned from her how to live together. "It was much like the convent," she said. "Major conflicts over cleaning up the kitchen and replacing toilet paper." She learned to adapt to challenges like the donation of six dozen sneakers, all size 8 and all lefties.

Carol raised a foster son, a boy given to her by an impoverished woman just before her death. His marriage and fatherhood have given her three delightful grandchildren who find in her a rapt audience for school yard intrigue and Michael Jackson impersonations.

She shares an apartment with Katherine, a community organizer for thousands of politically active senior citizens who lobby most effectively for the rights of the frail elderly.

Frances and Sonya teach English to Russian immigrants whose values have been molded solely by pragmatic concerns. So, the students copy answers and even ask for their papers back once they've discovered the correct responses. The challenge is greater than any offered by mere academy sophomores; there is no resort to ten commandments or good old-fashioned religious guilt.

Many of us in poor areas live alone or with one other sister. Our primary community is no longer under one roof. We meet quite often in one another's apartments, or at a local restaurant if we're too tired to cook. Concerts in downtown churches are fun; so are visits to former sisters. The line between the in's and the out's is gone.

We are saddened by so many of the diocesan priests, once good friends and team members, who are now party-line orthodox misogynists, nervous to the point of apoplexy when approached by a questioning nun. They find us too uppity now. We took seriously their offer to become associates and challenged them to consider systemic change. They backed off, most of them, and resorted to the hierarchy's time-worn cover-up — tradition. There are a few for whom we pray, the intelligent and courageous few who refuse to bow to present day conservatism. They are very lonely men.

So...VOCO exists. We are the clergy's worst nightmare: well educated, articulate women bent on living a decent Christian life for which we need not be ashamed. We are in daily gritty touch with women and men whose suffering is palpable and we bring it home with us each night. We no longer fear anyone.

That last sentence demands a pause. Once, our religious formation depended greatly on fear: fear of being "singular," of intellectual pride (whatever that was), of a superior's displeasure or a pastor's discomfort. We shuddered if the altar linens were wrinkled or the Kentile showed waxy buildup, if our students were noisy or our veils the wrong length.

But now, we are honestly unafraid. The unthinkable has already happened. Our religious life has cracked to pieces and will never be the same. The sheltered retirement, once so firmly there, is, we know, unlikely.

So we turn to this day and counsel crime victims, care for AIDS babies, open shelters. We pray less formally, more passionately. We are very, very happy. Another startling thought, that if we had enemies, we'd surely be unsettling foes. We are deeply happy, intelligent women afraid of absolutely nothing.

Yes. Thank you so much for asking.

Elissa Kamaka
Franciscan

Coordinator, Religious Education Parish Team Member

Bachelor of Arts, Silver Lake College, Wisconsin

Master of Theological Studies, University of Wisconsin

Doctor of Philosophy, University of Saint Louis, Spiritual Direction training

Job-related ministry

Elissa enjoys reading historical biographies, painting in watercolors, teaching basketry and other crafts, going to art shows. Someday she would like to write a story about her father's spiritual legacy to his family, and to travel across the United States, visiting family and friends. She would like to learn the Hispanic language "so that I can speak it fluently," and someday would like to become involved "with base communities here in the Midwest as the shortage of ordained priests continues to grow."

Elissa Kamaka

Transitions

Looking back forty-one years, it seems like another life time when at the age of nineteen, I left my native land of Hawaii to begin my chosen lifestyle as a nun in Wisconsin. My family background and culture were to become significant struggles in another culture. Mother did not approve my decision to enter religious life. She was not a Catholic. The spiritual force in our family was my father. He was very supportive and encouraged me.

Why did I choose to enter religious life? Because Catholic education was highly valued and my parents sacrificed much to give all thirteen children the best education. I went to Catholic elementary school and was baptized on May 23, 1938. My baptism has remained a crystal-clear memory.

During my high school years I was very involved in the activities of the parish. The women religious who taught us had ingrained in us strong Christian values and principles. We were welcomed into their convent, not only in the visiting parlor, but also in their kitchen, chapel and living room. We captured their sense of being women with a vision.

My childhood and young adulthood were happy and centered around my family, school and church. Though I was a normal adolescent, that inner call to become a nun was always a nagging aspect of my being. In an all-girl high school we were instructed that each class had the responsibility to pray that some of us would heed the call to service the church through religious vocations. Out of my class of fifty-four seniors, twelve of us answered that call to various religious congregations. During the fall of 1990, while on the west coast, I had the greatest pleasure of meeting a few of my classmates who have persevered in their religious communities.

In August, 1951, I had my first flight across the Pacific Ocean. It took twelve hours to reach California. It was a great achievement to have traveled across that Pacific Ocean and the North American continent to a place called Wisconsin. My life journey had begun.

I traveled on the train from California to Chicago. It felt adventurous. People were curious as to why I was traveling alone. Of course I told them where and why I was going to Wisconsin. Their questions: Why go to a convent? Did I know how life was for a young woman shut away in such a place? How naive I was then, because I was very proud about my decision, and confident that I was going to do my best in the life I had freely chosen.

The first years in the convent were filled with joy and peace, struggles and challenges, pain of separation from my family, and the first taste of what it meant to be from a different culture and nationality. So many aspects of living in a Midwestern state with the four seasons of autumn, winter, spring and summer were for me, a whole new way of living and learning.

During the thirty plus years in that Franciscan congregation , I was professionally trained as a teacher and taught in the elementary and junior high grades. My educational background included graduate degrees earned through scholarships at two different universities. I was very involved academically, and all my energies were poured into my professional life. During the last eleven years in that community, I ministered on the college level in teacher education.

My parent congregation was once known as progressive and visionary. As the leadership changed, so did the emphasis on community values. There was a more restrictive stance on the interpretation of religious life. Conformity was the description of a good religious; diversity was not welcomed in religious life. In reality there was more control, and conformity to the outward material symbols and their values on religious life. The garb became a constant source of critical contention within the community. Sisters who dared to go without their veils were called on the carpet. At times it was more common sense to be appropriately dressed for recreational events in slacks than in the garb. Such common sense could not be a decision of the individual sister but rather, permission had to be obtained from a superior.

166

I remember the anger I felt during a meeting for sisters who ministered at the college. We were given the chapter results. As I sat listening to the *do's* and *don'ts* of conformity to the wearing of the garb, my inner being felt the violence of being dehumanized and controlled by meaningless symbols.

The gist of my response stemmed from these facts: as women religious, we ministered to men and women on the college level. Many of us taught day and evening classes. We made professional decisions regarding the lives of people. We were firm in our dedication and commitment to our call as women religious. We were aware of the human temptations inherent in our ministry. After all, we were human persons with strengths and weaknesses. I personally felt that as women religious we deserved to be treated and respected as mature women in community as well as in our professional lives.

That was only one example of why I began to question the essence of religious life for me. Did I want to live the rest of my life in that kind of environment? By this time many of my friends in the community had left, and I kept hoping from chapter to chapter that there would be diversity.

After a series of physical illnesses I received a statement by the doctor that if I wanted to live healthier, I needed to take control of my own life. My discernment with my spiritual director clearly gave me the first step. I decided to take a leave of absence from the college. So much had happened; I was totally burned out. To distance myself I took a job at a Catholic college in Baltimore, Maryland. I stayed there for three years and loved every moment.

Through my soul searching I came to terms with what I wanted to do with my life. At that particular time I was gifted with a spiritual director who knew me very well, and understood my conviction that religious life was for me.

What was I looking for? Did I have the courage and strength to transfer into another congregation? Would I be a compatible fit? Could I withstand the intense and deep pain, the separation from friends I had grown-up with in my parent community? Would my lay friends understand why I needed to transfer? Emotions were raw. I was in turmoil!

The struggles in discernment were tough. My relationship with God was like the dark night of a soul. There was a continuous tugging in my heart regarding the relationships I valued in the congregation I was leaving. The hurts were unspeakable. Yet in the midst of all the chaos, there were many who understood and supported my decision.

There was no heavenly messenger who announced which congregation I was to choose. My intuition and gut feelings were my guides in the final analysis of choice. Once the decision to transfer was made, the dying process was over and a new life began.

August 1, 1985 was the beginning of my transfer process in the new congregation. The theme I wrote to express my feeling and experiences was:

Sifting Sand

(Theme of a Transfer)
Stinging grains kiss my face
Flying particles grit my eyes
Pricking fibers tickle my ears
Whistling winds touch my lips
Sifting sand, sifting sand.
Feet searching rocky debris
Hands changing ready swirls
Body dancing misty vastness
Mind capturing desert glory
Sifting sand, sifting sand.

Since 1987 five sisters of transfer and I formulated a team under the name, *Divergent Path*. We are committed to share and help other sisters who are discerning a transfer into another congregation. This is done through transfer workshops scheduled each summer at a designated site. It is not the purpose of the writer to detail the history of *Divergent Path* in this anthology.

May, 1991; my life was on a roller coaster. My medical check-up revealed breast cancer. A biopsy was done. There was no option. A bilateral mastectomy was done in July. Such a reality made me face my own mortality. I learned that peace comes when there is acceptance of the cancer and its consequences. Life takes on an unbelievable perspective for me. I now live a different lifestyle.

At the present I live in an apartment by choice. I wanted this special quietness to process my illness, to grieve the loss of my breasts, to truthfully face my mortality, to reorganize my priorities, to change the pace of my life, to become more in touch with my God, to listen attentively to the *why's* of what is happening to my whole being, to make meaningful things happen, to share my creativity with others.

As each day dawns I am grateful. Each day my tolerance for the chemotherapy drug improves. Each day I read and learn how to live with breast cancer. Each day I am thankful that I can live and enjoy a normal healthy life.

Eleanore A. Kilcoyne
Former Franciscan

Married, four step-children

Periodicals Assistant, Elmhurst College Library

Bachelor of Arts, Loyola-Marymount, Los Angeles

Extensive training, Lay Ministry, Diocese of Joliet

Ministry to the Aged, Immaculate Conception Church, Elmhurst

Eleanore hopes to become more involved with lay ministry when she retires from her current job. Her other love is in genealogy. At present she is tracing and researching her family history. Eleanore would like to expand this project with an eye toward publishing it.

Eleanore A. Kilcoyne

June 4, 1969

The time is 1:30 p.m. I sit in the outer office of the Vicar for Religious of the archdiocese. Earlier today I said good-bye to my seventh grade students and wished them a happy summer. Now I wait for my appointment to sign a decree of dispensation which will officially release me from my religious vows. No longer am I wearing the black serge habit which was my uniform for twenty years. I have changed into a bright yellow dress, and it reflects my feelings well. My tears and fears are gone; I am filled with an inner peace that is like the morning after a summer storm.

My thoughts are interrupted by the receptionist's announcement that Father McCartney will see me now. He is sitting behind his desk as I enter, some papers spread out before him. We are not strangers to each other, for I have been in this office many times in the past three years. Father greets me, commenting on how calm I seem. Then he begins to read to me in English the decree which is written in Latin. When he finishes, he reminds me that, upon signing the decree, I shall no longer be a religious under vow. I reach for the pen he has laid in front of me. "Don't sign until you are very sure you understand what you are doing", he warns. I look at him, and beyond him to the window behind where he sits. Do I understand what I am doing? Does *he* understand the path I have walked — from nagging doubts to sleepless nights, the years of holding on when there was nothing to hold onto? Can he understand the anguish in which I have given birth to this moment? I smile and assure him that I do, indeed, understand what I am doing. I sign my name and leave. Walking out into the street, I enter the world again as I first entered it thirty-nine years ago. I am once more Eleanore Ann Birmingham.

How did I get to this day? For a child of Martin and Elizabeth Birmingham, a life of dedication to Christian ideals seemed most natural. My parents were not only devoted to the practice of the Catholic faith, but were leaders in social and civic issues in the rural community in the Midwest where I grew up. The greatest gift and the heaviest burden I received from them was a sense of fairness — you played fair and you worked fair and expected others to do the same. I was the twelfth of thirteen children. My oldest sister was Sister Mary Martin. She became a Franciscan nun before I was born. I scarcely knew her; her visits home for one week every five years left little time for us to become acquainted.

I took my faith very seriously even as a small child. Shortly after I made my First Communion I had my first problem of conscience. Foul language was neither spoken nor tolerated in our home, but I had heard my two older brothers use some pretty wicked words, away from my parents' hearing. I decided to use my new vocabulary to chastise my pet cat. Though the cat didn't seem shocked, I felt I had become quite a woman of the world. Then came Saturday afternoon and time for confession. Of course I had sinned, but what did one call this sin? All sins had to have names. Finally I remembered that one term Sister Mary Ella had said was something "very bad." Trembling I entered the dark box and announced, "I committed adultery." There was a loud sniff from the other side of the grille. Immediately I was asked, "How old are you?" I could barely whisper, "Seven." Next came "What did you do?" To this I gasped, "I said bad words." ("Please, Jesus, don't let him ask me what I said.") He assured me that I had not committed adultery but had used "vulgar language." The second term didn't make any better sense than the first one, but I decided that maybe religion wasn't meant to make sense.

People who knew me as a child and as a teenager described me as "quiet and serious." I hated both words, but I really didn't know how else to be. In a large family being one of the youngest meant being quiet a lot. And, as for serious, there was much in life to be serious about. My parents were older than my friends' parents and I worried that they might die before I grew up. So I become very responsible and did more than my share of chores on the farm, especially after my two older brothers went off to the military during World War II. Socially, I had many girlfriends and held my own until came adolescence — and boys. Boys in the 1940's didn't care much for girls who were quiet and serious. But I was an excellent student, so I stayed clear of the popular group and carved my niche among those who admired my academic ability. It hurt, but I had already learned never to let anyone know when I was hurt.

The idea of a religious vocation wasn't something I gave much thought to in my early teens. I wasn't especially close to any of the Franciscan sisters who taught me. (They were the order to which my sister belonged.) Two things changed my outlook. First, my brother Joe, four years older, went away to the army. Having been close, we wrote to each other often. Joe had been in college before the war, with plans to enter the seminary. His letters kept telling me that I should do something important with my life, and not marry a farmer and raise kids and chickens.

The second event was the arrival in our parish, for the first time, of an assistant pastor. Father Wilmer Pieffer was young and full of enthusiasm. He taught in our high school and coached our basketball teams. We loved him at once. More by his example than by words, he planted the idea in my mind of a life dedicated to God. When I broached the subject to him, he was most encouraging but not pushy. I told him I was definitely not interested in the order of sisters who staffed our school. He advised me to write to other communities and he even took me, with a couple of other girls, on a day-long tour of motherhouses in the diocese. More and more I realized that this was what I really wanted in life.

In my junior year of high school my world fell apart. Because my dad's health was failing, my parents retired from the farm to the small town where our parish church and school were. A month later Dad died of a stroke. His death left me very angry with him for abandoning me, and with God for taking him from me. Six months later, our beloved assistant pastor became very ill and had to leave the parish. Not long afterward he died of leukemia. I began to realize for the first time that life is not fair.

Why my mother made the decision to send me to boarding school for my senior year I have never been sure. Perhaps she felt I needed some direction in my life. At any rate, she told me that I could go to the

Franciscan academy where my sister, Sister Mary Martin, was stationed. I really did not want to go, and I knew it would be a financial hardship for Mom. But she seemed to want it so much that I didn't have the heart to oppose her. I felt she had had enough grief losing my dad that year. So I went without protest. That same month my brother Joe, home from the army now, entered the Jesuit novitiate.

Socially, that year at boarding school was dismal. The senior class was small — only twenty-three girls, and most of them had been there since freshman year. There were tight little groups, none of which seemed to want an addition. I was unhappy, but stubbornly determined to make it somehow. The answer was to throw all my energy into my studies. By the end of the first quarter I had earned the highest average in the senior class, which I maintained until graduation. It didn't make me a social success, but it won me respect, however grudging.

By far the most important happening of that year was seeing these Franciscan sisters in a new light. I found them to be wonderfully warm and caring women. My teachers were outstanding. And I became acquainted with my mysterious oldest sister, who was teaching in the music department of the academy and the junior college also located at the motherhouse. In the early months I saw her as another one of the sisters. Gradually our family bond developed. We viewed our family very differently: she as the eldest, I as the twelfth. My mother was nineteen when Sis was born, and forty-two when I arrived. I was proud of my sister, but fearful of becoming "Sister Martin's little sister" instead of me, Eleanore. Because the novitiate was in the same building as the academy, I observed the novices and postulants a great deal. More and more I found myself looking at the stairway that led to the enclosure and wondering, "Is that where I belong?"

Before the year had gone far, bad family news came from home. My brother Joe had left the Jesuit novitiate, filled with bitter disillusionment about religious life. His anger spilled into frequent letters to me, which I carefully concealed from Sister Martin. I was torn between worry over his distraught mental state and my own new-found doubts about the value of religious life. But I told no one. What was the use? I had to make the decision; it was my life.

During our mid-year retreat I wrestled myself to a decision of sorts — not to make a decision for a year. I would come back in the fall as a college freshman and wait to see what time would do to my indecision. When I proposed college to my mother, she told me there was no way she could afford college now. Maybe if I would get a job for a year — but I knew there could be no moving away from where I felt I had to be. The next day I applied for admission to the novitiate in September.

My first, or postulant year, was a happy one. Busy with college classes and the complexities of the daily schedule, I kept the demons of doubt at bay. All that changed the following June with the reception of the habit and the beginning of my canonical year of novitiate as Sister Mary James. During this year we were permitted to study only religious life and theology. The rest of the time was spent in the bakery, laundry and in other housekeeping duties. The physical work I enjoyed, being an active farm girl; the classes were another matter. The spiritual life, as it was presented, was not at all appealing.

Human nature appeared hopelessly flawed; only the most stringent asceticism would subdue it. Temptation was everywhere — in one's fellow religious, in one's family, in worldly desires. A bleak and joyless existence, it seemed to me, and yet, the fervent religious was supposed to be happy. I continually struggled with myself. Why did I feel that I was being brain-washed? Why couldn't I believe that kneeling down to ask to be excused from the recreation room would make me humble? Why couldn't I make the blind leap of faith that would enable me to accept as others seemed to accept? The few times I dared to admit my difficulties to the novice mistress or a confessor, I was told that these were little crosses one must bear. I didn't know how, but I was determined that somehow I would climb this mountain.

During the senior novitiate year my little crosses faded as I resumed college classes and student teaching. And a new novice-mistress was appointed that year. Her sense of humor helped me to keep my spiritual indigestion somewhat controlled as we studied the vows in preparation for our first profession. Six weeks before we began retreat for profession, my mother died very suddenly. Accompanied by my sister, Sister Martin, I went home for the funeral. Mother's death left me with a terrible emptiness — not anger, just overwhelming sadness. I had never been especially close to her, perhaps because we were so much alike. Now I would never have a chance to really know her as an adult. Once again, life was not fair.

My first assignment after profession was teaching second grade in a large suburban school. The transition from novitiate to professed religious life was very difficult for me. I was terrified of the principal/local superior, a tall stern-looking woman who seemed always to be looking for the dust in the bathroom I had just cleaned, or for the error in the report I turned in. Fortunately for both of us, I spent only one year there. The next few years I taught in rural areas with smaller schools and convents. The principal/superiors were teaching full-time, and were less concerned with dust. I breathed easier and began to enjoy teaching my first and second graders. I received much help and advice from older and more experienced teachers in some of our nearby schools. I felt myself growing into a confident and competent teacher. Sometimes my equipment was poor and funds scarce, but I loved the challenge to improvise and be creative.

As a religious I was far less secure. Why was I always analyzing, trying to make sense of things that did not make sense? All too soon came the time to make perpetual vows. I knew I could not in conscience make this commitment, yet I did not want to leave. Surely if I tried harder and prayed more, I would find the way. So I asked for an extension of my temporary vows for one year. It was hard to see my classmates make their final profession without me. But somehow, the decision brought peace, and the next year I pronounced my vows "forever" without reservation.

Two years later I was stunned to open the envelope containing my obedience for the year and discover that I had been assigned to California. In my wildest fantasies I had never imagined that I would join the small group of sisters who were opening schools in the far West. Perhaps the community did see me as a valuable member after all.

Saint Anthony School was located in a small town in California's San Joaquin Valley. Never having left the Midwest, I was awe-struck by the snow-capped Sierra Nevada, the lush fruit orchards and the endless rows of grape vines. Even the frequent appearance of black widow spiders could not dampen my enthusiasm. Our school enrollment was about 75% Mexican-American, with a sprinkling of Lebanese, Basque,

Portuguese, and native American. I was assigned to teach eighth grade. My students were not all typical eighth graders — many of the Mexican-Americans were fifteen or sixteen years old, a few were nearly eighteen. The reading level of the class was spread from third grade to that of a junior in high school. The first year was tough, but I loved every minute of it.

Because of the expense of traveling back to the motherhouse, sisters who were stationed in California stayed there during the summer, attending summer school and making retreat. The first summer six of us traveled to Los Angeles to attend Loyola University, which is today Loyola-Marymount. Our living accommodations that summer were unique. Loyola was in the process of building a new dorm, and the old ones were filled by the time we registered. Consequently, we were housed in the engineering building, whose classrooms had been converted into dorms, complete with white cell curtains in true convent style. All the rooms in this building bore labels on the doors. We had many laughs over the label on our quarters: "Reproduction Room."

The intellectual and spiritual atmosphere of the campus breathed new life into me. I had completed an associate of arts degree in education at our college at the motherhouse. Now I began studying philosophy and history in a program in which I would earn a bachelor of arts degree in eight summer sessions. My teachers were superb, so I didn't mind the fast pace needed to cover a semester's work in six weeks. Each year when summer session was over we traveled north to the San Francisco area to make our annual retreat with another community of Franciscans. These were precious years of spiritual peace and growth.

Early in the 1960's the winds of change began to sweep through our community. We in California felt the wind in the arrival of the first fruits of the Sister Formation program. Under this plan, the young sisters who had made first vows were not assigned to teaching positions; instead they were allowed to remain at the motherhouse until they had completed their college degrees, as well as additional training in religious life. Many of us who were teaching while completing under-graduate courses and who had made final profession, felt that we should have been given the first opportunity for full-time study. Our disenchantment was heightened by the coming of some of these newly-formed sisters to work among us. There was a definite air of intellectual superiority about them, as well as a marked aversion for any kind of household chores.

The direction of the community further changed at this time in the election of a new superior general. Mother Mary John Francis had been in office since I entered the novitiate. To me she was a woman of broad vision, possessed with a great deal of compassion and a wonderful sense of humor. Her successor was unbending in her literal inter- pretation of rules. Her leadership style was based on inspiring fear rather than confidence. Directives came forth from the motherhouse often, mostly chilling and negative in tone. I felt as if I were being covered with a cold gray fog.

In many ways the feeling of oppression I experienced at this time was similar to what I had felt in the novitiate. But there was one big difference. I was now in my thirties, with several years of religious life behind me. I had lived away from the mainstream of the community and had been influenced by teachers and spiritual advisors outside the order. Instead of turning inward upon myself, I began to look more critically at my community. What I saw was very distressing. There seemed to be so little respect for human dignity. We professed to follow the ideal of Franciscan poverty, but we were actually obsessed with money. Whether or not it was permissible to have something depended not so much on whether it was appropriate, as on whether you spent community funds to acquire it. We preached justice; meanwhile we ostracized some members as "problems", a label that could last a lifetime. Had we made hypocrisy a virtue, I wondered? And if I pretended not to see these double standards, was I not the biggest hypocrite of all?

The summer I finished my studies at Loyola, I returned to the motherhouse for the first time since being assigned to California. I had looked forward all summer to seeing my friends and family, and to making retreat in familiar surroundings. My homecoming was not to be joyous, however. The sisters were glad to see me, but it was a very restrained welcome — people seemed almost afraid to speak freely. Puzzled, but still upbeat, I went to the superior general's office to greet her, as was customary. Besides my diploma I had a letter from the chairman of the history department at Loyola, stating that I would be admitted to graduate school without probation because of my high scholastic standing. I had worked hard for this honor, and I was proud as I handed the letter to her. She read it, sniffed, and gave it back to me with the comment, "He didn't offer to pay your tuition, I see." No one else ever saw that letter; I returned to my room and tore it to shreds.

At the end of retreat I learned that I was being re-assigned to the Midwest. I was shocked; such transfers were not usually made from California without a serious reason, either on the part of the person transferred or her superiors. I could not imagine what I had done, or failed to do, to bring about such an abrupt decision. Again I approached the office of the superior general. I asked to know the reason why I had been transferred. What had I done wrong? I was coolly informed that it was "not your business to know. It is community business." From somewhere I heard my voice saying, "If the community is not my business, then what is my business?" There was no answer. I excused myself and left the room, holding tears deep inside me that would not be shed for a long time.

I struggled through two more years. Then I decided to ask for a leave of absence, called exclaustration. A priest friend with whom I had communicated for several years advised this step. I had no idea how, or if, I would survive as a civilian after eighteen years as a sister. But I know I could no longer keep on hanging to the edge of a cliff. I moved to a large metropolitan area where two of my blood sisters lived. Their support and advice helped my adjustment immeasurably. It was not difficult to find a teaching job in the Catholic school system where I was accepted as another lay teacher.

Two years passed and with the end of the second year I made plans to return to the community. I still believed that I wanted to be a Franciscan sister more than anything else in life. The vicar of religious of the archdiocese, who had counseled me during this time, was skeptical of my decision. He told me that he had known several women who had returned to their communities after exclaustration, but none of them had been able to stay. Even against these odds I knew I had to go back and try once more.

On my return I received a warm welcome from the sisters. During my absence a new superior general had been elected. But the unrest and conflict which marked all religious orders in the 1960's were building to a crisis. The younger members were clamoring for change; the older sisters were fearfully resisting what they saw as impending calamity. In the center was a group of sisters being pulled in both directions, yet not able to identify with either faction. Suddenly, as if I had always known it, I knew the truth: I could not, and would not be part of whatever the community eventually became. I had committed myself to a teaching position for a year and I would honor that. But there it would end. In the spring I made a weekend retreat at a nearby Cenacle. When it was over, I returned to the convent and wrote a petition to be released from the vows I had once believed were forever.

Hindsight supposedly makes all things clear; I have not found it so. Looking back over my years in religious life, I see many shadows. For my part, I know that I entered the community with a sincere desire to dedicate my life to God. That the community accepted me indicated their belief in me as a candidate. What happened in the ensuing years is more complex. Whatever gifts and talents I possessed were apparently considered insignificant, and little effort was ever made by the community leadership to encourage me to develop them. If I behaved in a manner that marked me as "troublemaker", no one was interested enough or honest enough to try to help me. As the years went by I felt increasingly unnecessary, however hard I tried. It was this sense of utter failure and rejection that eventually stifled my spirit.

Empathy and compassion were not popular ideas in the business of governing religious communities in those days. It was all there in black and white: the superior gave commands and you obeyed without question. If you were of a questioning nature, you were headed for a lot of trouble unless you could do violence to the part of you which needed answers.

As I brought gifts to the community when I entered, I also brought gifts from the community when I left. Twenty-one years of memories came with me. Some of them are sad. But there are good memories — warm, fuzzy memories, and crazy, funny memories. Sisters who patiently answered my questions as a new teacher; sisters who nursed me through bouts of flu; sisters who laughed with me over a first grader's antics; sisters who cried with me at the tragic death of my sister. It is, most of all, the gift of my relationships with these beautiful women that I treasure from my Franciscan years.

I have returned to the motherhouse many times since leaving the community. These visits have been a powerful step in my healing process. In going back I have gotten in touch with my spiritual roots. I no longer have a sense of having failed. I now realize that our basic commitment as Christians is our baptismal commitment. Whether we live as lay persons or as vowed religious is less important than how we live the gospel.

Where am I in relation to the Church today? I believe that I am a Christian who happens to be a Catholic. Being a Catholic is part of my cultural heritage. It is the way in which I fulfill my need for a relationship with God. There is much in the Church which grieves and saddens me, but I have chosen to remain an active member. Because my years as a religious have left me very wary of authority figures in the Church, I work in my parish in roles that do not involve me directly with administration. As a minister of care and as bereavement minister, I can offer a caring presence to my sisters and brothers who are suffering. They, in turn, reassure me that faith is stronger than illness and death.

Of all the influences that have shaped my life since leaving the convent, the most profound is my relationship with the kind and loving man to whom I have been married for twenty-one years. Because he has loved me and believed in me, I have learned to love and believe again. In accepting me as I am, he has freed me to be who I am. Free to look at the past without regret; free to look to the future with hope.

Margaret Peter
Franciscan

Franciscan teacher, multiple handicapped deaf children

Master of Education, University of Buffalo

Master of Special Education

Master of Deaf Education

Job related ministries

Sister Margaret hopes to retire in a few years, and then volunteer to teach English as a second language to recent immigrants, especially to those with Laotion, Polish, and Hispanic backgrounds. In the meantime, she continues her work at Saint Coletta's, living in a campus apartment with five other sisters. She is involved with developing a simplified sign language program using video tapes and card games. One of her hobbies is writing the biographies of her sisters who wish to share their stores.

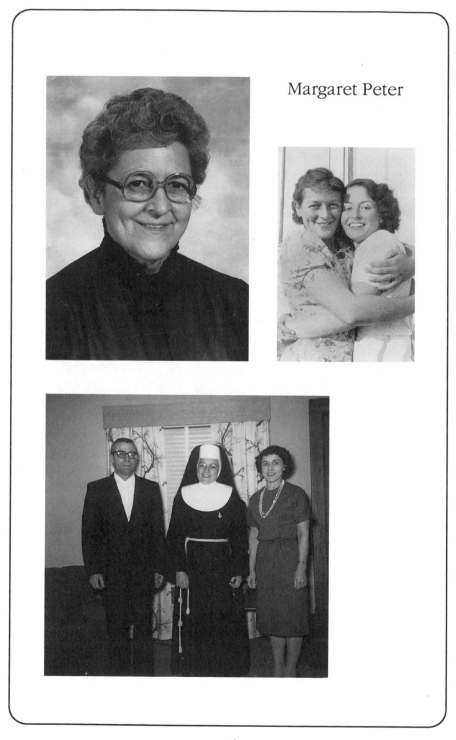

Margaret Peter

What Happened to My Life?

What have I done with my life? As a teenager I dreamed lofty dreams. I remember sitting on the highest rung of the steel ladder that reached to the top of the windmill on our South Dakota farm. From there I surveyed the surrounding countryside with its miles of farm land on every side. I had just graduated from high school as valedictorian. (Never mind that there were only six in my class!) Exhilarated by my accomplishment, and by the height from which I looked down on the earth, all the world was mine. I was strong, healthy, intelligent, ambitious, attractive. I could do anything I wanted to do, maybe even be the first woman president of the United States. It would probably be more fun, though, to travel all over the world and write books about what I'd seen. I wouldn't marry until I was real old — like about twenty-four — unless I found a man as smart as I was who also wanted to travel and write!

During the two years after I descended from the windmill, I worked at home or at whatever lowly jobs were available to women during the Great Depression years. Then came my twentieth birthday and a need to decide what to do with my life. My mind was filled with the scores of books and magazines I had read — a mixture of Wild West stories, Catholic Mission magazines, and romance novels. Out of all that reading, and out of a strong Catholic home life, I retained high ideals and a longing to do with my life the best thing I could possibly do. That, I figured, was to be ordained a priest and work in the foreign missions. Even though I knew such was not possible, I cherished the dream. The Mission magazines, especially the Maryknoll magazine, had appealed to me more than the Wild West stories or the romance novels. I had dated young men and liked most of them, but, after three months of quiet reading, pondering, praying and searching for the special life that would please both God and me, I decided to join a religious order that sent sisters to the foreign missions.

My parents, when I told them my plans, were proud and happy. My brother and six sisters were surprised and less than enthusiastic, but they accepted my decision to join the Sisters of St. Francis in faraway Milwaukee. Although I had struggled against giving up dreams of adventure and vague plans for having a family of my own, I knew that I truly wanted to be a sister.

In September of 1940, when I joined the Sisters of St. Francis of Assisi in Milwaukee, I walked into the motherhouse with great excitement and anticipation. Meeting the twenty-three young women who would be my classmates was a delight. They were far different than I had expected. There were no quiet, withdrawn types, no spinster types, no types at all, but just a group of individual personalities who shared my excitement and anticipation. During the following three years of living, working, and studying together, most of us would become life-long friends.

I thoroughly enjoyed the three years of preparation required before taking vows as a Franciscan sister. Each morning I awoke at 5:00 a.m.. to the sound of a bell and to white curtains surrounding my bed in the large dormitory where all twenty-four of us slept. Each morning I exulted, "I'm a Sister! Me!" That fact kept surprising and cheering me for years to come.

I loved going to college — the fulfillment of one of my dreams. I was pleasantly surprised at the fun my classmates and I had during free times, especially the time we spent in the gym playing basketball, volley ball or badminton. We also learned square dances, circle games and relay races — whatever might prove useful in later years of teaching.

At the end of the three years of preparation I proudly professed the vows of poverty, chastity and obedience. Then came the challenge of teaching forty-nine second graders in a large city school. The kindness and helpfulness of the other sisters helped me do a fair job that first year, and to decide that teaching was what I like best. However, I still dreamed of going to China and had volunteered to do so. Those dreams collapsed when the Communists in China took over our schools there in the 1940's.

Then, in the spring of 1951, the mother general asked for volunteers to teach at St. Johns' School for the Deaf in Milwaukee. "Not me!" I thought. "I don't know anything about deaf children, except that they seem rather strange."

The following summer I overheard one of our sisters who taught there say, "Nobody volunteered! Nobody cares about poor little deaf children." I pretended not to hear, but the remarks persisted in my memory. Shortly after that our class made a seven-day silent retreat, a time of prayer and reflection. Between conferences and prayer times in chapel, I allowed those words to echo in my mind and heart. Deciding to volunteer for St. John's would be as difficult as my first major decision to enter a convent. The retreat master, a Jesuit priest, spoke much of doing God's will, whatever that was for each of us.

On the last day of retreat I wrote a note to the mother general, volunteering to teach at St. John's. Hoping such was not God's will, I thrust the note into mother's mailbox, thinking she wouldn't really accept my offer. Surely she would send me back to St. Joseph's School, the rural parish where I had been teaching. The pastor there wanted me to come back and to enjoy the beautiful new school that was being built that summer.

Then came August and the exciting appointment day when the mother general would give each sister a card with the name of her mission for that year. Mine said I would be going on to school to earn a Master's degree in deaf education. The idea of more education set my spirits soaring, but the thought of leaving the lovable children at St. Joseph's saddened me. As for teaching deaf children, probably for the rest of my life, well — that would be the most difficult part.

During my year of further education in Buffalo, New York, I would be getting my Master's at one of the largest universities in the United States. That excited me. The practical classes in Deaf Education were taught at St. Mary's School for the Deaf where I would be living for one year. There I learned, to my surprise, that deaf children were lovable, whether they were nursery school tots or high school seniors. The forty Sisters of St. Joseph and ten lay teachers who staffed the school were models of dedication and expertise. I marveled at their ability to communicate via speech, lip reading and sign language with children who could not hear. Another surprise — deaf children were happy and friendly — not strange or distant, as I had feared.

The school year of 1951-1952 was full of new awakenings. I learned to do things I never dreamed I could do. By following the instructions of pre-school teacher Sister Rosemary, I could work miracles. Teaching a three-year-old deaf child to imitate her first intelligible basic speech sound "bububu' filled me with awe. It had taken scores of tries, with me pressing the little girl's hand against my cheek, then against her own, while I spoke "bububu." At first Judy watched me with curiosity, then she imitated my lip movements, and finally she vocalized "bububu." That was an important beginning. By the end of the school year Judy could speak, in her soft deaf voice, nearly one hundred words. She could lip read more than that, and sign even more.

That year was unique in many ways. Our group of twelve student teachers visited various institutions for multiple handicapped children. Each was an adventure, but not at all like my youthful dreams of adventure. Each institution seemed to me a whole different world, but the experience of learning and working at St. Mary's introduced me to a new and unique world that changed my life. The sisters there helped me feel at home and a welcome part of the staff. They remain in my memory and affection now, forty years later. The students, with their eagerness to learn and their fun-loving ways, touched me deeply, convincing me that the best thing I could do with the rest of my life was to teach deaf children. At the end of that year of observing, teaching and earning a Master's degree in Deaf Education, I thought I was well prepared to teach deaf children full-time.

My first year at St. John's School for the Deaf proved to be quite overwhelming. Teaching was one thing; supervising children outside of school hours quite another. It took several years for me to learn that such times could be enjoyable. The next thirty years of my life would be intricately bound up with the lives of deaf children, their families and our deeply committed staff. For the first twelve years the staff consisted of fourteen sisters, two priests and several lay people. St. John's was a residential elementary school for nearly one hundred deaf children. Most of the children and staff lived and worked in one old four-story building under very crowded conditions. No one complained about that. We knew St. John's was a great school, rated among the top five of its kind in the nation.

All the sisters worked overtime, often double time. People said that St. John's operated on a shoestring. The school was the largest charity of our Franciscan community. For nearly forty years the sisters had worked without a salary, since that was the only way the school could survive. For another twenty years we would be paid a small stipend. No state or Federal assistance was available for our private school at that time. Hiring an adequate lay staff was out of the question financially, so the sisters willingly took on multiple roles. We saw the need for our services, knew that we were being effective, had compassion for the parents, and most of all, loved the deaf children in our care.

After teaching all day we took weekly turns supervising on the playground, in the children's dining room, in the dormitory morning and evening, in chapel during Mass, or in playrooms. Through our constant presence with the children and with each other we formed close family relationships. I felt that in the classroom I was respected and loved as a teacher, while at other times my relationship with the children was more that of a mother or big sister.

After overcoming initial discipline problems, my favorite job was supervising the children at play. Sometimes, while watching the younger boys play basketball in the gym, I would sit on the sidelines and laugh aloud at their mad scrambling for the ball. The self-appointed leader of the group, a black lad from Atlanta, claimed attention by grabbing the basketball and sitting on it. With all the boys gathered around him, R.P. would share bits of wisdom: "Play ball. Don't fight!" "Don't cry. Be tough!" The boys played with such earnestness and concentration that they seemed oblivious of my presence.

On the other hand, when I supervised the girls, they never forgot my presence. They often asked me to join in their games, interpret a program on TV, or just tell them things I remembered about them when they were little. One evening at bedtime one of the girls asked if the group could stay up late that night. Feeling exhausted and anxious to go off duty, I said, "No!" Gayle was taken aback by my impatience. The next evening she said to me, "I was surprised that you were so crabby last night." Appreciating her honest remark, I excused my mood with:

"Gayle, last night I was very, very tired." She smiled brightly and said, "Oh, I understand. Sometimes I'm crabby, too, when I'm tired." We shared a knowing smile, and our bond of friendship grew stronger.

I found being on duty with the girls in the dormitory one week out of each month a pleasant task. It was an important family time for everyone. The girls were like sisters to one another and they knew I cared about them and their families. Each girl would kneel at her bedside for a short night prayer before hopping into bed, but once Cathy, a hard-of-hearing girl, forgetting I could hear, prayed aloud in her bed after lights were out. She had just told her parents good-bye at the close of her weekend at home. "Dear God, please bless my family. Please carry my kisses to my family. Here's one for Mommy (smack). Here's one for Daddy..."

We formed lasting friendships with the parents. I felt a deep sense of responsibility to them, for they relied on us for so many things: to give their deaf child early understandings of God and religion, to teach their three-year-old deaf children to speak for the first time, "I love you," and to enable them to communicate via speech, lip reading, sign language and writing, while also teaching regular school subjects and being care-givers nine months of the year. Parents often admitted feelings of helplessness in dealing with their deaf child and I acknowledged my own frustrations while also sharing successes and precious moments.

Frustration led me to fulfill one of the greatest dreams of my teenage years. It would be in my struggle to teach young deaf children to communicate that my creativity would be forced to the hilt and beyond. I would do things I had dreamed I would do, but I started with very small steps.

In school I strove to make each day a perfect one. Failing that for even a single day, I settled for "as good as possible." In any case I had to learn to keep the alert, willing attention of each child. It was obvious to me that deaf children, in order to learn, must watch and must want to learn. The most important subject they had to learn was language, which was key to all other subjects. They could see things happening all around them, but could not communicate in speech or sign language what was happening.

192

I noticed that the children loved wordless comic strips. They studied each picture of the Julie and Jack comic strip at the end of our weekly first grade *Little Messenger* and chuckled with glee. "That's the way deaf children see life!" I realized with sudden insight. They see things happening but don't hear what's happening. In the comic strip the complete story is told in pictures so they understand it. Now they need to learn to tell the story in sign language, speech and writing.

I could hardly wait to try out my new idea, which I did the following week. I kept group attention by holding up an enlarged copy of each picture of the comic strip. My students told me the story, word by word, as I elicited answers to fit under the blackboard headings: Who, Verb, What and Where. They followed my every move. At last I had perfect attention! Teaching expressive language became fun. The Julie and Jack comic strips became an important part of daily lessons. When I needed more such comic strips, I wrote to former students I had taught at St. Joseph's, asking whether they had saved their first grade *Little Messengers* from past years, and would they give them to me? They had and they would! Those comic strips were destined to travel far beyond my classroom.

The following autumn a national convention for teachers of the deaf was held in Milwaukee. One day was reserved for open house at St. John's. All classrooms were open for visiting teachers to come and go at will. Usually I found visitors observing me teaching quite an ordeal. That day, however, proved to be very exciting. For every teacher or group that came to my room I put on a demonstration using Julie and Jack comic strips. Teachers from various states showed great interest. "Where can we get picture stories like that?" they inquired. I promised to get the publisher's permission to make copies and share them with anyone interested.

That was the beginning of a series of ten reading and language workbooks that I developed with and for deaf children. My dream of writing books had been fulfilled! Gradually the books sold to most schools for the deaf in the United States and to one or more schools in thirty different countries. Writing, producing and marketing the books kept me much too busy. The other sisters helped when their schedules allowed. Volunteers helped with collating, typing, packing and mailing. My greatest encouragement to keep up all that extra work came from more than 500 teachers who wrote appreciative letters telling how much they and their deaf students enjoyed the language lessons based on comic strips.

By 1960 St. John's School was bursting at the seams. Classrooms and dormitories were filled. Prospective students had to be turned away because there were no more beds. One mother told us her boy, Tom, could bring a sleeping bag and sleep on the floor! We did make room for Tom, and better yet, by 1965 we had built a large new school, including a high school.

With the opening of the new school more staff members were hired, mostly lay teachers and child care workers. The latter took over many of the Sister's extracurricular duties. With extra time on my hands and energy to spare, I found ways to expend both.

In the new school I taught upper primary students. They were a bright group, bubbling with enthusiasm and ready to learn whatever appealed to them. Keeping their attention was often a problem because they wouldn't tolerate a moment's boredom. The Julie and Jack books were too easy for them. One day, to teach a sentence pattern, I used a "Family Circus" cartoon from the Sunday Comic Section of *The Milwaukee Journal*. In the cartoon Billy, Dolly, Jeffy and PJ were bringing gifts to their mother, so I wrote and signed the sentence, "Billy brought Mother a flower." The children quickly caught on to the sentence pattern and signed, "Jeffy brought Mother a card," etc. The group identified with the Family Circus characters and wanted "More! More!"

After sharing my idea with other teachers and asking them to try it out, I wrote to Bil Keane, the cartoonist, and to the sponsoring syndicate for permission to use past and current cartoons in language books for deaf children. The syndicate approved the idea. They sent me copies of original cartoons from the previous two years. They even called the Milwaukee Journal asking them to publish an article in the Green Sheet, which they did. Cartoonist Bil Keane also liked the idea. The only royalty he wanted: "Pray two Our Fathers and Hail Marys for me every Sunday!"

During those busy years, I heard hundreds of times from the other sisters: "Margaret, don't work so hard!" My response was always the same: "But I enjoy working!" The job that kept me overly busy was keeping up with book orders. I loved it because of my belief in the value of the books and my pride in the fulfillment of my fondest dream — being an author.

I lived in a world of deaf education. Everything I read, wrote, watched or listened to had to do with deaf education. I experienced a real high at the beginning of Saturdays when I was free to work in my classroom all day. I hardly knew what was going on it the world outside.

Then, in 1972, at the urging of another sister, I joined the Milwaukee Archdiocesan Sisters Council. Here was another whole new world. More new awakenings. More new adventures, however distant they were from the dreams of my youth. The Sisters Council, made up of delegates from ten or twelve different religious communities, was involved in works and causes that I hardly knew existed. At one meeting a sister amazed me by speaking her belief in the ordination of women. Until that moment I had told no one of my early dreams of ordination, feeling that it was somehow wrong for me to even think about. Some sisters agreed with the idea, some did not.

Life at St. John's moved briskly forward, filled, for the most part, with success stories of most of our high school seniors going on to college, other students doing well, the basketball team winning games, some funding available for many out-of-state students, faculty members, students and parents proud of our school. But we were having financial problems. We were borrowing heavily from the Milwaukee Archdiocese.

Then came February of 1982 and the tragic news that the Archdiocese could no longer afford to help fund our school. The priest director and sister principal met with the sisters to break the sad news: St. John's must close in June! The eight of us had given most of our teaching years to St. John's. It was the contributed services of the sisters that had kept St. John's going strong for 106 years. We felt devastated, not because we couldn't easily find another job, but because the children we loved would be parted from us and from each other. Our close-knit family would be torn apart. It seemed to us that no other school could possibly take the place of St. John's.

The day after the sisters heard of the closing a meeting was called for the entire faculty and student body. We met in the chapel. In a strained voice and in sign language, Father Zerkel explained slowly and clearly that we were no longer able to meet expenses and that our beloved school would close in June. After a moment of intense silence, students and faculty expressed their grief in gasps, startled movements, tears, sobs, frantic signing to one another and shocked disbelief.

No one was ready to accept that decision. Faculty members immediately started planning ways to raise enough money to reverse the decision. Parents were notified. An emergency meeting was called for all parents and anyone who could possibly help. The local Knights of Columbus promised to raise $20,000 a year. St. John's would not go down without a struggle.

The closing of St. Johns' would be traumatic, especially for parents who were already sacrificing to keep their child in their chosen school. They put forth heroic efforts to keep the school open. An early meeting of parents from several states was covered by the three Milwaukee TV stations. They televised the parent spokesman shouting: "We'll go to hell and back to save this school!"

Newspapers, radio and television stations kept the public informed on a daily basis. Scores of people wrote letters to us, to the archbishop and to editors of all local newspapers. Telephone calls, letters and cards of support and sympathy poured in. We were heartened and gratified by the unexpected generosity and support of many people: local parishes, former students or their parents, former faculty members, high school students, neighbors, friends and total strangers.

In the next few months, as we bowed to the inevitable, our bonding with students and parents grew stronger, enabling us to support each other in the final sad closing of a great residential school for deaf children. The blow was softened somewhat when the high school was allowed to remain open for one year so that students who had attended St. John's since they were three years old could graduate from there.

Those months of fighting a losing battle for a great cause constituted the most difficult period of my life. Saying good-bye to so many loved ones, most of whom I would never see again, was heartbreaking. But I know with new certainty there is a heaven, and I shall see them again.

Some of them we do see on special occasions, times that are like family reunions — heartwarming and filled with reminiscing. Our former students will always be a part of our lives. We rejoice when they do well, grieve when they fail, and keep them in prayer always.

During the ten years since St. John's closed, I have let go of many things, including the workbooks on which I spent so much time. They are now published by a company in Illinois. However, letting go has opened up new avenues. I have been working part-time in Jefferson, Wisconsin at St. Coletta's, a school for persons with mental retardation. This, too, is a great residential school and, once again, a whole different world. I now teach several deaf children who are multiply handicapped. This is far more difficult than teaching normal deaf children, but I rejoice at every inch of improvement. I am often surprised that life continues to offer new experiences and new opportunities for growth.

Looking back over the fifty-two years that have passed since my decision to do the best thing I could, I believe that being a Franciscan Sister and committing most of my life to deaf children has been my very best.

Today, the pace of my life has slowed. I take more time for prayer, community activities, reading, letter writing, leisure time and keeping up with world events. I'm not climbing any windmills to contemplate the future, but the past holds enough memories, and the present enough challenges to keep my life rewarding and fulfilling.

Josie Kelly Welch
Former Dominican

Married

Career and Life Planning Counselor

Group Facilitator

Master of Science, Educational Psychology, University of Utah

There will never be a boring time in Josie's life — she has too many interests and dreams! At the present she combines her professional life with related volunteer work in nursing homes, visiting old women. Her reading list is varied, and definitely includes spiritual and metaphysical works. There is music, too, jazz, piano and Celtic. The last holds a key to her projections beyond the now, for in addition to co-writing a life story with her spouse, and doing Elder Hostels in the United States, England and Ireland, she hopes someday to do professional counseling for women in recovery, "possibly in Ireland."

Josie Kelly Welch

A Collage

Recently I was part of a wonderful workshop led by an intensely spiritual, wise woman, probably a few years older than I, so late sixties. She guided us through some thought, quiet time, and exercises which had a focus balancing the inner and outer life. One idea she shared with us, not really new but especially significant, struck me: each of us has a story to tell. Certainly there is much in common as we share. Paradoxically, each is unique, and to tell it is to let ourselves be known, and to know ourselves better! So as I begin my own story today I am Josie, sixty-one years of age. To remember all my sixty-one years is to remember so many different selves it's almost as though I'm recalling other lives and other times.

Who am I today? And what does it mean to be sixty-one? These days I'm especially open to my own growth and each day is different! As I write I'm thinking of a good friend — she, too, is sixty-one years of age. She lies paralyzed in a hospital bed, breathing with a ventilator and sitting with a rod up her spine to support her. For her, a few months ago, being sixty-one meant being an alive, athletic, energetic, happy family woman. Today, after a split-second, life-threatening accident, sixty-one looks and feels very different to my friend.

Today as I write I'm taking a ferry ride on Elliot Bay. The weather here is so beautiful. It's the end of February and the air is lovely and kind, the sun casts a sparkle on the water and it warms my heart. For Seattle the season seems rushed. Usually we have some mild and rainy days, or sunny and crisply cold ones. Rarely at this time of year do the sunny and warm join hands. It's hopeful and speaks of newness.

We — my spouse and I — came here to Seattle seventeen years ago. It is home to us, and even after so many years the mystical beauty of the place nourishes our souls. The water and greenery that surround us are comforting and life giving and I often wonder at our good fortune in having found our way here.

The way for me has been circuitous, sometimes tortuous, always challenging. My sixty-one years have seen many places. Eighteen of them at home in Ohio and Illinois. Twenty-one and one-half years as a Dominican Sister, teaching and schooling and living in twelve different homes in Arizona, Illinois, Indiana, Michigan, Virginia, New Mexico. One and one-half years as a woman alone, working and going to school, living in Illinois and Utah, Twenty-one years married, living and working in Utah, New York, Denver, Seattle, and having nine different places to call home. This journey has left me always a little restless, trying to "land," feeling a bit alien, not belonging.

As with most women who entered the convent in the forties, I was very young when I left home. Two weeks after my high school graduation, three weeks before my eighteenth birthday, my whole life transformed and I became caught up in a life that I never really owned. I say that now with sadness; the anger that I felt toward myself and the world for so long has dissipated and I have a peace and joy of heart that for years escaped me.

My choice to be a nun began when I was in sixth grade. I still remember when the principal said to me: "Jo Anne, have you ever thought of being a sister?" The caring way she said that and the wonderful twinkle in her eyes touched my heart. I felt so honored and thrilled with the attention. That spark stayed with me even as I dealt with deep doubts about life and God and faith.

And then my sister, my dear friend and confidante, took that step and left me to "join the convent." I felt bereft and abandoned, and the spark that had lit my heart to be a nun three years before took hold and seemed to burn within me all through my high school years. I would follow her as soon as I could. In fact I did consider entering before I graduated. Somehow the push I needed in order to do that never surfaced, and I stayed home to graduate.

Although the boarding school I spent four years in was fairly close to my home, I boarded. That meant my closest friends did not share my home life, and my home town friends often fell away because I was gone. So my social life failed to thrive and I was very much a girl without a date. I mention this because I would often, in the midst of my loneliness and wallflower tears, think "I will be so glad when I get to the convent. I won't have to worry about getting a date!" I don't remember sharing that thought with anyone. I guess even then I realized that that probably was not a good and spiritual motivation for entering. Ironically, during my senior year I did finally get a date. In fact, I fell in love, and the memory of all that still tickles me. I finally could hold my head up and be counted as a normal, attractive young woman: someone really cared for me.

As the time to leave home drew nearer and my somber wardrobe of black stockings, black shoes, black skirts, blouses and capes grew, I began to feel trapped. For years I had talked about entering. My dad was so proud, my sister excited; my aunt spent hours getting me ready for my leap into the unknown. And I was in love! When I told Daddy that I wasn't very anxious anymore to go (and I did that with great fear in my heart) he chuckled, and advised that, since I had wanted to go for so long, why not go? I could always come home. I remember his words with very mixed feelings. As so often happened, I had followed someone else's head, not my heart. Neither of us could know what that would really mean.

And what it did mean was a roller coaster ride of depression, little spurts of some genuine joy, and always trying to fit in, and wondering why I didn't. Even though I had not really wanted to enter, the fact that I did committed me to be happy and to be a good nun. Both frequently eluded me.

So for twenty-one years I struggled for meaning, for peace, for a sense of the commitment I had voiced. Much of this I did through sickness. Depression, with its many faces, plagued me and I fought to stay alive. Because I was a survivor, I did, barely, and in my mid-thirties I found a psychiatrist, a wonderful old man truly ahead of his time. He, through many trials and frequent errors, found a medication that gave me back my life. And as I moved through the terrifying downs and hope-filled ups of recovery, I finally found the truth in my heart: that the choice I had made need not be irrevocable. I needed to follow the wisdom of my body and my soul. One day I just knew what I must do to be true to myself and to be honest with those who were my sisters. After twenty-one and a half years I closed that door of my life, and went home.

The other day Joe and I joined a group of friends for a private liturgy. The theme that the host couple put out for consideration spoke to me in significant ways. "Living in the present moment" reminded me of a phrase that one of the nuns or priests taught me years ago: "the grace of the present moment." I love that idea, and yesterday's theme reminded me again of its value in a truly spiritual life. So often I regret all the years I wasted living a way that was not appropriate for me. Or I fear for the future — the Bag Lady Syndrome. All too often I forget that the present moment and who I am today is because of who and where I've been before.

On Good Friday eight of us were at a wonderful spot on Puget Sound; an old, renovated fort sits right at a point. The stately old officers' homes provide comfortable, affordable vacation and week-end get-aways for families and groups like ours. We have a couples' group, a renegade offshoot of Marriage Encounter. About nine years ago we did that program and have been meeting ever since. That particular week-end was our annual retreat. We walked, rested, shared our stories and enjoyed the wonderful openness and beauty of the place. It is there with those friends that Joe and I deal with old stuff that keeps surfacing over the twenty one years of our marriage; we find new meaning in our relationship. This year it was so clear that all of us are on a spiritual quest, and more importantly, are talking about this at a deep level with one another. We learned that we had been afraid to reveal this intimate aspect of ourselves and have finally broken through. Sex and sexuality, too, had been somewhat taboo until that weekend. Nine years of meetings, years of marriage, and these had been our topics twice!

It seemed that as someone found courage to share a little deeper, another did, and another. And finally, we were free to share two of our most vital gifts, our spirit and our sexuality.

As I experienced myself in the convent, spirituality and sexuality appeared as contradictions; if one were spiritual, one was not sexual. For most of my convent days I paid no attention to my sexuality, and my spirituality consisted of trying to make some meaning for myself in all the spiritual exercises of the day.

When I first met my spouse in the mid-60's he was teaching a class I was taking as part of a Masters Program in Religious Studies. I remember him as a breath of fresh air, telling us things about God and life and

204

choices that I knew in my heart were true and had been afraid to talk about. At that time in my life I was very ready for newness and hope; life was certainly shaky for me. Still trying to make convent life work for myself, I had gladly immersed myself in studies, and the summer program began to restore my spirit. I remember vividly my connection with Joe. One time in particular stands out. Prayer time summoned the nuns to chapel, and to get there we had to go outside. The afternoon rains had come, and I had chosen to wait until they calmed. A couch in the sitting area by the door seemed a good place to wait and as I enjoyed my few minutes of liberated rest, Joe came along, joined me, and there began a beautiful friendship!

It wasn't until two years later that I saw Joe again. Surely it was meant to be that we re-connect, because there really wasn't any rhyme or reason for doing so. My work in campus ministry took me to the Southwest, where I worked with a group of priests. Joe had come to visit his priest brothers there. So when we met again, it seemed to be providence, since neither of us had planned it. After that we continued to keep in touch by phone, letters and visits. I gradually fell in love, although at the time I felt mostly confusion, obsessive worry, and an emotional excitement I didn't even recognize! However, when I made my decision to leave the convent, I left thinking that Joe would remain in the priesthood. So I left knowing nothing of my future, just knowing that it was the right thing for me to do. The integrity I experienced in my decision fully outweighed the fear and uncertainty. Joe would have to follow his own path, as I did mine.

Happily his path and mine came together. He, too, came to an understanding that his journey must take a turn and found that he wanted to join me in mine.

And so, May, 1971, in a mountain lodge in Utah, surrounded by old friends and new ones, we said: "O.K. together we move on. Hand in hand we climb the mountain, go down to the valleys, rest in the meadows, and swim upstream and down." Sometimes we drop hands and find our own pace. Sometimes we abandon each other for a time. Always we come together, pick up and go forward. Our lives are separate and together — that is our new journey.

Shortly after I left the convent the disease of alcoholism took hold of me. Peace and joy do not flourish side by side with this disease. The dark holes of addiction and depression can be so deep that these gifts get stuck in the mire. They don't die, but the smothering sludge buries them with barely air to breathe. For the first ten years after I left the convent I lived in that hole. Often the disease claims marriage and job. Gratefully, my spouse stayed with me and I did not lose a job during that ten years.

The disease is an ugly, shame-filled one. People who don't have it often "know" how to control it — just say no! And those who have it have had to struggle through craziness and hopelessness and a terrible fear before finally coming to a place of recovery and peace. I am thankful every day of my life that I am among the living. In my fifty-first year I had a miracle of a crisis and began my healing journey.

The wisdom of the body and soul never cease to amaze me. They certainly move at their own rate. Since I left the convent, my life seems to go naturally in ten year phases: ten with my alcoholism actually controlling me; ten spent experimenting with various ways of recovering; now, at sixty-one, feeling better than I ever have, physically, emotionally, and spiritually. I'm not ready to ascend yet. The angst will probably always flavor my life. But certainly I have wings and am ready to fly!

On the first day of this spring, one of my delights was walking in a beautiful Desert Preserve. I came to the Southwest to take part in a program for personal healing and growth, and to look at what I want to change in my own life and in my relationships, especially with my spouse.

The beauty of the preserve is powerful. The stream that circulates continually gives a wonderfully comforting wash to this desert in miniature. I sit and listen and look at the prickly cactus and the stately little tree right here next to me, the saguaro that rises up like a tower, lording it over these strange creatures; the tiny blossoms that thrive on the dry, scrubby floor of the preserve. I made metaphors of all of this unique life. Painted and prickly, arid on the surface with richness just below, beautifully colored flowers next to some of the most peculiar combinations. Certainly my story.

Looking back on the vignettes of my life is like sitting on this bench here in this place. I'd be crazy to lean against a saguaro or pick a cactus. And I would kill the plant if I were to pick the flowers. Getting too close reveals pain and limitation. Seen from some distance, all of the extra-ordinariness demands, perhaps not understanding, but surely appreciation and awe.

Today my spouse got a memorial card in the mail. A priest who had been an associate of his in the Dominican Order had died. The card read:

Born: June 22, 1929 in Denver
Professed: June 25, 1949
Ordained: December 18, 1954
Died: February 26, 1992.

When I first began writing I had thought about "Maybe that's all I have to say!"

Jo Anne Kelly Welch
Born: July 25, 1930. Lakewood, Ohio
First Profession: December 31, 1949
Final Profession: December 31, 1954
Left Community: December, 1969
Married: May 22, 1971
Still alive: April, 1992

Happily, as I have sat and remembered, the blanks have filled in, and I am relieved — I did have a life! Looking back on it, I make no attempt to put it in any order. The glimpses, the brief moments of remembering — they are pieces of my life and they pop in and out with no sense of sequence or time. They are a collage — a picture here, a word, an overlay of thoughts and insights. These are how I remember. I will write again and the collage will be different. That is my life, too.

As I look ahead to sixty-two and growing, I feel excited and peaceful, scared and hopeful, most of all wonder-full.

Who is this woman?
Lately she (I?) looks different.
It's funny: looking in the mirror,
I see a beautiful person.
Thinner than yesterday.
Yet somehow bigger.

The power of self smiles back.
The eyes sparkle.
The woman looking out
Seems friendlier.
She's older — and lighter.
Remembering the woman
At twenty-one; fifty-one;
I remember humps and sadness,
A few smiles, some wrinkles.
Today, at sixty-one,
The humps are flattened.
The wrinkles smoothed.
There is gladness in her eyes!

Pat C.
Sisters of Providence

Pastoral Associate, Director of Adult Education

Director of Parish Marriage Preparation Program

Director of RCIA

Director of Christian Parenting, Preparation for Baptism

Facilitator of a Scripture Program

Bachelor of Arts in Education, English, St. Mary of the Woods

Master of Arts in Religious Studies, Spaulding College

Master of Arts, Administration, Indiana State University

Basic Units, CPE, Baptist Hospital in Louisville

Sister Pat lives in a community convent, but is greatly involved in the parish community in which she works. In addition to her many official ministries she finds time to visit a limited number of shut-ins. Her personal interests are as diverse as her professional involvements, and include walking, cycling, calligraphy and printing. "I am a young Golden Jubilarian this year, and look forward to continued ministry as long as I am effective."

Now Nun

Many things happened to the Good Sisters of days gone by. When I look back and reflect on those days they seem so far away and in the distance. It is like a dream.

When I entered the community in January of '42, it was another step along the way, since I attended high school at the motherhouse. The sister in charge of this small high school certainly did not understand teen-age girls and was well on her way to a complete nervous breakdown. She had introduced us to "profound silence", which of course we didn't understand. We made yearly retreats (which she gave) and we trooped in and out of church every morning and evening. The novitiate simply enlarged on the basis begun in high school. I began to understand the meaning of these actions. This helped make sense out of a lot of things.

We were a group of fifty to sixty novices trained to pray, to work, to play together. We had a strong sense of community after those two and a half years. Every minute of our day was filled, and when the directors were at a loss to fill every minute, we took another long walk.

We asked permission to speak to someone. We even asked permission to go up a flight of stairs to another floor. I formed close friendships, but was always warned against particular friendships. I was never clear on the *why* of this great danger, but was well aware that I must stay far, far away from it.

The professed Sisters were also off limits. We were not to talk to them except on special days when they could come over and visit.

We were imbued with a deep sense of the charism in our community and studied the life of our foundress to use as our role model.

We had to acknowledge our faults and make reparation for our failings. The novitiate and the army had a lot in common! I took on persona other than my own, and my family were the first to notice this. My personality is extraverted, my enthusiasm normally high, and my determination is very strong. I am very much my own person. Going through a spirituality emphasizing humility, piety, shutting self away from the world affected these strong personality traits. I thought I had to imitate Therese of Lisieux.

I come from a large family of eight and grew up during the depression years. Doing without something was part of my childhood. We had to share whether we wanted to or not. My older sister had already joined the community and she was a great influence on me. We had always been and always remain very close. My parents tried to give us a great reverence for the Catholic faith and a respect for one another.

Novitiate years were also war years. Most of us had brothers and relatives in the armed forces. My brother was a Marine. We had no idea what was going on overseas and we were not to ask. We were removed and apart from the world. The entire family was present when I received the habit in '42, including the Marine brother, who was scheduled to join the South Pacific forces in a couple weeks.

In those days, dressed as brides of Christ, we processed up the long aisle to receive the habit. It had been decided that no bridal pictures would be taken for the families this year, as several novices had left the community and they were hanging their religious bridal pictures in their homes. This was frowned upon. It was not a problem for me, as I felt completely detached. I had forgotten that my older sister, who preceded me by three years, had had her picture taken. This was quite a blow to my mother; she would not receive a picture of me. We were also directed not to have any pictures taken of ourselves during the day. My mother was in tears since my Marine brother was leaving for overseas, and she felt this would be the last time we could all be together.

My older religious sister solved the dilemma. She directed them to get the picture set up, let us know when it was ready, and the two of us dashed into the picture and out just as quickly, lest anyone see us breaking this important rule. That picture has been multiplied many times over and passed on through the years. It is the only picture I ever had taken as a novice. When I look at that picture today, the circumstances always reappear vividly in my mind. I peer at that young, shy, self-effacing good little sister, not the now nun of today.

212

I was professed with temporary vows in '44 and went to Chicago on my first mission. I was nineteen. There I was handed a class of fifty-two fourth-graders. Needless to say, I was very ill-equipped. The principal stopped at my classroom the first day about an hour after all were in the room. I remember telling her that I had told them everything she had directed us to tell them, and what was I to do now. She was distressed.

In those days, if we had a free day while other schools were in session, we spent the day at another school observing and learning from a master teacher. The in-between times were still very difficult. I admired the master teachers who could teach and still keep 52 fourth- or sixth-graders in good order. My principal took great interest in the young sisters, and spent many hours coaching us. Without her support and help I would have been lost.

There were five young sisters on the first mission in Chicago, and we enjoyed the support and humor of our peer group. We tried to fulfill the expectations of the older sisters, some of whom were very loving and some of whom were the opposite.

Our schedules were set. We followed the bell for school, for recreation, for prayer, for retiring. The bell ruled our days. During the summer we returned to the motherhouse and spent the time working on our undergraduate degrees.

My peer group was very important to me, and even though we were not able to stay in close contact since we were shifted to fill the slots, I still remained close to those who had shared those early teen and formation years with me.

My work occupied most of my time; work became me. Week-ends were spent on preparation for the coming week. Gradually I became a professionally educated teacher. That was something to be proud of, but close relationships with the outside were discouraged. Not only could we not visit the homes of our students, we could not visit in our own homes with our families. We were in the world but out of it. I was a paradox.

In the early sixties, when everything was beginning to pop open as a result of Vatican II, I was a principal of a large school with over 500 students in a southern Indiana town. Besides acting as principal, I earned a Masters' in Administration during the summer months; I also taught a class of forty-five to fifty sixth grade students full time, and tried to fulfill the role of superior of the convent, and that of treasurer thrown in for good measure.

When I look back on those six years, I marvel that I did not completely unravel. The pressures were very great, but the expectations were even greater. The pastor was a puzzling person. He wanted me to get everything done neatly and cleanly and not bother him in the process. His words are still vivid in my mind, "You stay on your side of the fence and I'll stay on my side of the fence; just make sure you stay on yours."

It had always been expected that we would accept whatever we were assigned, and not question it, but I was never one to accept blindly. I was forever questioning and probing, trying to piece it all together. By the time my six years in this impossible situation were over, and Vatican II had opened all those wonderful doors and windows, I had had it. This was the beginning of the Great Exodus. I took a long, serious look at this possibility, and then decided this was a chance to help move, change and renew a community that had molded me; I was now willing to break that mold. I was definitely a now sister.

I took advantage of everything my community offered, and it was an offer. There was no pressure. I attended workshops and became active in the area of peace and justice. I retrained, and studied for a Master's in Theology. I took two basic units in Clinical Pastoral Education to prepare me to help those in crisis. Because all my training, except my degree in Administration, had been in a Roman Catholic setting, I chose to take CPE in a Baptist Hospital. My supervisor was a young Irish, Baptist minister who was gentle and wise beyond his years. That opened a lot of awareness for me.

I found a job in the field of Pastoral Ministry in a small southern Indiana parish. This was the first job I had found completely on my own. It was a good feeling. My experience and background stood me in good stead in my new work. I did not regret leaving the classroom.

My experiences in the clerical club have left me much wiser. The first experience of being abruptly fired and dispatched prepared me for the second. I was completely devastated the first time; the second time I was just plain mad and angry, and I refused to accept the unilateral decision made by the pastor. The now-nun in me came to the forefront and with the help of compassionate and caring laity, I decided to hang in.

In my present ministry I direct Adult Education in a large Midwest parish. Since I enjoy many and varied projects instead of the sameness of a daily schedule, I love what I do. I have made my peace with the pastor who fired me. I helped him to see that women do have an important place in the church. Our day will come for ordination. In the meantime, I know I can never change people trained in clericalism and pre-Vatican theology, but I can try to understand them and accept their personhood for the struggles they, too, experience.

What is it like today compared with yesterday? It's like a different world, a different Church. I am my own person. I can better accept others since I better understand myself. I am not sure my community will survive, but I am sure that there will always be vowed women in the Church as an important sign.

The struggle for an emerging, meaningful recognition of women in the church is very much a part of the sister of today. I have had my share of patronization, being taken for granted. My early training falsely led me to believe that I was being humble when I allowed myself to be trampled on. That is no longer true. Respect for myself includes demanding respect from the clerical world.

Just as my counterparts in the secular work field, I have always felt the need to excel simply because I am a woman invading an all-male club. The constant need to accomplish a juggling act, to excel and to relate, sooner or later produces stress. If I cannot deal with stress and tension, then I must make the decision to stay and cope in my way, or leave. I credit myself with enough common sense to deal with this. Perhaps I can sum up my true feelings by stating the maxim, "One Day at a Time."

Jane Wilcox
Sisters of St. Joseph

Secretarial work in community Archives

Credo Program, Gonzaga University, Spokane

Creation Spirituality, Holy Name College, Oakland

Jane lives within her community, and her official occupation is closely connected to that community. A poet, as her work included here proves, Jane is interested in reading, sports, and walking. Her quiet life explodes in the fire of her poetry.

Jane Wilcox

Images of a Woman

The passionate women
He calls
From the earthiness
Beneath
She walks and walks
The long stretched way
In quietness and life.

And through the failure
Turned away
There yet still dawns within,
The fiery passion
Of a woman's' strength
Poured out in the Universe.

Maiden

The young maiden languishes
    by a still pond
        Water rippling
            against the sand.
                Then treads warily
                    frightened steps
                        Hiding, hiding.
                            Away from them.

Polarity

O swirling, turning darkness engulfed,
And holds sway in mind and body —
Pressing its suffocation
The tears wrenched from deep within
Shivers in isolation.
Extremes of my own person

Wrestle and lose ground
Against the darkness.

Deep silence and darkness.
No movement there.
And then, and then
Body and mind races around
To force the depression out.
Agitated, racing form,
Until there seeps inside
The nothingness
And the soul breaks down
And cries.
Energy spent away.

Books that I have sought
Comfort now no more,
But one sure way
To wait the darkness out.
And waits and waits
Not in the patience
Of my younger years
But in violet agitation.

Does not the soul of a gentle woman there
Covering the hidden strength lying
And battles through terrifying battle after battle
Tearing the darkness from my soul
And wanders far in safety.

And yet there comes a day of peace again
Hearing the birds chippering in the trees.
The river water rippling down the stream.
All that stirs in nature come alive
The wind blowing through my hair,
Body from its sleep becomes alive
Filled with infinite passion.

Manic-Depressive

The formless form
moves across the horizon
groping for life
hidden in self-destructive behavior.

Overcome by the darkness
a sad heart
scathed naked in a crumbling form.
Desperateness of a woman.

Wending her way
looks at a thousand faces
in the market place.
City swallowing up the loneliness
and tormenting the woman.

Deepest isolation and crying heart
Tears flowing and flowing,
as a dam gives way,
A woman in deepest poverty,
a human person in isolation.

Compulsive behavior drives her onward
as one compulsion replaces another and another
and driven, drives deeper still
in search of God.

The barren wasteland
of a country place
she stops for breath

As moods mercurial force
sky rockets high
and pivots on the abyss,
Then crashes down.

Manic energy flows fast within
in surging crescendo and swift current.
The lie of the manic energy
Rebounds against itself
in blocked regressive form

Dragging slowly in deadly stupor
Depresses, depresses
its own depths.

Restructuring

A woman
    connecting
        intimately
            with the Light.
Earthiness
    reshaping
        magnificent form.
Darkness
    receding.
        Prince of Peace
           reigning.

Dawn

Dawn awakens the woman
And stretching, reaches toward life.
Rhythm of energy
Emerges on its blessed way.

Ah! the beauty of a woman
Standing there
Caressing and embracing
The gentle flow of life.

Images of Creation

At the dawn of creation
A woman mystically created
And wonderfully made
Evolving consciousness.
The antithesis of androgyny
The Self not divided.
The Universe Erupting, rhythm,
Expansion and contraction,
Flowing life. Dawn
The breathless beauty
of a woman in gentle movement
Caressing the dawn
and awakes
to new splendor
Across the earth.

The Dance

Her body moves in an unending dance with life,
Now spiraling downward
Now stretching outward
And beyond. She, lost in the darkness
Aerobesques

Notes to Myself

Ah! ecstatic wonder
And liberated soul
Stretching, stretching
Beyond myself.

Connection

Listening to the heart
She lives at one

With God and creation.
Inner attitude welling up
In grace. Isolation set aside
Content with my own space.

Personality falling asleep
Essence emerges.
Pay attention Jane.

Hands folded, breathing
Lifting up and out
I become a flower.

Tyrant rearing
Bring Centre
Back to yourself
And transcend the suffering.

No contradictions,
No positions,
Perceiving the world
From calmness.

Hurt, anger, upset
Never meant to be
That way.
Connection with God,
With ourselves,
And the world.
Choice important. *Peace*

Peace flows through
in gentle rippling waves
The body calm
Betrays that dark night
As disintegrated human thought
That filled the mind
Disperses for yet
Another while.

Rosalind Camardella
Former Dominican

Married, one child

Part time teacher of writing

Free Lance writer

Bachelor of Arts, Siena Heights College, Michigan

Master of arts, Mundelein College of Loyola University, Chicago

Rosalind is currently studying quantum physics to see what that field has to teach us about living together on this planet. Related to that is a book she is writing on education and a new vision, one "to reconnect us to the earth and one another." She stays in touch with her former community by attending annual reunions of former sisters, and by "crowd" reunions. She is deeply involved in promoting ecological awareness, and says, "I'm not good at projections, but I'm convinced that my experience as a religious has profoundly enhanced whatever contribution I am able to make to the world."

Rosalind Camardella

With a Grateful Heart

When I was growing up, the thought of entering the convent never crossed my mind. In fact, I assumed that such a holy calling was reserved for girls named Mary Agnes. Everyone remembers them. They were Sister's special helpers; girls who had "Sodality, 4 years" next to their names in the yearbook; girls who served their apprenticeship by helping Sister pass out crayons and coloring sheets at CCD classes on Saturday mornings; and they were always the ones chosen to crown the Blessed Virgin Mary. Sweet and smart and already other worldly, we all knew they were destined for nunhood. Choices being limited, many of us cherished dreams of marriage and motherhood, babies and bake sales. We understood that we didn't have a vocation and would become instead the devoted laity of the local parish and the faithful members of the Ladies' Altar and Rosary Society. But as Kierkegard reminds us, though life is lived forward, it is only understood backward. This, then, is a loving backward glance at my years in religious life.

The church of my youth was full of ritual. The heady fragrance of incense, gently spiraling from ornate, gleaming vessels, the comforting flicker of red votive candles, even the unintelligible Latin prayers all served to wrap my belief in reverence and stir my young soul to awe. No need to understand doctrines and dogmas; my sense of God was immediate, direct, and real.

As a child, I remember penciling little prayers on small squares of paper and slipping them into the slot of the old wooden petition box on the far end of the communion rail. I was certain God listened and just as certain that He cared. I remember coloring soft pink and yellow angels in my second grade religion book, angels who hovered over two small children as they crossed a dangerous bridge, and I felt safe. But most of all, I remember the immense silence of the empty church.

Often after school or during recess I'd slip in from the playground, exchanging the bright, chattering world outside for the cool, aromatic darkness within. I'd visit the half-lit alcoves and gaze at the solemn statues; I'd watch as candlelight shadow danced against the peeling gilt along the walls; I'd run my hand along the warm, burnished wood of the well-worn pews; I'd listen to the quiet. I was only eight or nine, but this sense of the sacred stirred a longing in me. Now, years later, I recognize that it is this same longing which has led me along a somewhat circuitous route on my journey of faith.

The wonderful community of religious women to which I would eventually belong, first came into my life in high school. Without a doubt, that experience with the sisters tapped into my early faith life and carried it forward. At thirteen, I saw them as spirited, joyful and intelligent; warm, prayerful and self-reliant. I can still see their faces and hear the echo of their voices. Those women were never so "nunny" as to seem distant or separate. I remember one young sister eagerly sharing the writings of Thomas Merton with a small group of us. We began to meet after school. Each week that lovely woman patiently spoon-fed *The Seeds of Contemplation* to us, one paragraph at a time. The loving attention she paid to our spiritual awakenings was a great gift, one which affirmed my fledgling discoveries and encouraged a life-long commitment to spiritual growth. They were always right there beside us, decorating the gym for prom or building sets or pinning costumes. They moderated club activities and coordinated service projects. I remember thinking that "my" nuns were not like other nuns. Mine belied the sad stereotype of Sister-Mary-Knucklecracker or Sister Prunella the Prude. They seemed quite natural, down to earth and human. So I spent my formative years admiring them, loving them, and, much to my surprise, deciding at nineteen to join them.

One ordinary Sunday I came home from Mass, announced that I wanted to enter the convent — and burst into tears. The source of the tears as well as the decision remained a mystery to me for a very long time. My only awareness was of something intangible just below the surface of day-to-day life, something which tugged at me, a desire as yet unnamed but, nonetheless, insistent.

My family greeted the news with much hugging and great happiness. In all the excitement, however, we forgot one important consideration: I was engaged to be married. When Bob and I finally talked things over, I told him not to worry, that this was just something I had to get out of my system and that I'd be home soon. I now wonder if I wasn't protecting myself against the claims of a genuine call by saying to God, "See, I tried it and it didn't work."

Well, Bob waited patiently. After three years, when more relaxed rules allowed us to receive letters from people outside our family, he wrote a long, lonesome letter which closed with these words: "P.S. Have you seen *The Sound of Music?* And have you thought about how it ends?"

I smiled, warmed by memories and abiding affection. I don't know if I ever answered him, but several years later another letter arrived. This time he shared news of his job promotion, his new wife and their beautiful infant son. I felt happy for him and for myself. We were both content with our lives.

That contentment lasted for many years. I have no horror stories about my fifteen years in the convent, years that, for the most part, were full and happy. Saying this does not diminish the pain other women have known. They have a different story and mine is not intended in any way to discount theirs. It is simply mine.

Over the years, I lived with women of all ages and temperaments, each with varying degrees of spiritual and emotional maturity. And although community life generated all the petty irritations and personal foibles common to such close living, I was amazed and often inspired by each one's unwavering commitment to live a life of service and sanctity. Under the best of circumstances, such commitment on a daily basis is heroic. Yet, in spite of being bound by medieval traditions and hampered by rules which, in hindsight, seem psychologically unsound, the women in our congregation achieved such heroism time and time again.

However, families (and religious life is family in the very best sense) sometimes blame themselves for uninformed behavior. They apply what they know now to what they did then and often feel guilty. Or angry. Or both. But since we can only act on what we know at any given moment, such reactions are pointless. Subsequent knowledge is irrelevant when judging past actions or second-guessing former decisions. That is why it saddens me to recall that as we started to re-image religious life following Vatican II, we began by criticizing our past.

Yes, some of the rules by which we lived were archaic: wearing night caps to bed and requiring lights out by 9:30. Some were mere annoyances: needing to ask permission for everything from a new tube of toothpaste to accepting a telephone call. And there were some that seemed truly misguided: the censoring of personal mail, not being allowed to stay overnight with our families, or the infamous prohibitions against close friendships. But what we must remember is that outmoded and distorted as some aspects of religious life had become, it still produced many selfless women of deep faith and human wholeness, women who while privately acknowledging the serious shortcomings of the system, upheld the public image and, in reality, transcended it.

I was already out on mission when the radical changes began in the late 60's. As life-giving as the changes were, they were unsettling at the same time. We knew who we had been: Brides of Christ and dutiful daughters of a patriarchal church. But now that John XXIII had thrown open the windows and let in fresh air, who we would become was a great unknown. Changing our lifestyles and modifying our habits actually signified something more profound: a fundamental shift in our sense of ourselves and a radical new vision of our mission. Religious life as we had known it would never again be the same.

Now comes the hard part: explaining why I left the convent. In trying to share this briefly — and "briefly" is part of the problem, given the serendipitous nature of life — I found my reflections took me back to the reasons that I entered. Simply put, I wanted my life to be of service to God and to the church; I wanted to live a deeply spiritual life; and I wanted to do this freely, unencumbered by other obligations. Were my motives purely spiritual? No...but I didn't know that. Were there psychological undercurrents which influenced my decision? Of course. I was, after all, barely nineteen, and had more than my share of adolescent idealism. I never tried to imagine what life inside would be like or even considered what work I would be trained to do. Without doubt, the decision was more intuitive than reasoned, but graced, nonetheless. It felt right, and even now, I believe that it was.

In fact, I've come to view my years in community as a most significant stage in my life, and while not a permanent one, still vital to my development and a rich personal blessing as well. The decision to leave was one which evolved, one which had no single precipitating event and one with which I was very comfortable. I didn't leave in anger or in haste. I wasn't terribly dissatisfied with life as I found it in the convent and only slightly (and I confess naively) disillusioned. Actually, only two issues ever crystallized into real concerns for me. One was the issue of dependency and the other of comfort.

At times, it seemed to me that the basic tenants of religious life discouraged, if not directly thwarted, essential kinds of individual growth. While our professional and spiritual lives were nurtured, our emotional and psychological lives were not. It's not even so much that our personal development was neglected; it would be more accurate to say it was simply overlooked. This was evidenced dramatically for me when I was a young sister on my first mission.

One Saturday, we were gathered in the community room when a call came for a sister, by then in her eighties who was living her retirement with us because her family lived nearby and new regulations permitted more frequent visits. That much sister could accept, but when her niece called to invite her to dinner, she still came to the superior, knelt down and requested permission to go. The superior explained gently that it was her decision; she was free to go or free to stay. A look of panic flashed across her face. Again she asked if she had permission to go and was told once more that the decision was hers. After a few silent moments of visible agony, she raised her bowed head and with tears in her eyes said, "I've been a religious for over sixty years and in all that time, I've never had to choose. Please tell me what to do." Mercifully, the superior told her to accept the invitation from her family and to go and have a good time.

The damage such dependency caused was certainly never intended. And while I was not unaware that many women had matured remarkably well under the very rules I deemed unhealthy, I was equally aware that I could not. Today, of course, things are quite different. The notion of substituting a system of higher authority for one's personal responsibility is gone as religious women embrace the challenge of living out their dedication consciously. It is important to note as well that women, not girls, are entering. Women often with established careers. Women in their twenties and thirties with the education and experience we didn't possess when as wide-eyed teenagers, we appeared at the foot of the motherhouse steps.

Perhaps more crucial in my decision to leave, however, was the issue of the comfortable life. Following Vatican II, when our semi-cloistered view of convent living gave way, we put on ordinary clothes and went out among the people. We began to identify ourselves less altruistically and more directly with their lives and their pain. And we began to see first hand, that a world of suffering existed just outside the safe boundaries of our well-ordered lives. What followed I remember as a time of healthy unsettling.

In many ways our lives had become too easy and definitely too comfortable. Not comfort in the sense of luxury, for our convents were simply, even sparsely furnished, and our food and clothes quite plain and ordinary. But we were secure. We never worried about having to do without; we didn't need to fear for our jobs or plan for our future. Everything was taken care of. So, when real need and lack and even desperation appeared alongside our snug existence, many of us became uneasy and even more became adamant about the need for fundamental changes. Our mother general once remarked after visiting her brother, sister-in-law and their five children, that although she took the vow of poverty, it was her brother and his family who truly lived it. Even the predictable routine of our daily lives unwittingly invited a comfortable compliance and too seldom required us to ask hard questions of ourselves or our congregation.

Yet, valid as these observations may be, it is clear to me now, almost fourteen years later, that they did not cause me to leave. In fact, both concerns were well on the way to becoming non-issues by the time I left in 1978 and courageous innovations were already being thought-fully, prayerfully put in place. So the question remains: why did I leave? And the truest answer is simply that it was time. I left with the same sense of rightness and peace with which I entered. And one thing more: a grateful heart.

Because of the congregation, I was able to attend college. The opportunity for an education prepared me for a life of teaching, instilled in me a deep sense of ministry regarding my profession, and helped me discover, as well as develop, gifts I never knew were mine. Because I was immersed in daily prayer and meditation, and exposed to a wealth of spiritual and theological studies, both my faith life and my prayer were enriched; they continue to deepen and grow. And because of my experience with the sisters, I fashioned a sense of womanhood secure enough to balance compassion with conviction, and a concept of selflessness consciously tempered by self-awareness. I consider it no small thing that, in great part, because of my years in religious life, I now lead a life firmly grounded in hope. For all this and for much more, I remain permanently (and happily) indebted.

My life today includes a devoted husband (himself a former member of a religious community), and a delightful eleven-year old son who is bright, athletically talented, tender-hearted, and growing up much too quickly. I juggle the typical demands of family, community, and church involvement with the professional commitments of teaching and writing. The daily struggle to live what I say I believe is still with me. So is my desire to serve. In many ways, life has come full circle.

Though I don't pretend to see the final pattern of this beautiful tapestry my life is weaving, I must acknowledge with gratefulness the wondrous interlocking of each strand. In the words of Dag Hammarskjold, may I, at last, give public voice to my personal gratitude as with admiration and affection I say to my sisters, "For all that has been — Thanks. For all that will be — Yes."

4
TIERCE

For our soul is greatly filled;
We are a reproach to the rich,
And contempt to the proud.
And so in Sion was I established,
And in the holy city, likewise, did I rest,
And in Jerusalem was my power.

Pauline Grady
Adorers of the Blood of Christ

Contract Chaplain, U.S. Medical Center for Federal Prisoners

Province Historian

Translator

Bachelor of Arts, English Literature, Saint Louis University

Master of Arts, Theology, Philosophy

Special Training: Journalism, Corrections, Library Science, Italian (Perugia)

Parish Adult Education

Pauline lives with two ASC sisters in a rented duplex close to her parish and work. They enjoy common prayer, meals and conversation several times a week, and have fun together when they can. As part of a cluster they meet and share whenever possible. She is active in the RCIA process and adult Scripture classes in both her parish and in prison. Pauline would like to "water the seeds of the future" by planning with others in her parish and congregation. She continues to write essays on interracial and ecumenical matters, and "as it becomes necessary to lessen direct action" hopes to continue as inspirer and counselor.

Pauline Grady

Ripeness is All

—Mark 4: 29

Whether we think of a generation as the passing of three decades of time or as the experience of a fundamental change in environment and life style, I would say that I have lived in three different generations in my fifty-eight years as a Catholic sister.

Where has this "good little nun" gone since her profession in 1934? In terms of geography I have traveled much, but am again living in the Midwest where I began. In terms of inner development, what I am today is rooted in what I was in the beginning. I'm a prison chaplain now, and one of the inmates I work with asked me in all seriousness if I were some kind of maverick, or if I were in good standing in my order. He had gotten the idea from reading, without knowing any sisters personally, that somehow sisters were not realistic and present to life as it is. Maybe I don't act or look official. However, I think that what I am now grew directly from the seeds planted in my early religious life.

The time from my profession of vows in 1934 to the beginning of Vatican II was a generation in experience as well as in calendar time. The first twenty-five years after Vatican II was another. And, because a generation can be counted horizontally, by maturation, as well as vertically, by the passing of three decades, I believe that I am in a third generation in the 1990's.

Looking back over six decades as an Adorer of the Blood of Christ, I see the first thirty years as a period of the planting of winter wheat; good seed in good soil, even though the weather was wintry and the winds blew harshly at times. My adolescent enthusiasms were at first expressed in mystical images of myself as a Bride of Christ, and the children I taught as lambs. Those images faded and I was jarred into a

239

different level of reality when I was sent into the inner city, and was motivated by fellow sisters to work against the prejudice and injustice that prevailed there, situations which were entirely absent from my experience growing up in the Illinois corn-land.

At the beginning of my first generation as a sister, I was a young, inexperienced woman, without a liberal education or a completed human formation, sent into a parish to teach before I was seventeen because a sister had died unexpectedly and her place had to be filled. All that was required of me was docility, hard work, and the ability to fit into a tradition whose role models were our pioneer sisters. They had subsisted on little. The teachers in pioneer days, the older sisters told us, had sometimes earned their inadequate wages twice, first by teaching and then giving plays to get the money for the parish to pay them. They did all that was expected of them, even to firing the furnace and cleaning the schoolrooms. The nurses were sometimes engaged for 365 days a year, caring for the patients even during retreat time because there were no substitutes available. The housekeeping sisters raised vegetables and kept chickens and did the housekeeping chores, and helped the nursing or teaching sisters sew and mend. Ideally, there was no free time. One filled it with crafts or productive undertakings such as gardening.

Our traditional lifestyle, we were convinced, throve on miracles. We heartily subscribed to the principle give us by Mother Clementine Zerr, our American Foundress, that "there is nothing you can't do if you are obedient." My less-than-distinguished performance as church organist, on an ancient pipe organ pumped by mischievous high school boys, proved that in my case such miracles were not inevitable.

The role model offered me as a child had been Therese of Lisieux — meek, obedient, separated from family, not even reading the newspaper. As a girl I had had no direct contact with sisters to adapt that role model to what was happening in the 1930's. Yet, when I entered a province of the Adorers of The Blood of Christ in rural southern Illinois, there were always one or two — a wise old chaplain, a far-seeing teacher — who talked about the changes that were bound to come in liturgy, religious mission, historical consciousness, and who encouraged us to be vocal and down-to-earth. In our formation, lock-step as it was, the seeds of change were planted. I'm told that this was unusual, that few other novices in the thirties had a course on the history of the Roman Mass and the likely changes, or were led to question common interpretations of Scripture, or were quietly told that, once formation was over, they could be themselves again.

The formal life we lived was based on a European model of security and compliance. Those who had attended Catholic schools were especially formed in this pattern. Canon law and our image of ourselves had not kept pace with the burgeoning of our congregations in the nineteenth century as caregivers for the poor, or even with the actual experience of our pioneer sisters, whom we tended to emulate. We might run a hospital or school or library, we might deal maturely with real and pressing problems among our clientele, but within the community we prided ourselves on submitting to regulations like a child, unthinking and unquestioning.

Since we were part of the American culture of individualism, emphasized all the more because our immigrant forebears had come here precisely to become independent, there was a built-in problem. This was all the more true because many of us entered as adolescents, not pre-programmed to submission. When the excitement of the new life ebbed, would not unrest be inevitable?

I'm told that I never did really submit to being formed in the community mold, but I wanted to. Those who had attended Catholic schools had been exposed to a formalized presentation of religion, but I, as a public-school student, learned my religion from my parents' practice. I remember a session of choir practice when the choir director remarked that she did not see why Psalm 130, commonly used as a prayer for the dead, was included in Christmas Vespers. Inwardly I wondered how she could be so dense. How could she not see that the psalm applied to Jesus, speaking to his father from the depths? Somewhat typical of the current culture was this inability to make adaptations, even of Scripture, that differed from the prevailing one. Yet buried seeds were being broken open by the moisture in the soil. There would soon be sprigs rising above the ground.

I remember, too, bursting into tears when I was told I would be sent to the university for higher studies because I thought that, if I became a real scholar, I never would be like everybody else. After all, most of the sisters did not have master's degrees at that time, or even bachelor's degrees, and my priority was to be acceptable, even at the cost of my own mental and social development. My inner ideal was to be that acceptable person, the good little nun, who was not important or famous, but only dependable and obedient.

Perhaps untypically for the time, I was called for by our creative-education director who had already chosen my major, but wanted to check it out with me. She told me to plan on developing my gift for writing. She made the profound statement that current religious superiors were sending a sister to school for a year and expecting her to produce for twenty-five, when it would, perhaps, be more sensible to offer a sister twenty-five years in which to develop her power to do one year of creative work. I was deeply moved and thought of her words many times during my years of study.

We were expected, in formation and to a great extent in common life afterward, to eat what was served, to play and to pray in common, and always to be in a certain place at a certain time, doing what we were assigned to do. We carried with us to the required monthly interview with our local superior a "permission book," a listing of all the conceivable daily actions for which, by getting permission first, we could gain the merit of obedience. Each year we made a carefully revised list of our possessions, down to the precise number of handkerchiefs and home-made panties. Even the clothing was to be perfect in every detail: seven tassels on each end of the red sash in honor of the sorrows of Mary; no personalized tilt to the headdress; no eye glasses or shoes that were out of the ordinary.

Spiritual reading was a sensitive area. I remember receiving a scolding in confession because I was reading with some excitement Teilhard De Chardin's *The Divine Milieu.* Visits to our fellow sisters on nearby missions were limited to three times a year, since we had no car and would have to depend on some parishioner's charity for transportation. And our families were to be left, definitely, even though on occasion we could go to the houses of perfect strangers in their time of need.

There's no doubt that life in my first generation was stable, but it allowed for a certain stagnation, a gradually formed lack of sensitivity to the real needs of the real people we were sent to help. But, in fact, seed has been scattered in the land, and, in Jesus' words, "It is as if a man were to scatter seed on the land and sleep and rise night and day and the seed would sprout and grow, he knows not how. Of its own accord the land yields fruit, first the blade, then the ear, then the full grain in the ear."

During this first generation, because of my quality Catholic higher education (St. Louis University rather than a sisters' college), my theoretical positions veered toward social justice and adaptation, toward philosophical and theological progressiveness, but there was not always an obvious connection between these ideas and the way I lived and worked as a high school and college teacher.

At times, regular observance gave way to imperative grace. One evening after school a student of mine, a junior in high school, stopped at my desk and made a remark I did not understand. I knew she trusted me to figure out her real meaning. I went to a fellow teacher to get help in interpreting, and we decided we'd better get to the girl's home before another hour had passed and she had had time to hurt herself. Two problems: it was 5:00 p.m. and we were not allowed out of the house after sunset. We had no car and no pocket money for the bus. We called our superior on the telephone, told her we had to do something for which she could not give permission, and gave her a phone number in case of an emergency. Once the crisis was successfully met, we went back to regular observance.

When the summer of Vatican II arrived, with the fresh air pouring into opened windows, the winter wheat was already appearing above ground. Sister Formation was a formal expression of a ground-swell of burgeoning life which made the sisters leaders in the post-Vatican II church. In 1962 I received the assignment to go to Italy, the land of origin of our congregation, and write a biography of our foundress, Blessed Maria De Mattias. Almost simultaneously came my felt need, as a teacher of young women in inner-city East St. Louis, Illinois, to protest on the streets, to court arrest, to "put my money where my mouth was," to become "the wasp on the rear end of the Church," as one of our advisors put it.

So my second generation as a sister arrived with apocalyptic excitement erupting everywhere. The formal restraints of our previous semi-cloistered lifestyle gave way to an era of experimentation. Therese of

Lisieux gave place to Thomas More and Teresa of Avila as our role models, and to Malcolm X and Mahatma Gandhi as well. Our understanding deepened as we studied our roots as a congregation and our original mission to proclaim the Good News of Christ's death and resurrection and the glory of Christ's Blood (we now spoke of it as the Paschal Mystery). That brought me into the women's movement, inevitably, since Maria De Mattias, now beautified, had been in frequent conflict with the local bishop who could not accept her charismatic preaching and her concept of mission.

This was a period of reckless experimentation and perhaps of some lawlessness. You might say that the weeds had invaded the wheat. We had underground masses, got ourselves arrested, appeared dramatically before church people. I remember when our United Front appeared in protest before the local bishops of the Lutherans, Catholics, and Methodists of E. St. Louis, all in one day. We worked with the League of Women Voters and the United Front, prayed ecumenically, called on the Lord together in darkened rooms as we burned the plastic tops of six-packs of soda for candles, got ourselves debriefed after every election, fought for cleaner city government, served on city commissions, and expressed our liberation even in the way we dressed.

Fellow laborers began to leave the congregation at this time, almost without exception remaining part of our community of friends. This second generation was like the time in a person's life when he or she experiences the need for independence and leaves home. Those of us who did not leave home stayed because we trusted that we could get the institutions to change. Perhaps, at times, we tilted Peter's boat, trying to hasten change. Often we were a source of pain to well-meaning church people, who considered us very much at risk, and even prematurely mourned our passing.

Assigned to be historian for my province, I finally entered the field of writing, as my teacher had foreseen in 1938. I found myself digging for roots in the past, coming to understand better the charismatic quality in our founding mothers before their work was frozen by the 1917 Code of Canon Law, knowing that, with God's grace, the refounding would also be the work of the Spirit.

There was also a whole new set of experiences to manage that arose from our diminishing numbers. No longer were we assigned to meet a

244

community commitment with little consultation; now we had to work with our superiors to obtain an individual contract, and take personal responsibility for earning an income for the needs of the province. No longer did we have a sister assigned to do laundry and cooking, and may of us, having entered the community as teenagers, had never taken responsibility for these tasks at home. We simply did not know how to cook! We sisters went through a cycle in which the community scuttlebutt passed on new recipes rather than old rumors, when arguments about the use of the car superseded quieter discussions about teaching methods or doctors' peculiarities.

Six general assemblies and many, many voyages to other lands later, our international congregation has drawn strength from its widely differing members in twenty-two countries. The need to think globally about changes in life style and ministry in rewriting our constitution has sharpened our awareness of what it means to be international and multicultural, united in diversity, with our ministry rooted in our charism of the Paschal Mystery, rather than in accidents of nineteenth-century history.

In the last few years I have felt that we are arriving at a new point of growth, harvesting the crop that was planted in the winter time, and that sprouted and grew, weeds and all, in spring and summer. I sense the approach of fall, the season of mellow fruitfulness.

I've become adept at small-group living. I no longer live in a community of thirty, or ten, or even five, but with one other sister with whom I share in a matter-of-fact, honest way as we take full responsibility for who we are. If I had the needs and characteristics of an adolescent in my first decades as a sister, and matured into young adulthood during the disorderly days of a second generation of change and imbalance, I know at this point that my companion sister and I are adult in our reactions, not expecting what community cannot give, gratefully receiving what it can, joyfully sharing Christ's work without needing to be either perfect or ever-present.

In my position as a prison chaplain I put to good use everything that I have ever done: teaching, counselling, encouraging, healing human relationships, meeting the nitty-gritty daily reality of the prisoners in a way that allows them to find Christ present through me. I've come nearer than I ever imagined to the real priesthood which I have longed for since I was six years old. As a friend told me, when the Spirit's work through us women becomes obvious, the Church will ordain us, so I go merrily on dispensing what I have, and the inmates go on asking for "the woman priest." I no longer panic as my human limitations increase with age. The focus is no longer on my lifestyle, or my personal development, but on Christ who has died and risen and has, in this troubled world, already come again.

Roseline Joseph
Former Sister of St. Anne

Married

Seeking employment as school social worker

Bachelor of Arts in Humanities, University of Dharwar, India

Bachelor of Education, University of Mysore, India

Masters of Pastoral Studies, Loyola University, Chicago

Roseline, a member of St. Michael and All Angels Episcopal Church, is truly a "woman at service to all." Her reading interests range from children's literature to short stories, dramas, and of course, poetry. She hopes to write in those genres, and would like someday to lead seminars and retreats, "to help the people become aware of the richness of life."

Roseline Joseph

Turning Points

Home, sweet home, filled with love,
Filled with laughter, fun, play.
We flew like butterflies, merry, gleeful.

Home, our sweet home, first school of love,
Ample training in prayer and principles,
Principles and values of human life,
First place to God, center of life.

A rainy season in June...
I leave my beloved at home,
Going to a distant land
To give my life to God, His people.

To love, to serve — my only goal in life.
And life became easy to follow,
In spite of struggles.
Life, entirely different within a convent,
Stress on rules and structures.

Hard to train me, under Western rules,
Me, who knew only South Indian life style.
I remember the initial days of struggles,
Putting my feet in socks and shoes, unfamiliar.
Feeling funny, feeling strange,
No option but to obey or quit.

God's will in everything that happened...
So, everything for God's glory.
No room for question or complaint.

I, just a nice, gentle nun
With no complaints.
Pleasing character that pleased everyone,
A name so suitable — Smiling Sister.

Found worthy, capable, efficient,
Chosen to train others.

The studies that trained me as animator
Opening the dark corners of my being to light,
Hundreds of questions, systems, structures
Before me, to be answered.

Questioning the meaning of my life,
Opening before me new thoughts, reflections, insights.
Silent moments of prayer, reflection,
Directions opening before me a new road to journey.

Convent life, too rigid, mechanical,
Filled with rules, decrees, systems, structures.
Following the letter of the rule,
While values and principles are left unnoticed

The second turning point of my life —
The decision to leave religious life, choose to be lay.
Prayer, guidance and direction sought
And God's continuous care over all.

New goals, plans, and visions ahead
To be accomplished before my journey's end.
Believing that God's unending love and care
Is before me to guide, support, and strengthen.

June 29th 1968! Indeed it was a day of rejoicing and sadness! Joy in heeding God's call to be a Missionary, sadness in leaving my loving folks behind, and traveling to an unknown distant land. At the age of sixteen, though, it was not a hard decision to make, having been brought up in an atmosphere of religious discipline. To be a priest or nun was considered great, and it was an honor to the family. To be a missionary rather than a local nun was again highly prestigious. I don't remember what drove me crazy to be a missionary, away from my dear home. Anyway, one thing I remember clearly: when I was little, my maternal uncle left his home for the priesthood, to be a missionary. I think his sharing of experiences had some effect in my decision to be a missionary. Indeed, it was the first turning point in my life.

Today at the age of thirty-nine, I have taken another road. It is indeed a turning point of my life, the beginning of another chapter, adding newness to my life. Twenty-three years of life as a nun had both positive and negative aspects: any other field brings both merits and demerits, too.

Life was just fine and easy in the convent initially, as my only desire was to be a nun, no matter what struggles and hardships convent life brought. Everything was done for the glory of God and the salvation of others. With the teaching of the religious rules, principles, customs and habits, I found I couldn't think of anything else. I was taught what was right and wrong; I had no time to think for myself. Obeying blindly was the policy then. But things don't stay always the same. God has created man with the ability to think, reflect, question and criticize, and he must be functional at one or another time in his journey through life.

I was sent for studies and given responsible positions. The major part of my ministry was among young women who joined us in the novitiate. It was as easy for me to confine them within the religious principles and rules as it had been easy for my directors to do so with me. I enjoyed being with those young girls.

The God given capacities of thinking, reflecting and questioning started to open up their shoots during the later part of my convent life, i.e., from 1981, when I had the chance to do a course in the ministry of formation. Indeed, it was an eye opener to me, and I questioned the very meaning of my own life as a religious. My questioning was always to myself, as I didn't dare to question the existing authority, the systems or structures. I gave myself ample time to think, reflect, question and pray. It took me about ten years to take a bold step and quit the convent. Indeed it was a risk, a challenge. But I could see the hand of God supporting me all through, and His voice resounding in me, giving me His *yes* answer of assurance.

Leaving the convent life in India is a very difficult task. It is considered a curse: it brings a bad name to the one who leaves and to her family and relatives. A decent leaving is out of the question. But I had a different situation from the other folks; I was still holding a responsible position.

The reason for my leaving is quite obvious: I didn't want to be a part of the system that preached one thing and practiced another; a system that didn't follow the spirit of the law, but the letter; one that failed to practice the fundamental human principles of love, justice, equality and forgiveness; one stressing the observance of "Holy Poverty, Chastity and Obedience" although few practiced.

I am proud to be what I am today. I am a simple human being, free and liberated to do my service to the society within my capability, not restricted to so-called rules and regulations that are really a hindrance to what I want to do. I am grateful to God for the twenty-three years of experience He allowed me to have, and the beautiful lessons I was taught, and those lessons I was able to teach others. I have no regrets or hurt feelings. I think I am a better human being now than before, when I was a nun.

Gandhi says, "Hate none, love all." I still love and cherish the goodness of all those who have helped me to grow as I am today. I am grateful to my community for opening avenues that gave me new visions and insights in life.

I pray, think, reflect and question as before, and I have visions and goals ahead. I am trying to complete a few courses, and get back to my country among my folks, where I can help them to be better, free human beings. My purpose is to serve the society at large.

I wish and pray that religious life placed more emphasis on human principles and values. Let them try to eradicate poverty rather than taking the vow of poverty. Let them help the poor prostitutes by educating them to live a dignified life, teaching them the value, worth and decency of their lives rather than merely proclaiming the vow of chastity. Let them choose to obey freely rather than obeying blindly. Let them love, forgive, understand and accept people just as they are. Yes, let them be just human beings, never trying to be supernatural.

Anonymous
Former Sister of Providence

Married, two children

School Social Worker

Bachelor of Science in Elementary Education, Saint Mary of the Woods, Indiana

Master of Social Work, University of Illinois, Chicago

Special Training: School Social Work

This anonymous author loves to keep up with friends who live far and wide, and while letters help, getting together for lunch, shopping and reunions are favorite pastimes. She loves sports and will travel far and wide to watch just about any kind of team game. This year saw her in Minnesota for the "Final Four!" She has been married almost twenty-five years to "a great Italian" and hopes when retired to travel to "sights yet unseen."

St. Peter's Barnacle

Years ago my ex-nun story was rejected outright by many well known women's magazines: one rejection letter stated in so many words that the women of the USA just weren't ready for such an article. Would you believe I can't find that article?

True, much has happened since writing that article some twenty-odd years ago; do you suppose women and men are ready now to hear the hows and whys of all those empty convents? I was one of the first to leave those convents; nuns refused to speak to me once they knew I was leaving; I was referred to as a "Barnacle on the Boat of St. Peter" by my superiors; I was given no money or support to live on, though I had lived and worked freely with them for ten years. Unfortunately, those terrible conditions ceased once the ranks were leaving in huge numbers. The nuns in authority became more humane and support-ive, even financially so. I must say that my friends in the community of sisters never abandoned me. In the end they all left, except for a small minority. I'm sure they would have left, too, if the rules and regulations had not changed rapidly once they started. I never felt they would change fast enough for me to endure that type of life. These friendships have endured and enhanced my life.

I was never convent material: I never looked holy, never prayed a lot, or was ever a serious person. I shocked my family and friends when I announced towards the end of my senior year in high school that I was entering the convent. I was somewhat of a hell-raiser in those days; I was always trying to have fun and enjoy life. I came from a family that spoiled me with love and attention; I was certainly not used to deprivation and hardships. I did have a totally Catholic education, grammar and high school. And I had this enormous, exaggerated desire to give myself to a cause, but at that time there were no Peace

Corps or Vista Volunteers. There were a few sisters that I looked upon as role models, but not a one ever approached me to say I had a vocation! I'm sure I shocked the Good Sisters as much as I shocked my family and friends.

I remember thinking that once I entered religious life I would probably never eat bacon or chocolate chip cookies again. How wrong I was: if we didn't eat and gain weight the Sisters thought we didn't have a vocation and were unhappy! Actually, it was just the opposite. I had had my share of boyfriends and the thought of no sex and/or babies really didn't seem like much of a sacrifice. Remember, in my day we weren't allowed to think about sex and/or babies anyway. I'm from the generation of "Black Patent Leather Shoes".

Since my family was not wealthy, poverty didn't seem to be too depressing an idea. I forgot about the obedience part, how difficult it would be for such a head-strong person as myself to bow to the capricious will of another who often required you to do the most inane things, things that had absolutely nothing to do with holiness or spirituality. Like asking permission to wash your face, to go upstairs, to write a letter, to talk to someone. It was humiliating for me, but I thought I could live through the training part; surely it would not be like this once I was out teaching. Meanwhile, I was still the fun-loving person, making friends and trying to outwit the sisters in authority.

I found a way to shave my legs and underarms: razors were not allowed. I found a way to sneak in hamburgers and fries on visiting weekends. I found a way to write and mail letters. On the exterior I sometimes resembled a mild, meek sister, but I never ever bent my will to theirs. My friends in the community were my salvation: we would get hysterical over the noontime prayer: "Jesus, Jesus, Jesus make me constant." We would sneak up to the attic anytime of the day or night to talk: we would watch TV shows long after the older sisters had gone to bed. There is no way I could have endured the ten years without my friends. Perhaps I should have left sooner, but every time I tried to leave, the authorities told me I had a religious vocation. Everytime I asked to stay, they doubted I should stay. And if I had left sooner, I would not have the life I have today. Thank you, dear friends.

Having sent children off to college, I now have just an inkling of what our parents endured when sending their daughters off to convents. We were not allowed to eat in their presence, for whatever reason I will never understand. We could see them and/or write home about four times a year. What terrible sacrifices our families endured! They suffered much more than we did; we had our routines and friends while they had nothing but memories. Other friends of our parents were launching children into college, jobs, marriage and grandchildren while ours were not allowed to see or talk to us.

My mother died before I left the convent; I'm sure that along with the pain of her disease was the pain of not having her daughter with her at the end of her life, much less present for the support of her husband, my father. I was told I could either visit my mother on her deathbed or attend the funeral, but not both. Who was that punishing? Certainly the family more so than me, and certainly my mother most of all. As it turned out I went over the head of my local superior and did both. However, that local superior was furious and when I returned from the funeral she never once expressed sympathy to me over the death of my mother.

This brings up the main reason for leaving the convent; the total lack of basic Christian Charity. Over and over again I witnessed sisters not speaking to each other, sisters who fought each other, sisters who would play dirty, rotten tricks on each other, tricks like telling a classroom of children that their teacher (a sister) was having an affair with the parish priest. Yet these same sisters could mouth holy platitudes on a dime, would never miss Mass and Communion, were pillars of the community. While I was going through the rigors and trials of deciding to leave, I would often consult a priest via telephone; another sister would listen in the adjoining phone booth. I was later accused of being in love with this man! One sister even pulled a gun on a sister-friend of mine — talk about tricks! The gun-toting nun was a superior in an inner-city convent, and apparently had the gun for protection.

Homosexuality was an ever present fear (or reality) of our superiors. In training we could never spend recreation time with the same person twice in a thirty day period. Of course we did, but we were often forbidden to continue to do so. *Particular friendships* were strictly forbidden. Most of us were barely eighteen and had no idea what they were talking about! They were trying to prevent lesbian relationships, but their methods were so stupid that they only achieved in having us circumvent their rules and regs. I'm convinced the Great Silence in many religious communities was not to prepare us for Holy Mass and Communion the following morning, but to insure we could not visit one another's bedrooms at night. I don't think it ever prevented the lesbian relationships. What it did was keep many sisters isolated and fearful of getting close to people.

Once the training was over, I gleefully left the motherhouse for a teaching career and some semblance of the real world. I now had a classroom to mange, meals to cook and I was actually allowed to make decisions. What a shocker to discover I did not like teaching; I was bored with the job.

This was a point in my life when I clearly thought I should leave community, as teaching was about all one could do therein. However, one of my superiors — a good sister — convinced me that one semester of teaching was not enough time to make such a drastic decision. This woman and I became life-time friends, though at one point we were forbidden to see one another because of the particular friendship syndrome. Because I got along with the superior so well, I was transferred.

As I became more comfortable with teaching, especially in the inner city schools, I became more perceptive and mature bout the workings of the community. It was also the 60's, with the women's movement, civil rights and Vatican II. I grew up and out of the mold in which I had been cast in the Fifties. I was teaching fifteen-year-olds in seventh grade, from a third grade reader. I had not been trained for this! My middle-class value system was coming apart at the seams. Most of what I had been taught to teach would not work in the inner-cities where I lived and taught.

I read authors: deChardin, King, Malcolm X, Richard Wright, Eugene Kennedy, etc. I literally intellectualized myself out of the community. My personal heroes/heroines became Martin L. King, Jr., JFK, Betty Freidan and Bella Absug. The winds of change were blowing strong, and I was in the mainstream, or wanted to be. There was no way I could rationalize being a sister anymore. This, of course, did not happen overnight, but it was a fast-moving process in a fast-moving decade. The pettiness of convent issues: how clothes were folded, hairs in your hairbrush, too many pins in pincushion just would/could not compare with real life events of the 60's. The sisters were becoming more and more divided among themselves over issues; I was fortunate (in the inner city convents) to live with younger, more up-to-date thinkers like myself.

However, the powers that be were hidden away in their ivory towers, and trying to put a lid on the changes that were blowing in the winds. I was told that I would be given a superior who would teach me the meaning of obedience, and I was moved to another rapidly changing inner-city parish. Actually, this superior was a wonderful educator who inspired me to love teaching and who instilled in me a respect for authority because she treated me with respect. Too bad it was her last year as principal/superior in that parish, as her successor left much to be desired, and I returned to complaining about how awful things were. Of course I was moved again! This was always the community solution: move the trouble maker; keep the awful status-quo.

My spirituality was and is caught up with my fellow-man. My credo has always been: "Whatever you do to the least of my brethren, you do for me." I found that the sisters had forgotten that; they had lost their vision for the poor and downtrodden. The Church itself was closing parishes and schools even back then, while the Vatican Museum was filled with treasures, one of which could have kept a school open for a year at the very least. I believed in birth-control; I saw how being unwanted and unloved could stunt the physical and emotional growth of children. I came to understand why abortions could be necessary. Having lived and worked in inner-cities, I understood about the quality of life that had been denied to the poor.

I left the sisters because I did not believe — and do not believe — Jesus would have approved of the kind of life the sisters were living. I eventually left the Church because I came to the belief, still held today, that Jesus would not be a Catholic were he to live today on Earth. I cannot reconcile what the authority of the Church believes and tells its followers they must believe.

When I left the Community I worked for a county welfare program and came to my first real experience of community. We were a diverse group of race, age and life-style. Yet we were a community in the real sense of our professional commitment to the poor. I also came to live in my first real community in my personal life, as I lived in an apartment complex that held many ex-religious. These were men and women who were struggling financially and emotionally just as I was. They became my safety net for testing the social life, for learning to associate with men, for coping with an entire new world. Most of these friends are still my friends today. We may have grown wiser and older since those days, but bonds were forged that remain unbroken. Thank you, dear friends.

I began to experience the true meaning of poverty once I left the sisters! In community you may have had to ask for toothpaste, or shampoo, but you always got it. Now, I had to save money to buy what I used to consider necessities. I was determined not to get involved with ex-priests or brothers in a romantic manner as I felt one person trying to adjust to life in the real world was quite enough! Looking back, that was probably an unwise decision; for me, personally, it was wise. I have to say though that many of my friends did marry "exes" and, for the most part, have wonderful marriages and families.

I was ecstatic to be free of the vow of obedience; I was now on an even par with my work-world bosses. They were no longer my superiors, but equals; I could speak my mind now, and not be sent off to another place. I was very fortunate in having as my first boss a gentleman who thought my explosions were humorous, not sinful!

I have always been lucky in my personal relationships. It was very difficult to leave my friends in community and branch out into a strange big city, but wherever I went and whatever job I held, it was always the friendships that nourished and sustained me. I did not go home because in those days the ex-religious were not highly regarded, in Catholic circles especially. My family and friends back home were loving and supportive, but their lives had taken different paths.

Nowadays, one can leave the sisters and not feel in the least stigmatized. That is how it should be, but such was not the case in the 60's. I still tell no work colleagues of my religious past because of the fear they will treat me differently. Most Catholics still cannot understand it, and my beliefs have gone so far-afield from theirs that no one would probably believe it anyway! My name will be withheld from this article; actually, since it has been almost twenty-five years, telling means very little to me anymore.

In order to keep sisters in community the rules finally changed in the 70's and 80's. Sisters can now do and live whatever, wherever. Changes came slowly, but they came.

I found real community in the world I was supposed to detach myself from. I find community in the family I build with my spouse and children. I find community in the friends I have made through the years. I find community in the work-place where individuals are dedicated and committed. Isn't it a shame I couldn't have found it in the religious community? Was it my fault?

I grew and developed into a mature woman during turbulent times. I credit the religious community for assisting me becoming the woman I am today. They exposed me to opportunities that a middle-class white woman from the Midwest never would have known, opportunities that have made me the person I am today. Believe me, I am out of synch with most women of my generation. I am proud of that.

I do not regret the years spent with the sisters; I cannot honestly thank them either. I was a lucky one; I came out an intact person because I never truly turned myself over to them. Some women who departed have been permanently harmed by the Good Sisters; they will never be the same. The community was cruel to them in ways beyond measure because they gave them all they had, and when they discovered they had been deceived, it was too late to recover. That is probably where my anger, if I have any, lies. These women are still not healed; I weep and pray for them.

One of the themes in this article is *endurance*; I used the word endure more than just a few times. It's a sad word, but it does sum up the ten years! I endured them. I was told that that was probably all I could expect when and if you are "dead to the world"! I endured the years of teaching, the ridiculous rules, the "guard of the eyes", all for a higher, purer goal.

I believe that we Good Sisters are still out there; we are not dead to the world, but have embraced it in all its human conditions. I'm sure if truth be told, most of us are serving our fellow man in some capacity. We have found our communities where we can truly be at home.

Mary Ann
Felician

Reference Librarian, Pastoral Counselor

Bachelor of Philosophy

Certified member: National Association of Catholic Chaplains

Mary Ann uses her professional skills in loving ways. She creates nameday and birthday cards for the sisters in her provincial home, for the Montay Community College Community, and for the Good Counsel High School Community. Mary Ann also distributes large-print literature to the sisters in the Manor Care Center. She would like to continue "making people happy through pastoral visits, little visits" and, importantly, "taking time to listen." She is active in a telephone prayer and counseling ministry.

Mary Ann

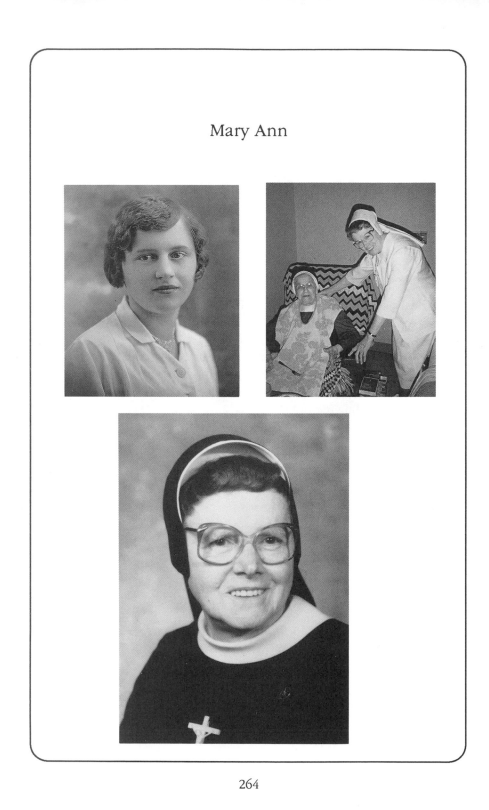

A Legend

On a beautiful spring day of March 23, 1915, a little girl was born into the family of Mr. and Mrs. Philip Baldys, in Calumet City, Illinois. Her brother Walter, eight, and Stanley, only two, were delighted to have a little sister, who was baptized on April 4, 1915, at St. Andrew the Apostle Church by Rev. B. Nowakowski and named Mary, since her birth preceded the vigil of the feast of the Annunciation.

Mary received her First Holy Communion on August 2, 1923, at Holy Rosary Church in Medford, Wisconsin, where her parents moved when she was four years of age. Rev. Gregory Reuter was her instructor for this event. However, it was Sister M. Salomea, OSF, who attracted her to religious life when Mary first met her at the age of five. She graduated from elementary school on May 27, 1929 and received the Sacrament of Confirmation from Bishop Reverman of the Diocese of Superior, Wisconsin, on November 24, 1929, taking the name of Anne.

After a year as a freshman at Medford High School, Mary Anne entered the aspirancy at Good Counsel High School in Chicago, on August 27, 1929. She graduated from there on June 16, 1933 and entered the postulancy of the Felician Sisters Mother of Good Counsel Province on June 29, 1933, and was initiated into the life of a Felician Sister on August 23, 1934. On August 23, 1935, Mary made her first profession of annual vows until she pronounced her final vows on August 23, 1941.

She celebrated her fifty years of religious life in the Felician Congregation with the Most Rev. Wurm of Belleville as a celebrant and the Very Rev. Msgr. Schwaegel as Bishop's assistant, at St. Mary's Convent, in Centralia, on April 11, 1983.

I am Mary.

I have had my ups and downs in life, for who is without trials and problems, many created because of success, others because of lack of foresight, and others because of personality differences and clashes.

My elementary school days were times of joy, challenge, and vision. In fact I expressed in an autobiography that if heaven were as beautiful as my childhood days, life would be worth living. From childhood on I was a nature lover, and often composed poems and plays on the beauty of the nature around my home. I also wrote skits which my brothers and sisters would dramatize for my parents.

The angelic smile of an elderly sister at my home parish and her outgoing hospitality and love ignited in me a desire to enter religious life. My first six years in religious life were days of happiness which earned for me the title, "Happy Felician," *felix* in Latin, meaning, happy. Because I idolized all religious and put them on the pedestal, and because I was considered the ideal student in class, I was dismayed and shocked when, after my final profession, I learned that all people were not saints, and there was often jealousy in religious life. For a number of years this took a toll on me; I was a very sensitive individual.

The happiest day of my life was when I was assigned to the Alabama missions. It seemed too good to be true and I was afraid that the train would break down before I reached my destination. Despite difficulties, such as teaching in a garage with a cement floor and rain dripping down from the ceiling, my first year was one of heavenly joy. In fact, I was so happy that at the end of the year after making my final profession, I asked the Lord to deal with that joy if He so wished. My prayer was granted; the next five years became days of hardships and pain because of my success in schoolwork, and my excellent rapport with supervisors and students.

When I think back, any large success of mine was followed by a cross, as if the Lord did not want me to become haughty. For example, I was changed from an assignment because the pastor praised the performances of the operettas I wrote, or was responsible for. In Pastoral Ministry I was called on the carpet because the doctors asked for my presence and counseling with their patients before surgery, and with those who were critically ill. In education I was snubbed because the supervisors made favorable comments about my teaching methods and handling of students. These are but a few of the problems which I had to encounter. With the Lord's help and an understanding provincial administration I survived them and became stronger in accepting difficulties as a part of life, although most of my former life was honey and roses.

The day before my final examination for a Master's degree in Library Science I was called by phone to volunteer for a Brazilian mission. A qualified librarian was needed to set up a library for the American Embassy students who were to graduate from a recognized school. I accepted, and left within five days, asking a companion student to pick up my diploma. Within four months I had the school affiliated with the Catholic University of America and accredited in two years by the United States Southern Association. The library was constructed according to the American Library Association standards: only recommended books and periodicals were purchased, and with the cooperation of the administration, my mission was accomplished.

From there I went to Chicago where I became chairman of Chicago's Region 14 Education System. Our specialty was the encouraging of growth within the system by having various educators and teachers demonstrate new techniques and advances. We held district meetings, arranged demonstrations and showed model programs.

Years later I was awarded the Clinical Pastoral Certificate of Education by the United States Catholic Conference through the National Catholic Chaplains Association. That was in 1982. Shortly after that I went to Centralia, Illinois for my next mission. I was commissioned as Pastoral Associate at St. Mary's.

I did that work for three years, resigning when I became seventy years old. However, I was able to serve and use my training in the Marian Care Infirmary, counseling the elderly in my own Felician community.

In 1991 a serious surgery led me into a part-time ministry, using my professional experience in library administration. God continues to provide me with the ability to reach young and old through the process of communication.

I think a lot about Heaven these days, and I am thankful for all the blessings I have received, for all those I was able to touch. In May of 1993 I will have lived sixty years of service as a Felician, years filled with joy, hope, tears, gladness, fears. *Magnificat.*

Rita Bresnahan
Former Franciscan

Single

Psychotherapist

Bachelor of Arts in Education, St. Ambrose College

Master of Social Work, Psychiatric, University of Illinois

Doctor of Philosophy, Counseling Psychology, The Union Institute

Licensed Massage Therapist

Neuro-Linguistic Programming

Certificate of Study in Aging

Ministry to the Aging: Retreats, Workshops in Aging as Journey

Rita uses her own "spiritual underpinnings" as a basis for her professional work and avocational work with the aging. Her interests are varied, ranging from the outdoors to travel and theater to "surprise and wonder and celebrations and laughter." Her dreams of beyond the now include aging gracefully for herself, and the creation of a spiritual community, a retreat center.

Rita Bresnahan

Spirit Journey:
Ebb and Flow

I was raised by gentle affectionate Catholic parents in a little Midwestern town where our lives literally revolved around our faith and its practice. From earliest memory, my every day ended with my father coming to my bed, sprinkling me in blessing with holy water, leaning down, kissing me and whispering, "G'nite, Reet. I love you."

There was some unspoken expectation whose origins I still cannot trace (for it was not that of my parents), an expectation that the oldest son and the oldest daughter in good Irish Catholic families were to dedicate themselves to the Church. My older brother had entered the seminary at age thirteen, and it remained for me to do my duty as well. Besides, the nuns told me I had a vocation; they could tell. It felt almost as if I didn't have a choice, that it was my destiny. And if truth must be told, I had been a very immature teenager, scared and uncertain. I was particularly frightened of my own sexuality, ignorant and in the dark as I was about that mysterious part of life. The convent offered a safe harbor and a lifetime direction.

In many ways that undeveloped part of me loved being tucked safely in the convent. Some deeper part of me, however, knew early on that convent life was not healthy for me, especially with its detached, impersonal demands. Ours had been such an affectionate family, and every day of my convent years I longed for a closeness such as I had known at home. Yet I was a person who kept my promises. I was too ashamed to leave, too guilty, and too scared. On my reception day something inside of me chilled and congealed, clicked into place and entombed itself, closing off my very depths.

When I was thirty-two or thirty-three something began stirring inside me which helped to open my eyes and pry loose some of my doubts and fears, and especially some of my lifelong beliefs. One of the most profound discoveries came the year I could not bring myself to recruit girls into our aspirant school. I knew what it was like to be naive and malleable and to be caught in a premature commitment, and I wanted none of that for them. That was the beginning: I had dared to question, to think for myself. I began to acknowledge how I longed to give expression to my human self — to enter into deep friendships or intimate relationships, to be myself, to be appreciated, to make my own decisions, to come and go as I pleased, not to have to feel guilty so much of the time. In a word, to be whole.

Ultimately it was my own body that both betrayed and salvaged me. In the midst of enormous conflict and confusion, my face began to break out in the most ugly acne. When all ministrations and dietary precautions proved futile, the dermatologist I had been seeing told me frankly, "Sister, you are suffering from nervous exhaustion. Something is wrong. I'm not a psychiatrist, but I do know that if you don't change what's upsetting in your life, there will be serious consequences." He was right. I was crying a lot, for no apparent reason. I didn't care any more, and I could feel myself slipping away. I felt a terrible failure as a religious. I had tried. God, how I had tried.

Feeling guilty in reneging on the promise I had made publicly to serve as a Sister of St. Francis for all the days of my life, I felt helpless in my attempts to silence my conscience. How I bridged this gap and reconciled the discrepancies I cannot specifically remember. There simply emerged a deep and primitive survival instinct assuring me there was a law greater than my young promise — one that must be obeyed.

So, at the age of thirty-six I walked unnoticed out the front door of the Franciscan motherhouse I had known intimately for eighteen years. Just as resolutely as I had signed the document granting me a dispensation from my religious vows, I crossed out with an angry definitive slash the life I'd lived there, as if it belonged to somebody else. I crossed out, too, the nuns who remained, together with all the ideals and associations connected with that eternity of dissonance and self-desertion. Closing that door marked the official start of my second life, and all the fear and panic of beginning a new life flooded over me. I'd like to remember my step as light and airy when I headed to the waiting car. But I felt no sense of joy or of freedom. Only a heaviness. A terrible heaviness.

Tierce

I'd turned eighteen in that place. From a strong Irish Catholic family, shy, naive, and untried, I had dutifully followed my vocation — the call from God, eagerly exchanging my "Rita" for the romanticized, detached "Sister Mary Sharon." When I left the order, I'd known Sister Mary Sharon longer than I had known Rita. In fact, Rita was nowhere to be found that leaving day. My adult identity fell away when I stripped myself of that familiar habit. No one was inside. "Who can I be," I'd ask myself, "if I'm not a nun — not a teacher?" Neuter: certainly not a woman. Having revoked my vows, no longer a good person. Who then?

For many long months I was unable to answer that haunting question, struggling as I was to survive in an alien world. My growth had been stunted in many ways during those years; the day I left the order I was instantaneously whisked back in time—a thirty-six-year-old woman just turned seventeen. Never had I felt so painfully self-conscious, never so ugly, so scared, confused, and dependent—so totally inadequate to meet the world.

Straddling two worlds, I didn't know who I was, what I could do, what my options were. After an eternity of acting and thinking like someone I was not, even believing at most levels that I was that shadowy someone, I knew no way of unearthing the real essence within. That new Rita was a mysterious, elusive creature, one I had never met before.

How could that nun-shadow — a shadow that for eighteen years had clung closely to the walls, moving only when directed by the authorities in her order, changing shape, alternately magnified or diminished, as the light allowed—be transformed into person-substance?

What compounded the tortuous struggle to infuse substance into shadow was that now Rita refused to allow any part of Sister Mary Sharon to re-enter her new life. Rita was embarrassed about that convent life, that spiritual life —angry with it. With its guilt and self-betrayal and free floating fears, it was excess baggage. So I buried it.

Over the following years a recurrent dream plagued me. Still in the order, fully habited and veiled, blindfolded, I would be lying in a narrow white metal dormitory bed with huge concrete blocks placed all over the top of my body, my arms and legs strapped to the metal slats below. Nobody remembered I was in that dark, closed room. Time and again I'd awaken with a jolt, sweating and shivering, relieved to discover that

273

I was only dreaming, I was no longer a nun. Yet I was somehow still bound; the immobilized, helpless, alienated mood stretched into my days. What still had a hold on me? How could I loose myself from that?

I moved from Illinois to Colorado, hoping that a change of locale and the mountain air would grant me a freedom I had not known. In Colorado I avoided anything smacking of religion. I forgot about the order, convincing myself I was no longer affected by that unlived life there. One piece of convent identity I retained was my need to be perfect in whatever I did. Driven to achieve, I became successful—professionally, socially, economically—in every way possible. At least that's what it looked like from the outside. But inside, in spite of having it made, in spite of traveling extensively and long vacations, I grew increasingly restless, dissatisfied during those six years. Something was missing.

At the age of forty-three the possibility of lung cancer reawakened my habit of soul-searching. In the weeks of testing and overwhelming anxiety before the operation something inside me changed. After the benign tumor reprieve I turned my life around, not knowing toward what destination. I knew only that it was from the parameters I'd allowed to define and confine me: role, status, money, having to have the answers , having to be perfect. I resigned from my position with the mental health center with no clear notion of what I was going to do, or why I had made that choice. I knew only that it was important and that the time was right. In my journal at that time I quoted Goethe: "Whatever you can do or dream you can, begin it," I did begin it.

That departure from old patterns, from established expectations, from having to have everything in place, became a quest to discover what was truly important to me. Once that was in clear focus, I trusted myself to have the integrity to live accordingly.

I set off vagabonding, leaving my home in Boulder, Colorado, and heading to the West Coast, with visions of catching a freighter to the Orient. My first stop was Salt Lake City. I had anticipated that my stay there would be brief and insignificant, but it became a time of tremendous meaning. I reclaimed an integral part of myself there — the religious, mystic, spiritual self that had in some way reigned supreme for eighteen years, but that I had carefully and deliberately abandoned and denied upon leaving the convent.

It happened in the Mormon Tabernacle, where two friends had taken me to hear *The Messiah*. I cannot describe the process that began inside me, nor how long it lasted. I only know I crossed some unnamed line, felt myself suddenly open once again to spiritual levels of experiencing and knowing. Such a relief to be free again, tears streaming down allowing the spirit to encompass me, without all the resistance and negative overlays. Just reclaim, embrace, the spirit within. It had been there as a constant, or course, perhaps even growing more insistent as its years of denial continued.

I was deeply touched by each section of that oratorio: the voice crying in the wilderness, people walking in darkness seeing a great light...eyes of the blind opened, ears of the deaf unstopped, lame persons leaping, the tongue of the dumb singing. And each of these spoke of me — now opened, unstopped, leaping, singing: "Behold, I tell you a mystery . . . We shall be changed in a moment." I was changed. In that moment I understood that what I had actually meant to renounce years before was the religiosity of those years: the hypocritical, authoritarian, guilt-inducing, sanctimonious manipulation that bears no relationship to the spiritual. A realm of phoniness where so much was mouthed me-chanically, preached and practiced and imposed under the guise of good — yet whose end result in so many cases is a devastating one: that is what I had rejected.

But much of what had been called evil and traitorous — the question-ing, the renouncing of my vows — on that day became not only acceptable, but holy. What had earlier looked like betrayal was, ulti-mately, only truth. I was following my own truth. And whatever God is — truth, wisdom, oneness, healing, trust, congruence, life, meaning, love — that is the faith I profess, the religious life I now choose to lead. It was, and is, impossible — indeed, immoral — to deny that.

Buoyed up by this new discovery, I headed on to the West Coast, where I gardened for my rent in Berkeley, struggled with a deep love, worked on the bottling crew in a winery, decided against hopping a freighter to the Far East in search of lost treasures. Periodically, during some twenty months of vagabonding, I crisscrossed the country, find-ing myself back in Illinois — a surprise even to myself. Roots country, yes, where I had grown up and where my mother and brothers still lived. Ten miles away loomed another magnet for me, the pull and push of which I did not fully acknowledge: the motherhouse. I carefully avoided that area of the city as if it were condemned; the times I did approach within even blocks of those areas, there welled up in me a feeling of nausea, a sense of my own powerlessness and absorbing fear. Tenaciously, something in that place held me in its grasp.

Gradually, near the end of my vagabonding, tiny flickers of light began to illuminate the darkness of those eighteen years. The first was provided by a workshop in which we participants were encouraged to look with new eyes at the background, learning and context of signifi- cant people in our lives. Flash: the nuns from my order are mere human beings — and women. I couldn't believe they were women, too. Even those who had been in positions of authority and with whom I had known such conflict? They, too, could be scared and confused, and very uncertain? Lonely at times, longing for the comfort of a human touch? Suddenly the *bete noire* was tamed, lost its hold over me. The order was no longer an all-powerful judge disposing of me at will. It could not swallow me, suck me in, consume or punish me. "It" was powerless. I held my power in my own hands.

Shortly after that workshop came an invitation to visit at the motherhouse from a friend still in the order . It was not the first such invitation, but it was the first carrying the welcome of a new administra- tion, and the first I'd felt inclined to accept. I toured the motherhouse with her, awkwardly meeting the nuns again, revisiting sites of my immense joys and deep hurts, remembering what I had tried to forget. It felt reminiscent of going through a loved one's personal effects after a death. But here I was — the deceased and the survivor. At the time of that visit I was in no condition to decide what to keep and what to dispose of.

That same weekend, we went to see the movie *Julia*. The opening scene struck me forcefully, particularly in the context of the convent weekend: the solitary figure in the rowboat out on the lake, and Hellman's words, taken from the frontispiece of *Pentimento*: "The old conception, replaced by a later choice, is a way of seeing and then seeing again...The pain has aged now and I want to see what was there for me once, what is there for me now." Ah yes, what was there for that painfully shy, confused, but intense and sensitive young nun — and what is there for her *now!* At that moment I determined to open myself to that gift.

I was at the time a doctoral candidate in psychology and was studying how the process of change comes about, especially for women in their mid-life years. One focus for the study was women who had left the religious orders. My doctoral advisor and colleagues challenged me: "What about interviewing those who stayed? Haven't there been great changes inside the religious orders as well?" "Yes, but — ."

No excuses were sufficient, particularly to quiet my inner divining rod that discerns what is right for me at any given time. It hovered and trembled and finally dipped down: *back to convent.* "All right, all right!" I hollered. I gave in. Yet how could I, still harboring much of the old anger and bitterness, return, if even for the three to four weeks that would be needed? In such a charged situation, how could I be objective, as befits a psychologist? In examining my own changes, I drew a blank when it came to the convent years. Getting in touch with that past was much of my reason for returning. But how would I know when I was ready?

And then came the dream! I was fully habited and veiled. Smiling broadly, laughing. And *dancing!* My body was moving freely! Through psychedelic swirls. No longer strapped down. No longer in the closed darkness.

I wrote the president of the order asking to spend a few weeks back at the motherhouse. By return mail, without requesting an explanation, her unequivocal response was, "Come!" That note of welcome brought with it relief, but unbearable anxiety as well. There was relief because the connection had been made and I was following my own sense of what I needed to do. But there was also anxiety: could I survive the ghosts of my past? Would reviving them jeopardize the security of the now? With this ambivalence I crossed the threshold of the motherhouse once again, nearly ten years after I had angrily left it all behind.

I was totally unprepared for the enlightenment that came during those four weeks.

What struck me repeatedly was how the nuns who stayed and I were really on the same journey. Quotes from letters sent to members of the community by Sister Joan, president, revealed how many metaphors we held in common: "...the quest for understanding requires that we give up the search for certainty and go on a voyage of discovery...letting go of what we have for what we do not have...deeper solidarity...ministers of healing...moving toward new visions, open to where they may take us provided we are willing to move in darkness and uncertainty...hoping to see many hidden barriers released and lifted, wounds healed, harsh judgments let go of...growing awareness of what it means to be a woman...and freedom to be oneself."

So, they, too, had leapt over many walls. How dramatically my perspective changed, from seeing them as so different from me, to seeing that we are all sisters, pilgrims traveling together. "Sister" now is much more than a title, a form of address, but speaks tenderly of the bond between us. For we are all sisters, we who were "Sisters" for eighteen years without touching upon so much of what sisterhood could really mean: the kind of love and support and trust and sharing at the core that began to manifest itself those weeks, reconnecting us gently but irrevocably to one another.

Gradually, following those weeks at the motherhouse, I could begin letting discounted parts of myself return. In the past, certain of my behaviors and attitudes had been referred to as "nunny," and I hated it. Even when a friend had insisted, "But Rita, it's your nunny parts I like best!" I had still cringed. I felt it meant naive and innocent, Pollyanna-ish. "Nunny" also meant being reflective, often seeking solitude. It meant a heightened sensitivity and response to the needs of others, a way of being of service. For years I had withheld myself, had performed no such action that might give me away, make me feel nunny or be perceived as such, thus unknowingly crossing out another important part of myself.

A graduate student in one of my classes helped me understand what I was about, without the nunny label: "Rita, I have felt more ministered to in your Tuesday night class than I ever have in the Sunday morning pew." At the last class session I received a card quoting Camus— "In the midst of winter I finally learned that there was in me an invincible summer," with the added note, "Rita, this is what your class has meant to us." The light began to dawn. I welcomed my nunny self back: she who is not only quiet and meditative and introspective, but she who responds to what she cares about, offering an ambiance of love and tenderness that nourishes the depths.

The enlightenment embedded in my return to that formidable site also assumed another critical form. By reflecting in silence and through tears I began to understand the movement and the meaning of my own life process: what had brought me to the convent at that tender age, what had kept me there such long years, why I ultimately had had to leave it all behind me, and what forces had drawn me back for the reconciliation. It was a seeing with new eyes and fresh perspectives — a coming into a new kind of ownership of my life.

For me, the core issue in the journey revolves around sorting out beliefs about "the way the world has to be," as I had been taught to view it. Once I had started to question, my whole world began to topple. When that "crack in the cosmic egg" appeared — when I realized the extent to which I had been lying to myself, denying my own authority — there was the unspoken but haunting and pivotal question: Can I trust myself to know what is real for me, what is true, what is right? Or do I have to continue to rely on someone else to determine that for me?

In my struggle with traditional religion, that was my ultimate dilemma: the discrepancy between the what-should-be of dogma and what I knew in my depths to be true, as my life experience revealed it. The mistake had lain in cutting myself off from my feelings, from my own experience, in attempting to build a spiritual life before I understood or appreciated my humanness. My "spiritual life" cannot exist in a vacuum, splint off from the rest of me. The highest goal in the convent had been somehow to rise above the humanness, to conquer it. However, at the height of my religious perfection era, when I had risen above, I had felt curiously hollow and shallow; I had felt, ironically, that I had somehow lost my soul. Not in the sense of having committed some act that meant I was irrevocably damned but, rather, that the very depths of my being were closed off to me.

Was I wrong all those years? Were they a waste? Not at all. The key is not to see my earlier perceptions and choices as wrong but to be able to say of them, "It was important that I entered the convent and that I dedicated my life to the church for eighteen years. But it is also important that I left the order. Life changes. So did I. I love myself where

I am, at each step of the way, for I understand how I got there. Each was right for its time. I can understand my decision at age seventeen. I understand, — and honor what it was that I needed and what I wanted at that time, given my upbringing, my assumptions about the world, my resources."

That may be the secret in dealing with past issues or commitments: not denying them their place in time, but transforming them into what makes sense for me now — values emerging from my own experience as opposed to "shoulds" imposed from without. Coming to terms with my past and understanding the assumptions in which I was immersed lay the ground for knowing my present, for understanding myself. Leaving the order did not constitute failure; staying would not necessarily have meant success. Both were simply life experiences, choices, as are all of the paths along which we travel. The ultimate failure is not to allow myself to know with a deeper knowing, not to learn from experience, to fight the ebb and flow of my life.

It is this process of ebb and flow that best symbolizes the movement of my spirit-journey. Many months ago a force I called "my water-spirit surfacing" brought me to the Northwest. Now each day deep and mysterious waters graciously present to me the gifts of life itself — ever present though ever changing; gentle, wild, daily reminders, magnificent manifestations of the ebb and flow that makes all things one. I am learning not to separate my world into what is spiritual and what is not, for I perceive and embrace the sacredness in the stuff of even the most ordinary of happenings. I also know myself to be a part of a larger whole, part of a community; and that is much of what my life, my vision, is about: fostering relatedness that emerges from honoring the place where each person stands, from sharing vulnerabilities as well as strengths, from honoring the darkness as well as the light, from being open to lessons from all quarters.

Shortly after much of this story was published in the anthology, *A Time to Weep, A Time to Sing: Faith Journeys of Women Scholars of Religion,* I returned once again to the motherhouse, this time to present an autographed copy of the book to the convent library, and to read my story aloud to any sisters who would like to hear it. They packed the recreation room. I read for forty to fifty minutes, a timeless period of almost breathless silence except for the sound of my voice, a time punctuated periodically by my own choked tears and those of the listeners as well.

After I had finished reading, and as I was about to leave, the sisters began gathering spontaneously around the entrance, almost as in a reception line, one-by-one hugging and blessing me, thanking me and wishing me well. It registered in my bones as the good-bye I had longed for when I had had to disappear under the cover of darkness, departing through those same portals nearly twenty years before, in silence, unacknowledged, as in disgrace.

Periodically, people look at me quizzically, as if I am an alien from some distant planet/time, and inquire, "Rita, what makes you tick?" The clearest answer I can give is my intention, renewed daily, to live in the *Namaste* consciousness. "Namaste" is the greeting people use in India when they meet one another. Folding their hands, each bows to the other, saying "Namaste", which means, "The spirit in me bows to the spirit in you." I am keenly aware of the spirit-life in me, and begin each day with "I inbreathe the light of the Spirit; I radiate the life of the Spirit." To know that spirit in me and to recognize and honor that in you is my most sacred calling.

Today I experience life as a continuous and ever-changing process of responding to the truth of that calling in whatever form it appears at any given moment, moving with a sense of reverence and mystery, of caring and wonder and exploration. All this emanates from a life-affirming and joyful sense of my own spirit, of our interconnectedness to one another and to the universe itself.

Just this quarter, a student in one of my classes commented, "At lunch we were talking about you, Rita, and decided that the description that fits you best is "pastoral". That is true, I believe. However, for many years after leaving the convent, I struggled with co-dependency issues, although there was not a name for them then. I think I am learning the fine art of attending to my own needs, while also being of service, pastoral.

I am at the core not much different a person today than I was as Sister Mary Sharon. The major exception is that now I live my life in such awareness, whereas for so many convent years I had lived as if anesthetized. Through therapy and spiritual direction, I have dealt creatively with the issues of identity and of sexuality that played a part in my entering the convent. I have taken my life back into my own hands. I have reclaimed my own authority. The same desires which brought me to the convent still propel me: to make the world a better place, to share my life with people who carry a similar vision. I continue to hope for a family/community context in which to live out my days and my vision.

The substance presented to me by my parents is printed indelibly on my heart as well as on the patterns of my everyday living: to love my neighbor, to rely on the kindness of others just as they can count on mine, to walk gently and to live simply on this earth, to appreciate what I have, to be generous in sharing with others, to know what true riches are, to laugh at life's surprises, to live gracefully in the Spirit.

And so it is.

Margaret M. Trepal
Exclaustrated Franciscan

Elementary school administrator

Future RCIA director and part-time student

Bachelor of Arts, DePaul University

Master of Education, DePaul University

Adult Education RCIA

Margaret hopes to expand her background in order to begin working in adult education in theology and scripture. She and another sister share a house rented from the parish in which they work, and she stays in touch with her community through mailings and the like. She would like to pursue a Master's degree in Theological Studies, and is exploring the possibility of affiliation with a new Franciscan community of religious women in the summer of 1993.

Margaret M. Trepal

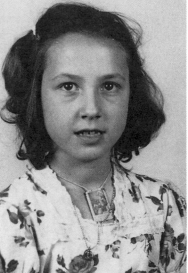

284

To Be the Face of God

After thirty years as an active and involved member of a religious community, I requested excaustration. In June of 1990, I began again.

I was nineteen, eager and idealistic when I began the journey that led me to choose a Franciscan religious community. It is quite a joy for me to think back upon those youthful days because I am still energized by them. This is the story of how, after almost a lifetime, I am recapturing the ideal of my youth and experiencing the joy of it while turning my thinking into action at deeper levels than I thought possible so many years ago.

"When I grow up," I boldly declared, at age fourteen, "I'll drive a red convertible, take a trip around the world, have plenty of money, clothing, anything I want." Such was my attitude before I really knew and fell in love with Jesus Christ. After a year of college and some powerful prayer experience, I found myself turned around, now only wishing to know the Lord better, and to share this knowledge with others along the way. Living with like-minded women in community seemed to be just the place for me. My understanding of what it meant to be a religious was, and still is, very simple.

So began my membership with the Sisters of St. Francis. The Franciscan tradition and life style are well suited to my prayer and temperament. There is a simplicity about this tradition that has attracted and held me. Contemplative prayer, along with an openness to the world, characterize it. The entire world is sacred space to a Franciscan: all are our brothers and sisters. For a Franciscan, *being* is better than *doing*. A Franciscan presence is a ministry in itself, therefore the works that Franciscans undertake can be as varied as Franciscans, but ministry that brings healing and reconciliation is most appropriate. Love is to be the motivation of a brother or sister of Francis. But I am getting ahead of myself here, because these are insights that I have gained throughout years of living, learning and praying. They were not those taught to me in the novitiate of 1959.

While I was being taught how to walk — with my hands tucked modestly into my sleeves — I longed to learn to pray without words, the way my spirit was calling me. When one of my students was killed in a traffic accident, I was restricted in the amount of time I could spend with the grieving family, even though my tears, mingled with theirs, were bringing consolation. Throughout all of this I kept trying to adjust myself to the expectations placed upon me by written and unwritten standards. I didn't expect religious life to be like this, but if this is what it was, then this is what I would do, even though it didn't feel quite right. I kept discounting my uneasiness.

In those early days I eagerly read and studied all I could about Francis and his early companions. They were my heroes and I loved to read their stories. As I matured into my middle years, my ideals began to solidify. It is one thing to hear stories of centuried saints; it is quite another to translate that ideal to my own era.

For thirty years I was a teacher or administrator in parish elementary schools. I liked that. Living and working within a parish was so grass roots. Here was real life: birth, growth, death; old and young; real people with real stories. This was Church: not distant, antiseptic, or manageable, but certainly real and demanding honest service. This was a great place to be a Franciscan. To bring the love of Jesus to children and through them to touch families was a fulfilling way to share faith.

I was growing and changing. Through the ups and downs of living I learned what it meant to be, to trust, and to really *like* myself. My relational skills developed and so did my ability to be an effective minister. It was wonderful to discover that when I functioned as "Sister," I was first of all Margaret and this was the person that the people came to know and love.

But the more involved I became in the lives of others, the more I began to see that the attitudes and the prevailing opinion within the community frowned upon such involvement, and discouraged creative solutions that would directly affect the sisters and the quality of service they could provide to the folk. I began to doubt my own dream and journey.

And worse, I began to abandon it for the safer, more comfortable route: conformity. In confusion, I turned inward and began to pray.

Many good friends left the community during those years. Some of them were fine religious, but they had had enough of frustration and had decided to turn to other lifestyles. Others, discerning that religious life was not their call, left the community for marriage or career. Throughout all this upheaval, I could not bring myself to make that decision. I was called to be a religious and wished to live my entire life as a member of this community. This was a difficult time full of doubt and pain. I must admit that there were times when I was more out of the community than in it. Still, something held me there.

How can the Franciscan life style be interpreted and lived today? Can religious life have meaning for the people who live it, as well as for those for whom we live? Was my community making efforts to answer or even to ask those questions?

As the years passed, I felt that this was not happening. The community had settled into a comfortable pattern of living that did not accept challenge or debate. In my opinion, it was in decline. Surely this was not life-giving for me. I became disillusioned and restless. This Lord whom I had come to know so well was calling me to something beyond my present situation. What do I do about this, I wondered? How do I go about making changes so that my lived experience matches my inner convictions?

Getting involved seemed to be the answer. As a chapter delegate, elected in 1981 to leadership in the provincial council, I was interested in building a community vision, believing that changes in focus and attitude could be made through my efforts. But this proved to be a dead end. There were no imaginative ideas being generated in the administration; I was not being encouraged to generate them, either. When my term as a council member was up and a new administration was elected, I threw myself into committee work. I became more vocal and willing to share my ideas and desires. Now my motives came into question. Perhaps there is a hidden agenda, I was told. I felt that my efforts were leading to blind alleys and darkened passages that led only to frustration and mistrust.

This was not right. Rather than initiate change or at least the thought of it, my increasing involvement was causing mistrust and discord. Neither the community nor I needed more of that.

It was difficult to find other sisters within the community who shared my discomfort. I wanted to bond with others who could dream, discuss, and pray with me and who shared my desire to achieve much needed harmony between lived reality and religious experience. As yet I had no words or specifics to define my vision, but I knew that my community was not responding, nor was it allowing me to respond to a need for change that I sensed called for a new community focus.

Whenever small groups of sisters would get together and begin discussing such ideas, there would be questions. Someone, not sympathetic to our thinking, would find out about such meetings and carry reports to the provincial who might then call upon one or another of the group, questioning the motives of the sisters involved. This was certainly not solving the problem. I continued to search, to pray.

Discernment of this kind is not to be undertaken alone. The Spirit's wisdom is given to all and truth is known because many share in that wisdom. I considered myself blessed because in 1988 another sister expressed views similar to my own and decided to join me in this quest.

One day the two of us decided to have our own meeting and to come to some decision concerning our values and the direction they would take us. There among the hamburgers, fries, and fun of a fast food restaurant called Fuddrucker's, we formulated an outline of what we considered the basic tenets of religious life.

Armed with this list we approached the provincial superior on April 2, 1990, asking to be given an opportunity to live out this new expression within a small intentional community that would be sanctioned by the province. Ours was a simple vision of religious life: a life lived with others in mutual respect for the uniqueness of each, with emphasis upon individual responsibility. It included collaboration and openness to the constant growth and change of individuals and of the group.

It demanded a contemplative stance based in Scripture which would lead to the Franciscan values of fraternity and conversion of heart. Most of all, we could see a community develop that spoke to ordinary people offering hope and an experience of the love of God. There was nothing radical in this request. We felt a strong desire to renew religious commitment by peeling away the layers of oddities and less-than-honest structures that had developed around religious communities. The request was to form a group of women interested once again in probing the heart of religious commitment.

I thought this a good idea, but the provincial certainly did not, and said that the community at large would not be ready for such a vision for another ten years. We didn't have ten years. We only had now, so each of us decided to request exclaustration.

Exclaustration is a canonical term which means that a religious is given a period of time freed from the restrictions of community membership while keeping her vows intact. The purpose of this time is the discerning of her vocation. After one to three years she can either return to the community or request a dispensation from vows. This was the only option open to us. We did not feel that we were discerning a vocation, but we did want to preserve our religious vows while searching out a deeper expression for them. This was very important to us.

Life is a series of beginnings calling for honesty and clear judgement. I am not afraid of beginnings — even though they are risky — because they are also challenging, exciting, and fresh. My life had taken on new directions; I was forced to face what my inner sense was telling me about society today. Materialism, hunger for power and control, violence and injustice are eroding human worth and dignity, even life itself.

I measured that with what I understood to be the purpose of a religious vocation, and felt that this change in my lifestyle was needed in order to respond to these two realities. I wanted to bring the two together in an way that would restore my sense of harmony and wholeness. My life, however successful, was disjointed and out of balance. I sensed that the values that characterized society also characterized religious communities, and I needed to be free of community obligations so that I could make a healthy decision regarding my response.

It is good that the two of us have been together. We have learned to pray and to share Scripture with each other, keeping open hearts and minds in order to hear the truth as it is found within our individual personalities and strengths and in our life together as well.

At first we wondered where would we live and how would we support ourselves. The pastor and people of the parish to which we were assigned at that time were overwhelming in their affirmation of us, and asked us to continue living and working within their parish community: I, as principal of the elementary school, and my companion as pastoral associate. This proved to be an excellent situation for many reasons. Our experience was not unlike that of newly divorced middle-aged women beginning life alone without the emotional and financial support of a spouse. Being able to continue in the same positions and live in the same home minimized the difficulty of adjusting to a new status. It provided some security in an otherwise insecure move.

Now we continue living a community life: praying together, supporting each other, sharing expenses and finances. We are on our own and responsible to each other. We are becoming ordinary people and we are comfortable with that. The people have become our community. It is a joy to receive from them.

Stepping out of my community has proved to be a good way to view its values and customs more objectively, to observe other groups of religious women, and, more importantly, to take time to define my beliefs and goals. I realized how often I had been ashamed and impatient with my community's irrelevance and backwardness. I was embarrassed to be a member. There is such relief in being free of that heaviness. Coming to the decision to request exclaustration was painful; living free from the community brought me joyful relief.

I am finding the seeds of new directions by looking back upon the motives and ideals that prompted me to answer the call to live in a religious community in the first place, thus redefining what I believe the call is about. This is a powerful place to be.

There are many men and women in various stages of membership in religious community as am I. Each person struggles with questions and finds answers in ways that are unique to him or her. In fact, it is only through these shared struggles and resulting wisdom that new understandings and definitions of religious life will emerge for future generations. I see religious communities developing and changing. Some will cease to be, new ones will be formed; others will grow and flourish. This is, indeed, an exciting time to live and I am honored to be part of this development.

Religious life is a response to the reality of a God who is one with his creation. Religious are to make this God real and within the grasp of the ordinary person. Through their corporate witness, religious demonstrate the compassionate God at work. I have come to see that religious are called to give human dignity back to those who have lost it. Empowering people to take their places within the church and society, and helping them to gain the understanding that faith in God and in themselves can be a strong force in their lives, is my focus.

In this process I am learning to live by faith and to take risks. It is risky to begin a life apart from a group that I had come to depend upon for many years. It takes courage to carve out a new lifestyle within a culture that voices a value system different from that which is considered the norm. Once freed from the structures of active community membership, it is a challenge to hold to the ideals and vision that brought me to this place. I believe that through my experience I am beginning to have something to say to religious communities, to the greater church, and to those who are not members of the Catholic faith.

How does a new or refounded religious community look? I don't know. Defining specifics is not easy, but I can identify my discomfort with elements that allowed or even expected that religious be different from ordinary people. I am just an ordinary person. To be set apart, to be different is not comfortable to me, yet totally to commit myself to lived faith is.

Some individuals desire to espouse the basic values of a culture, creed, or ideology so totally that they are willing to give their lives to its witness. For me, this is what it means to be a member of a religious community. Since their origins in the early centuries of Christianity, religious communities have continually changed. Communities always have responded to the needs of the times, as members put their lived faith at the service of their fellow human beings. This principle is true and still at work today. Because of it, I and many other religious, are beginning anew. Finding our inner balance as ordinary people within our culture and within our church is the key to responding to the needs apparent in our times. We have to be who we are, each with her own individuality, then we can be for each other as community members. The community which is solid has something to say to the Church, but it is said without words.

For me the challenge is to continue to live an authentic religious life even though some of the look that characterized my conservative former community is changed. When my leave of absence or exclaustration became effective, I was faced with decisions. What is that basic kernel that needs to be preserved? What do I hold fast and what do I discard? People who lead authentic, healthy, and satisfying lives are honest with themselves about who they are and realistic about finding their places in society. So the basic kernel is self.

We start with ourselves. The first value that I uphold is a belief in the goodness and the importance of the individual, and the necessity that each develop God-given gifts for the good of self and others, always acknowledging the Creator's wisdom. Following upon this value I espouse the goodness of a community of persons of faith whose sense of self-worth reaches out beyond the group itself to touch the needs of the greater human family.

Years ago I chose to become a Franciscan sister. Living as a member of a Franciscan religious community had been a source of happiness for me because it gave me companions whose values matched my own. We shared a common vision and a spiritual language with which to shape our dreams of knowing the Lord and sharing this knowledge with others. I found that it was a good life for me, learning and growing in my personal knowledge and love of the Lord, in ministry, and communal living.

The three vows that I professed — poverty, chastity, obedience — came to shape my life and give it meaning. Lived within the context of the community, these vows, in particular the vow of celibacy, made a space within myself that could only be filled by a loving, deeply personal relationship with the Lord of life. This love grounded me and gave great purpose to my commitment. Continuing this relationship is essential to me.

I also came to believe that religious communities are of and for the larger community of humankind, and only make sense when members reach out beyond themselves. They continually discover how to live the Christian life so as to give others hope, joy, and courage in their faith journeys.

In order to do this, religious have to be very much in tune with the problems and values contemporary culture presents. Being in tune with societal values implies that religious people can see when those values erode the dignity of humankind and need to be challenged.

Through the years I began to see the difficulty that my particular community had in getting in touch with the persons that we served. I felt that we were becoming a closed society, molding on to a traditional style of living that impeded the growth of both the individual and group. Members were not encouraged to explore their talents, nor were they expected to voice opinions or interests that were not sanctioned by the group. We were different from the other ordinary people around us and fast becoming an anomaly.

This is proving to be an exciting and grace-filled time for me. Along with independence, the uncertainty is as exhilarating as it is challenging. There are unknowns to face, such as health and retirement costs. Perhaps I am just another foolish middle-ager going off on a quixotic adventure that will lead to destitution. I had visions of myself dying in the county home. But then I thought that if I do, as many of God's poor have, it is all part of the vow of poverty I have professed. Haven't I promised to rely upon the goodness of the Almighty so that I might be free to offer hope to those who do not have it? I certainly can't say that I wish to be one with humankind and then balk at the reality of it.

We had to face other considerations. Is our vision unique? Should we consider building our own religious community and encourage new membership, or should we seek affiliation with an existing group? We asked these questions and decided that before we could claim this of ourselves we needed to investigate other communities in order to evaluate them in the light of our evolving understanding.

We have begun visiting with other groups of sisters. Some groups have made many ministerial and lifestyle adjustments, but we did not see what we believed to be the radical shift needed. In our view, these women still maintain the old veneer. As corporate entities they are not taking risks and, in our opinion, they are not uncomfortable enough to search for new realities.

We are continuing our candid search and are opening ourselves to the possibility that an existing group holds some of our values and would willingly assimilate our vision into theirs.

I feel that a religious community is not to be characterized as a group of professional women whose lifestyles reflect the values of middle

America, but rather women whose prayer and community living are strong witnesses to faith and to the dignity of all. I believe that these two elements are the very basic foundation of religious life; it is there that we can find our true identity.

The Franciscan tradition answers this for me. As a Franciscan my interest is in being a loving person of prayer who is accepting of others. What I do does not matter as much as who I am, which leads me to affirm the dignity of all . My presence more than my action is important in the lives of others. A community of Franciscans has much to say to those among whom they live, first by being a community and affirming each other, and then by helping others to find their own power.

The task is not simple nor is it ever completed. Searching for the kernel of truth within time-honored structures takes energy and implies risk that many cannot or will not undertake. To truthfully explore the purpose of this lifestyle I must be willing to question it in its entirety, accepting that this is an ongoing undertaking. Since religious life is an expression of lived faith, the lifestyle should always evolve reflecting the faith of members and non-members alike. There is collaboration and mutuality operating here. This is what it means to be a church.

For me, the profession of the vows of poverty, chastity, and obedience has been a source of purpose and a sign of my dedication. This public commitment has been a joy and is important to defining my personal and corporate identity. But, I see the need to come to terms with these vows and to ask a painful question: Can I still be a religious without the public expression of these vows? Is public profession necessary in order to live in loving relationship with God and humankind?

In other words, can I still live a religious commitment without professing these vows?

If I come to the conclusion that my vision of religious life differs from any group that I have met and I choose to remain alone, then I will need to seek a dispensation from vows because they tie me to my former community. While it is possible to profess private vows that are not relative to a community, I am not satisfied that the answer is here. This is a hard question to ask and a painful one to answer, but it must be faced.

Obviously there are many people in society for whom faith is a driving force. These people live in a loving relationship with God and everyone knows it. How are vowed religious different from them and yet the same? How essential is a corporate witness in addition to a personal one? I don't have answers to these questions, but continue to explore them.

At this time we are solidifying our values and gaining an identity from the people to whom we minister. By their affirmation and acceptance of us they are shaping us and letting us know what kind of ministers they seek. Because of these good people, I see myself becoming more attentive to listening for and recognizing goodness in the people and events of everyday life. I have learned to encourage and affirm them in their struggles. If I am effective at all, it is because I am someone who can be counted upon. They are calling me to provide stability and faithfulness while being a person who is vulnerable and in need of the support they can provide.

We see that our value to them comes from our community sharing, as well as from our individuality and gifts. These people are defining and affirming us beyond what we would have expected. We are coming to see that it is who you are and how authentically you proclaim that truth that reveals faith. Accepting others and reaching out to them speaks volumes.

This post-modern period is a challenging time in which to live. Structures that seemed so solid and unchangeable are crumbling, leaving people searching for meaning in their lives. They find that the old answers don't fit the new questions. Do standards change? Have human needs changed? While people desire stability and comfort, many are finding former institutions, such as the family, shaky at best, disintegrated at worst. Rapid scientific and technological changes are resulting in confusion and dehumanization. The desire for a faith that provides answers to life's mysteries is as strong as ever, yet people are skeptical and unsure about its form.

The Church, perceived as unchanging, offers more questions than answers; it, too, is in a state of flux. Because the Church as an institution is made up of people who are experiencing uncertainties, its leadership and members struggle to balance faith with the life-and-death realities of our era.

In my own small way, I desire a religious community life lived in a simple, prayerful style that can be an anchor for its members, as well as for fellow searchers on this journey.

Because I believe so strongly in this principle, I have seen that developing new or renewed religious lifestyles cannot be the task of one person or small group, but requires many working within and without religious communities. Thus the human community becomes the agent that shapes and defines the religious of tomorrow because it calls for people whose fidelity gives them hope.

When property, institutions, and corporations provide religious with elitist standing, we believe that communities should divest themselves of them. Religious will then have the freedom to be downwardly mobile, losing control, but gaining a moral and spiritual power that is surely perceived and welcomed by those who need to know the consuming goodness of an all-loving Being.

This story is not ended. I am still engaged in the search, aided by many whose presence gives me courage to continue. In every age people are called upon to be the face of God to each other. It is in human relationships lived in honesty, giftedness and equality that we are most human and thus able to share the Divine.

Kristin Neufeld
Former Sister of St. Joseph

Married

Children: Adopted, international and racially mixed: Terumi, Sayumi, Wayne

Retired liturgy/music coordinator

Private piano instructor, ESL tutor, organist

Bachelor of Arts, Music, College of St. Catherine, St. Paul

Master of Arts, Speech and Drama, University of Notre Dame

Special Training: Graduate, Franciscan Institute of Japanese Studies, Tokyo, Japan

English as a Second Language, Japanese

Board of Directors, Manna House shelter for women and children

Weekend organist, accompanist for parish adult choir

Kristin's interest are varied, and include music, travel, crafts and teaching, but "above all, camping." She recently spent three weeks in a pop-up camper exploring Newfoundland. At present she is one of a small group of women who ritualize together, and would love to be part of forming a base community. Kristin would like to travel to places which pique her interest and has a dream "to teach in a Third World country, helping women realize their potential."

Kristin Neufeld

They Simply Got Better

The question "Whatever happened to the Good Sisters?" is a little like the question "Whatever happened to the little screens and huge cabinets of early TV?" My answer to both of these would be, "They simply got better!"

I suspect that this question is asked, not out of genuine curiosity, but with an agenda hovering beneath the surface. The good-sisters-advocates are often nostalgic about a church of the past, and they are remembering 1) women who could be expected to do any task asked of them, 2) women easily identified by their distinctive clothing, 3) women who often demeaned themselves and who made as few confrontative waves as possible, and 4) women who worked tirelessly, for no pay.

Now, what is so bad about that? A lot. As a former religious woman I would compare the person who, in the 1980's and 1990's is looking for this kind of religious, to the frustrated parent of a rebellious teenager. "Why can't I just be a parent to a nice, docile kid instead of the real thing: one who defies, who questions, who fights for independence, and who wants to become an adult?"

I remember vividly my first day of religious life. I was a little late arriving at the novitiate, having been a bridesmaid that morning at a brother's wedding. My parents brought me to the gates of the motherhouse, flushed from the excitement of the wedding reception and nervous at what I was about to do.

Years later, as they reminisced about that day, they still remembered their heavy hearts as they drove back to the reception. For, having seen me whisked off to the dormitories to be clothed in the postulant's uniform, they sat all alone in the convent parlor, awaiting my return. Although they were thrilled at the prospect of a religious vocation in the

299

family, it was a bit of a shock, not only to see me totally changed from bright colors to solid black, but more so, to be allotted about four seconds to say good-bye and to wish me good luck — because I was due in chapel for afternoon prayers. It is hardly surprising they felt as though they had abandoned me to a new life which was certainly a tightly-structured one, albeit of questionable warmth.

That postulant's outfit changed, six months later, to full religious habit. Along with fifty-four other young women in my group, I wore it proudly and lovingly; we thought it was the best-looking habit in all of Catholic sisterdom. Now, when I look through old pictures, I am amused at the unnatural shape of our heads and the grotesque look of those stiff white bibs. As a young religious, however, I thought our habit was beautiful.

Somewhere in the mid-50's, the technology of the textile industry brought to convent life a wonderful new fabric, polyester. What a boon to personal hygiene when we could wash our habits (even though only every month or so) instead of de-spotting them, or airing them, or, in Minnesota's generous winters, taking them out and rubbing the heavy wool in a pile of snow, presumably eradicating spots, stains, odors, and wrinkles.

The old snapshots which today give me so many good laughs include some wonderful ones from visits home during the summer. They prove to what lengths one can put ingenuity to work in order to overcome the handicaps of long skirt and flowing sleeves. When playing baseball or volleyball with countless nephews and nieces I managed to alter lines and lengths, but never did I feel free to remove any part of the habit.

My mother, now in her nineties, still recalls hot summers, with ninety-plus heat, when she would urge me to get rid of at least the white plastic bib, or the thin sleeves worn under the voluminous, flowing ones. (God forbid that anyone should see arms or skin.) What was my reply to her urgings? "No, it's not necessary, Mom; I'm not even warm." I actually believed that someone would see this infraction and report on me. What is incredible is that I could ever believe anyone would think it worthy of reporting.

It took over fifteen years of wearing and tending that habit before I began to realize just what it both gave to us and took from us. What did it give? A sense of belonging to a group, not unlike the effect of wearing a baseball or football uniform. It brought a sense of security; wearing it, we could walk into any of our convents and feel welcome. It gave us the feeling of being special or different and, in a hostile milieu, of being odd.

When we walked down the street, heads turned, and although most sisters never abused this, that habit gave us seats on the bus, deference in a doctor's office, and often an unchallenged advantage in the classroom. It gave to many of us a kind of indifference to our bodies, almost as if they were non-existent. Its voluminous folds allowed us often to be careless about our posture and maintenance of a healthy weight.

It was a kind of psychological armor which erased any feelings of sexuality we might have had about ourselves; it was intended to protect us from any advances from the outside world. Ironically, it sometimes produced the opposite effect. My husband, whom I met in language school in Tokyo, once admitted that the habit was just mysterious enough to create in the viewer a tremendous curiosity about the person inside it.

As Vatican II began to alter our thinking about religious life, changes in the religious habit were made cautiously and often, ridiculously. Hemlines got higher (sometimes it took the equivalent of a plenary session to knock off two inches) until they became short enough to necessitate something a bit more fashionable than the well-known "nun shoes" and black stockings. In my community those of us in the mission field of Japan were given little encouragement to experiment in the very country where the traditional habit was inappropriate to begin with. Not only did its symbolism mean little to a non-Christian culture, but the white color of our summer habits was the Japanese color for death.

When we finally did begin making a few timid changes, the reaction from some of our native Japanese sisters was interesting. By and large, the majority of them did *not* want to change; some admitted that, in a country where conformity and anonymity are so valued, wearing the habit was the only way they could feel unique. Wearing clothes from another time and place gave them a sense of being foreign-looking, a quality relatively popular at the time.

What did the religious habit take from us? At the risk of sounding overly dramatic, I think it took away a sense of personal identity, and of pride in being a woman. For many of those whom we served, it also had the subliminal effect of their perceiving our worth by how we looked, rather than by what we accomplished.

In the course of making my decision to leave the community, I returned one summer to my small hometown to earn a little money working for a very conservative older brother. His biggest concern was that, because I was no longer wearing the habit, nobody in town would know what I stood for. It was as though people couldn't try to find that out by talking to me. I replied by quoting a statement that Bernard Cooke, then teaching at Marquette University, had made about religious habits. He felt that it made much more sense for religious and clergy to dress like everyone else so that fellow Christians would feel compelled to imitate their good works rather than say something like, "Well, acting justly and leading a good life is what they're supposed to do; it's their job."

I have concentrated on the significance of the religious habit, along with a few images of the good sisters because to me, the nostalgia about the habit symbolizes how the church used to think all the time, and still thinks much of the time. Most religious habits, when traced to their origins, were the daily garb of the women of those times. They had nothing to do with religious life or vows as such.

The fact is that some of the European communities sent young missionaries off to America, where conditions and climates and ministries should have dictated another style of dress. However, the long skirts and veils eventually came to be synonymous with religious and, to many, symbolized the unchanging rock upon which Peter built his church. It set special, religious people apart from society and reminded a Christian world of past traditions.

On how many levels are we still seeing these concepts operating in the 1990's. Many Catholics have managed to romanticize their early formative years as positive ones. They have forgotten the sense of moral guilt, the fear of a vengeful God who would cast us to the fires of hell for looking at a bad picture, or for not memorizing the answers to our Baltimore catechism. The nostalgics would love to return to a time when "Father said so," and when they felt exempted from making any moral decisions.

Some leaders in the church are still fighting change. For example, for centuries the Eucharist, in its fullest meaning, has been considered the

302

cornerstone of Catholic Christian worship. Yet these leaders ask, "What does it matter that worshiping communities of God's people are without ordained clergy? Let them struggle on, with pre-consecrated bread and some prayers, and the distorted belief that Eucharist means physical bread rather than the communal blessing and sharing of that bread. Don't trust those people of God to choose, from among themselves, a leader to help them celebrate Eucharist. Above all, don't let a woman be the voice of the Spirit."

Let us return to my answer to the original question: "Those good sisters got better." What happened to give religious women the courage to break from traditional convent life to live among the poor, or with those to whom they minister, or in more intimate, meaningful settings with a few of their sisters? What happened to give them the voices to say they will no longer staff schools that cater to the affluent, or to grin-and-bear-it, frustrated in a classroom when their individual, personal talents lead them to work other than teaching?

What happened to give them the courage to grow beyond being taken care of by the community and to go out to interview for jobs, like other people; to work for salaries, sharing their earnings with their retired sisters whose ministry is now one of prayer? What happened to free them to respond to people's needs when and where those needs arise, even if doing so interferes with a scheduled prayer time? What happened to give them a sense of being women—of their importance in society, their compassion, their ability to be healers, their sexuality?

I suspect that a very small number of creative, indignant, courageous women religious have slowly, slowly, made all these things happen. They are women whose names may never be remembered, or even known. Just as well, for theirs would be added to the lists of leaders in the Church who need to be watched, controlled, and silenced.

Today, twenty years after leaving religious life, I am proud of and love what I still refer to as *my* community. I am proud of those steadfast women who entered that community with me on a hot September afternoon, and, led by the Spirit, continue to live out their vocations to the religious life. *Note:* I do not say their "religious vocations" because that is the task of all of us. I am convinced that those women are today touching lives in countless ways that were just not possible in the good old days of the good sisters.

5

SEXT

May the Lord bless
Thee out of Sion;
And mayest thou see
The good things of Jerusalem
All the days of thy life.
And I took root
In an honorable people,
And in the portion
Of my God
Is my inheritance,
And my abode is in the
Full assembly of saints

Mary Josetta Prondzinski
Franciscan

Art Therapist, United Stand Family Counseling Center

Bachelor of Science in Education, DePaul University, Chicago

Master of Education, University of Minnesota

Art Therapy Program, Oasis Center, Chicago

Non-degree studies, The Art Institute of Chicago

Architectural Drafting, Chicago State University Job-related ministries

Sister Josetta's hopes for the future are related to her present job and ministry: she would like to become more proficient in the creative process of image and symbol as therapeutic value for non-verbal communication and to become a specialist in sand-play therapy. These will be coupled with her desire to become a specialist in drug/alcohol prevention. In the present she lives in a mixed-congregation community house and stays in contact with her community with membership in that community's Wholeness in Living Committee, by acting as a summer art instructor at a community college and by being the community artist. Her interests range from art to music, playing the guitar, playing cards, travel and camping and gardening.

Mary Josetta Prondzinski

The Gentling of Time: My Story

My grandfather was an alcoholic. My uncles were alcoholics. Alcoholism is the disease of my family of origin. My father was an alcoholic. I grew up keeping it a secret. I wasn't allowed to sit in my father's lap as a child. He kept me at a distance. I was afraid of my father, never sure of what to expect of him. Anxious and fearing my father's behavior, I wouldn't bring my friends home. I was ashamed and confused. My friends' families weren't like mine. I felt I was different. Terror gripped me when he came home drunk at night to awake me from sleep in rageful accusations and threats. Nothing I did made my father proud of me. He made promises he wouldn't keep. I made my first Holy Communion and Dad was not there. The pain of that abandonment was just the beginning. He didn't know how to love me. He abused my mother until she would have it no more and divorced him. She kept alive the growing shame within me with reports of Dad's disgusting behavior.

I was to have no male role model. Because of my Catholic school upbringing, I was devastated by the divorce. The Church of the Forties didn't recognize divorce. I struggled with the Church's rejection of my mother from the Sacraments. How was I to reconcile this action with what I was taught? I was so preoccupied with this secret and my feelings that I couldn't study and lost interest in achievement in school. Failing grades appeared on my fifth grade report card and I was not promoted to sixth grade. I felt I was a failure and I had a report card to prove it. My behavior changed. I defied Mom's admonitions and constantly brought neighborhood kids in the house when Mom was at work. Because I continued in my rowdiness and did not heed the landlord's warnings and complaints, we were asked to move. Luckily,

I didn't have to repeat the fifth grade in the same school with the same teacher.

An only child, I was left with Grandma or the neighbors while Mom worked each day. I was a latch-key kid, coming home to an empty house. Mom and I were frequent movers. When we couldn't make the rent payment in one place, we moved to another. I hated being an only child, pulled from one school to another, unable to make friends because I would be moving again. I became quite adept at playing alone, lost in a fantasy world and at home with my imagination.

My mother kept company with men who sexually abused me and probably my mother as well. More secrets to keep. I was a freshman in high school when my mother married again. I had to adjust to a man receiving my mother's affection when I wanted her all to myself. Suddenly my world turned upside down again as I struggled with this intrusion in my life. Wasn't it enough that my body had been violated? This was a violation of another part of me.

It was long before I accepted this man. He did not abuse me. He was patient with me. He wanted to be, for me, the father I didn't have. I was rebellious toward him, feeling misunderstood, confused and angry. I manifested behaviors that puzzled everyone around me.

As a teenager walking home from roller skating late in the evening I was molested and abused in a neighbor's yard. I was saved from rape when the neighbors returned home unexpectedly. One thing I learned from my abuse experiences is how to be abused and to endure it. My dating experiences as a teen testify to that. My dates were allowed too many liberties. Instead of learning to protect myself, I learned I couldn't protect myself and was convinced that I was worthless and deserved the abuse anyway.

It was at this time that I turned to the sisters in school for comfort and support. It was in the sixth grade that I first thought of being a sister but I kept it quiet since it didn't match my rowdy image. It was my admiration for the sisters and the mystery that surrounded them that first set me thinking that I wanted to be just like them. The mystery left me when I came to know their humanness in my eighth grade teacher. The admiration stayed because of her kindness, love and concern. She was my first mentor, model, guide and confidant. I loved her. I felt her love for me.

During my high school years the sisters were an integral part of my life. Because I was very impressionable, stories of the saints, especially St. Maria Goretti, sparked heroic ambition in my young heart. I questioned how I could be like her when I was already too "impure" to brave what she did. When Sister would make the sign of the cross on my forehead, I would think I was in heaven and that everything would be fine. My cousin entered a religious congregation, paving the way for me. We corresponded. I visited her and finally entered the same congregation. To everybody's surprise, I did not enter the same order of sisters that taught me.

Having been raised in a dysfunctional, codependent environment, I was attracted to a helping profession. Entering religious life satisfied my need to be looked up to. As an only and predominantly lost child, I found in the religious community an environment where I could get lost in the crowd. Here was a place I could hide the past and continue keeping the family secrets. I chose religious community to punish my mother for abandoning me emotionally. I thought community would be the solution to my aloneness, and that no one would leave me anymore as my father did. On the other hand, I wanted Mom to be proud of me. I wanted to please her, to be somebody and be successful. I could hide behind the habit as someone good and acceptable.

Early religious formation reinforced the need to keep the secrets through the rules of silence. Having grown up with unreliable adults and broken promises, I learned not to trust. I found the same patterns among those I came to live with in novitiate and continued not to trust. I had no role models for intimacy in my own family, nor in this new family I came to embrace. All my energy was focused on trying to fix my mother and father. I would save their souls in order to save my soul. I was determined. If they couldn't, I would. You can be sure I was doing the same for my new religious family.

The patterns of distrust continued as the rules discouraged personal attachments and close relationships. I saw celibacy as a flight from intimacy which further reinforced emptiness, isolation, loneliness and depression. In order to be accepted and approved of by authority figures, I pleased them at any cost, and lost myself in the process. My early training taught me that loss of self was something good and was to be commended. Low self-esteem was encouraged. Feelings were to be ignored and subdued. Submissive obedience was the norm. Constant permissions kept me in submission and dependent in the name of obedience. Quotes from community Constitutions, the Rule and Canon Law were used to manipulate my behavior. Any infraction of policy resulted in consequences and punishment in the name of humility. Today this is a *victim* role; at that time it was a *noble* role.

I was comfortable in it. It was familiar. I entrenched myself in guilt and low self-esteem. I convinced myself that my self-worth is from what I do rather than from who I am. Though praised for work performance and encouraged to deny feelings, I felt rejected and grew to distrust authority. I became confused about loyalty, my human condition and sense of self. I worked hard to be perfect. I looked at accomplishments and workaholism as virtuous. I had been super-responsible at home; now I fit community life since responsibility was expected, admired and familiar to me.

Canonical novitiate rules wouldn't allow novices to receive mail. The night before first profession of vows, we were to receive a letter of blessing from our parents. I was not given my letter; I was punished for failure to be on time for some function earlier in the day. I don't remember the circumstances of the tardiness, but I do remember the pain of deprivation and the anger I felt. Truly my childhood prepared me for such moments. Wasn't I the best candidate for a life of self-denial?

My perception of religious community has changed since those early days. Being Franciscan embodies ideals, values, and traditions that hold tremendous challenge and opportunity for union with God. In my confusion about intimacy, I turned to intimacy with God. It didn't seem to be the same for me as for the saints I read about, yet I had my grace-filled moments.

Our provincial house has daily exposition of the Blessed Sacrament. I was drawn there for quiet, prayerful adoration. I drew strength from God's presence and I experienced inner peace and the serenity in the conviction that I was called to this life and really didn't choose it on my own. I had the sense of being in the right place; God would see me through. Sister companions brought and bring me friendship, joy and laughter. From them I have learned to value my own person, my gifts, talents and even my weaknesses.

312

I was prepared for the teaching profession. My first assignment for this career was the fourth grade. This has always been my favorite grade level, even to this day. I never gave much thought to being a teacher or what I would do as a sister. I just wanted to be a sister. Back in the 50's facing sixty-five lively youngsters for the first time was a lot easier then than it is now. I felt needed and important to those kids. I was listened to; I was in control. They didn't question and neither did I. I prepared that first class for their First Holy Communion, taught them all the subject matter and was still taking college classes. I don't know how I did it.

My teaching experience has included elementary schools in Illinois, Minnesota, Wisconsin and Alabama. Numerous roles and experiences abounded: school librarian, director of school plays, children's liturgies, art instructor, art fairs, science fairs, conventions, Teens Encounter Christ, Cursillo, Youth Conferences, Sisters' Encounter, Charismatic Conferences, lector and parish Eucharistic Minister. I have taught all grade levels and CCD. During my last year in elementary education I taught religion in the morning to grades five through eight. In the afternoon I taught art to all grades, two classes each day, kindergarten through eighth grade.

I did not want to leave elementary education so I met my assignment to high school education with much resistance. I was at the peak of my career, successful, well-liked, promising, fulfilled, ambitious, and untiring. My superiors told me not to worry for I would do well. I embarked upon this new venture with uncertainty and fear. I did not like the discomfort of leaving behind a small-town country environment for a big city. I had to leave friends and projects just beginning.

Shortly before this I had major surgery and needed more time to recuperate. I didn't know it at the time, but I was experiencing several losses. I was grieving, struggling to hold on. The uprooting, the adjusting, the pain of letting go finally took its toll, emotionally, physically and spiritually. I had repeated illnesses, relationships weren't going right, my spirit was drained and I distanced myself from God. I found it increasingly difficult to live with myself and the uneasiness that things were not going right. I was no longer comfortable being controlled, having decisions made for me. Simple setbacks and inconviences became major problems; I would either become extremely withdrawn or I would fall apart, out of control.

Since I had lost significant relationships and was experiencing serious illness and long term depression, a friend suggested I see a therapist. I was ready to admit I couldn't manage my life without help. Slowly I realized it is healthy to express my feelings. I had become so numbed-out that I didn't know what I was feeling. Through reading, retreats and workshops, I became aware of a more wholistic acceptance of self. I learned I have characteristics of codependent behavior, and realized I grew up in a dysfunctional family. I was beginning to understand that I'm the only one who can change my situation. I could make choices. I began to look at what my options were. I told myself there are no right or wrong choices, right or wrong feelings. Feelings just are, and choices are always the right choices because they are me. If what I choose puts me flat on my face, then I've learned something more about myself and I move on.

I became aware of my tendency to take charge of matters that would be better left to God. I learned what the Twelve Steps of Alcoholics Anonymous were and how to apply them to my life. I began a spiritual search of my past and present attitudes, actions, and reactions. I had to understand and be honest about my behavior patterns and motives.

I sought help outside my religious community because I hadn't yet come to trust that I would find the support and understanding I needed within it. When a congregation has little knowledge of terms and issues of dysfunction, of being shame-based, or being addicted, then the recovering sister must turn to those outside the congregation for maintaining healthy behavior. I do not want to imply that healthy living is not possible in a religious community. It was my not knowing how to live it in a healthy manner that presented problems for me.

The rewards of community living are manifested in the bonding of spiritual companionship, praying together, coming together to share Eucharist, community ceremonies and celebrations. I am content to live a simple life as I struggle to harmonize a deep prayer life with dedicated service. I know joy-filled moments of sharing fun times with my sisters. The swimming, the card-playing, bike riding, going to movies, throwing a party for a names' day or birthday, talent shows, jubilees, picnics, going for walks, traveling and vacationing together will ever hold significant memories for me. I know more serious times of working on projects together, cooking a meal for the household, challenging one another in our professional work, days of reflection and study, weekend retreats, dialoging in collaborative discernment, visiting sick sisters and sitting at the bedside of a dying sister.

I began a regular program of recovery with counseling at the Adult Children Center in Lombard, Illinois. To strengthen my counseling experience, I attend weekly meetings of the ACOA self-help support group for sisters, an Incest Survivors support group for sisters, and monthly meetings at ICAP, the Intercongregational Alcoholism Program in Chicago. In addition to these, my annual retreat is with sisters who are in a Twelve Step Program and come together for Twelve Step Spirituality. As life goes on I find myself delivered into situations I do not choose, discover attitudes in myself of which I have been unaware, and have been asked to abide by decisions I only later discover I myself had made. Sometimes I refuse to accept what happens to me; other times I surrender with grace.

In some instances sisters are taken out of treatment and programs of therapy too soon because of cost or because they are not serving a community need while in therapy. Members who do not understand look at these sisters as lazy or selfish. Some recovering sisters are regarded as becoming worse, troublesome, assertive, different, non-conformists or disobedient; this threatens control. Recovering sisters may even be shamed and abandoned by other sisters. My experience has been the latter.

Attitudes are changing in regard to sisters needing therapy. We are beginning to understand our families of origin and our individual role in the revitalization of religious life. As community we are beginning to look at our wounds, to face our denial that anything could be wrong with us, to own our anger, and to claim the fear that paralyzes us from taking risks that move us into growth. We are responding to God's will that we choose life, lest we die. I join with my community in looking to the future with hope.

By learning to accept myself exactly as I am, without hiding, disguising, distorting or rejecting any part of mystlf, I embrace the poor part of me. This is when I begin to use the gift of forgiveness. Any harm that has come to me because of my family or religious community, I forgive freely and completely. The sooner I can do this, the sooner will I be relieved of the grudges and resentments which continually gnaw away at me and block my spiritual growth. I do this by recognizing my personal poverty and at the same time acknowledging my inner spiritual richness received as a result of struggling through the past traumas. I heal when I release my family and community, turning them over to God to care for them and to see that only good comes to them. I then no longer need them to be different from what they already are. Having freely forgiven others for wrongs done or imagined toward me, I can and must come to forgive myself for all past wrongs I have done to others and to myself. The pain I have experienced must be turned around to help others in their personal pain.

I will work with others who need and ask for my help, because only by trying to help them, can I help myself. Only by freely giving away what I discover and receive can I keep it and use it in my life. I sometimes deny what I don't want to own, so I need to be honest with myself on a daily, instantaneous basis. In addressing my needs, in accepting recovery and allowing healing to enrich my life, I continue to explore my issues in hope of carrying the message to those who have experienced similar difficulties and may not know where to turn for help or know that they need help. Then I will know peace and acknowledge that God is doing for me what I could not do for myself.

After thirty-four years of teaching, I decided it was time to pursue a new career. I was no longer using my creative energies productively. I was completing twelve years as a high school art instructor and I needed a change, a new challenge. I also needed opportunity to express my own art work more fully as artist. When I express my own messages through art, I heal and nurture myself. My interest in art therapy came about through reading and the opening of our community-owned family counseling center which had a need for an art therapist on the staff. I am attracted to integrating the art process with the therapy process. I want to use my background experience, giftedness and teaching skills in a theraputic setting.

In searching for a school or program in which to study art therapy, I found Oasis Center in Chicago. The Center offers ATIRA: Expressive Arts Program. When I read the description of the program, I said, "This is for me!" I immediately applied. After two years in the program, and going for a third, I have found the program to be both an experiential and didactic learning model in therapy training. The program provides me an environment of support, encouragement, and discipline, for personal, professional and spiritual development. ATIRA offers a place for continued practice of personal competence with the satisfaction of immersion in art making. It is here I learned the Plains Indians lore, Atira goddess, from whom all life has emerged and to whom all life will return. It speaks of the new life emerging within me and I responded with my poem, The Dawning of Atira, dedicated to Evadne McNeil, director of ATIRA program, and my co-learners at Oasis.

At present I am an art therapist intern serving our client population at United Stand Family Center in Chicago. I use my skills to aide and assist in the assessment and treatment of children, adolescents and adults who are troubled and behavior-disordered by planning activities for creative expression of their needs in a non-threatening environment. When I complete my internship, I will apply for credentials as a Certified Expressive Therapist. The days ahead hold vision and venture for me, filled with dreams and daring, always new, always refreshing.

The Dawning of Atira

The bright dawn of Atira awakened a yearning for the creative to be satisfied.

Waiting
Inviting
Anticipating
Beginning anew
Surfacing potential
Dispelling uncertainty
Hungering for release
Flowering promises
Visioning hope
Dreaming dreams
Choosing serenity

Between the Exhilaration of beginning and the satisfaction of concluding is the wonder of Atira.

Reaching
Touching
Venturing
Marveling
Experimenting
Brightening the path
Opening
Widening
Challenging "to be"
Strengthening
Expanding wild energy
Delight in the birthing

Gentle flow the answers from deep within intimate rhythm is the vision of Atira.

A poetic searching
Affirming the divine
Freeing
Discovering
Integrating
Transforming
Eventual fulfillment
Truth
Light

Anne
Former Franciscan

Widowed, four children

Elementary school teacher

Bachelor of Science, small Catholic college

Master of Science

SUNY ESL student at the University of California

Anne is a Charismatic Catholic; this is a very important part of her life. At present she is "just now learning to start over again after the tragic and sudden death of my husband." She is vitally concerned with raising her children to be happy, well-adjusted Christians and in furthering her professional possibilities. She likes to dance and entertain and is making new friends, having left others behind in her cross-country move. She tries not to project too much, letting "God direct my life."

Anne

Why Would Anyone?

A few years ago my friend Marilyn and I were planning to return to the motherhouse in the mountains of New York to join our ten bandmates in celebrating their Silver Jubilee. A tragedy interrupted our trip, but we are still planning to revisit the site where forty-eight of us entered the convent one September Sunday more than thirty years before. Although it has been more than twenty years since I sought dispensation from my vows and reentered the world, I cherish many of the relationships from that period of my life. I exchange Christmas cards with a few sisters, and Marilyn and I have remained friends. In fact, ours is the friendship of longest duration in my life.

Recently a colleague in Southern California, who stumbled upon the information I neither flaunt nor conceal, that I am an ex-nun, asked a question I had not considered in years. Why did I, why would anyone, enter the convent? I decided to consider the question once again, to see if the intervening years would add clarification and fresh insight.

As I see it, many of those scores of young Catholic women who entered religious life a few decades ago did so for one or both of the same reasons that seemed to motivate me. The more lofty one, the conscious one, was simply that there did not appear to be any other avenue of service or path to personal holiness in the Catholic church of that period. The Vatican Council had not even been heard of when I traded my last pack of cigarettes for a postulant's veil.

I did want to love the Lord with my whole heart and mind and strength, and my neighbor as myself. No psychoanalytic conjecture from critics inside or outside the Church changes that fact. In the years following my departure it became popular to speculate about what propelled us to select such a restrictive and mysterious lifestyle, and to impute motives that were groundless, sweeping and often scurrilous. I wanted more than what I saw as typical in a Christian family life.

To these motives one could probably add others, deeper and more controversial. It is true some aspirants were introverted, sexually repressed, chronically immature, psychologically impaired and socially maladjusted. In my judgment most who entered were not. Most were moved by a combination of the two motives I still see as determiners in my decision: I wanted more than what I thought was typical in Catholic family life; I wanted to make a difference and I wanted a personal God.

But is that what happened? Was there someone in charge of forming all those young women with high ideals, albeit less than perfect motivations and resources? Not as I recall.

This is not an opinion I form in retrospect, for I remember knowing from the start that the means employed were not going to lead to the end I had envisioned. Those endless picayune details about where to put one's hands while walking down the shiny corridors, to say nothing of how rapidly one might walk without compromising religious decorum, how one might muffle the sound of the large rosary beads hanging from the waist if they perchance rattled against one's side, how carefully one had to avoid looking at another sister passing just inches away without violating custody of the eyes. On and on the monotonous litany read.

What could these incidentals have to do with forming a contemplative prayer life? In what unexplained way would they fortify me to bring the message of Jesus' love and acceptance to the crippled family and society from which I was inadvertently fleeing? I was prone to ponder such matters from the beginning, though most seemed to accept them without much question. Why did we always have to walk in threes on our daily outing during those early years, when I'd have something to talk to Marilyn about, something I did not want to share with another? We were told it was to discourage particular friendships, a cloaked phrase for lesbianism. But a lesbian is a lesbian whether she walks in groups of two or three. And, incidentally, the number of them I met throughout the years was minuscule. So why have an all-encompassing rule to cover a minute fraction of cases?

Religious communities of women specialized in those rules when I was a member. They thwarted the imagination, weakened the resolve and crushed the spirit of many. To this day, I am in a state of mute rebellion against minutia. I seem compelled to disobey little rules. If it isn't purposeful, don't do it, I silently exhort. If the sheets aren't dirty, don't wash them just because it's laundry day. I wonder if I am ever going to stop reacting to the infinite number of rubrics and customs, rules and regulations which, in my formation days, seemed to vie with the Sacred Scriptures for significance. I have a residual disdain for the externals of religion in particular, for fear they will obscure the reality of the message.

If I saw this dichotomy between the reality and the dream from the beginning, one might wonder why I stayed for nine years. I thought the situation would improve once the training years ended. I hoped that once I got out into the local communities, I'd get to the heart of the matter. Maybe there was some significance to these formalities, and I'd piece it all together out on mission. I wasn't ready to give up!

I received my first assignment in a sealed envelope while seated in chapel at the motherhouse among dozens of other apprehensive nuns. At that time there was no choice as to type of work, geographic location, or any other specifics defining our future. The annual reassignment day was a cause for dread among many. If you didn't get a letter, you stayed where you were: if you got a letter, you filled the post it designated. It was that cut-and-dried and arbitrary.

Generally whether an individual convent was considered a good place to live depended on who the local superior was. It was, after all, a totalitarian system in every way. Next in importance were the other sisters you lived with in the local setting, for these women formed your family for that year. After these concerns came the actual work to which you were assigned. Important as this was, it was secondary in much the same way a married woman's happiness and peace of mind are primarily determined by her home and family life and only secondarily by her job.

My first assignment was to a house of about twenty sisters who staffed an elementary school and a high school. Many were as young as I was and proved to be good company. My superior was a lovely, supportive, level-headed, capable woman who made life pleasant for those in her charge. Nevertheless, in that pre-Vatican setting where the full traditional garb was worn at all times, where all contact with the laity was shunned, where daily life was regimented and individuality frowned upon, we basically lived more like young children than like educated, responsible, dedicated adults. No one seemed to question this arrangement.

My next assignment came a year later in a vastly different setting. I was sent to a large boarding school for girls in the West Indies. Within the community at large it was well known that once a sister became acclimated to the climate and culture, she would be left there for years, decades. There were very few young nuns; they were only needed when someone retired or died. I found the atmosphere oppressive, the workday interminable. and our treatment of the boarders like something from Charles Dickens' day.

During the nightly recreation hour each of the forty sisters sat in seniority, from oldest to youngest, at a long table where we visited with those in close proximity, knitted, or played a game. We also sat in the same order of seniority for all meals, many of which werc eaten in imposed silence. One memory I can recall at will because of its poignancy involves the olympic-size swimming pool at the boarding school where I lived seven days a week. I saw it every day, I thought about it a lot, but I never got to swim in it. Once during spring break, when only a handful of boarders remained on campus, I got permission from the superior to go for a swim if I could get another nun to accompany me. I couldn't! I got a negative response from every person I asked. They were all afraid the boarders and the domestic help would see them in their bathing suits. My reaction to that fear was exactly the same then as it is now. Who would be interested in seeing me in my bathing suit? Who would care! I was twenty-four years old. That experience was only one of many similar frustrating and nonsensical limitations imposed on us.

Life seemed an endless succession of such depressing practices, none of which had any bearing on loving God or neighbor. Another related incident in this particular local community involved a severe reprimand I got for playing tennis one Saturday morning on the school's tennis courts. One of the eighteen-year-old boarders was an accomplished player and offered to show me a few strokes. The entire incident lasted fifteen minutes, but the aftermath remained in the form of dismay and growing discontent. I was chastised and humiliated for removing a small part of my habit, playing without permission and fraternizing with a student in my care. Shortly thereafter a family emergency precipitated my return to the States to be nearer my needy parents. What a welcome relief that phone call brought.

It was about 1967 when, not so figuratively speaking, all hell broke loose. I was living in a local community in Florida with eight sisters. Someone suggested as a possible outgrowth of the open window policy initiated by the recent Vatican Council, that we might begin experimenting with modification of the traditional medieval habit we wore. Someone else questioned whether we had to sit in seniority in chapel, at the table, during evening recreation and for study hour. Maybe we could even rethink recreation and come up with some "non-sitting" ways to relax and refresh ourselves. Perhaps one day of the week could remain unscheduled and each could rise when she wished, eat whatever she wished, and so forth.

Some select sisters, it was rumored, were permitted to study at secular universities. Nuns began to serve on an occasional parish committee, even though that necessitated contact with members of the laity. We were told maybe we didn't have to sit in the back seat of the car anymore when riding with our dads or other males. Perhaps there wouldn't be any scandal after all. Sometimes we might even go out and drive alone without a companion sister. And what a furor it caused when someone intimated that just because the Blessed Sacrament was present in the convent chapel, maybe the nuns didn't have to wear a silly little night cap to bed when we finally disrobed at the end of a long, demanding day. Once I had had a severe outbreak of psoriasis, and the tending dermatologist prescribed at least a couple hours of fresh air on my scalp every day. He might as well have sent me to Athens; the trip would have been more easily arranged.

Reactions to these impending changes were varied. Our loving and supportive pastor took an active interest in negotiating the transitions. He started coming to dinner once a week, something that had been unheard of before. He used to look down the long dinner table and ask individual sisters what they thought about this or that. It was a terrible shock! Some were unable to respond. They had spent years cultivating an infantile absence of thought, assuming it was related to piety. Now the pastor wanted to know what they thought. Why didn't he just ask the superior? She was sitting right next to him. Often her response was downright hostile. Why was he bothering the sisters with these questions when he could just as well ask her? This situation was a threat to all she treasured.

He publicly encouraged the sisters to become more actively involved in parish life. Although most resisted the suggestion, some few of us responded and began participating. I recall one night when I attended a parish renewal meeting conducted by the pastor himself. I was reprimanded the next day because I didn't make it back to the convent before the night silence bell rang. Actually one of those global warnings appeared on the common bulletin board, reminding all the nuns that no outside activity should ever interfere with our convent schedule. It was like being caught in the middle of two conflicting camps as the battle raged.

It seems a bit too easy to recount these incidents now without reference to the human cost, the pain and suffering factor. The sisters, many of whom had entered with high spirits, impetuous dispositions and passionate causes, had been meticulously groomed to act one way and were now being challenged to act another. For many the structure had become the substance, but who knew that until the facade began to crumble? Chaos ensued, interior as well as exterior. It seemed few could judge wisely; after all, what experience did any of us have making decisions? Once the rigid common prayer schedule was modified and individualized, many ceased to pray regularly. Once contact with the laity was tolerated, some nuns formed frivolous and even suspect relationships. One sister actually showed up at a First Communion poolside party held in a parent's home, dressed in her bathing suit. This case was extreme, but that was her interpretation of a modified habit for that occasion. Another sister in our convent, who couldn't drive, got so involved in outside affairs that she ended up with twelve weekly appointments to which she had to be driven and then picked up. It was a dreadful burden on those of us who drove, but the superior lacked the prudence to curtail these activities. She had become unsure of her boundaries in the changing structure as well, and was now loath to impose any restrictions.

During those transitional years, I lacked the foundation of a genuine spiritual life. I was no more aware of my dignity and worth in God's eyes than I had been before entering the convent. As I was unaware of his personal and sustaining love for me, I turned to a life of good works. After teaching school all day I now had the freedom to make home visits, counsel troubled teenagers, serve on parish committees, visit prisons and hospitals and attend graduate night classes. I engaged in perpetual social projects to give meaning and value to my existence. I am in no way suggesting that a Christian should do less than care for his brother, but only that the solicitude be a reflection of God's love rather than the caregiver's need.

Finally the hectic pace over an extended period aversely affected my health. It was at this time, the decade of the 60's, when in the country itself the institutions and conventions became subject to scrutiny and reformation. There was turmoil, not only within the confines of the convent, but also out in the streets. Couple this extrinsic disorder with the fragility of my personal state: the byproducts were stress, grief, and extreme anxiety.

I began taking tranquilizers, some under prescription, some available without prescription in the large sample boxes the hospital sisters used to share with us. I was coming to the painful conclusion that I would have to leave the community, and the wrenching experience was not dissimilar to that of a woman contemplating a divorce after many years of marriage. I had to go; the environment had become destructive for me, and this insight caused me anguish. I am sure a similar pattern manifested itself even in the lives of so many of the nuns who left during the post-Vatican days. There was little stigma associated with such departures, even after the taking of perpetual vows.

Mentioning the taking of perpetual vows offers me one final opportunity to underscore the tenacious adherence to arbitrary regulations taken by the community's hierarchy. In the midst of all this turmoil came the day I was to cease renewing my annual vows and make my perpetual commitment. But how could I conform to such an absolute that did not take into account my current dilemma? My life had become an open wound, the pain of which I can still feel twenty-five years later. Whenever I tried to weigh the pros and cons of leaving or staying, I developed such a severe headache that I had to suspend the thought process. I recall speaking to Marilyn about it as we arrived at the motherhouse from our respective posts around the country, with just days left before the final profession ceremony. At her urging I summoned the courage to request an appointment with the mother general to seek a year's extension. She was a tall, gaunt woman who looked like Abe Lincoln. Upon hearing the account of my predicament, her maternal advice was to make up my mind because she was not inclined to assemble a last minute meeting of the general council whose approval would be necessary to grant my extension. Eight years had been long enough, she reminded me sternly, and I should either decide to go or decide to stay for good. Since I was incapable of doing either, I made my final vows and left the following year. It was the summer of 1969, and I departed a pretty broken young woman. My nerves were frayed, my dreams dead, and my general health precarious.

Among my ex-nun friends, including Marilyn, there seems to be some concensus as to one source of the pain of leaving the convent. It centers around the quality of friendship and love among the members of the community. Marilyn recently told me that she has never replaced those friendships with any of comparable depth and value. We were, after all, each other's parents, spouses, children and extended family. In addition to that loss there was the fear of the unknown, the perception of personal failure, the absence of material security, a social awkwardness and an ignorance of basic survival techniques. On the positive side in my case, the community had paid for my education; on the negative side, I was handed fifty dollars severance pay after nine years of membership.

I did eventually find all that I had been looking for. A year after leaving the convent I met a man named Mike at Marilyn's wedding. He was the groom's best friend, both having been teaching brothers in the same community. I was reluctant to become involved, feared any form of commitment and was afraid of failure, but Mike was a persistent man. I even joined a commune of lay Catholics in New York in the hope of finding a Christian community. Mike followed me there, but wanted no more of communal life. We eventually married. He proved to be a loving, supportive, wise, and happy mate whom I loved dearly. We had four children and enough years together to supplant the tarnished image of Christian family life I had had from childhood. The fear of an unhappy marriage had been an underlying reason for my chosing religious life. Through my husband's unconditional love and friendship I came to know God and believe in his unconditional love and friendship as well. It was not until Mike's death that I realized God was not a reflection of Mike's love, but rather Mike had been a reflection of God's. I may have known it theoretically, but I didn't really understand it until I no longer had Mike's earthly presence. Then I realized that my personal relationship with God remained firm, which after all is what I had sought when I entered the convent that September Sunday.

The day after Mike's heart attack, when family and friends had been notified, I groped for an additional source of strength and asked, "What else can I do to comfort myself?" I called the switchboard at the motherhouse and identified myself as a former sister. I explained that my beloved husband had died and I needed to get in touch with my former bandmates and friends from about twenty years ago because I needed their consolation and prayers. I don't know whatever happened to all the good sisters, but I do know where a select number are. My phone rang for days with messages from friends whose voices I had not heard in years and I was greatly consoled. I don't analyze it much, but I find it strange that, surrounded by a great number of loving relatives and close friends I still had the impulse to reach back and draw strength from that part of my life and those who shared it with me. What is not so strange at all was their spontaneous and loving response.

I am trying to get on with my life now. I moved to Southern California to be near family members and to give this endeavor a boost. I have wonderful children, excellent health, a good job, and incomparable memories. If there is truth to the idea that there are no wasted years in one's life, then the experience I just retold must be helping me to start again — again.

Margaret Jankoski Kreuzer
Former Sister of Notre Dame

Married, three children

Director of Religious Education

Bachelor of Science in Elementary Education, Our Lady of Cincinnati College, Ohio

Master of Pastoral Studies, Loyola University of Chicago

Job-related ministries

Margaret's family is fortunate in sharing the fruits of her hobby, which is cooking. She enhances her natural gifts in this area by using the extensive collection of cookbooks she has amassed. Her hopes? "To someday receive my doctorate and to survive my children's adolescent years!!!"

Margaret Jankoski Kreuzer

The Answer to Why

Over the years many people have asked me why I entered the convent and just as many people — often the same — have asked me why I left the convent. Hopefully, both of these questions will be answered as I write my story.

Why would the Sisters of Notre Dame want *me?* What made *me* special? Why was I wooed, however subtly, by the Sisters who taught me both in grade school and high school? I believe that from the time I entered school I was a joiner, a volunteer for anything and everything. Ask for a leader, a contribution, a committee and there I was with my hand up. Pick me, please. Coming from a good middle class family, being bright and organized and spending many hours after school helping the sisters correct papers, work on bulletin boards, clean vigil lights, most likely were assets, too. Yes, there was a desire on my part to do God's will. I wanted to be a sister, to live the mysterious life of a nun. Never in my grade or high school years was I ever given even a hint of what it was really like to live this life. All of the sisters I had contact with were great actresses and through the years I became one too!

On December 8, 1959 in the convent chapel of my parish in Chicago, Illinois, I signed the papers requesting to join the Sisters of Notre Dame. The next few months were spent waiting for an answer. Was there something that I had done or not done that might make the sisters *not* want me? Being accepted a few months later was a joyful moment only to be overshadowed by many moments of doubt in the months between March and September when I was to go to the novitiate.

The last months of high school and the following summer flew by as no other time in my life had. There were so many "lasts" that I was reeling by September. In the style of my family, all of my aunts and uncles took me out to dinner for the last time and my parents had a huge going away party! There were many "firsts" too during this time, all of which revolved around my getting ready to leave. Gathering together everything on the list that was sent to me was a major feat in itself. Luckily, my best friend was also entering the Sisters of Notre Dame with me, and we spent days hunting down our dowry items. Our plans included flying to the motherhouse town and since I had never flown before, a good friend of mine arranged for me to take a short flight that summer so I wouldn't have this to worry about in September.

September 8, 1960 finally arrived — the ultimate day of lasts and firsts. Only many years after did I find out that the last morning at my home was even more traumatic for my parents and brother and sisters than it was for me. They kept the cup I last drank out of in a special place for years! My parents were always supportive, wanting me to be happy. I did not know for years the anguish they were feeling. As I boarded the plane with the nine other young women from my high school graduating class, I looked back at my family and cried. My tears were for me, thinking I would never be able to go home again. Little did I know all the tears that were shed over the next ten years by those who loved me.

As the two taxis pulled up to the novitiate that afternoon somehow, deep down, I knew that my life would never be the same. I was grateful to have arrived, exhausted from the last few weeks at home and terrified of what was to come. I became part of a group of forty-one postulants — the largest group they had ever had! We came from all over the area. All of us had been taught by the Sisters of Notre Dame in grade and/or high school and we were all just out of high school. We were black (the first ever) and white, tall and short, thin and not so thin! Because there were only seven novices at the time, we were overwhelming just by our numbers!

Our mistress of postulants possessed the qualities of a drill sergeant and a grandmother! Both were needed to deal with us. We were to be taught the intricacies of eating convent style, all courses from the same bowl, for example; the fine points of folding a nightgown which was large enough to be a tent; the proper way to make your bed by completely unmaking it, folding all sheets and blankets in threes and flipping the mattress before remaking it each morning. We learned hundreds of other convent etiquette rules. We also learned how to clean, peel, cook, wash dishes and clothes, iron and fold laundry. Prayer and play were also part of our daily routine and we were taught about silence! And taught and taught and taught.

I also remember waiting in line to ask for soap or shoelaces or to ask if I could write a letter or get an aspirin.

During this time we started taking some college courses and someone on high decided that I would become an elementary school teacher. I'm not sure why. Most of our group were destined to become elementary school teachers, and those who were chosen to teach high school were looked upon as being privileged. Why? I do not know.

Needless to say, during this time some chose to leave. The rigors of awaking at 4:55 a.m., the loneliness, the silence proved too much for some. When a place was empty at breakfast it usually meant that someone had left during the night. No time for goodbyes, just an empty place.How we ever formed a group and made friendships was a miracle. We weren't supposed to spend time with those with whom we had gone to high school nor were we really given the luxury of making new friends, since this was warned against.

Visits from family and friends were to take place on Sunday afternoons from one to three. Because my family lived far away and could only come to see me three or four times a year, the visiting times could be accrued. A weekend of visiting with my family was more traumatic than therapeutic; the setting was so unnatural and I was not allowed to eat with them. My sisters and brother were eight, ten and twelve, and spending six hours just talking or walking with me was sheer boredom. Every gift that I received had to be turned in, most of the times never to be seen again. I remember having to choose between two sweaters on one occasion. My aunt had made me a sleeveless one and I had one which had sleeves. What a decision! I chose the one without sleeves since it had sentimental value. I had cold arms for a long time !

The style and timing of the visits stayed the same for the next four years. I never felt comfortable with my family until after leaving the juniorate and beginning teaching.

In spite of all that was so foreign and new, I felt I belonged. This was due in a very large part to the love I received from our postulant mistress. Her shoulders were broad and I cried on them so many times. I know that I wouldn't have stayed without her to take care of me.

The year passed and on August 13, 1961, I was allowed to enter the novitiate; I received the name of Sister Mary Beth. I also received the habit which I so longed for. Little did I know that as beautiful as it was, it was complicated to put on correctly. Morning routine, already a time-juggling act, would become even more chaotic! Trying to pin myself together without the help of a mirror, added to the bed-making ritual at 5:00 a.m., almost did me in! I can still see myself running to morning prayer not wanting to be late.

Our first year of the novitiate was very contemplative. We didn't take any secular college courses and we were taught how to pray by our mistress of novices, a truly spiritual woman. We also learned about Chapter of Faults. We were given the "Instruments of Penance": a chain with sharp points to be worn on one's arm during the mornings twice a week, and a discipline, a small hand-held knotted rope instrument which we used to flagellate ourselves with on the back of our thighs.

We also began kneeling for breakfast on Fridays, kissing the floor if we were late, praying the rosary with our arms extended for every other decade, prostrating in the refectory and kissing the feet of the other sisters as well as telling our faults to our novice mistress and receiving a penance. All this was done at regularly prescribed times and intervals. We also cleaned and cooked and washed and ironed and peeled until we thought we would drop.

During our second year of the novitiate we traded our scrub brushes for school books. We were finally allowed to go out to school. We were bused to an all girls school run by the Sisters of Mercy. I loved school. It was so good to be a little free. But, alas, it was also difficult for me as I was always being reported to the novice mistress for "talking on the school bus and to others at school". I received many penances and reprimands for my behavior!

Somehow, I made the grade and was allowed to take my first vows on August 13, 1963. It was truly a joyful occasion with my family and my sisters. This is what we had been working so hard and praying for.

We became first year juniors — still in formation, still going to school, but very different from the novices, whom we weren't allowed to talk to except on special occasions. The juniorate was a relatively new idea in religious formation and with it came a blessing and a curse. The blessing was that we were allowed to finish our college education before being sent out to teach; the curse was that we were not very well liked by those sisters who were just a few years older than we were, and had been sent out from the novitiate to teach with only two years of college. They had to spend their Saturdays and many summers going to school to complete their degrees. Through no fault of our own we eventually lived with some of these sisters who were jealous of us!

The two years in the juniorate were full of ups and downs. We were given the privilege of staying up as late as we needed to study, but we were also expected to be in chapel at 5:30 a.m. We could drive because of our varied schedules, but still weren't supposed to talk in the car. We did student teaching, which was truly rewarding. I'll never forget the fifth-grade class I had. One of the highlights of these two years was called Little Missions. During our long breaks at Christmas and Easter we were sent out to smaller communities to help teach. What a breath of fresh air!

Our junior mistress was a woman who truly wanted us to be the best that we could be, but getting to this point was a rocky road for most of us. In our minds, we were divided into three groups: the small, elite group of the favorites, the small group of those who seemingly could do nothing right; and the rest of us who tried to do what was expected without getting into trouble. I remained in the large group for the most part and even when I had a minor accident and hit a tree with one of the cars, I wasn't punished severely. I think just having to tell what I had done was punishment enough!

I will always be grateful to the juniorate mistress for what we learned. It helped me to deal with some of the bosses I've had in my career.

Would the day ever come for us to leave the motherhouse? Finally, on Pentecost Sunday, 1965 we were given our missions. Most of us still had one summer left of college but there was a light at the end of the tunnel. The last few months were not unlike the last months at home. We knew that we would only see each other on occasion; in spite of our size and diversity, we had formed a real, loving and caring community in the past five years. We lived through the lasts as we prepared for the firsts.

My mission was to teach first grade at St. Aloysius School in Columbus, Ohio and to live at the Rich Street community as St. Aloysius did not have a convent. Little did I know that it would almost become "Mission Impossible".

At St. Aloysius my first grade class consisted of fifty-three children, half of whom had never been to kindergarten! My principal was a first-time principal and the one person who could have helped me the most was one of the sisters who, though not much older than I, was still going to school and resenting me. If I had questions she would always say that I should have learned that in school since I had a degree! I really believe that the children learned in spite of me rather than because of me. I still cherish those children and their parents who were so supportive of me that year.

Living at Rich Street proved to be as much a challenge as teaching first grade. The community was large, eighty sisters, and I was the youngest. For the first time in my convent life I had my own room, but what a room. It was up four flights of stairs in the condemned part of the building! I remember it being very hot or very cold — no happy medium. I got many colds, conjunctivitis and the flu. I think it was a combination of spending the days with the children and the nights in my room.

My sisters here were on four or five different faculties; there were so many conflicting schedules that I never sensed a real community. We did pray and eat together for the most part, but I don't remember having any fun together or sharing.

This was the first time I could go out with my family and ride in their car. They were as thrilled as I was. It was fun to show them my classroom and have them meet some of the parents and children.

I finished college in the summer of 1965 and our graduation was to take place in May, 1966. I was allowed to attend, and my family came to share my joy.

May also brought new missions and although I don't remember verbalizing my frustrations, someone obviously knew that this wasn't the best situation for me. After spending the summer as the cook at Rich Street (a real treat for me) I was to move to St. Susanna's in Mason, Ohio.

The town of Mason, Ohio (population 6,000) and the Convent of St. Susanna (population 6) were obviously light years away from the Rich Street community and Columbus, Ohio! Our convent was a small home with three bedrooms (no more private room), a large yard and a large front porch. It was across a highway from the school and church and we each had a flashlight which we used each morning as we crossed the road in the dark at 5:30 to go to church!

I was assigned to teach fourth grade, a much more delightful age for me. I loved the children and really liked the rest of the faculty. The principal of the school, who was also my superior, was a big help to me. She knew what a hard year I had in Columbus and really tried her best to be supportive.

The three years I lived in Mason provided me with opportunities and challenges which made me mature and even today have ramifications on my life.

Two major "happenings" occurred during these years. The first one was my summer assignment in 1967. I volunteered to do missionary work in Mexicali, Mexico with a group called LAMP (Latin American Mission Project). Four other sisters and I rode the Greyhound bus to Phoenix, Arizona, the first part of our journey. We stayed in one of our convents for a few days and then went down to Mexicali to begin our adventure.

Even though Mexicali is a border town we were soon immersed in Mexican culture and lifestyle. As a group we were to do two main things: provide water and medical supplies, and evangelize by having classes and working on validating marriages. We lived in two houses, one for the men, and the other for the women. Our house had no air conditioning and the average daytime temperature was over 120! At night you could feel the cockroaches crawling across your back and it wasn't unusual to step on one when getting up!

We met each morning for prayer at 8:00 and then went out into the field until 1:00 when we would return for lunch and siesta. After siesta we would go back out until nine or ten when we would come back to have supper, and often to party! The local restaurants and bars knew us as the missionaries even though we did not wear our habits and clerical garb.

During these weeks I worked with some of the best people in the world, and I still keep in touch with some of them. One person in particular changed the course of my life. His name was Larry, a Deacon from Worland, Wyoming. Although we became good friends in Mexicali, it was only after returning to our homes and regular assignments that we realized what kinship we shared. We wrote to each other often, shared books and tapes and talked on the phone on rare occasions. Even though by this time our mail was no longer read by our superiors, my superior questioned me about the volume of the mail I was getting.

Larry was working in a parish somewhere in Wyoming and was preparing for his ordination, which was to take place in May, 1968. I, too, had hoped to be allowed to take my final vows in August, 1968. Larry's bishop and my superiors had other ideas. Larry was not ordained; I was not allowed to take my final vows. I still find it hard to believe that this happened, since we were over 1500 miles apart and hadn't seen each other since the summer before. There never was anything inappropriate in our minds, and we were both devastated. Thinking I had nothing to lose, I asked if I could go back to Mexicali in the summer of 1968. Surprisingly, I did. Larry was in California and I did see him once, even though he did not work with LAMP.

The second summer in Mexico was just as great, but in a different way. There were some of the same people from the year before, as well as new friends to be made.

I will always be grateful to all my Mexicali friends for the good times and especially for encouraging me to be *me* again. I blossomed. Much of what we did those summers was never shared back in Ohio, needless to say.

I lost touch with Larry for several years, but now we write to each other occasionally. I visited him and his wife when we were in California a few years ago. We had shared so much those years that it wasn't hard to pick up where we had left off. He still has a special place in my life.

Our community in Mason often included Bill, the pastor. He was invited to dinner whenever his housekeeper was off or away and he took us on many day trips during vacations. He and Ann, my superior, always seemed to get along so well that it really wasn't such a big surprise, to me at least, when in the summer of 1969 they left Mason to get married. I was sent to St. Pater Canisius that summer and worked in a hospital lab as a receptionist. I had expected to be in Mason to teach in September but the provincial superior thought it best that I not be in

Mason; I wouldn't have to answer questions. I was given a day to pack my things and had no chance to say good-bye to my friends.

During these years in Mason the sisters of Notre Dame were going through radical changes. We could change back to our given names if we so chose; we didn't wear habits anymore; and we were given allowances. So much happened so fast!

I was assigned to teach sixth grade at St. Peter Canisius. The superior here had lived in Mason and knew Ann and Bill very well. They came to visit us on occasion, and I was allowed to go to their wedding.

Community life at St. Peter Canisius was almost nonexistent. I really didn't think that I was living my vow of poverty very well; I was in charge of doing the grocery shopping and was given a blank check and never worried about the price of anything. I knew that the families I was working with were living more poorly than I was. Also, at this time we could do almost anything we wanted to.

Where was obedience? I also felt that I was living in a hotel for single women where it was O.K. (or not) to pray together or eat together or have any form of community.

It was during this year that I made the decision to leave the sisters of Notre Dame. I told my local superior and the provincial superior when she made her visit. To my surprise, no one asked me to stay. At this time so many were leaving that a booklet was put together about how to buy a car, how to find an apartment, how to open a bank account.I chose to stay until August of 1970, even though the other three sisters who left from St. Peter Canisius left the day school was out. I chose to do this because I had planned to move to Phoenix where I was to teach third grade in a local Catholic school. Even though my family still lived just a few blocks away from the convent, I chose not to go home for those two months. I know that it was very difficult for my parents. They couldn't understand why I wanted to move so far away, not really knowing anyone. At twenty-seven I really didn't think that I could move home.

When I left St. Peter Canisius in August the sisters gave me a shower, and I left knowing that if I needed anything I could always call. I was given a check for $1500 and was told that if I needed more money to let them know.

I really am grateful for all my years with the Sisters of Notre Dame. I never would have made the friendships, received such a good education nor had some of the opportunities I had if not for those years with them. I still keep in touch with several people, both in and out of the convent, that I met during those ten years. I did not leave bitter, only grateful that I had the support and courage to try to be me again.

Moving to Phoenix with no community and only one friend was difficult. I tried not to let on to my family how lonely I was (and poor). The pay in the Catholic schools was pitiful and I got another job during the summer and on weekends working in the Emergency Room of a local hospital. I taught elementary school for three years and then decided to apply for a job as a Director of Religious Education for a Mexican-American parish. With my background and experience in Mexico I was hired and although the pay was not much better than being a teacher, I really liked my job and the people I was working with.

It was during this time that I met my husband. He was a seminarian studying for the Diocese of Phoenix, and had been assigned to our parish to do a census during the summer of 1975. I went back to Chicago for my sister's wedding and I was told of a parish in the suburban Chicago area that was in need of a Director of Religious Education. I applied just to appease my family, and to my surprise was offered the position at almost double my salary in Phoenix, plus an opportunity to go to graduate school. The decision to leave Phoenix was difficult. I really liked the people, had made a great many friends and was reluctant to get back into the fast-paced life in Chicago. While in Chicago, trying to make this decision, I had to call Phoenix several times to talk to the pastor. He had no idea I was about to leave. During these calls I also talked to Mike Kreuzer, the seminarian. We weighed the pros and cons of this move and he was my sounding board in Phoenix. Finally I decided to move back to Chicago. I went back to. Phoenix to resign from both of my jobs and to pack my things. Mike was a big help and we started spending a lot of time together.

Mike was from Riverside, California and a senior in college at St. Meinrad in Indiana. He was also ten years younger than I. We were good friends and when he returned to school in September and I moved to Chicago, we started to write and call each other. Because his family lived in California and he wasn't able to go home for Thanksgiving, I

342

invited him to spend the weekend with my family. It wasn't long after this that we decided to get married. The age difference seemed to bother everyone else but us. Mike graduated in May 1976 and we were married in October of 1976. We have been married for more than fifteen years and have three children, two boys and a girl, ages thirteen and a half, twelve and ten and a half. The years have been filled with joys and sorrows, births and deaths, good jobs and lack of work, but we have become stronger because of our faith in God and each other. Mike is gentle and kind and rock-solid when I need him to be. I love him and my children so much, and am so grateful to God for them.

I received my Masters Degree in Pastoral Studies from the Institute of Pastoral Studies at Loyola University in Chicago, and after spending a few years as an Admissions Counselor in a school of nursing have been a Director of Religious Education for a large suburban Chicago parish for the past six years.

In 1985 one of my friends who had left the Sisters of Notre Dame and I decided to plan a twenty-five year reunion of our group. To our surprise, twenty-three of the original forty-one of us got together to spend a weekend. We had letters and tapes from nine others and it was as if we had never been apart.

Even though it has been over twenty years since I left the Sisters of Notre Dame, I still feel a kinship with them and their mission. Their values, along with those of my parents and husband, have made me who I am today. Hopefully, they are as proud of me and my work as I am in having spent ten years with them.

This is my story.

Marguerite
Sisters of Saint Joseph

Intervention Specialist

Job-related ministry

Bachelor of Science in Education, College of St. Rose, Albany

Master of Science, Marriage and Family, College for Human Development, Syracuse

Theology, the Catholic University of America

Home Economics, Marywood, Scranton

Marguerite stays in touch with her community through regular attendance at assemblies, local gatherings, committees and community days and mail! She lives in a house close to her work, and is interested in movies, reading, and Scrabble. Her hope is to someday "work with women in recovery."

Marguerite

Sensible Shoes

Today I was having lunch with one of my favorite friends. As we were finishing up, Diane, who is many years my junior said to me, "So have I told you before how much I love nuns?" Of course she had, because we talk a lot. "Until I was sixteen I wanted to be one. I just knew that they 'knew'. I loved it." She went on, "Then when I 'came out' I knew it didn't matter. Lesbians and nuns are the same. They seem to love unity and diversity. They see the bigger picture." She paused. "You know, I think it must have been the sensible shoes that attracted me to the convent."

I was born the fourth of nine children. My parents were young and poor and they loved us the best they could, given the many difficult circumstances they had to endure. My dad had gone to the seminary. When he left he went to work as an accountant. He and my mother were then married, much to the chagrin of my grandmother and aunts. My father was the youngest of four and had been raised by the women in his family after his father died when he was very young. My mother's mother died when she was very young and her father was in the service. She was raised by her grandmother and her only sister was sent to a home. As soon as my mother and father were married, my aunt came to live with them.

My mother worked until she began to have children. With children came problems. She had lung disease, three of her five sons had hemophilia, my father had alcoholism and they were poor. We moved a lot and my father changed jobs often.

I never knew what was wrong with my brothers. I was five when the first died and I had never heard the word "dead," nor had I ever heard the mention of hemophilia. At that time my older brother had had hemophilia for at least ten years. I also never saw alcohol in my house and did not know that it was possible that alcoholism was the cause of my grandfather's early death. It was only when my father had been in recovery for a good many years that he shared this with me. I experienced my aunt's addiction to pills in my own relationship to her, particularly in her dying. It was she who provided me with most of the drugs I later came to depend on.

We grew up in a place called "Tipperary Hill", the only place known to have the green light over the red. My father told us the stories of the"Stone-throwers" who would keep on breaking the light until it was changed permanently. People lived there as if there were some privilege to being second generation Irish: anyone else was second class. My parents were not prejudiced. My mother was not from the hill and did not have a lot going for her that endeared her to my father's family. Today I choose to believe that the greatest legacy I have from my parents is the freedom that comes from lack of acceptance on the part of the reigning powers. My family seemed too busy organizing themselves around illness and what today would certainly be classified as poverty, to be involved in any kind of struggles for power or notoriety. I am grateful for that. My uncle, the priest, often kept us alive. He was parent, banker, nurturer and doctor. He was the calm in many a storm. Neither he nor my mother ever said much, yet I shall never forget all that they taught me.

We were taught by the Sisters of St. Joseph for all of our education. With them we felt safe, loved and significant. At times I think the sisters related to us in response to what they saw, a sort of family persona. Church and prayer were very important in our lives. Many of us went to daily Mass. We said the daily rosary and participated in all of the Advent and Lenten services. The sisters and the priests had no idea what our struggles were at home. I only told the nuns about the new babies or my mother's illness, my brothers being in the hospital. They put the religious practices and our troubles together to define us as a special family of faith. We were. And we had alcoholism, fights, fear and poverty that went unnoticed intentionally.

When I was twelve years old my oldest sister decided to enter the convent. It was a shock, and it wasn't until she left religious life thirty-six years later that I realized how angry I was with her for both decisions. When she entered I was the oldest girl, in charge when my mother was pregnant, sick, recovering. So at twelve I knew two things: I was now in charge, and I would do the same thing my sister had done when my time came. I kept my promise. In the meantime I managed to live a normal life as a cheerleader, dancer, dater.

Now I am aware of the inner conflict. I wanted to be a normal high school girl and I was set on being a nun. I know, too, that I hadn't a clue about what either of these were all about since my primary role at the time was mother, homemaker, parent. My mother was in a sanitarium for TB throughout my high school years. I recall saying to her on one of my visits that the sisters did not see how I could enter the convent and leave my family responsibilities. And I recall my mother's response. These were not *my* children; she was the mother and it was my parents' responsibility to care for the family. That's how she was. Any burden I may have felt was of my own choosing. That has not changed much for me.

My decision to enter the convent was made long before I actually entered. It was a decision made out of anger, a feeling of abandonment, feeling abused and a bit overwhelmed with it all. I also think that I believed that entering the convent might give me that feeling of acceptance, of being holy and worthy of redemption after all.

I believe I lived the first ten years of religious life seeking holiness and trying to be good. Neither pursuit helped me to know myself any better than I had when I entered. In the 50's we prayed and played together; we worked and remained pretty isolated from the rest of the world. I loved most of it because I did not know any better. None of us did. I remained isolated and lonely for most of those days. I found community difficult and became known for my work, my teaching and my rapport with the students. My drive for holiness, as I saw it, kept me isolated from anyone who would see through the cracks.

On the other hand, I gravitated to superiors who saw my work and my drive and thought that was who I was. I got attached to being treated as special. It was in these days that my disease was manifest in illness, which now I know was my need for medication, of feelings of loneliness, inadequacy and a host of others. I was defined by my work and I would work till I dropped, get sick to be taken care of with pills and alcohol.

Only much later did I make the connection between alcohol and medicine. Since I had pledged not to drink, my mind had to justify my desire for and attachment to alcohol. Most of my earlier years of religious life were lived under the influence of mood-altering drugs, including alcohol. One day while not under the influence I snapped at another sister and withdrew to my room for the remainder of the day and night. The next thing I knew I was taken to a hospital where I was treated for six weeks for a breakdown. This was my first "bottom".

Because my sisters were embarrassed I was not permitted to return to the high school. I was recruited by the diocese to head up one of the diocesan offices. That began an "I'll show you that I'm good" phase of my life. I accomplished a lot of good without the notice of those whom I was out to show. I went elsewhere for affirmation and praise. Now I was different; I had power. Thus began the upward spiral of importance and the downward twist toward the admission of powerlessness.

Today I am very different. I work as an Intervention Specialist full-time in a public high school and one night a week in a parish. All I have to do is show up. Today I know the true meaning of ministry. The focus has changed from work and being important to being myself and seeing with new eyes.

It is wonderful to be back in a school and to know that I am good at it. My first ten years were spent in teaching and I loved it. When I left teaching I did not know how much I had loved it. My new drive toward power had blinded me. With change came the need to re-examine everything I had grown used to. Now I was on my own. I could not depend on anyone or anything being there for me. God truly became central to my life and my commitment was definitely to the God of my understanding. God had always been a personal friend; this change had sort of given me permission to choose that God rather than the one I had often felt was offered with no alternative.

I was now able to choose religious life and to live it one day at a time, to the best of my ability. I stayed and I stay even though separated from some of my dearest friends. These women continue to enrich my life and I am grateful that it was our choice of religious life that first brought us together. Among the many wonderful things religious life has given me, the greatest of all is my connection with so many wonderful women all over the world in many walks of life. I love women and the life we bring to this world. I feel like my friend Diane. I believe it is the sensible shoes, the unique way we came to view ourselves and the world.

Church is very difficult for me. I find it next to impossible to participate in Eucharist separate from a context that includes a relationship with others. The reason I loved daily Mass as a child was that we were a community. It didn't matter what language the priest was speaking, we were one; we knew each other and we touched. Eucharist is the central tenet of my faith, and it began back there. Today I know many Eucharistic moments. I feel called and drawn into the brokenness of life of the ones I have the privilege to serve. I feel Eucharist at A.A. meetings and with persons I sponsor. I thoroughly appreciate the liturgy at our provincial house. I gather with women for prayer and I enjoy my opportunities for facilitating retreats for women who are in recovery programs.

Community is like Eucharist for me. I have lived in all sizes of communities. For the past six years I have lived with another sister who is away this year. I have lived alone this year and have no intention of doing this forever. However I will not live with others just so I will not be alone. I could live with any small number, provided we had a common vision and a mutual commitment to the ongoing struggle.

Friendship is like Eucharist also. For a very long time I felt that I had a number of good friends. Today I have a few very special friends, and I am able to be myself with most people. I know the difference. It seems to me that the common denominator for Eucharist, community and friendship is intimacy or in-to-me-see. It is in those moments that I am able to look deeply into my soul and tell another person the truth that I believe, Eucharist, friendship, community happens. Friends are the greatest gifts, and I feel blessed with mine.

This leads me to vows. Because of my upbringing, my inclination as a young woman was to serve and seduce men, and to resist or create conflict with women. This mindset had caused most of my problems in life prior to my entry into the wonderful world of Alcoholics Anonymous. I once spent a lot of valuable time competing with other women, and being mad at them if they won. Today I am likely to fall back into these patterns when I am not talking to other women in recovery and practicing the principles that keep me sane. Alcoholism, or acceptance of my own alcoholism and addiction, has made a world of difference in my life. Everything I do is better, especially the vows because I now know the meaning of living one day at a time and staying in the now.

Celibacy means that I am willing to continue to grow in my relationship with God, with others and with myself. It means that I am willing in all things to be honest and open. I learn to be more loving in all of my relationships.

Poverty is difficult for me because of my upbringing, I had no idea about how things ought to be. I am still more obsessed in this area than any other. I love money and things and I usually feel guilty when I spend. A priest friend of mine once told me that poverty was not about being a miser. It's about being responsible for time and money and possessions. I couldn't get it for a very long time. I have gone through periods of depression about having or not having money. I have neglected myself and my health rather than go to a doctor or a counselor. I know that this has little to do with living the vows, and it has taken me a lot of pain and time to get to the place where I know I deserve to be cared for, no matter the price.

Obedience has never been a problem for me, and I am grateful. I am respectful of designated authority and have always been grateful for those who would serve. I am willing to do my share in serving on committees. My gift is to intuit and affirm leadership qualities in others. I am good at this, and I make my business to do it.

One constant theme in my life has been illness, death and grief. Until my recovery in Alcoholics Anonymous began, my entire life was somehow bound up in unresolved issues around these themes. Because of this it was never possible for me to even consider the possibility of living in the present. As I said earlier, I had three brothers who had hemophilia. The first died when I was about five. I was in a very difficult place when the second one died. It was one of those "You go to the funeral and get back to school," experiences. Between 1970 and 1979 I had six family members die quickly. By then I was drinking and using medication, and was able to keep up the image of being in control. I needed no one.

Then I was given the gift.

My youngest brother was already in recovery and he was one of the significant others in my life. I had raised him. I saw what the program was doing for him so I went for it. I was in about one year when he died while running. That devastated me, and I still had to deal with all of the other deaths. So I began, and I know today that recovery has changed everything for me. It was this gift that brought me to the recognition and acceptance of my own lifetime dependence on medication. I came to realize that although I thought I had been drinking for a short period of time, I had really used alcohol from the time I entered the convent. And when the superior called it medicine, my alcoholic brain bought that.

I continued to be sick. I never knew if I got sick to have alcohol. What I do know is that even today when I get sick, I want to be medicated rather than to ask for help. I am better at that or I would not be writing this. What I do know for certain is that as soon as someone said alcohol was medicine, I forgot the pledge. If I could characterize my relationship with alcohol and other mind-altering drugs it would be about hiding. So I hid behind sickness and the word medicine. Later when I gave myself permission to drink, I drank only in secret. Prescriptions were always legal. I would protest that I was unable to swallow pills, yet I was always under the influence.

I have been in therapy on and off for a number of years. After ten years in A.A. I was diagnosed as being bipolar. Now I was mentally ill. That was a very difficult truth to take. I see a psychiatrist, and I take the medication as I am directed. The doctor knows my fear of medication and I am very careful to do what I am supposed to do with it. It seems that a very large number of my women friends are also on medication, and I am able to talk with them about this, too. The thought just occurred to me that there are very few of my sisters I would share this with. I know that it's because I am still into perfection with most of them. I did share it with one sister; our relationship changed immediately. I am thankful for my friend with whom I live.

Sometimes I feel just a little schizophrenic. It seems that my life as a sister has little to do with my real life. I try to be careful with that kind of thinking. I am a most respected member of my community. I learned that when my sister chose to leave after thirty-six years. I had always lived in her shadow. When she left one of my friends said, "Well, Margie, now you're on your own." That was a shock. I had to give up competing.

By that time I was in A.A. and had already begun my own process of looking at myself separate from anyone else. While people in A.A. know that I am a sister it is the principle of anonymity that has kept me humble and helped me put being a sister into perspective. Anonymity is the great leveler, the unifier, and it helps me more than anything else in my life. As they say, it is the spiritual foundation of all of our traditions. When I am into my old stuff of competing, or feeling sorry for myself, I need a meeting, a phone call. I believe, like Diane, that sisters are wonderful. I know, also, that some of us are terminally stuck. Left to my own devices I will go back to all that kept me sick.

I am first a woman; I am a woman called to religious life. That life is nothing like what I thought it would be or what it was when I entered. I am grateful that God and my life in A.A. have become the focus of who I am and all that I do. Today that means being a sister who ministers in a public high school, and who is ministered to by a variety of persons who share my disease. That makes me who I am. I believe I am a better sister because I am a better person, not the other way around, as I used to think.

Mary Cecilia
Former Religious of the Sacred Heart of Jesus

Single

Retired nurse

Red Cross Bloodmobile Volunteer

Bachelor of Arts, Psychology, Marymount Manhattan College

Registered Nurse, St. Francis Hospital School of Nursing

Coordinator, Right to Life

Eucharistic Minister

Librarian, Parish Choir Holy Family Parish, New York

Mary Cecilia wishes to "continue to live out my life to its fullest, giving and ministering to all who need me." Her life-long dedication to such ministering, including years as a head nurse in Cabrini Hospice, has laid a firm foundation for that desire. Church activities, a little office work, and her volunteer activities keep her very busy.

The Center of My Life

When in high school I thoroughly enjoyed my friends and my social life, but there was always that inner something that made it most important for me to spend time each day in quiet prayer in a church. Often I just sat and let the Divine Presence fill me. These precious moments gave me a longing for a life where I could spend a longer time with Him. After high school I went into nursing and there I experienced His presence in all I cared for. So finally I felt religious life was my place for the future.

During my postulantship and noviceship I became convinced I had made the right choice. Silence was the rule to give us a chance to build an interior life. There was a book of rule and constitutions to be read, commentaries to enrich our understanding, daily Mass, yearly retreats, frequent days of recollection, and, of course, the religious habit. We looked forward to the day we were to be clothed, and the habit was worn with pride and respect. It showed we belonged. First vows, and then out to the apostolate. Final vows, and with them the joy of knowing that now I had launched out on my road to becoming a true religious dedicated to my God.

Then what happened to the good sisters? We heard Pope John III was opening the windows and doors to let in fresh air. The fresh air was more like hurricane winds.

The habit was to be modified; the habit was optional; we could wear secular clothes. Silence: no more; talk all you want. The Rule: was it possible we heard correctly? "We rescind all we taught you, a new rule will be compiled." Cloister: no more, the doors are open, go out shopping, take trips, go home. We had not been out since we entered. Retreats: you are on your own, plan as you wish. As for community life, break up into small groups, choose those you wish, make your own community Our mother superior no longer existed. Classes in the academies were slowly taken over by secular teachers. We were told, "Go out and find jobs. Just turn in three-fourths of your salary." Then the unthinkable: some were smoking and drinking.

What is all this, I wondered? My life has been pulled out from under me. There is no longer any need to stay. I felt I could find a great job using my nursing, serving and loving the Lord, still so dear to me, in all I met and cared for. Have I found happiness? Yes, lots of it. I know deep down I have again made the right choice. I hear people say, "You are so wonderful... so different... it's as if you came into our work place from another planet." It's nice to hear. I have never told any one my past. I just thank God. He still is the center of my life.

Margaret Lynch
Former Sister of Charity

Single

Director of Education, Health Insurance Company of America

Bachelor of Arts, College of Saint Elizabeth

Master of Arts, Duquesne University

Margaret, as her story reveals, is a gifted writer who uses that gift in her professional life as well as delighting in it as an avocation. She enjoys theater and music as audienc, but also as performer. Her wish for beyond the now is to "grow older with grace and creativity expansion."

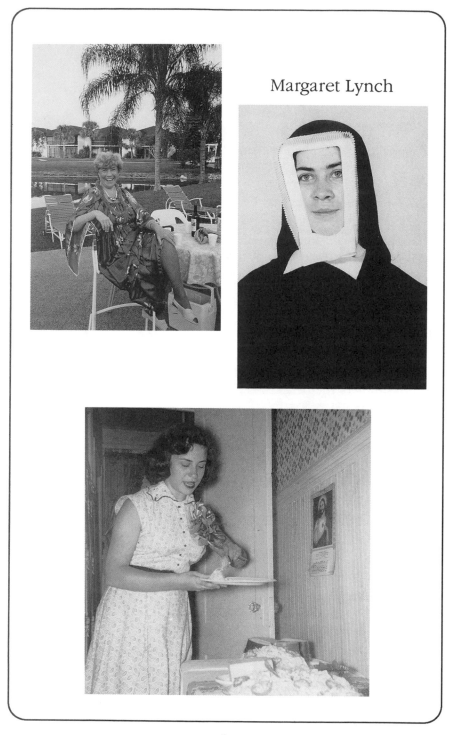

Margaret Lynch

The Myth of the Good Sisters

A multi-level, somewhat ironic, question this: Whatever happened to the good sisters? My sixteen years spent as one of them had indeed been a happening — a long one. Things had happened to and by and because of the *them* that used to be *us*. I recoil from the trite phrase indicating categorical goodness; yet, the polarity term "bad" certainly does not apply. The women I knew who called themselves Sisters of Charity commingled the good and the bad in varying proportions, inseparably, not in orderly bar graphs. Eventually, each individual sister made the appalling discovery of her own humanity.

This discovery, when finally made by Catholics at large, shattered an underpinning of the belief system of many of them who felt enriched by others' denial of this troublesome condition. For had not God selected certain females to be the perpetual fire tenders, the vestal virgins, the servants of the servants of God?

To them, the "good sisters" were desexed, hence abnormal entities with a specific function — to ultimately suck ordinary Catholics through heaven's pearly gates by force of their saintly nature, separate enclosure, and medieval garb. When the myth finally collapsed, many of us literally ran for our lives.

We lived in the land of Maxim, where the motto "Who lives to the Rule lives to God" was displayed above the crucifix. An aspirant was welcomed for a trial in the novitiate, and that promise was kept. Major sins included running giddily through the house, breaking night silence, and taking much-needed sleep in the pre-dawn hours of morning meditation. Instructions to the novices stressed that feelings, although not failings, were very poor guides, and readings from *The Imitation of Christ* reminded us that "Sufficient for the day is the evil thereof." The good and the positive never got equal mention.

This, of course, is a retrospective view. For the age of fifty-six encourages, almost enforces, reflection. At this life point time becomes tangible, and losses and separations are both feared and expected. Reconciliation and acceptance are essential keys to continued life and future self-development. It was in this spirit of search for closure and connectedness that I, and others who had chosen to remove themselves from convent life, responded to a second calling to the motherhouse of the Sisters of Charity one spring weekend several years ago.

The journey had both physical and mythic dimensions when I again boarded a train, this time from Washington, D.C., as I had on that long-ago day in September, 1953 when I took that seemingly much longer commuter train ride from Hoboken. That simple act moved me from the known to the unknown, from being one of the Lynch girls to being one of the *sisters*. The question of who *I* was probably was not apprehended and certainly not confronted. I wanted to be something. Only later would I realize that I wanted to be someone: somebody, and that endings and beginnings were merely terms to identify specific moments of critical choice, integration, or realization.

My world had been a circumscribed one, a mile-square city broken down into even more manageable segments. I had packed my yearnings and my future into a small green suitcase that matched my green skirt and fled the limits of actual poverty to pursue the poverty of spirit I had read about, to escape the demands imposed on the married women I had observed, and to pour out my love of the God Who would love, lead, and protect me while I served others in His name.

The novitiate, this boarding school for would-be nuns, was more joyous than trying for me. I loved the solitude that aided the inner search, the communion with soul and prayerful conversations with divinity, the walks among trees, the companionship of other young women who shared my ideals and goals. The limitation of campus could be felt at times, as well as the onus of constant surveillance. But we had the creativity and the audacity to find ways to be ourselves to a considerable degree, and to find places to gather, and spaces within, that our "captors" could neither locate nor enter.

Our lives together continued and broadened with the introduction of the Sister Formation Movement within the Church. My band, as it was called, became the first group to stay at the motherhouse to study towards their college degrees, and we even were asked what major area of learning we preferred! I had not completed high school and was able to make up these credits while taking college courses. As an English major I wrote and read and met the great authors whose names were new.

But these halcyon days ended, and at last, I embarked on the reason for all this preparation — the fulfillment of my mission. An initial assignment to teach sixth grade at a Jersey City elementary school jolted me into the real world. I pronounced myself a failure after that first year, attempting to control fifty-six children in an initially deskless basement classroom. My vocation, fortunately, did not permit me to quit and seek employment elsewhere. So I mastered some techniques, relaxed, and crafted my skill during the ensuing years, and truly grew to look forward to my days in the classroom. After five years and the receipt of my bachelor's degree I was transferred to teach high school English at a suburban parish.

But the word was out about that convent and its sister servant, and the experience met all expectations. St. Vincent dePaul wisely decreed that the sisters he founded should not have a superior. He believed that their leader should be reminded by her title that her role was to serve, not command. Work was continual: school; convent chores; prayers; preparation of meals; taking care of the needs of the middle-aged sisters who demanded attention and the elderly sisters who required it. Full, exhausting, repetitive days blurred into late nights of preparation for classes and early mornings of drug-like ritual. And all of this was performed in a mean atmosphere of constant criticism and suspicion. Even worse, these same characteristics permeated the school setting, where the convent superior (for superior she indeed made herself) ruled as principal.

After two unhappy years I was transferred. But during that time I had found some expressive release in my studies for a Master's degree at Duquesne University. Summer study continued for six successive years at this urban university in the heart of an area ravaged by the decline of the steel industry. It was the 1960's, the onset of a frontal attack on all our social structures: religious, educational, and societal.

In Pittsburgh, during those summers from 1962 to 1967, men with expressionless faces stood on corners, and woman in shabby cotton house dresses entered and exited from stores where I saw the sign "food stamps accepted" for the first time. Children scurried around — dirty anklebones, no socks, open shoelaces. Yes, I looked down, for it was easier to follow the convent maxim to avert one's eyes so that I could protect my inner child who had lived in like circumstances. I avoided leaving the college buildings and buried my questions, my compassion, my guilt, and my sadness in the library.

The feelings were aroused and could not be quelled. The Sisters of Charity had lost sight of the mission assigned to them by St. Vincent dePaul. Their schools had followed the upwardly mobile into their safe suburban sanctuaries. The poor were still with us and their neglect was apparent. I saw my life as a sham and my community as an escape from reality.

The papal edict for religious communities to convene chapters for renewal brought some hope; perhaps enough change would occur to allow me to stay within the religious community whose ideals I still embraced. I threw myself into the preparation that involved review and evaluation of rules, customs, and overall activity. I found myself endlessly challenging, vocal, and explosive. As an attendee at the sessions to vote on renewal, my voice was effectively silenced. I heard the dread of change, and witnessed the fury that defended the status quo. The delegates changed the concluding sentence of my report on collegial leadership and distorted its message and intent. I judged most of the sister attendees as stupid, vicious, or willfully blind. I could no longer survive among them. I had to get out.

Determined to leave and seek a life among ordinary mortals, I resumed my quest for that life at age thirty-four. From my current vantage point this seems young indeed, but at that life juncture I felt old and tired and used. I was unaware of the societal roles assigned to women which, even today, leave them with those feelings. Nor did I yet even suspect that victimhood was common and frequently self-chosen, albeit subconsciously. I hoped for a good job and acceptance in the world and, more muted, for someone who would both love and make love to me.

In the months after making my decision I filed application after application for a teaching position in local New Jersey school districts. I had no replies. Aware of the nepotism of local politics that included teaching jobs among its awards, dread of the future contracted my stomach and intruded on my hopes. I left the safety of the convent without a job, spent the summer months in the apartment of a friend, and moved back to Hoboken to live with my younger sister. Now desperate for income and some security, I accepted a job as office manager at the Laboratory of Psychological Studies at Stevens Institute of Technology at a salary of $125 a week, net pay $98.22 — a huge sum for a woman who had for the past sixteen years worked for nothing. I was satisfied. I would earn, save, and continue my search.

But the sense of safety was a chimera. I was driven by anxiety and inability to understand finances. Everything cost money; I counted it daily. My sister called me Silas Marner, and the name was apt. I felt I had circled, returned to the place of my beginnings, and feared its entrapment. I had escaped once; I must again. I *wanted* to teach; I wanted the status and stability. In November I received an offer to teach in a suburb of Trenton. I took it.

I was struggling, but I was free. I began to feel alive. Yet, establishing credibility and achieving acceptance within a public school setting was no easy task. The title sister had insulated me from the creating and sustaining of boundaries and bonds of respect, unity, and affection with students and fellow teachers. I had no "in" with the administration and no assurance of continued employment. In addition, I felt timid and shy among my colleagues who joked and communicated easily on matters of daily living. I felt I carried an embarrassing secret that, if known and discussed, would make me a curiosity. I did not know how to approach my colleagues on non-professional matters, convinced that their lives and life experiences so differed from my own. Male teachers approached but found me too well-armed. I behaved only slightly better with the women. My life in good part echoed the convent routine: I taught, went back to my apartment, prepared the next day's lessons, and took the train to Hoboken on Friday afternoons. I lasted for two school years.

I would do better in the business world, I rationalized. I registered in a career development seminar and got some good ideas and positive feedback. I began slowly to feel less tentative. I landed a job that bridged education and industry and worked for a middle-aged woman who had overcome an abusive marriage and mental illness to arrive at career success. We talked and shared a lot—intellectually and emotionally.

But the work became repetitive, dulling. I again performed what had become almost an avocation; the reading of the want ads. I fine-tuned my resume, and lateralled into a new venture. Bestowing on myself the title of Director of Cooperative Education, I accepted a position to create programs for a new community college that would exist only as a concept. For a lesser tuition supplemented by county funds, needy students could earn an associate's degree by using the facilities and faculties of local area colleges. I did not like the way the concept was executed, but I liked *me* better after the one-year grant expired. I had met two men who found me desirable. I had laughed and felt young for a while, and it was good.

When another job offer came in New York City, I decided that I would probably stay with this one until retirement. I wearied of the search for the perfect job and reluctantly acknowledged that a successful career was not enough. I was over forty, unmarried, childless, and essentially empty. I continued to function well, but could not ignore the caverns within. I sought therapy and learned to mourn my losses and acknowledge my gains. I tried theater and fulfilled a long-harbored fantasy of performing in a musical. I used therapy as theater, and theater as therapy. I grew up a lot.

My job took me to Washington, D.C, in 1985 shortly before my fiftieth birthday. There, I bought a house and got a promotion. Currently, I am paid (I dare not say earn) a salary almost fifteen times greater than the annual salary I was so proud of twenty years earlier when I took my first non-nun job.

I was returning to the motherhouse a successful woman. The fact that I would materially equal, and probably exceed, others who had shared my early dreams and ambitions pleased me. I was ashamed a bit of my competitive gloating. I didn't want the worldly to be so important. I wondered what had become of old friends. I wanted to meet on the more common ground of the spirit and the search for life's meaning that were still vital to me.

And I did. The trip proved worthwhile. I readily shared deeply with the women who also had come back, both those whom I still knew after many years of silence and those whom I had never met, but who had shared the same formative experience.

But this satisfaction did not extend to most of the sisters present who had remained Sisters of Charity. They seemed to exude a feeling of welcoming us back into the fold, of forgiveness. We would need but a day, their agenda told us, to verbalize our pain and we would be restored to them. We could again commingle and interact. They wanted something from me, but could not drop the pretension that they were the donors.

Uncomfortably and reluctantly I defined my feeling: I hated and despised their show of benevolence. How dare these women assume they had something to offer me? I rejected their need and connected with my own. I had anguished and moved onward and grown. I perceived that they had essentially stood still. I was angry that I still cared.

I left after the weekend and returned to my home, pondering what had occurred. That probing continues and probably will for life. As a Sister of Charity I began a lifetime quest for the fullness of life in a narrow, doctrinaire world of shoulds. But internal worlds had opened for me through the routes of education and contact and contracts with the spiritual.

I no longer call myself a Catholic or affiliate with any organized religion. I avoid groups where I feel faceless. I do not perform acts of charity nor do I involve myself in missions of rescue. At times I allow myself to consider that awful possibility: somewhere, deep in my heart's Grand Canyon, I may be just one of the sisters on a solo flight.

Alvernia Witek
Felician

Director of Community Outreach, Saint Andrew Home for the Elderly

Editor of Newsletter

Bachelor of Science, Loyola University, Chicago

Masters in Social Work, University of Wisconsin, Milwaukee

Pastoral Care Certification, Saint Mary Hospital, Kansas

Sister Alvernia says she lives by the words of Paul: "I can do all things in Christ, who strengthens me." Her life is proof of this. At present she lives in a local convent with eighteen nuns who have meals and recreation in common. She stays in touch with the community at large through monthly meetings and special celebrations. Sister Alvernia believes that all can achieve their potential if they respond to the Spirit. "In the twilight of my life now, I trust the Spirit will continue to guide me until I arrive at the foot of the Cross."

Alvernia Witek

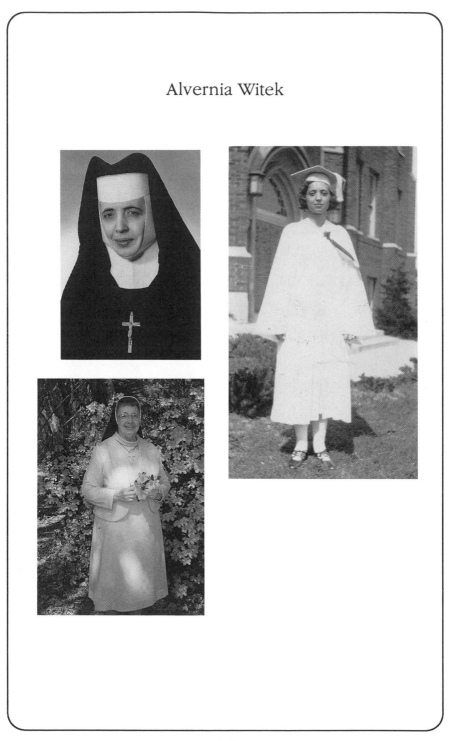

The Myth of Progress

Each individual must decide if his or her efforts over the years can be called progress. We have emerged from the Norman Rockwell age to the dark days we've endured since.

Most of us recall the days of calling the "fridge" an icebox. Deposits on soda bottles were only two cents and seven bottles generated enough hard cash to get into the theater on Saturday, where 500 kids squealed and hissed at cartoons and Jackie Coogan. We remember mid-calf dresses, bathing suits with skirts, hats and gloves for church. Milk was delivered to the door, cream still on top; it froze in winter, popping the lid. My father smelled of cigars and worked as a flagman. My mother, with my sisters Jean and Stephany, earned good money as dressmakers in our Bridal Shop. Purchasing thread, beads and materials and paying bills monthly was my responsibility at age ten until I entered the boarding school at age fourteen.

On December 7, 1941, an event made a profound change in the entire world, a change which continued for the next fifty years. The real world opened to us and got smaller every day. Maps came alive with names like Dunkirk, Anzio, Midway and Iwo Jima. Blue-star service flags hung in windows; some changed to gold. We watched John Wayne movies with sneering Japs. Nobody could have prepared us for the German Holocaust or for Hiroshima.

We survived on Spam during the depression. We bought white bricks of margarine with a yellow spot to squeeze to make it the color of butter. Mothers washed clothes in wringer washers, used bluing rinse, and hung them to dry in the yard. We got along without plastic, frozen foods, contact lens, electric can openers and nursing homes.

There were Scripture books and, once in a while, *National Geographic* and *Life* magazines.

Pastors delivered brimstone sermons and we, in remorse, went to confession to confess to sins of which we were not guilty. Once at the communion rail the pastor asked me, in a voice loud enough for others to hear, if my mother didn't have a strap to punish my sin of disobedience.

During the 1930's I spent most of my life secluded in a convent environment. I entered Good Counsel High in Chicago. In high school I struggled through algebra and Latin translations. Nineteen of the forty girls in my senior class crossed over to the adjoining building to become Felician Sisters. My reasons for applying were "to become a teacher and to escape the evils in the world". I accomplished both.

When I took my vows, I honestly believed I knew the real meaning of poverty, chastity and obedience. It took many years thereafter, through living, reading and the media, to grasp the losses and the gains experienced by a person taking such vows; fortunately, my gains far exceed my losses.

The one year in novitiate before I started my career in teaching gave me a little firepower. I was taught responsibility, motivation and teamwork. These gave me an edge in life and I succeeded quite well in teaching for twenty-five years and in administration for thirty-five years at our different institutions.

As a teacher for twenty-two years and principal of St. Turibius School for three years my goal was to make learning interesting and exciting. The minds of children are ripe and inquisitive; I believed that growth could be nourished through good education coupled with wonderment, high ideals, encouragement and excitement.

As Administrator of St. Joseph Orphanage in Milwaukee, Wisconsin for twenty years, I was involved with the renovation of the fifty-year old, huge building and, more importantly, the improving and updating of the curriculum and programs for the 120 children. In 1960 the Ladies' Auxiliary and the St. Joseph Athletic Association helped finance a $95,000 Villa St. Joseph, a very lovely recreation and vacation facility on twelve acres on Upper Lake Nemahbin in Oconomowoc, Wisconsin.

Holidays are nostalgic for me. My memory of past, happy experiences is kept alive by letters and telephone calls from pupils and friends to whom I was a substitute mother at St. Hedwig Orphanage (now Niles

College Seminary) and later at St. Joseph Orphanage in Milwaukee (now South Day Care Center of St. Joseph).

My proposal to build 250 apartments for the older Americans under HUD on the sprawling grounds of St. Joseph Orphanage, Milwaukee was too premature. To kill the idea quickly, since the board members and south side community had begun to voice interest in it, my higher supervisors transferred me to Centralia, Illinois. My prediction that the proposed project would become a reality in ten years was short only by two years. It took twelve years to see Villa St. Francis constructed, and at a much greater cost.

When President Nixon stressed the need for day care for pre-school children, my vision came into play again. I immediately took action with the board members.. Within one year St. Joseph Orphanage was converted into 12 classrooms and playrooms. It was staffed by certified teachers, teacher aides and nurses from St. Francis Hospital. The South Day Care Center is (and has been since that time) operating at its maximum capacity of three hundred youngsters.

The south side Milwaukee community supported whole-heartedly all of our proposed projects. I received the Pal Joey Award from the Athletic Association of Milwaukee for distinguished service to children. My name is engraved among other community leaders in the Hall of Fame in the entrance to the Milwaukee Arena.

After earning and receiving my certificate in Pastoral Care Education at St. Mary's Hospital in Kansas City I became director of the newly opened Pastoral Care Department at St. Mary Hospital in Centralia, Illinois.

Ministering to the dying and grieving has been to me the most rewarding experience. My small world has been widened by cherished friends I would not have otherwise met, friends who have been most generous sharing their deepest pain and most fearsome inadequacies with me. Most of all I learned how little room the Lord needs to move freely. Even I could be the Lord's presence for the ill and wounded.

Looking back into my life, there was a time when I hated to hear any discussion of death and dying. I abhorred the last day of our annual retreat in the convent because it was devoted to meditations on death. To this day I remember one mediation on death very vividly. The retreat master asked us to close our eyes and to visualize ourselves in the coffin surrounded by our friends and enemies. We were to tune in and listen to what was said about us. I was very young then and thought such meditations were proper only for the senior citizens.

Then, too, I had always worked with young people and young folk are symbols of life, health and joy. However, with the new assignment to the Pastoral Care Department at St. Mary's Hospital, my scenes have changed. The majority of the people I meet now are the elderly, the sick and the dying.

The Lord initiated me to the dying with a bang by leading me to Room 309 in my first week of arrival at the hospital. As I walked into the patient's room I was shocked to see a man with a badly deformed face. To me he looked like a monster. Cancer had eaten half of the right side of his face and his eye had popped out of the socket. The smell of rotting flesh was offensive in spite of all the efforts of the nurses. His speech was affected and he couldn't carry on a conversation with me. I was told he was a very successful banker, had traveled extensively, and had everything that Americans prize. His only visitor was his eighty-one-year-old sister from Florida. She lived in his house now while he was in the hospital. Each day she would arrive with six fresh roses. Since they were so alone I visited with them daily. We would discuss our experiences; we would pray and sing hymns so our sick one cold hear voices. Each day as I came into the room, the patient's hand would come out to greet me. The same thing happened when I was leaving the room. It was his way of saying, "Thanks for caring".

I saw many people go through the stripping process before death in the hospital. One business man was dying of lung cancer for over a year. He shared his feelings and thoughts on dying on a very personal and confidential basis with me. I saw this man stripped of everything. He still grieved for his wife who preceded him by three years. He gave all his money to his grandchildren, establishing trust funds for their education; his health failed him, his business companions deserted him; finally he even signed off his name from the home he loved so dearly. He died in the nursing home very shortly after that.

I have seen this man and others in their last days, overflowing in thanksgiving in spite of their suffering. So much has been accomplished, experienced, enjoyed and passed on that is of material and spiritual value to others around them. Some had time to do everything that had to be done.

Another man whose dying I witnessed was a deacon in his church. He spent his retirement days teaching Bible to large groups of men. His lovely wife, ministers and family gave this dying man meaning and worth to the very end. This patient requested that we sing hymns in his room daily. One morning as I entered his room I noticed the patient staring at the ceiling and the family around his bed. I joined hands with them and we prayed. I then intoned "Nearer My God To Thee" and all joined in. When we got half way through the song the patient breathed his last. We continued the song until the end. We all felt the presence of the Lord and spontaneously we all embraced each other, thanking the Lord for coming in our midst. When we were leaving the room the wife said, "We all loved him dearly but decided to give him up to the Lord so he wouldn't suffer any more." This patient had time to prepare for his death. His bed became the altar of prayer and praise of God.

Some death is logical; some death is illogical. It is logical to see an old person depart from this world. It is expected when a man is old and had a full life, but it seems illogical when death takes a young person. Then death seems cruel and unwarranted.

Two unforgettable scenes of death of young children are with me. One was a crib death tragedy. The grandfather came rushing into the emergency room with the dead baby in the hope the doctor would revive the baby. The next car brought the shocked mother, still in her bed clothes. She asked me, "Is my child dead?" and collapsed at my feet. Luckily her father emerged from the waiting room. He scooped her into his hands and held her on his knees like a child. She sobbed uncontrollably while we stood speechless at the scene. After an hour, when she began accepting the reality, the nurse called us to view the baby. One nurse had the mother sit in the wheelchair and the other put the baby in the blanket in the mother's lap. We and the four nurses surrounded her in silence and watched the mother's tears wash the baby's face. About a week later the mother wrote a note of appreciation for the support we gave her by our presence and concern.

The other traumatic scene was the death of a burned boy of eight years of age. His clothes caught on fire while he was playing with matches near a gasoline tank. He ran through the field in flames to his mother in the kitchen and she smothered the flames. The mother drove the screaming boy to the emergency room. I supported the mother in her agony; she was blaming herself for the tragedy. I admired the mother, who in her awful pain asked me to get the boy baptized. Since the helicopter was going to take the boy to St. John's Burn Center in Springfield there was no time to look for any minister. I performed the Baptismal rite over the scorched body. The boy died three days later. The mother's Christian values came through in spite of her agony.

I had one other occasion to baptize an adult employee. She was dying from cancer of the stomach. In the course of my daily visits we came together to a deep understanding, trust and faith. She admitted that her married life was very difficult and that she had no church affiliation. One morning she asked me to baptize her as she did not want a clergyman. No one knows what a solemn moment that was for both of us as I poured the water over her head and pronounced the words of Baptism. She died shortly afterward. What we give to others, especially the sick and the dying, cannot be measured. What we give to one another I know and I treasure.

Next I was challenged with the appointment to be administrator of a sixty-bed Maria Care Center for six years, an infirmary for the sick and retired Felician Sisters of the Chicago Province.

My sensitivity to the needs of the elderly brought about many physical, structural and recreational improvements. Little things, like the purchase of comfortable lawn chairs and tables, enabled the convalescing to enjoy the outdoors. A six-passenger golf cart was purchased so handicapped nuns could enjoy a pleasant ride around the beautiful gardens surrounding the motherhouse.

I was also blessed to accompany my sister, Jane Adriatico, on tours of several countries — Japan, Taiwan, the Philippines, Poland, Rome, Hawaii, Jamaica, the Cayman Islands and Mexico.

Each trip intensified our appreciation for being born in America. When our airplane tires touched the ground of the O'Hare Airport we felt safe and secure again. The poverty and suffering of so many people in these countries overwhelmed us, especially in the Philippines and Mexico.

At seventy-eight years of age and after sixty happy and healthy years of service in the consecrated life, I am currently a Director of Community

Outreach at St. Andrew Retirement Home in Niles, Illinois and editor of St. Andrew quarterly Newsletter.

Today the big questions are: "Have I made a difference? What can I still do in the few years ahead, provided I am willing to make peace and to live fully in the faith I profess?"

The best example of goodness I encountered was during my vacation in Florida. My brother-in-law, Venancio Adriatico, was planting 240 young orange trees to replace those destroyed by the heavy frost. Why, in his nineties, was he planting trees? He said: "Won't they look lovely from the back porch? Won't future generations enjoy them?" How wonderful!!

What these seventy-eight years have taught me is that taking the extra mile in life has its rewards. Deep faith and that hope always bring satisfaction and fulfillment if you allow the Spirit to guide you.

6
NONE

My soul hath relied on His word;
My soul hath hoped in the Lord.
I was exalted like
The cedar in Libanus,
And like a cypress
on Mt. Sion;
Like a palm tree in Cades
·Was I exulted
And like a rose plant
In Jericho.

Cheryl Murphy Wollin
Former Franciscan

Married, one child

Teacher: Political Science. Oakton Community College
Niles Seminary, Archdiocese of Chicago

Alderman, City of Evanston

Bachelor of Arts, Saint Theresa College, Minnesota

Master of Arts, Northeastern Illinois University

Eucharistic Minister; former RCIA teacher

Cheryl continues to develop and use her leadership skills in her avocation, local politics. She has enjoyed a twenty-one year marriage to Jay, a professor. Beyond her family and politics Cheryl is interested in "travel, art — good books." Her future plans are well defined. In January of 1993 she plans to begin her campaign for the office of Mayor of Evanston.

Cheryl Murphy Wollin

Reflections on My Past

One of the clearest memories of my novitiate experience concerns a lesson in leadership. It was shortly after the amazing Vatican II council that a leadership training conference was scheduled at the order's college for women about twenty-five miles away. Five senior novices, including me, were selected to attend. We were delighted about the opportunity to go — both to have an outing on the college campus, mingling with students in the real world , and to discuss the hot topic of Vatican II. The day-long seminar was inspiring and intense. We returned to the motherhouse exhilarated, enthusiastic, and exuberant! As leaders in the future Church, we were ready to step up to the plate. We shared our new-found energy with our chaplain, who listened attentively to our ideas and seemed pleased with our involvement. Unfortunately, our novice mistress was not equally impressed.

I can remember, in the weeks that followed, how effectively she managed to stifle the joy of our experience. She gave us each routine and menial tasks through which she urged us to "show leadership." Whether we represented a threat to her management style or simply her authority I still do not understand; but I know that she was determined to squelch our enthusiasm. In one of my conversations with her, when I made an attempt to honestly deal with the situation, she was very clear. The gist of what she said was, "You are too young to be involved in the decision-making process. You have the potential to be a leader. Perhaps when you are in your forties, you will be a leader in our community, but for now just follow directions."

Wait twenty years to voice my opinion? Was she really serious? The more I looked around me, the more I was sure that she definitely was. This was during the 1960's. Radicals, hippies and flower children were emerging. But the five of us — young, well-meaning, and basically obedient — buckled down. We were all good students, and we applied our energies to our studies. There was an unspoken bond between us, however. We knew that somehow, something went wrong. Our spirits were dampened, and a part of us never quite recovered from that lesson in religious obedience.

It was a foreboding of trouble within religious communities. If the young could not be catalysts for change, if resistance (with the force of authority) met every new idea, how would religious life function in the fresh air of post-Vatican II? It was a time of conflict, consternation, and uncertainty as we all struggled to adapt to "The Church in the Modern World." I remained in the community another three years after this episode, trying to reconcile my own place in religious community life with my ideals. Growing up in a democracy definitely skewed my ability to adjust to blind obedience.

What positive lessons do I carry with me today — besides being the only one of my friends who is able to eat a banana with a knife and fork? Actually, quite a few. Living in a houseful of women made me better able to balance diversity, to understand the necessity of listening, and to appreciate the benefits of forgiveness. I am sure it made me more patient, more caring, and more careful of other people's feelings. I recently read the Great Decisions 1992 analysis of the Soviet economic problems which said that in the communist system "the rewards of hard work were denied to the general population." Well, that wasn't a problem in the convent. We worked hard and shared the burden together. And the psychological rewards of a job well done are substantial.

I value the rich academic education I received, and still appreciate the liturgical awareness that I developed during my six years as a sister. It enriches my spiritual life even today. I was trained to be a teacher, and am still teaching college courses twenty-five years later. Happily married for twenty-one years, I think those years of religious communal living helped me learn to share and care, especially through the trivial annoyances of daily life.

To complete the circle of my earlier memory, let me comment briefly on leadership. This whole flashback on my novitiate experience occurred when I was recently invited to accept an appointment to the National League of Cities Leadership Training Council. How ironic. This is the kind of thing that got me into difficulties in the first place! How right my novice mistress was after all. I am now in my forties. I am a member of the City Council in my city of 75,000 people, and I am planning to run for mayor next spring. Whether I win or lose, I've already learned that to risk nothing is to achieve nothing. To listen to one's own heart is just as important as listening to authority. Just because "we've always done things that way" doesn't mean that we can't forge new ways in the days ahead. Some spirits are hard to squelch!

Janet K. Schenk
Former Benedictine

Married

Free-lance writer, editor, social worker

Bachelor of Education, St. Benedict College

Master of Social Work, University of Kentucky

Special Training: journalism; writing for children; editing, computer.

Involvement as a Unitarian Universalist, Chicago

Janet lives an active, productive life, with emphasis on "having fun, reading, biking, aerobic walking, enjoying nature, being with people, having time alone," being with her siblings and traveling. She is writing ten to twenty hours a week. This writing is a must for her, a part of her being. She can't see life "settling down," and is looking forward to being able to work part time as a school social worker, or with an agency that works with children. This will help her writing for children to be more productive.

Janet K. Schenk

Piecing it Together

I have been out of the convent of the Sisters of St. Benedict three years longer than I was in. I celebrated the nineteenth anniversary of my leaving, shaking my head with disbelief. That year, 1989, was one of an overall life evaluation. What had I been when I entered the convent at age sixteen? What had I gained in the nineteen years? How have I developed since returning to lay life?

It has been slow. I had much to catch up on. The first feeling this past fall, as I read the quarterly report of the convent I left, was pain that those who remain seem farther along professionally than I am. Then immediately I admitted that I would not have survived spiritually or emotionally had I stayed. I felt the pain and then rejoiced at who I am — my whole life progression. I wrote this in 1979:

> The pieces I'm in
> Are all very thin
> And very, very fragile.
> They keep changing shapes,
> While listening to tapes
> Of what they ought to be.
> It's so hard to see
> How to be free
> With so many demands all around.
> While seeming curt,
> I allow the hurt
> Until life pulls together again.
> I gradually change
> As the pieces rearrange
> And a new form does emerge.

The Benedictine convent I joined when I was sixteen is about ten miles from where we lived. These nuns taught me through grade school. There I went to boarding school for my sophomore year before I entered the convent. The nuns seemed so peaceful and happy in contrast to our home, always in turmoil because of its rule by a very domineering mother. Maybe she was just venting on us her grief at losing her oldest daughter at age fourteen.

Subconsciously, all I wanted to do was get away from home.

I suppose all through my life I have been conscious of the fact that each person is a whole — spiritual, mental, physical, and emotional. Spiritual reading emphasized this fact, which probably helped me realize during my postulant year, when I developed stomach ulcers, that I really didn't belong in the convent. I didn't have enough strength within myself to leave, nor was there help from other nuns or from my family. I shiver to think what would have happened to me had I left at that time. I was so immature. I had to learn to make and trust my decisions. To do what thought was right had been discouraged throughout my childhood.

This training began in earnest toward the end of my novitiate. It was the day before we made temporary vows. My skill at sewing, developed since I was ten, was used well at my daily work making habits. We had been told to take some time during that day to write our vows. I was too petrified to make the decision to leave my work at a particular time of my choice in order do as I had been told. I was hurt, surprised, and confused at the strong reprimand I received. In a place where obedience was one of the vows, was I supposed to make a decision? Decision-making was so foreign to me that it took years to perfect the skill.

I was in a class of thirteen. We did have some fun times and some mischievous times but they were always initiated by others because I was too shy. One such was playing a Caruso record on an old wind-up victrola in our study room. We were caught when the novice mistress took a short cut on her way to chapel, and we were reprimanded. I don't remember a punishment; we were just postulants.

Then there was the serious side. I finished my high school during that first year. It took a full twelve months. I was sick of school, and happy to do more sewing than studying during the year of my novitiate.

The summer before my perpetual vows was spent in counseling with my juniorate mistress. I again felt an intense desire to terminate my life in the convent. Again I received only encouragement to pursue my religious vocation. I was an ideal member of the community; I was docile and made no trouble. God was showing me the way—how else could I interpret the lack of a helping hand to do what I felt was right for me? I joyfully celebrated my commitment with community and family.

I taught for fifteen years in parochial grade schools. I was a loner, and very easy to move around; I taught only two or three years in each school. I was never commended verbally —which is important to me, and necessary — for the work I did. During the last few years that I taught I was given the responsibility of being the supervisor of one new nun and was appointed the coordinator of grades three and four. But for me this was not enough to make me realize I was in the right profession. I needed to be told outright.

During the last two years of teaching I also realized I wanted to do more for individual children than I could do in the classroom, so social work became an attraction. The nun who was principal asked me why I wanted to leave teaching, since I was so effective.

My response, "You're too late in telling me."

In my convent days fear of two possibilities reigned — ego inflation and lesbianism. Praise was therefore withheld; friendships were greatly discouraged. I envied others who dared to have close friends. But I didn't have the courage to reach out because of my inability to go against authority and because of past personal losses. My oldest sister, with whom I was very close, died when I was four, and several friends had moved out of town during my grade school years. Fear of loss bound me tightly until the last four years in community.

My feeling of frustration in the spring of 1966 made me adamantly resolve either to find peace within the convent or to leave. I was on much medicine and I was sick of it. I felt that to find resolutions I had two needs: a good friend and a good counselor. One of the nuns I taught with became the friend and our confessor referred me for professional counseling. I began a journal during these years in order to process the change taking place within. Tearing the pages into the smallest pieces didn't totally allay my fears that someone would take what I had written from the wastebasket of my private room, piece it together and read it. I now continue a loose journal when in need of processing. The first thing I wrote was "I want to write!"

My friend turned out to be a very dominating person. The psychiatrist helped me grow through this 'friendship,' through my change to social work, and through my heart-rending decision to begin severing my mother's control of my life by leaving the religious community. Through all this my dependency on medicines decreased to only those needed for the control of my epilepsy.

When I left the religious community I also, more or less, left the Catholic Church. I needed community; being the seventh child in a family of eleven, I was born into community. My family was very religious when I was growing up. Now we are from far right to far left in our beliefs. Three years and an invitation from a classmate in graduate school completed the transition from the Catholic Church to Unitarian Universalist Church. This newly found religious family allows me the elbow room to have my own beliefs, and the freedom to change these as I have need. What a relief after the rigidity of my earlier years!

Through those nineteen years of protection within convent walls I had gradually become more self confident, self assertive, and conscious of what was going on around me. By 1965 customs within the convent were liberalizing. We changed from a long habit, with long scapular and pleated coif to a shorter habit with waist-length scapular, a white collar, and a simple veil. I became part of the active voice for further changes. Nuns in our convent were beginning to apply for dispensations from vows and were leaving.

By 1967 I was aware of the contradictions in the thinking and decisions of our mother superior. For example, the work of our convent was teaching. One of the nuns wanted to go into nursing, but permission was denied. She requested a dispensation. Then she was told she could become a nurse, but she decided it was too late. I was puzzled by this hypocrisy and spoke to our mother superior about it. She told me it was none of my business, that I should speak to my counselor about what I was feeling. By the time I returned to the place where I was teaching two hours later I was very irate. I called her to express this and was called before the council. I told them it had nothing to do with rules or regulations, but was simply between our mother superior and me. From then on I was only tolerated because of this and because of my other activities to promote change in our community.

In 1969, my last year, I was readily given permission to go into social work. I began wearing regular lay clothes as did the three Providence Sisters with whom I was living and working. I didn't ask, but simply informed our mother superior that wearing lay clothes was what I would be doing. When I went to the motherhouse that year I reluctantly hid in my habit. By that time we were pushing hard for the freedom to wear what we pleased. It was a great shock just this year to see on a Chicago bus an elderly Benedictine nun still wearing the old antique long garb with pleated coif.

By the following spring I realized that the parish social work I had joined was going to crumble. What was I going to do? I spent seven weeks in mental crisis making that decision. Even though I was thirty-five and had become very assertive, leaving the convent seemed to mean that my mother would resume control. I was not keen enough to see that since three of my brothers and two of my sisters had left religious life, Mother had become less domineering.

I would miss meditation dreadfully, so much so that five years later I began giving myself time for it each day. It was the help I needed to deal with the frustrations of continuous life changes.

When I asked for my dispensation it was suggested that I stay and go to graduate school in social work instead. My lack of success in my first venture in social work made me doubt the wisdom of this change. I also needed my freedom. My personal life needed my first attention.

Leaving was socially painful. I had finally, during those last four years, been able to reach out and allow others to touch me, physically and emotionally. But then I found a need to pull away. I kept in touch with some, wondering how they could stay. I finally decided that maybe their early days were not as uncompromising as mine had been.

I moved from this community into another one with my two sisters for a year and a half. This proved too constraining for my growth. They made decisions for me. So what a beautiful relief to have the privacy of my own apartment, to learn, to develop, and to grow at my own speed.

After leaving the convent I found a social work job, not with children, as I preferred, but with the elderly who were my second choice. I would prove wrong my mother's saying: "I'm too old to change."

I was still not used to standing up for myself. I was expected to take care of all the emergencies as well as to see fifteen clients a week. After three years in Louisville at this job I finally questioned this unrealistic expectation, then resigned and went to Lexington to graduate school. The campus was like a large safe cocoon and I did well. I was there at the large Unitarian Universalist Church when I met my husband.

It took me the whole summer after I graduated to find a job, part of which was to work with unwed pregnant teenagers. I told them that because I had joined the convent when I was sixteen I knew that they would need to make up for their teen-age years. It overcame the pain I felt at seeing them miss out on the carefree, growing years of their lives.

During the first few years out of the convent, when encountering something new how many times did I say, "How old am I now?" I had to grieve over the years of maturing that were put off until I was thirty-five, thirty-six, thirty-seven. Learning about the process of grief was a great find. I was in and out of grief — feelings of numbness, anger, guilt, confusion, loneliness, and healing. Long before *How to Survive the Loss of a Love* was published in 1976 I was insistent that grief was for any change in life, not just for death. This acknowledgment made all the new roads I was traveling more bearable. I knew there was a beginning and a closure to each encounter.

Guilt loomed as the greatest feeling I had to shed in the process of readjustment. With emphasis on the commandments, confession, and chapter of faults, being sinful had been like a large cloak engulfing me. Positive reinforcement from friends, counselors, and a new church community has gradually decreased the injunctions in my vocabulary, "I have to..." or "I should..." to near extinction . I catch myself, every once in a while, laying on the guilt, and I change my thinking. I do more of what I see is good for me and for others. What I want to do is have more fun in life.

It took me about ten years to reconcile myself with the nineteen years of wasted time in the convent, to see the value of it for me. The process began in earnest in 1976 when I had moved with my husband to

Kitchener-Waterloo, Ontario, Canada, where he became concertmaster of the K-W Symphony. Though I had made a contact at the university before we moved there I realized, after two and a half years of job searching, that I was in a triple bind: not only did I need a work permit to find a job and a job to find a work permit, but I needed to obtain my M.S.W. in Canada.

My decision: I will do what I have always wanted to do. Write!

Another few years and more counseling were needed for me to be able to write. I had to dig up the grief of my oldest sister's death, when I was four, and deal with it. Writing poetry showed me the way in this process. I had several articles and several pieces of poetry published during the following three and a half years. It was especially during this period of becoming self-aware, from 1980 to 1984, that I realized the positives of my years in the convent, a time of maturing.

Change happens slowly and sporadically whether in a group or personally. It has taken me from 1980 to 1991 to feel that my writing is an integral part of me again, never to be lost. With this conviction I can reach back to pick up my work with children, which has been dormant during the past few years. I am sure that the pain of rediscovering and retrieving will raise its head again and again at various times of change. I know that a greater peace will settle overall when I have one hand writing and one hand soothing and bringing hope to children. At least now I know I can do both well. I know I must do both to have peace within, the peace I have struggled to find and am struggling to retain. Though I have done some work at Children's Memorial Hospital here, and with Big Sisters in Ontario, school social work seems to be calling me. This summer I will probably take the two courses I need to renew my certificate and then find a job.

Whenever I am at a point of change, (am I ever not?) of greater change, I feel a power greater than myself. I have been uncomfortable with the word God for the past twenty-one years, probably because of the male connotation. From my childhood through most of my convent days I was taught that all power was God's. I was simply an instrument. This began to change during my last several years in religious life. When I stepped out into lay life as an adult of thirty-five, I felt I had to take complete charge. Gradually the events of my life have taught me that what I used to mean by God is the combination of a power within, that I have control of, and a 'power without,' that is beyond me.

Now in times of great change, after finally shedding the powerful childhood experience of death that buried my creativity deep within me, I feel a great spiritual influence of the power without. I ask myself, "What does spiritual mean?" I finally found a definition in the *Chicago Tribune* that feels good, feels right for me: "For me, spirituality, which is the same thing as personal growth, means being able to risk change— re-think the stuff that doesn't work as well as it did before." (Actress/ singer Cher)

I have the clipping taped up in my study.

Jean Kenny
Sister of Providence

Dean of Girls, Religion and Drug Education Teacher,
Saint Benedict High School

Bachelor of Arts, Saint Mary of the Woods College

Master of Arts, Religious Education, Loyola University

Master of Education, DePaul University

Job-related ministry

Living in Chicago has advantages for Jean. Here she can attend Bears and Sox games regularly. She lives in Immaculate Conception convent with ten other sisters who share daily prayers and meals. She likes movies, Chicago beaches, cycling and taking counseling classes and workshops. "I would like to enroll in deaconate classes, but have been excluded because I am a woman and class participation is for male candidates and their spouses." Like many women called to serve, she would like to be ordained someday.

Jean Kenny

The Path of Providence

"Woe to us if we depart from the path marked out for us by Divine Providence, the path wherein our holy founders and those who have preceded us have walked with so much courage and generosity."
—*Mother Mary Cleophas Foley Last Circular Letter, 1926*

In her book entitled *Reweaving Religious Life*, Mary Jo Leddy reminds me of a truism:

"Jesus attracts women and men, inviting them to follow Him. Such an invitation evokes the desire to respond with the whole of one's life. Yet how this response takes concrete shape depends not only upon our personal timing but also upon a general assessment of the world and times we live in."

I do not want to go back to the way things were in religious life and I am confident that as Sisters of Providence we will reflect Christ to the people we minister to and with in the decades that lie ahead. A spirituality of providence gives me the sense of time that recognizes a *kairos*, a providence time that is very different from the day to day time, *chronos*.

I made the decision to join the Sisters of Providence during my senior year at Providence High School in Chicago. I wanted to serve God in a special way and liked what I saw in the Sisters of Providence throughout my twelve years of Catholic education. I still have the letter of acceptance into the novitiate in my well worn scrapbook.

Sisters of Providence were my teachers at St. Mel Grammar School (1955-1963); in those days students had mostly sisters as their teachers. Sister Bernard taught all four of us and we were referred to as the Kenny Kids long before the Brady Bunch became popular. My mom and dad were active in the parish and had a good relationship with the sisters and priests there. St. Mel Parish was a great one; it was so big that we had two grammar schools.

My formative years with the Sisters of Providence were happy ones. I still remember my first grade teacher asking me to read for the principal/superior and how proud I was to be chosen to read for her and my classmates. As a sixth grader and junior high student I joined the track team and basketball team and did well in both. In 1963, when I graduated, I was one of five students who won a scholar/athlete trophy and was proud of this achievement.

Attending Providence High School was a logical choice for the next phase of my education. My sister Maureen preceded me there by one year. The school was close to our house, and it was staffed by Sisters of Providence. I received a quality education there. This summer we will be celebrating our silver anniversary high school class reunion.

I experienced my vocational call from God during my senior year when I met a special teacher. She was very friendly and outgoing and a great role model of religious life. At the end of my senior year some of my classmates were showing their engagement rings to their friends; I was showing my letter of acceptance into the novitiate to my friends. They were surprised with my decision, yet supported my choice. I was the only student of a graduating class of 126 to enter religious life.

My sister and brothers were shocked with my decision and took bets with each other on how soon I would leave the novitiate and return home — how was that for a sibling vote of confidence? My parents were pleased with my decision. My mom always wanted two of her children to become a nun and a priest. Well, she never got the priest, but there is still hope, though maybe at a later date when women are ordained. I believe I am called to ordination in the Roman Catholic Church. I believed this long before the Women's Ordination Conference existed. It is frustrating and unfair not to receive this sacrament because of a gender difference. The people of God are the losers because of this outdated patriarchal decision. I firmly believe a John XXIV is needed to attend to this.

My family drove me to an unheard-of Terre Haute, Indiana on a hot and humid day in 1967, August 30th to be exact. It was one day before my mom's fiftieth birthday. I was the first child to leave the nest and when I waved good-bye to my parents from the chapel my mom nearly broke down.

The novitiate experience was a five-year program consisting of four years of college and one year called a canonical year. My band started out with thirty-six women, mostly between the ages of seventeen and twenty. I was the youngest one and was referred to as the "baby" of the band.

During the postulant year we attended Saint Mary of the Woods College with the other college students for some of our classes, and had other classes with only the postulants. Our day-to-day living was structured with a 5:15 rising bell and in the evening profound silence after recreation together in the community room, then off to bed. We had instructions each morning, did daily employments, and then went to class. Several postulants left quietly that year. No good-byes — they vanished; our band was smaller. We were told about their leaving during instructions the next day.

Becoming friends with Barb was the best part of postulant year for me. I invited her to eat lunch with me on our second day as postulants, and she said yes. She is like a blood sister to me, and I know we will always be friends; I treasure her friendship. The negative "p/f" (particular friendship) phrase was just about gone at this time. As I look back on our friendship it was *particular* in the best sense of the word, and was an unexpected joy during the postulant year.

In June of 1960 we became canonical novices. We received the white veil and began a special year in our formation program. We moved across the road and were separated from the other people in formation. During canonical year the emphasis was on learning about community history and serving the community at the motherhouse in the infirmary, helping with housekeeping chores, and making hosts. We also continued our study in theology.

Several more band members left during the canonical year for various reasons. I was not bothered by this; they realized religious life was not meant for them. I thought it was better to go when you realized that fact instead of staying and being unhappy. During that canonical year I missed not going to college full time, but took advantage of the slower pace getting to know our retired sisters better.

On May 31, 1970 I professed my first vows and received the black veil. My family came down for this special mass, and it was a memorable day. During the next year we became scholastic novices and went back to college as full time students. I finished my last two years of college. Some of the life was less structured and I enjoyed myself more. Going to Pizza Hut and/or to a show was fun.

Graduating from college was an important accomplishment for me and I was invited to teach social studies to junior high students at Saint Francis Borgia School in Chicago. I did so and enjoyed my four years there.

I lived with eleven other Sisters of Providence and once again I was the youngest. I especially liked Sister Ellen Angela, the oldest sister there, and when she died I cried, felt sick, and missed her a lot. But it was great being back in Chicago and being close to my family and seeing them often. After Saint Francis Borgia School I was invited to teach religion at Mother Theodore Guerin High School in River Grove, Illinois. This school was only a few blocks away from Saint Francis Borgia. I was complimented that the principal asked me to come to Guerin. I worked with her for ten years and learned a lot from her.

After being there for five years I created alcohol education seminars for freshmen and taught this drug education/prevention program there for five years. I am especially proud of this course and thought it to be worthwhile for the students.

A humorous story always comes to my mind when I reflect upon my teaching years at Guerin. One day in a morality class a junior asked me what year I graduated from high school and I told her in 1967. She asked me if I went to Woodstock and joined the hippie revolution. I laughed and told her no and mentioned that going into the convent was a very countercultural thing for me to do.

While I was at Guerin my mom died during Easter vacation on April 13, 1982. That was the saddest day of my life. I was thirty-two and she was sixty-four. I lost an important part of myself and nobody could ever replace her. Ten years later I continue to miss her very much. There is no way to adequately express this deep loss and painful separation. I received a lot of support from the sisters at her wake and funeral.

I was a pastoral associate for five years from 1986-1990. I enjoyed this new ministry for women in the church. It was as close to ordination as a woman could come in a parish setting. I touched adult lives in more personal ways than I could ever do as a teacher. Parishioners were so grateful for hospital and home visits to their sick relatives. They appreciated my presence at wakes and funerals, and invited me to their homes for meals and parties. I truly enjoyed teaching adult religious education courses because the adults were hungry to know more about Scripture, morality, Mother Teresa, Vatican II, Leo Buscaglia and John Powell. They were there faithfully because they wanted to be there, not because they had to take a religion course like the high school students I had taught. What a refreshing change! I remember helping a woman with her annulment, and how grateful she was, and how comfortable she was talking with a woman instead of a priest about her abusing husband and past life with him.

In 1991 I was invited to join the teaching staff at Saint Benedict High School in Chicago. I said yes to the principal, and I teach religion and a drug education course to freshmen. Right before the second semester began he asked me to join the administrative team as dean of girls and I said yes. Teaching and being one of two deans of students in this coed inner city school has been challenging to say the least, and at the same time a worthwhile and growthful experience for me. There are only two sisters and one priest in this high school.

I am twenty-five years older now and have welcomed the changes within our congregation; I continue to be a happy and proud member. I am glad I missed some of the strict observances the older sisters told me about, like kissing the floor and not being allowed to go home for funerals of family members. As a postulant I resented giving my unsealed outgoing letters to the postulant directress because I believed her reading them was an invasion of my privacy. At a later date she told us she did not read our letters. I will always be grateful to the sisters for the quality education I received during my novitiate and later at Loyola and DePaul.

Vatican II redefined the role of religious communities in the Catholic Church. The old structured and secure form of religious life is outdated. Now we are in transition and are undergoing the process of transformation required to relate to God and others in new ways — to cooperate with God in the 90's. This transformation continually takes place within us and among us. Because of these dramatic changes over the last twenty-five years, religious life today continues to be in the midst of a major transition.

I feel fortunate to have experienced the post-Vatican II view/lifestyle with the Sisters of Providence. As I await Vatican III, I am hopeful amidst the confusion that accompanies transitions. Living as a vowed religious person means developing new and different forms with the changing times. It continues to be a lifestyle where the central focus is God and not a spouse or a career.

I enjoy having adult friends of both sexes; I am enriched and empowered by their supportive presence in my life. These friendships are very important to me both personally and professionally. Time, effort and energy are expended to nurture these friendships. Spending some of my free time with friends at Bears and Sox games, going out to dinner and a movie or a concert (Neil Diamond) and going to the beach or bicycling are the ways I relax and enjoy life. My vocation is a complementary call to the married lifestyle and the single lifestyle, bearing witness to the belief that all of life is holy. On August 30, 1992 I will be celebrating my twenty-fifth anniversary.

Each day I try to spend some quiet time reflecting and/or reading — usually in the early morning before rushing off to work. I enjoy solitude as a quiet time to grow and recharge. I make a retreat each summer, and am fortunate to have this spiritually-deepening opportunity to nourish my faith life. I freely choose this style of discipleship as a vowed religious woman today. Being faithful to the movements of God's spirit in my life is a daily decision.

In 1990 my community celebrated our sesquicentennial anniversary. This unique celebration has been characterized as a journey — a journey in love, mercy and justice. It was a special year of remembering, thanksgiving and renewal for the members of the congregation and for all who are, have been, or will be part of our lives in providence. We continue our journey, quite certain that God's work will be brought to fruition even as our own joy is made complete in a future full of hope, lived for and with God's people, wherever they may be. Our hope continues to be in God, who has protected us until the present, and who will provide, somehow, for our future need.

Like other religious congregations in the United States, we reflect the changes in the church and in society. Women religious are assuming more visible roles in the life of the church and are finding many options for service available to them. What remains unchanged is a strong sense of the tradition of service handed down from Mother Theodore Guerin and the hundreds of courageous women who have come after her. The history of the congregation lives in the hearts and minds of present-day daughters of providence, committed to the service of God's people in the spirit of their foundress, and eager like them to continue the works of love, mercy and justice into the twenty-first century. I am happily saying yes to the providence quests that lie ahead.

January 17, 1992

Dear Dr. FitzGerald,

I was reading the NCR recently and saw your ad for some reflections on religious life for an anthology. I offer you my thoughts as a relatively young religious who has had a rather bumpy journey. I am searching for wholeness on my own.

At the same time, because I am still a member of the community, I cannot risk that these reflections be traced back to me. I would prefer to leave on my own rather than be asked to do so, should my superiors find out I wrote these pages.

If they are helpful to you, fine. This is the only copy and is now your property to do as you wish. I am not interested in any financial compensation.

—*Anonymous*

Freezer to Fire

I came to religious life some ten-odd years ago with all the sparkling idealism of anyone who is involved in a new relationship. I was sure that I was ready to make a commitment to a lifestyle which held the ultimate promise: eternal life. What more could a person ask for? I had known several of the sisters in my community for several years before I entered. They seemed like happy, holy women who were poised and professional. I admired them as noble women who were as selfless as the martyrs I had learned about in religion class. At the tender age of twenty I followed their example and the dictum of Jesus to "leave everything and come follow me".

Anxious to make this new mode of life work, I was full of zeal for the community forms of prayer, interpretations of the apostolic life and modes of recreation. All of us were guided by a novice mistress who was forming us out of a concept of obedience which was best described as blind, deaf and dumb. I vividly remember being told as a canonical novice that I did not have permission to think — literally. Of course I took that admonition straight to heart and tried to sublimate my intellectual curiosity for everything that wasn't approved. The biggest problem was that I liked to think. At the time I was sure my efforts would be greatly blessed by God, whose will was being voiced to me through my legitimate superiors.

During my second year as a novice I became good friends with a professed sister almost twenty years my senior. Of course this relationship was carefully monitored, lest the young one be adversely influenced or the relationship get too close. I started to realize that the concept of friendship was perceived as suspect. The questions I was asked by those same legitimate superiors seemed foreign to me.

I had left all the people who were close to me. Was the expectation of this way of life to remain that way? I wanted very much to belong to this new group. Little did I know that the interpretation of the word "group" meant just that: the *whole* group. I found out much later that my sister-friend was scrutinized about our friendship as much as I was. Despite the sometimes/sometimes-not-so subtle pressure applied to both of us, the relationship lasted about six years. It died a natural death because, in the end, our age difference made a great deal of difference in our outlook on life. That experience showed me a flash of the other side of the community, one that initially confused me. After all, wasn't life about relationships?

I managed to slide through the novitiate to first vows. My brain now out of the freezer, I continued through college and earned a teaching degree. The middle years of my formation experience were somewhat uneventful, and all meld together. As a new teacher I was very busy just trying to keep my head above water with the day-to-day work. Community structures were rote. I knew what was expected, and I had also learned how to produce the appropriate responses to practically any request. As I look back on it now, my behavior could be likened to any dog Pavlov might have conditioned.

Some of the most automatic responses I learned were: give complete attention and deference to the elderly sisters; always say "yes" to any request, even if it required you to stay up until three in the morning; be on time for community prayer; never complain; never have an opinion which could be interpreted as slightly left-of-center; bow your head at the name of the Holy Father; stay detached from everyone and everything. Somewhere in the back of my head the flash still existed and the question still remained: wasn't life about relationships?

As the time of perpetual profession drew nearer I was cautioned by the formation director to beware of a period of disillusionment immediately following final vows. I was given many suggestions as to what I could do to prevent this tragedy from happening. What nobody bothered to tell me in plain English was that I was about to discover the truth about the organization. The shield of formation, the fog, was about to be lifted and I would see the whole, uncensored picture. The time for full membership had come.

On the day of vows, I said "yes" with a heart full of gratitude to this group of women whom I had grown to love in the approved, detached way and who had accepted me and offered me a chance at eternal life. What more could a person ask for? I was sure that with this system of support, I could almost reach up and touch God. I could barely contain the exhilaration I felt on that day.

It didn't take long for the flash in the back of my head to become a raging fire. I was transferred from one place to the next on the average of every two years. During that fateful time (in which I am still involved) there was little discussion between myself and my legitimate superiors about what I wanted, or what kind of impact this vagabond existence was having on me. I began to identify with the nomadic peoples, feeling no strong attachments, neither accepted nor rejected, neither needed nor wanted, by anyone at any particular place — I was emotionally numb. I knew that each place was only temporary and that there was little hope for any relationships of significance.

Once I became conscious of what was happening to me, I purposely set out to find a person who would accept me for me and I began to shed some of the conditioned responses which had become my shell. Along with the release of armor, however, comes a great deal of intense pain. At the time of this writing, it is a pain which is beginning to call me to another level of existence — a sensitive loving, compassionate (dare I say human?) level.

Our community meetings focus on our impending financial doom. Our membership is declining; the median age of the community is rising at an exponential rate. By the time I turn forty there will be about thirty of us supporting two-hundred retired sisters. There are clamors from the periphery of the community to change those structures which are killing off any hope of a life of quality before it's too late. Sisters are leaving the community at ever-increasing rates and the community hierarchy still bows its head at the name of the Holy Father.

The call of the Church is toward greater participation of women in ministry; we are still assigned to fill slots in staffing patterns. The call of the Church is to compassion; we are not meeting the emotional needs of our own. The call of the Church is to wholeness; we continue to perpetuate that which is clearly dysfunctional.

Is this the time of disillusionment I was warned against? I think, more accurately, my reflections are an assessment of an organization which is holy, well-intentioned but naive. I have gained invaluable experience from the women who cared for me over the years. They still believe that this is the most direct route to God. Will I stay? It's doubtful. The cards are stacked against the healing of the dysfunction, and consequently against the wholeness of the members. The community can't be held solely responsible for its illness. It is a microcosm of the institutional Church.

Amy Therese Kenealy
School Sisters of St. Francis

Chaplain, American Healthcare Center, South Holland, Illinois

Project Director: Pastoral Ministry Institute, St. Xavier College, Chicago

Bachelor of Arts, Alverno College, Milwaukee

Master of Arts, English Language and Literature, University of Chicago

C.A.S. Educational Administration, University of Illinois

Master of Science, Counseling/Psychology, Chicago State University

Master of Arts, Pastoral Theology, St. Mary of the Woods

Doctor of Ministry, Chicago Theological Seminary

"Socializing with other sisters in the community" is a key to keeping in touch with Sister Amy Therese's community, as well as area meetings, letters and a telephone network. Sister Amy Therese lives in a rented house with another sister, and in addition to all her ministerial interests, cross country skiing and scuba diving keep her very active. "I have given up projections," says Sister. "I hope to be a pastoral assistant in a parish. God only knows what will happen beyond the now."

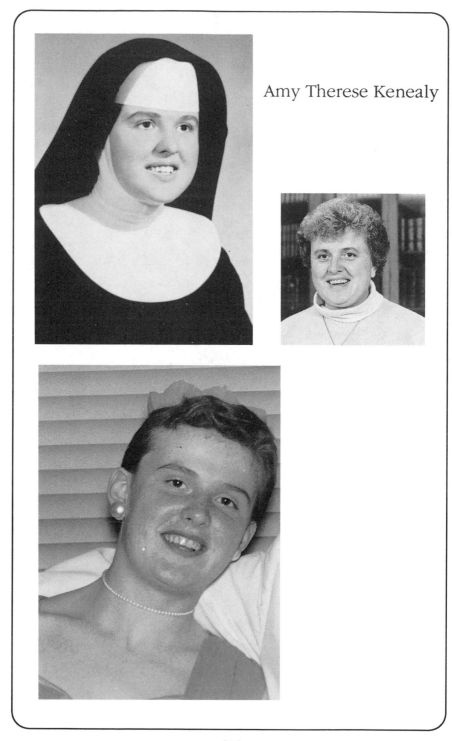

Amy Therese Kenealy

Whatever Happened to Sister Amy Therese?

As I begin to share my life I find myself the part-time chaplain at Americana Nursing Home in South Holland, and project director of the Pastoral Ministry Institute at St. Xavier University in Chicago. How I got here is an odyssey that will take me from a Jewish ghetto, through Catholic schools, to the School Sisters of St. Francis. Once a sister, I roamed (was missioned to) the affluent suburbs of Chicago, the rural missions of Mississippi, the housing projects in the inner city of Chicago, and finally to the southeast suburbs of Chicago, where I have lived for the past twenty-two years.

I was born on a cold, snowy December day in Chicago, a year before Pearl Harbor was bombed. The date was December 2, 1940. I had a brother who had been born sixteen months earlier. We were a blue-collar middle class family. My maternal grandmother, who lived with us, worked nights making bullets in the basement of the Merchandise Mart, my mother worked days at Montgomery Ward and later, at Sears; my father worked nights as a printing pressman after he returned from the Army. My grandmother died just prior to my graduation from eighth grade.

We were Irish and Roman Catholic, living in an apartment and neighborhood where the majority of families were Jewish. I did not realize the significance of that until I was older and understood the Holocaust. However, I credit my ecumenical openness today to those early times when I went to temple as well as to church. I entered Catholic grade school at four and a half years old and attended Catholic school through high school and college. During all these years I was taught by the School Sisters of St. Francis, whose order I entered after high school.

It came as a surprise to everyone, including myself and my high school nuns, that I entered the community. I had a steady boyfriend and a scholarship to Mundelein College. The call goes back to one day after school when I was a freshman. I was helping one of the sisters carry books to a locker. The sister said she knew I attended daily Mass at my parish. Somewhat defensive, not wanting to be considered a "holy roller" by my peers and teachers, I responded, "So what?" She replied, "So, it shows you love God."

I never gave her comment much thought, pursuing my life of studies, sports, dating and the like. But, periodically, the incident would surface, and I began to question: How much do I love God? Do I love him enough to give him my life? I thought I would give it a try for six months. Well, that was 1958 and, thirty-four years later, I am still a nun.

I had always wanted to be a teacher, so entering a teaching order who had taught me all my life seemed natural. The first nine years after formation became a whirlwind tour of seven missions. It was a" join the convent and see the world" type of life. These were the years where we went where we were sent. Oh, we could volunteer; I volunteered for Alaska, but look where I ended up.

Trained as a high school English teacher, I ended up teaching first grade at River Grove for two years; then I was sent to Wilmette to teach eighth grade. The superior/principal was a friend of mine, and I was happy. But after one year, and despite my objections, I was sent to Walls, Mississippi, to teach English, Latin, music, religion in an all-white grade and high school. That is, it was all-white until I got there.

The pastor decided that he would put the son of his housekeeper, who was black, into my homeroom. Not long after, on a Sunday morning, some men came to the convent door. They were members of the White Citizens Council by day and the KKK by night. They were looking for me, the Northerner, who had come down to make trouble. Young and naive, I told them if they did not like it they could remove their students from my class. Nothing happened, but I have never again seen such hate as I saw in the eyes of those men that day.

But I have jumped ahead of myself. I had not wanted to go to the South, but this was before Vatican II, when we followed orders. I, personally, did not like hot weather. But, there I was, in mid-August, clothed in black woolen serge and all wrapped up around the face, wearing a heavy, black veil. Did they send me at night in a sleeper car, on somewhat of an express train? No, they sent me in the heat of the day on a local train that seemed to stop every twenty minutes at another small town. I was wilted when I arrived in Memphis with my suitcase and my guitar. That was my first taste of the South.

After a year at Walls the high school was closed. I was sent to teach eighth grade in Barrington. Again, I was happy. Several of my friends were stationed there, but this was not to last. Six months later I was sent to Yazoo City, Mississippi, to an all-black school; one of the high school teachers had taken sick. After a year and a half I ended up at Holly Springs, Mississippi, another all-black school. Winters were spent teaching in Mississippi, but summers were spent in the inner city of Chicago around Holy Angels parish. I was sent to do CYO work in the Washington Park Homes, a public housing project . There I ran day camps for the grade-school children, trained teens to be peer counselors and offered them counseling services as well. This, of course, was during the years the Blackstone Rangers (later the El Ruk'ns) were starting up and the black power movement was growing.

I was still at Holly Springs, which was about a forty-five minute drive from Memphis, when news came that Martin Luther King was dead, shot by a white man. I was coaching an all-black girls basketball team, and the boys team had just started playing. The game was called at halftime. Here I was, the only white person, dressed in a long white habit, in the gym. I have never forgotten what it felt like to be a minority of one and a member of the race that had killed the hero of the rest of the people in the gym.

By the next year the administration of the school was taken over by the parish priests, who wanted to hire their own personnel. I took the opportunity to request time off to get my master's degree in Humanities at the University of Chicago. I received the degree in June, 1970, and my life began to settle down. By this time we were living under an experimental rule, were no longer in habit, had returned to our baptismal names, could choose our place of work and those with whom we wished to live.

I rented a home with a sister I had met at Walls. In fact, she was the one who picked me up at the train on that hot and humid August afternoon in the early 60's. She is now seventy-seven years old, has survived cancer and heart surgery, still visits the sick and home-confined, and will celebrate her sixtieth jubilee in religious life in June.

Having decided to live in the Chicago area, closer to where many of our sisters were, we searched for jobs — she as a school librarian and I as a high school English teacher. I had decided I wanted to teach in a public school for a variety of reasons: I wanted some stability; our order had only two high schools in the city and an abundance of high school teachers; I could earn a salary based on my credentials which would help support my religious community. We had no set place to live that summer of 1970 and, while we looked for something on the northwest side of Chicago, I got a phone call from the boy I had dated in high school. We had always kept in touch. He asked if we would live in his house for the summer while he took his family out west. We agreed, even though we had no idea where the suburb of Dolton was. I had never been in the southeast suburbs of Chicago.

One day that summer, while walking down Sibley Boulevard, I saw a beautiful high school building and went in to ask if they could use an English teacher. One of their English teachers had just resigned; after checking my credentials they hired me. I would stay at Thornridge High School for twenty years. On the first day of workshops for new teachers the assistant principal said there was an opening for a school librarian and asked if we knew of any one. One week later Sister Madonna joined me on the faculty.

I see the Holy Spirit in all of this. Had I not been asked to house sit, I would never have found Thornridge High School. Had there not been an opening for a librarian, Sister Madonna and I would never have worked together, having the same schedule and vacation time, as well as being able to use the same car. This was crucial, since in the Chicago province, each local house was responsible for buying and paying for their own cars and living expenses, all the while sending assessments to the community. We found a home to rent in Sauk Village, some fifteen miles south of the school, and joined St. James Parish where over the course of twenty years I became heavily involved in parish ministry.

I began teaching English at Thornridge in 1970. To advance on the pay scale we were required to take continuing education courses. Realizing that as I got older I would not be able to stay in the classroom, I started working on a graduate degree in counseling/psychology and another one in educational administration. By 1976, both degrees were finished and I was already a dean and crisis counselor, was qualified for most professional positions in education, and enjoyed what I was doing. I had planned to be in the educational field for the rest of my life. I was set for life, or so I thought.

It seems that God is never one to leave me alone for very long. Sister Madonna and I were always looking for retreat opportunities in a part of the country we had never seen so we could get a vacation out of it as well. Checking the *National Catholic Reporter* in the summer of 1976, I saw an advertisement: charismatic retreat for Franciscan sisters given by a Franciscan priest. I did not know anything about the charismatic renewal, but was attracted by the Franciscan flavor of the retreat. This retreat would disrupt my comfortable, happy, peaceful world. It would be a turning point in my religious and professional life. There would be no going back.

During this retreat I became aware of the Holy Spirit taking hold of my life and changing its direction. I felt a great urgency to spend much time in prayer, reading and meditating on the Scriptures. I was becoming aware of my desire and God's call to move into parish ministry, the healing ministry and spiritual direction. But before continuing down that path where the spirit was taking me, I want to reflect on what was happening in religious life—mine and others.

In 1959, my reception class had eighty-six people; eight years later, seventy-two took final vows. Today, there are less then twenty still in religious life. Naturally, I had concerns as members of my class and many others were leaving. I asked myself why I was still here. I guess I really never considered leaving, since I was doing what I would have done had I not joined the order — teaching. Would I have left if the changes of Vatican II had never happened? I really do not know. But with the ability to choose living arrangements and ministries, the option of whether or not to wear the habit, having a good circle of friends, both within and without the order, I was where I felt God wanted me to be. That is not to say these early years were not frought with difficult living situations, superiors and the like, but there were more good times than bad. And so, I stayed!

What happened to me after that 1976 retreat accounts for who and where I am today and my vision of religious life and ministry. I continued as a dean at Thornridge for fourteen more years. Being a religious sister and a dean of discipline in a public high school made for some surprising situations. I was criticized as to why I was in a public school, when there were not enough sisters in the Catholic schools. But many of the students at Thornridge were from Catholic schools and most others were Christians; I felt that my presence and guidance would help shape their lives.

As I indicated, these years also brought a change to my relationship with God, my spirituality and my prayer life. I was beginning to understand more deeply my commitment to belong to God. He became lover and best friend. The more deeply I meditated on the Scriptures, the more my prayer life began to change. During quiet times, I would write prayer and poetry to Jesus. As I look back on them, I find one that sums up my feelings during those years and still does today:

> "My heart leaps up," a poet said these words.
> And yet, somehow, they now belong to me.
> My heart can't help but leap, with bouncy ground of love
>   to lift it up.
> My love tonight is full and turns towards you;
> It longs to find the Heart from which it came.
> A Heart that loved so much when it was killed,
> Could not but help to pour its love on all.
> It flowed for centuries, across continents in search of me.
> Dare I say it!
> What Man could love with such a beating pulse
> To find my hidden and oft blocked-up heart.
> It entered on a cold December day, and there I was, alive!
> "So was it when my life began, so be it now that I'm a
>   woman."
> O Man of Heart and God of Love, I leap to You.

I also began to realize what the Peace Prayer of St. Francis really meant. I had to respond to God's love and care for the people he cared about.

In 1978, Deacon Matt came to St. James from a parish in the city. He urged the pastor, three years from retirement, to allow the ministries of the Church that flowed out of Vatican II to be initiated in the parish and to empower the people to serve in these ministries. Prior to this, women had not been allowed to serve in any liturgical ministries. Sister Madonna and I became the first people to serve as Communion ministers. We had served in other parishes and now were willing to become actively involved in the new ministries.

In the course of the next eleven years, I recruited, trained and nurtured all the liturgical ministers as well as the liturgy team. Deacon Matt and I would initiate the pastoral care ministry and I would coordinate and nurture these ministers for many years. Since I was making a good salary at Thornridge, I donated my pastoral ministry services to the parish. This consumed most of my evenings and weekends; my days were spent at the high school.

In 1985, I realized that I was being drawn more deeply into parish ministry and further away from working in school. I also realized that as a woman in the Catholic church who wanted a leadership role in parish ministry, I needed to update my theology and go for a Doctorate in Ministry. I received a masters, degree in pastoral theology in 1987, and my doctorate in 1989 from Chicago Theological Seminary in Hyde Park. Again, God was stepping into my life. One of my professors suggested that I come to teach in the Pastoral Ministry Institute at St. Xavier College. This was 1988, and now I am a project director of the Institute.

As I look over my years both at Thornridge and at St. James, I realize that I was wearing many hats all at the same time. I was student, pastoral minister, dean in a public school, instructor in a college. At the same time, I was pursuing graduate degrees in psychology, administration, pastoral theology and ministry. I never took a leave from working days at Thornridge and evenings and weekends at St. James Parish. Somewhere among all that I offered workshops for pastoral ministers through the Pastoral Ministry Institute. Today, I wonder how I ever managed. I even found time to learn to scuba-dive and cross-country ski during those years. I know God was behind it all or I would have never made it through.

By June of 1989 I had finished my doctorate. Six months later I would have twenty years of service at Thronridge. The current pastor at St. James was not open to my being a pastoral associate, so I put my name into the placement office of the Archdiocese. For the first time in my life, I had made no plans. I was open to whatever God wanted me to do. At least I was finished with my degrees and could relax for a while. But I should have known that God would not just let me be.

Barely three weeks after I received my doctorate, and after Thornridge had let out for the summer, I received a phone call from the pastor of an African-American parish on the southeast side of Chicago, about twenty-two miles from Sauk Village. He asked me to come up and interview for a pastoral associate position. In August I found out I had the position. Again, I had to change things in my life. I arranged to transfer my ministerial responsibilities at St. James to others in the parish and began serving in the new parish in September. I gave notice at Thornridge that I was retiring at the end of the first semester, January, 1990. I continued in the Pastoral Ministry Institute, which was only twenty minutes from the new parish.

Our parish staff consisted of two priests, the school principal (a sister), a deacon couple and myself. The pastor believed in collaborative ministry. He had just renewed his pastorate for another six years, so I planned to be there at least for that amount of time. But God had other plans as you will see.

A pastoral associate is a non-ordained associate pastor who ministers in many areas of the parish, just as the priest does. She shares responsibility with the priests for the daily care of the people of the parish community. This includes administration, pastoral care, catechesis and liturgy. I established and nurtured the pastoral care program (Ministry of Care), ran Bible Study groups, preached at weekend liturgies on a regular rotation basis, was staff advisor to the evangelization team and the youth, worked with lay ministers in training and liturgical ministers, visited hospitals and homes, and, one year, was also coordinator of the religious education program. In addition, we all helped out wherever necessary. The people of the parish were responsive and open to sharing in ministry.

I enjoyed serving in that parish. It was good to take off some of those hats I had been wearing for so many years. I was a full-time, salaried pastoral associate, doing part-time work at the Pastoral Ministry Institute and that was it! There was no school and no studies, although, for the next two years, I would spend little time at home because of the commute and evening meetings. I had responded to God's call to minister here and was prepared to stay for a while, but that was not to be.

In June, 1991 the pastoral associate position was eliminated because the parish could no longer afford to pay the salary. So, here I was, fifty years old, and in the short space of two years I had moved from being overworked and overemployed to being underworked and underemployed. It seemed to be another one of God's surprises. I looked for another position as a pastoral associate in a parish, but the situation was much the same. They already had one, or could not afford to hire one. Although we speak of a shortage of priests, there seems to be difficulty in finding a position in a parish for the non-ordained professional. I am still hoping to find such a position.

I find my situation somewhat of a paradox. I cannot find a position as a pastoral associate, and yet I initiated a Pastoral Associate Specialty Certificate program for the Pastoral Ministry Institute, writing the curriculum, creating an advisory board, recruiting instructors, and doing some of the teaching. I continue to direct the program preparing others for pastoral associate positions. It is a puzzle sometimes!

In December, 1991, I received a phone call asking if I would be interested in being a chaplain at a nursing home on a part-time basis. That, of course, was the farthest thing from my mind. Never had that been in my plans. Of course, I was training others to be pastoral care ministers in parishes, but I had never envisioned a chaplaincy for myself. The rest is now history.

By January, 1992, I was chaplain at Americana Healthcare Center in South Holland, only a ten-minute commute from my home. As chaplain I serve the residents and families as well as staff. I am responsible for the development and coordination of the overall religious programs, facilitating group counseling sessions, developing and leading in-service programs for staff, as well as serving as a liaison with community religious leaders. What an odyssey—from teaching first graders to being a chaplain for the elderly. Somehow, knowing how God has a way of continually breaking into my life in dramatic ways, I feel that this is only a rest stop in the journey. I am sure there is more to come! As I look over my life I see how God has moved in it, giving me an opportunity to share how I envision my life and ministry of the past few years and at this moment.

I am a woman of strong faith and deep prayer. My life is a constant reflection of who I am for Jesus. Everyday I place before Him my feelings, emotions, joys and disappointments. His message to me is always the same: "I love you and I am by your side. Believe in me and love me." I realized long ago that I cannot love God without loving those He loves, that I cannot care for Jesus without caring for those Jesus cares about. As a Franciscan sister who has lived in a community of dedicated women within the Church for thirty-four years, my strength for ministry comes from our common life of prayer, affection and care for each other.

I desire to share this vision with others, to nurture the laity who are called to minister to others in Jesus' name. I work with small groups of people, as Jesus did with his twelve apostles, nurturing them in faith and prayer, being a model of Jesus' service, so they in turn can grow closer to God and bring Jesus' love and mercy to those they serve. I see my ministry as showing others how to search out who God is and what He wants of them. It is the ongoing attempt to put my own search for God at the disposal of those who want to join the search, but may not know how.

I see my ministry as training others to serve as I have been taught to serve, to form them spiritually as I have been formed, to share with them what I have experienced. I try to listen to their needs and desires, affirming them in their success and weeping with them in their sorrow, being present to them, just as Jesus was present to others.

My model for ministry is Jesus. My textbook is the Scripture. That is what I see ministry being all about — to know who Jesus is and bring Him to others and others to Him. It is to witness to Jesus in my life and service and empower others to do the same. If someone asked me how I saw my ministry as a religious sister today, I could respond in one sentence: My ministry is to be available for others as Jesus was, and to enable others to go where Jesus wants to be.

Now you know what happened to one of the good sisters. You have shared my fifty-one year odyssey. Only God knows what will happen next!

Doreen Casey
Former Daughter of Charity

Single

Staff nurse in general hospital

Bachelor of Science in Nursing, Marillac College

Master of Arts, Counseling, University of South Alabama

Registered Nurse

Lector and Eucharistic Minister St. Philip Benizi Catholic Church, Jonesboro, Georgia

Doreen would someday like to work as a nurse in a jail. She's a member of Alcoholics Anonymous and is "vitally interested in ministry to addicts/alcoholics" in those jails. At present she teaches a weekly class to inmates. She hopes to continue writing for publication; she has had an article accepted by a major nursing journal.

Doreen Casey

A Good Sister Story

I entered the Community of the Daughters of Charity in 1955 at the age of eighteen. I entered in St. Louis, Missouri from my home in California. It was important to me to be far away from home. My sister had entered another community the year before, and my mother had been very interfering. I did not want this to happen to me.

I loved the religious and spiritual side of the life. I enjoyed the fellowship. I did not find the discipline difficult; I had come after a year spent as a nursing student, and that was a disciplined setting. However, I had to stuff my feelings about leaving home. We never talked about how we felt; it was as though we weren't supposed to feel. I never dealt with this aspect of entering. We wrote home once a month.

The community had a rule that you never went home, even for serious illness or death. Over the next few years I saw my family one time, and it was a surprise visit when I received the habit. I was already most uncomfortable with myself and my identity in this new dress, and then I received word that they were in town. It was a most upsetting experience; I was unable to relate either as a family member or as a nun. Over the next few years I lost contact with them except for letters; they moved, grew up. My dog died and they didn't think it important to tell me.

As for community life, I really enjoyed it. The life held a lot of meaning for me. I went to school, finished my R.N. and earned a B.S.N. I loved the liberal education; prior to this I had only been exposed to nursing. In high school I had done poorly, but now I did well academically. There was a great deal of emphasis put on using every minute. Thank God for monthly and yearly retreats. Prayer and spiritual reading were a priority in our lives and to this day I am glad of that. I was well cared for physically, spiritually and mentally.

427

There was a large group of sisters at the motherhouse and this gave me a real feeling of support. I think we were under a lot of pressure, however, during the time I was at the juniorate. Several sisters were admitted to the psychiatric hospital next door and they left the community from there. Years later, talking with the sisters who staffed the hospital at that time, I learned that they felt that going to the hospital was a way out of the pressure. A sister who developed symptoms severe enough to require hospitalization would always be advised to return home.

For myself, it seemed that leaving was the worst thing that could happen to you. "The community is the boat that will lead you to heaven, if you leave the boat you will be in the water and God knows if you will ever get to heaven; or what will happen to you." I remember a refectory reading we had about a sister who "took off the habit" and the despair and remorse she felt the next day. In those days there was no way to get back in; leaving was an irreversible decision.

I enjoyed the cloistered seminary year. We were a small group; there was time for prayer and study. I was happy and I felt safe, physically and spiritually.

My first mission was to the psychiatric hospital next door. I enjoyed it. I was well liked by the community I lived with, and I liked them. I took care of a lot of the older sisters who were chronic patients there, and I felt important. But after about one year of working in chronic psychiatry I started to burn out. I was not seeing any changes and the monotony was getting to me. I never did work any acute psychiatry, although I wanted to. It interested me, but they didn't put the young sisters on the acute floors because there were a lot of nuns and priests on those floors, and they did not want us to observe them. However, I was living with a lot of mentally ill sisters, sisters with scruples, handwashing compulsions and active hallucinations. All this was very frightening to me.

One year later I was sent to the Catholic University of America in Washington to study for a Master's degree in Psychiatric Nursing. It was a real honor to be chosen to study, but inside of me I knew they were all wrong. I had major problems with interpersonal relationships. Of course this showed up quite quickly in a school where this was the focus of study. My anxiety escalated rapidly. I could not visualize myself in any role that school might prepare me for.

I failed out of Catholic University after one year, a real disgrace. I was sent to work in a general hospital on a medical unit. The activity was good for me. I was supposed to be the supervisor, but I mostly did staff nursing, which consisted of filling in for absent nurses, giving medications, doing direct patient care. I was very uncomfortable in a supervisory role, but that's what sisters did. Fortunately, my head nurse was used to doing the supervisory role, and I was very willing to turn it over to her. This worked out well for both of us.

My sister servant (superior) at this hospital was the hospital administrator. For some reason, which is unclear to me to this day, we had a major personality conflict. I couldn't do or say anything right. I never argued with her or discussed this with her, but I wilted. I was always being called on the carpet. She suggested to higher superiors that I needed psychiatric help; by that time I could only agree. I was scared and depressed.

After several months of outpatient treatment I was admitted to one of our psychiatric hospitals in New Orleans and stayed as a patient there for six months. I did not live with the sisters, and did not wear the habit. I had a wonderful doctor and I did make some progress in learning how to talk about myself. I emerged from there a better adjusted and happier person and best of all, I got away from my superior.

I then worked in an Intensive Care Unit. Again I was supposed to be the supervisor; again I had a head nurse who liked and was used to that role. I was in reality a staff nurse, doing direct patient care. I enjoyed community life there immensely.

After working in ICU for one year I discovered I had some talent for teaching. I made my first independent decision about my job situation and asked to be transferred to the school of nursing.

This worked out very well. I loved teaching and stayed in it about twelve years. I was able to grow through adolescence with the students, something I badly needed. I gained a better sense of my own identity. I continued fairly happy in community life during this time. I was always very faithful to prayer and spiritual exercises.

When I left the psychiatric hospital after my six month stay in 1965, I had been given prescriptions for tranquilizers and antidepressants. I continued to take a variety of these over the next twenty years on a regular basis. Around 1972 I discovered that I had a drinking problem. I was drinking daily, and drinking to excess. I stopped drinking but continued to take tranquilizers. I resumed drinking ten years later in 1982 when I left the community.

Prior to my leaving the community I worked full time for a year in a nursing home as a staff nurse. This facility was not owned by the community. At the same time I was volunteering in a program for battered women. I realized that I had not begun to touch or understand the poverty that was out there. I felt the community was becoming sort of a cocoon for me. I looked with new eyes on the group of nuns sitting in front of the television each night. I heard with new ears comments like "Don't bring any of those women here." And I wondered about the entire second floor of the convent that was vacant. Our shelter was refusing homeless women because it was so crowded.

In the last five years that I was in community, we began to have a lot of community meetings, talking about where we were going as a community. I longed for someone to sit down with me and talk about where I was going as a person. But it seemed as though no one cared. I didn't feel they had their own answers, let alone mine. Finally, staying in the boat wasn't enough. I knew if I did that I would never walk on water.

I had reached a period where career-wise I was at a standstill. I had burned out badly in the nursing home. We were understaffed, the work was hard and I was very tired. So I quit the job. I did not want to go back to teaching nursing students. I would have to get a masters in nursing to stay in teaching. I had a masters degree in counseling which I had picked up part time in 1972. There really wasn't any job in the community that I had any interest in doing. Most of the hospital sisters did either administrative work or pastoral care, and I could not see myself in either of these positions. Also, I was coming to realize that, given the freedom and the opportunity, I could find a place for myself in the world of work. I had a vision of putting all my belongings in a car, driving to New York and working with the homeless, whatever that meant.

I wrestled with the thought of leaving, something I had never consciously done before. I had no idea how I would survive: I knew nothing about salaries; I didn't know what I could make; I did not know what it cost to live. I had never written a check or kept a bank account. I had been totally taken care of, with maids to clean the house and cooks to prepare my meals. All of this made me feel that I had never really taken responsibility for my own life. I wanted to stop being taken care of, to summon the energy I knew was inside of me, to live.

I felt pressured inside myself to either get a job in the community, or make the decision to leave. I had no help with this decision from within the community, but I did go for counseling to a psychiatric social worker for about two months. The decision was so difficult for me that I don't think anyone could have helped me with it. This was the most painful time of my entire life. It was a call to leave because I don't see how I could have done it without Divine help. I had been in the community for twenty-six years. I felt that I needed to grow, and needed some time on my own to do that, to find out who I was.

A frightening part of leaving was that I would find out if my relationship with God was truly a personal one or was "community property," something that would not go with me. I needed to find that out; it was frightening.

I left, moved into an apartment in the same city and got a job as a staff nurse at a local hospital. I began doing volunteer work at a shelter for the homeless, a ministry that was part of the local Catholic church I attended. This was lifesaving because it gave me a wonderful support group of persons who cared about the things I cared about. I drew strength from the shelter residents who were starting over as I was. They taught me a lot.

Looking back over the last ten years since I left, I can say that leaving was the best thing I could have done for me. I have grown tremendously in many ways. I have had numerous jobs. Like a kid in the candy shop, I wanted to experience what was out there. I worked in public health for two years, a marvelous experience of meeting some tough people who were making it and who led me to believe that I could, too. I worked as a clinic nurse for city employees and learned how to relate to adult males, a new experience. I have worked some jobs only to find out that they weren't for me. I got fired from two jobs. It took me a long time to learn that as a nun I ran things, but as a lay person I had to do the job the way "they" wanted it done or they would get someone else.

Financially, I have done well, paying rent, keeping food on the table and paying bills. I have only two years paid into a retirement plan because of my frequent job changes. But I don't have a saving or frugal mentality, so it is hard for me to plan beyond the present day.

I worked in a state psychiatric hospital in Georgia but quit after three months in fear of my life. I worked in Birmingham for one year with Health Care for the Homeless, assisting people to get off the streets. It was a wonderful experience. I worked in a drug treatment center for impaired professionals in Georgia. I worked in a county treatment center for indigent addicts and alcoholics. All of this has been a life-enhancing growth experience which I needed. During these last ten years I felt a need to place growth ahead of security, and have done that.

From 1982 to 1985 my alcoholism escalated. I began drinking again when I left the community, and drank until 1985 when I went into a treatment program. Thank God I never was arrested or involved in an accident, but with the alcohol combined with tranquilizers I had to leave work several times and missed appointments. I have six years of sobriety now, I'm involved with AA and love it. It gives me an opportunity to share my faith, something I never could do in community.

I had always believed that a call to be a member of a religious community was a higher kind of call than any other. I believed that the married state or the single state were lesser calls leading to lesser forms of holiness. I have been amazed at the spirituality I have encountered, especially in my black brothers and sisters. In them I have found the missing part of me. Without them I did not know the Whole Christ.

This brings me to another major change. While I was in the community I made preached retreats or silent retreats. These were marvelous experiences. When I left, the most convenient retreat houses were Jesuit-run, and I took the risk of making a directed retreat. I have made an eight-day directed retreat every year since I left. I cannot believe the difference this has made in me. I can talk about myself. I have a self-understanding and an understanding of my relationship with God that I never knew was possible. I learned to rage at God until I didn't need to anymore; I learned to make my own the gentle Jesuit answer to every problem: "What does He say to you?" I learned to listen for His voice. I have a spiritual director now and have the maturity to realize the importance of such for me.

I think that there were a lot of elements of the dysfunctional family in the community. "Don't talk, don't trust, don't feel," certainly applied. I always felt I was playing a role. If I took enough Valium, I could be the perfect nun. Everyone was surprised when I left; no one was more surprised than I was. I was the last one I thought would leave.

It is such a relief not to be wearing the habit. I can take a walk for exercise without cars stopping to know if "Sister is lost". I can wear my blue jeans and sit on the floor of the shelter with a homeless man and not be uncomfortable or make him uncomfortable. I can visit in the jails and blend with the inmates. I feel free to share myself with others. I share my background with very few people; I share where I am today with a lot of people.

I live alone; I have never married and don't plan to. My relationship with God is the primary focus of my life. Solitude nourishes that relationship. Daily prayer makes that relationship a living reality. I am happier than I have ever been. During my years in community, and through my addiction to drugs, I stuffed my feelings and therefore missed a major means of self-knowledge. All of that has had to be repaired for me to be a healthy person. I have had a good bit of personal counseling. I am much more comfortable with myself as a sexual being; I see my sexuality as an essential part of my spirituality.

I am getting to know my family better. Although they all live at a distance, I do have some contact with them and am finally comfortable with who I am. Therefore I can visit them with greater ease. Over the past two years I have talked with my mother weekly, a major miracle.

I am coming to know and accept myself, to know God and let Him in. I attended two reunions that the community had for former members, and they were very good and very healing times. However, I have not continued to go because it cost me a great deal to leave; I feel that disconnecting is very important for me.

I am very grateful for what I was given in the community; my entering was not a mistake and my leaving was not a mistake. I am very grateful that I was able to leave, and for all that has happened to me since

Betty McCafferty
Sister of Saint Joseph

Bachelor of Science in Education, St. John College, Cleveland

Master of Arts, English, John Carroll, Cleveland

Master of Science in Education, St. John College, Cleveland

Master of Religious Education, The Catholic University of America

Master of Arts, Religious Education, Fordham University

Liturgy Coordinator, Houston, Texas

Betty McCafferty is a seasoned writer and editor, teacher and administrator. At present she lives in an apartment, and maintains a good working relationship with her religious community, although she does "not feel the need to be highly active" in that community at present. Her job makes her highly visible in the parish community where she is involved in many ministries. What free time exists is spent in creative activities ranging from baking and crocheting to balloon sculpture. Future? "I would not mind doing further studies, but that's probably not feasible at the present."

Betty McCafferty

Reflections on Change

It Was Said . . . And We Believed . . .

1950-1959

It was said...

Sacrifice, die to self, live for Christ ...

And we believed...

We sacrificed, tried to die to self and live for Christ and we were determined and innocent and lived life hoping to mature, happy in our naivete.

1960-69

It was said...

Times are a'changing, renew without, within. Knock down, break out.

Release. This leads to peace.

It was said...

We were to be treated as individuals, have freedom, be free to create, be innovative, dare and do.

And we believed...

Then we became individuals, talked of freedom, tried to create, to innovate, dared to do, and we were not listened to, especially those not so young.

It was said...

Everyone is responsible, mature, makes decisions.

And we believed...

But found not all decisions to our making, but the responsibility to our taking, because we had had some experience in this, at times *our* ideas were valueless.

It was said...

Everyone had charisms, one should encounter, be counted.

And we believed...

Then our ideas were rejected, were not accepted, because we spoke what we believed and others did not want to hear. We were written off because we wanted community as we thought it should be: but we were not heard.

1970-1979

It was said...

commitment, challenge, collegiality without authority.

And we believed.

But someone forgot to mention what and how and why and we could not retrace our steps lest we be thought a coward, lest we be mocked, or not be jet-setted.

It was said...

Assert your ideas, do your thing, celebrate the sacrifice.

And we believed.

But we questioned the priority of individuals over group, could not always celebrate but at times had to be content with monotony, tried to pray, but found difficult our conversation with Him because so many other voices were raised in each's monologues and at times we felt old in heart,

Beaten, rejected, sighing.

It was said...

Be real. Life is the promise.

And we believed.

Was the fault ours in basing hope on false reality?

1980 - 1990

It was said...

Woman's rights, justice, be assertive. Equality.

It was said...

Dwindling numbers, aging personnel, responsible financing. Possible dissolution.

And we believed...

But regrouped and broke new ground.

But equality was lacking and age had a way of slowing down

And we felt the fear, the stagnation, the death knell

And prayed for new life, resurrection.

Into the 21st Century

We must go on, continuing to think, reflect, hope.

Perhaps that which was in the 50's posed by our forebears—

Perchance they were the prophets of truth.

They promised sacrifice and death ... to live.

Have we come full circle.

Lord, in you we trust!

The following was written in the days "when"...

Meetings were group discussions.

People had to declare if they stood on the right, left, or center.

Meetings were arranged so as to produce a specific outcome.

People were told to spill their thoughts, tell it like it was, listen only to the young whose ideas were the only ones that were important.

The concepts of poverty, chastity and obedience as lived and learned were questioned, and discarded.

Some were trying to hold on to the traditional mode of clothing.

New ministries were the vogue.

At mikes you were given one minute to "tell it like it is".

Meetings turned into battlegrounds.

The bishop (Prince) celebrated the closing liturgy

Communion was still received on the tongue.

A consultant (unbiased?) was hired to chair the sessions.

Holy Week:
A Viet Nam Assembly with Hidden Agendas

Wednesday:
Laughter.
Little apprehension.
Naivete; lack of awareness.
Defense barriers down.
"No camps." Congeniality, comaraderie. To live or die together.
That all may be one.

Thursday:
Morning as usual.
Run to groups. Clarify. Listen. Reports and interest areas.
A repast.
Three options. Cordon off the area, people, beliefs.
The tide gathers ... momentum.
Silence. A question or two.
A few seeds neatly planted.
Strategizing, watching, seething.

Good Friday: Blood Bath
Gathering for prayer.
Discussion,
Then ... the bomb. An explosion.
Rebellion. Open disbelief.
Who is the enemy? Where is she?
How can we tell since we are from similar origins. Confusion,
chaos, scrambling, threats. Pandemonium. We have met the
enemy and it is us!
"And the curtain of the temple was split..."
Attack—again—again.
Strike here, there, anywhere. Rationality. Irrationality.
Frenzy! Scare tactics? Psychology.
Shouts of repression, suppressed anger.
Ultimatums. Gnashing of teeth. Venting of pent-up spleen.
Cries of "Tyranny". We will now oppress the "other".

Regroup. Scramble. Break ranks. The powerful gain more numbers.
The leaders look on.
Let the battle begin again.
Quote. Requote. Misquote.
Strike the cheek; they turn another.
Strike that too. Sights on the target and full speed ahead.
Machine-gun punctuations.
Spume and phlegm spit into the air.
Heroic cries, thrown into the battle area.
Pleadings. Tensions.
The minority must be subjected, conquered.
Might makes right. Divide and conquer.
Holocaust. Indeed a burnt offering.
And some rejoiced to see the day while others regretted that they
were ever born.
This had to be so that the scriptures might be fulfilled.
Regroup. Be specific. Say it like it is. Get out the rest of the festers.
Not much time.
Rush! Haste! The process!
What is salvageable? Report quickly.
Gather the pieces. Pretend nothing happened. Talk but don't tell.
Apply a few band-aids when you go home.
"Father, into your hands..."
The Prince is here.
Respect his wishes for now.
"This is my body. This is my blood." Union and communion.
Communion on the tongue (but yesterday we took and ate!)
Strains of "Praise ye the Father."
The apparent victors:
Some rejoicing, triumphant, battle trophies won.
Complacent. Self-sufficient, smug. Seeming insensitive.
Cries of "We've got them where we want them". "Victory!" Pats on
the back.
Some confused, not sure of what happened.
The others ...
The apparent losers:

Heads high; eyes tear-stained. Terrified, shell-shocked, bewildered.
Reports from the front: "Radical differences in authority
concept, psychology, theology, philosophy." We might discuss.
(My God! Do we not believe in you? Isn't each of us a person?
Are there no semblances of vocation? Are there no common
grounds for obedience?)
We proclaim our radical differences. Divide the garment.
Cast lots.
Suppose widows, bent with age and meager possessions
Snatching at what little they have left.
Lives proclaimed worthless, wasted.
"Cursed are the barren and the wombs that never bore and breasts..."
Verbal euthanasia;
Yet, a few rise virile. Heads aloof; determined not to give in.
But a few "... begin to say to the mountains, 'Fall upon us'
and to the hills, 'Cover us'. For if in the case of green wood they
do these things, what is to happen in the case of the dry?"
(Unless the seed die... does it always have to die? or be killed?)
Agonizing death throes, or birth pangs ... or both.
Concern, derision, pride, humility, love-hate.
My life's blood.
The referee: non-committal, nothing to lose.
Objectivity. Non-subjective.
"Five minutes." "Take your ground." Timed precision. Everyone a
chance.
"Stand behind the cannon. You shoot. You! Your chance!"
Stored shells and mortar seized and used.
Carnage. Flesh exposed. Guts hanging out.
Was it wrong to have a belief? A few on middle ground.
Not in the heat. Not under direct fire.
Yet ... not unscathed.
Polite amenities.
A few onlookers, gathering up the remains.
"We are on the way to Peace, Reconciliation, Resurrection."
(My God, My God...)

442

Holy Saturday

Numb.
Disbelief.
Eyes puffed.
A nightmare?
Did it happen?
More to come? Was it an unrising?
Where shall we go?

Easter Sunday

"And on the first day of the week they went to the tomb..."
Was the battle justified and moral?
Was social justice achieved?
Did the end justify the means?
Who will be reborn?
Have some of the disciples gone back home?
Choose *Life* or *Death Now*
Has He risen?
Will He?
Will we meet Him on the way to Emmaus?

Geri Majkowski
Former Sister of the Holy Family

Single

Resident Manager, Senior Apartment Building

G.E.D. teacher, Lake County Community College

Bachelor of Science in Education, DeLourdes College, Des Plaines

Master of Arts, School Administration, Notre Dame University

Master of Arts, Gerontology, Roosevelt University, Chicago

Geri truly lives with her interests and her work. Her job as resident manager of an apartment house for the elderly keeps her in touch with the problems of the elderly. She stays in touch with her former community with letters, phone calls, and by donating in times of need. Writing is high on her list of special interests, ranking with history and genealogy She keeps active with racquetball and biking, relaxes by reading. "I hope to write more as times goes on. I hope to write more about the elderly — their histories, their dreams, their present difficulties."

Geri Majkowski

A Farewell, and One Day

January 7, 1992

Dear Sister,

The time has come for parting; not for saying "Good-bye" or "Farewell", just a time to be apart for a while. I am writing this just hours before signing my dispensation, and I am filled with many thoughts and reveries. I would not like the task of reporting my departure to be left to others. I feel that since I am doing this, I should announce it. I would like to take this opportunity to apologize if I have offended you or scandalized you over the years.

Also, I would like to thank you for all the many things you have done for me, for the good and bad times we have shared. I have grown to love each of you for your unique gifts, and have received much love and friendship in return. Love never dies, and will survive this parting.

What I am doing today is painful to you, I know. If you can, believe that it is also painful for me. However, this is not the time to discourse, debate or explain.

You can be sure that the charisma of Mother Foundress is carried away with me in my heart, and in some way, I will always be 'A Nazareth'. For now, all I ask of you is to remember me in prayer, and be assured that I shall do the same for you.

Yours in the Holy Family,
Fabia
aka Geri Majkowski

February, 1955

Forty-two second graders! The day starts at 5:15 a.m. when it is still dark. You rise to a knock on the door and to the words, "*Benedicamus Domino!*" You reply a sleepy, "*Deo Gratias.*" (Let us bless the Lord! Thanks be to God!) You crawl out of bed, brush your teeth, wash your face, and run down to the common bathroom in robe and slippers. Then you run back and put on the many parts of the holy habit, trying to say the short prayers that should be said simultaneously. Even the underclothes are unique. There is a simple band of cotton cloth snapped in front over the bosom. Long, loose split pantaloons that were popular in the Victorian era are worn over a whale bone corset from which hang garters to hold up your opaque, black stockings. Many young sisters were too thin to fill a whale bone corset.

After you lace up your black shoes, you don your long-sleeved undershirt and your short-sleeved day shirt (collarless, with three buttons down the front). Day shirts were made in the convent; undershirts were bought. Over this you put the two half slips: the first, made of coarse blue-striped pillow ticking material, has twelve inches of black material around the bottom edge; the second is all black. These two are tied at the waist. now you tie the 'pocket' around your waist, like a saddle bag. It hangs down your right side about twelve inches, and is about four inches wide at its widest, resembling, somewhat, a tear drop. It is large enough to hold a rosary, a hankie, a file to tuck your hair in, some safety pins, and anything else you want to keep private.

Finally you slip the long black dress over your head, snap it closed from the waist up, and tie the draw strings. Over this you slip the cape, often called a pallorine, which drapes you from neck to knuckles, all around your upper body. Like the long black dress, it has a line of cassock buttons down the front. It is pinned shut at the neck with a black-headed pin.

You kiss the profession cross and hang it around your neck by the black cord. When you received it at your first profession, you removed all three screws to see the relic inside. Yours is of St. Gerard Majella, patron saint of pregnant mothers. You already know the Latin inscriptions by heart. On one side, "*Ecce regnum Dei intra vos est*" (Behold! the reign of God is within you) and on the other, "*Ecce Ancilla Domini, Fiat mihi*

448

secundum Verbum Tuum" (Behold the Handmaid of the Lord; Be it done unto me according to Your Word).

When you put the pleated collar around your neck, the profession cross is visible right at the edge of it. You take the two tapes hanging from the collar and pin them to the back of the habit through an opening in the cape. You snap your cincture on and hang your large rosary right over the sash. The sash stops above the ankles and the rosary stops above the knees on the left, since there is an opening on the right for access to the pocket.

All that's left now is the cap and veil. First, you make sure that the cap has folded white netting basted to it so that an eighth of an inch shows around the edge of the cap. You put it on, cross the ties at the nape of the neck and tie them in a bow at the top of the head. Then you put the bonnet on, hiding the bow at the top of your head and tying it at the nape of the neck. Basted to the bonnet is a black veil that reaches down the back, but is not long enough to sit on. Since you have no alarm clock and no watch, you wait for the bell to tell you that it is time for chapel. More devout sisters have been there sometime already.

Whoops! Too late! You kneel down on both knees and kiss the floor. As mother superior knocks, you rise and make a mental note of the transgression, since you will have to mention it at the Chapter of Faults later in the week. On the pitch of 'A' everyone is chanting the Little Office of the Blessed Virgin Mary. You find the page for Matins and chime in. This is followed by a recitation of assorted prayers, the favorites of mother foundress, and the prayer to the Holy Spirit for enlightenment.

After this, the first point of meditation is read in Polish. You and other young Sisters have spiritual books in chapel to do your own reading in English. After fifteen minutes the second point is read, and when the half hour is over, all sisters kneel to thank the Holy Spirit for a fruitful meditation, recite the prayer to the Holy Family, and wait for Father to come and distribute Communion. All the Sisters will be attending Mass later with the student body, but there will be no time for breakfast then, and the Eucharist must be received before the midnight fast is broken.

Father has come and gone. You are seated in the refectory by seniority, which puts you at the end of the table. Everyone has said grace silently and is seated in silence, head bowed, waiting for the food to be passed. There is always juice and coffee, hot and cold milk, hot and cold cereal, and toast and butter. Today, the main dish is fried liver sausage slices. Sometimes there are hot dogs; sometimes there are scrambled eggs and ham. During Holy Week there would be no dairy products, but there would be sardines in oil, dry bread, and black coffee.

You're done, so you wash your dishes in the credence, return them to the drawer at your place at the table, and leave. After a quick stop in chapel and in your room, which has already been tidied up before morning prayers, you are on your way to your forty-two second graders.

The morning starts off briskly, with prayers and the Pledge of Allegiance to the Flag. That's how children mastered their prayers: they recited them daily. Then religion class was free for the recitation of memorized question and answers; there are about three a day, and only in English, not in Polish on alternate days, as when you were a child. Everyone is seated, roll is called, absentees recorded, and moneys are collected: tuition, milk, lunch, field trip, mission money and any fundraiser money, i.e., candy, Christmas cards, etc. This fund raising came about because the dollar a month tuition, which was the good sister's salary, was no longer adequate. Since the pastor would not hear of a raise, he allowed the sisters to make up the deficit in any way they could. All this money is put in a pouch and sent to the eighth grade, where the principal teaches forty-eight students all day.

After the recitation and the workbook pages, math class begins. Another workbook! Usually two pages were assigned the previous day. You make an effort to correct the work in class. You have the children trade books and call out the answers. This is good practice for them, but you know you'll have to go over them yourself. You check your lesson plan. It's in the required STOP format: Subject: math; Topic: Two digit addition with carrying; Objective: mastery of the skill; Procedure/Practice: PP.142-43 WKBK. Explain and demonstrate.

So you explain and demonstrate. Then you send some bright students to the chalk board and have them explain how they got the answer. You assign the pages and begin helping minutes, (assigned by state). You switch to phonics. This is where the robins, blue jays and cardinals come in. Placement in these groups has to do with reading tests, daily performance and teacher judgment. The reading groups and phonics groups are identical and usually stay frozen for the year, with few exceptions. This is the time before *Sesame Street* and *The Muppets*; it is a time when an educational radio program is being piloted for a half hour in the afternoon for the intermediate and upper grades.

By ten a.m. everybody is ready for a recess break, including the teacher. The class is marched off to the washrooms by two's and returned to class for cookies and milk. Then it's back to work until eleven-thirty.

At lunch-time, all rise to recite the Angelus and Grace before Meals. This is no longer the 40's, when everyone ran home for lunch at 11:30 and returned at 12:45. Almost all of these children will stay for lunch, and buy the one provided in the school hall. This is the Baby-Boom era. Classrooms are bursting at the seams. Some schools are teaching in two short day shifts and women are entering the work force in droves. There are still no lay teachers, so one sister from each level stays with the students in the lunch room while the rest return to the convent. You return, too, and hurry to chapel to examine your conscience. You're supposed to be thinking of your predominant fault, or the one virtue you want to become perfect in. Actually, the aroma wafting from the kitchen is driving you crazy.

After the examination of conscience and the Angelus, which you just finished with the children, everyone proceeds to the dining room to say grace and be seated as someone drones on about the life of one of the saints. You, however, are assigned to serve, so you go to the kitchen and don the white bibbed apron and cuffs. When all are seated you present each one with a bowl of soup. By the time the eighteenth sister gets her soup, you are ready to serve portions (a plate of meat, fish or poultry, rice or potato, and another hot vegetable). The cook was busy all morning!

After you put out the pots of coffee and pitchers of milk, you remove and fold the apron and cuffs, and you and your serving partner sit down to your own meal. The dessert is already on the table, thanks to the cook. Before you are done eating, all rise for grace after meals. Two sisters go to the credence to do the dishes and one goes to the kitchen to help with pots and leftovers. You and your partner finish your meal in silence while the other sisters return to the chapel to recite Psalm 50, the Miserere. Everyone hurries back to the children who are out on the playground by now. Those who had lunchroom duty are back at the convent grabbing a bit to eat.

An eighth grader rings a large cow bell and all the children line up by two's in their assigned places. What should be perfect silence is usually not. As in the convent, a second bell is rung. This is the signal to return to class, which they do, beginning with the oldest.

The afternoon is just as busy, and just as routine. This day, however, is interrupted by a fire drill. Since it is February it's not much of a surprise. We are told beforehand to have the children don their coats and hats. You are grateful for the interruption, since listening to oral reading is putting you to sleep.

Finally it's time for dismissal. After the students leave you stay behind to tidy up the classroom. Then you pack up all the math and phonics papers to correct, and lock the door behind you.

After a light snack you decide to have your half hour of adoration first. This is a time of private prayer, but the older sisters are quick to tell mother superior if you seem to be neglecting it. Then you take up your assigned chore, which is 'collars'. For eighteen sisters you have about thirty-six collars to do. That means scrub, rinse, hang to dry, steam and press. The collar is a yard of material, pleated to twelve to fourteen inches wide, with a band sewed on the underside, at the neck, and a one-inch hem at the bottom. For washing purposes the collar is threaded through the pleats on the underside, twice in the hem and twice between the hem and the neck band. You are expected to get them snowy white. You bleach them, scrub them and hang them up to dry in the laundry. The next day you will take them down and steam-press them and distribute them. This is hardly done when the Vesper bell rings.

After Vespers, everyone files into the refectory for a repeat performance of the lunch hour: a silent formal dinner to the monotonous sound of a reader. The reading is concluded with a maxim from the writings of mother foundress and an announcement of the anniversary of the death of the sisters who died that day anywhere in the world since the foundation of the congregation. The sisters proceed to the chapel to recite the De Profundis in their memory.

Everyone then proceeds to the community room for evening recreation, which begins with a signal from mother superior. Seating is again by seniority. Since you are the youngest you sit at the end of the table. Next to you are the two elderly lay Sisters who do the cooking and laundry. Since they know very little English, and you know very little Polish, there is much sign language, laughter, and mutual learning. They are fun to be with, especially Sister Notburga.

Sister Barnaba is a little off-center. You wonder what makes her that way. She tells you, seriously, that mother foundress and the pope tricked her into the Order; that someone keeps breaking her pencil tips, so she won't report what's going on here. You remember her alarm clock going off in her pocket during silent meditation and how you all giggled uncontrollably.

Anyway, after forty-five minutes of conversation and some hand sewing, the phone rings. The assigned sister goes to answer it, and returns to kneel by mother superior and whisper in her ear that the call is for you from your grandmother. Mother superior calls out your name, tells you to go to the phone and not to be too long.

Your grandmother asks if the family can visit, and when would be a good time. You go and kneel by mother superior's side to get an answer and return to the phone to tell your grandmother that the next Sunday would be fine.

By the time you return to the community room, everyone has had three pieces of chocolate candy (Jesus, Mary, and Joseph), and left three for you. All have responded *Deo Gratias* to mother superior's *Benedicamus Domino*, and now sit in silence listening to mother superior read to them from a spiritual book. This activity is closed with some exhortation from mother superior on general shortcomings she has observed in common life. When she is finished, all return their sewing to the drawer in the table right in front of them; they rise and return to chapel for night prayers. Although it is liturgically incorrect, Compline was recited right after Vespers, so now a 'homey' kind of night prayers are recited: ten Hail Mary's, each for a different intention, another psalm, and our traditional invocation, used whenever we leave chapel: to *Nos cum Prole pia* we answer *Benedicat Joseph et Maria*. This is loosely translated: "May the Holy Child Jesus, with Mary and Joseph, bless us.

Everyone has a chore and a cleaning. Your chore is collars, and your cleaning is the community room. You return there to dust, empty the waste basket, and freshen up the room. Then you go to your room to check the math and phonics papers and your lesson plan, and get ready for bed. At ten you hear a knock on the door and the signal for lights out, *"Benedicamus Domino"*. You respond, *"Deo Gratias."* You turn out the light and open the blind, hoping to finish some of your work by the street light.

As you finally crawl into bed, you make a mental note. At next month's private conference with mother superior, you want to ask to add one more permission to your small permission list: to stay up later than 10:00 p.m. Reason: all your weekend college classes need more attention. Last week, in an attempt to study after school, you fell asleep at your desk, slept right through Vespers and were late for supper.

Another day in the convent comes to a close. You fall asleep reciting the rosary, a habit you formed when you first entered.

For the next thirteen years you will follow this routine, with little change, four thousand seven hundred and forty-five times.

7
VESPERS

Because of the house of the Lord, Our God,
I have sought good things for you.
My soul doth magnify the Lord,
And my spirit hath rejoiced in God my Savior.

Claire Breault
Former Dominican

Single

Retired Teacher

Active Editor

Bachelor of Education, Chicago Teachers College

Master of Arts, Drama, The Catholic University of America

Master of Arts, English, Georgetown University

Coordinator, Rite of Christian Initiation for Adults Coordinator

Coordinator, Adult Education

Lector, Parish Council, School Advisory Board, St. Peter's Parish,
    Olney, Maryland

The fall and winter seasons are times of musical splendor for Claire, who for twelve years has held a season subscription to the Washington Opera Company. Warmer weather finds her in the garden, which she considers her best therapy. Each day brings "a new surprise, another interest to pursue." Her hopes for the future are tied to her ministry in the RCIA. "It would be wonderful to have the entire parish actively engaged in this process, not only as a welcoming community, but as partners on and sharers in the faith journey." A trip to Australia and New Zealand are in the long-range planning state.

Claire Breault

Happy Old Bones

Some of my best friends are now-nuns. They teach, nurse, lobby, administer parishes and government offices. They "do" spiritual direction and are involved in counseling. They are engaged in hundreds of useful, necessary professions and occupations. I know one who trains dogs!

They live in convents, apartments, institutions; they live in community of one kind or another, or alone. They drive cars, fly planes, have pets and pierced ears. They live close to God, and their emotional natures range from contentment to fury.

Some of my best friends are ex-nuns. They, too, teach, nurse, lobby and administer, work in parishes, "do" spiritual direction and counseling, and work in those same hundreds of other fields. They live in apartments or houses; they live alone or in new forms of community, or in family with parents, siblings or husbands and sometimes children. They are single or married; they are divorced or with a significant other. Some are churched and some are not, yet all seem to seek some sort of spirituality, a relationship with God, or a god. And, like the now-nuns, their emotions run the gamut.

Superficially they are alike. However, there are many differences, though not as many as there once were.

I am an ex-nun. I spent eleven years in religious life, from the age of twenty-eight to the age of thirty-nine. I was never unhappy; I wouldn't trade one moment of those years; I would never go back.

As my postulant mistress put it, with a grin, I gave my "old bones to God." Although my age and worldly experience would help me in many ways later on, in the beginning they seemed to work against me. In those early months and years the nuns in charge didn't know just what to do with me. I was degreed, and then some. I had seven years teaching experience in the Chicago public school system, more often than not in what we now label inner city schools. I had my own apartment, my own exciting social life, my own thank-you-very-much self-determined life style. And here I was, crowd "mother" to a bunch of teenagers.

That crowd has had one reunion, "ins" and "outs;" we are planning another. We had a lot of laughs at that first one, and a few tears. We shared for the first time our early perceptions of one another at those opposite ends of the age scale. We found that the thirty-some years since our novitiate have brought us to the point where there is little, if any, age differential. We've all grown up wonderfully well.

What amazed me at that reunion was that some of the youngsters had been acutely aware of my own painful moments during those two years of training — moments which I had forgotten — and were oblivious to the small perks I had received because of my age. I could not really remember some of the hurtful things that they remembered; it was the good which stayed with me. The passing of years seems to do that — gloss over the pain and highlight the joy.

But I am jumping around in time.

I came into religious life, age twenty-eight, in September of 1956. I came from a period of spiritual renewal, and was at last fulfilling a desire for that life which circumstances had ruled out many years before. I certainly did not have the educational needs that most of my crowd had, so the next day I found myself back in the classroom as teacher. While other postulants started college, or in some cases finished high school, I met daily with a group of enthusiastic but wiggly third graders.

This job occupied most of my time and gave me a degree of independence. However, it took me out of the formational core. I was not neglected in any sense, but I think I was not quite integrated.

I wanted that integration, though I could not have named it then. Perhaps that was one of the magnets which had drawn me to religious life. My relations with my family had been fragmented.

I remember a moment in my postulancy so vividly. We were all in a flurry of activity, preparing a welcome for our returning mother general (that's really what we called them then — a veritable oxymoron). I paused for a moment, absorbed in all that happy busy-ness, and my postulant mistress stopped beside me to say, "You have never known family like this before, have you?"

She was right. I loved that sense of family, community. Fortunately, I have been able to retain that kind of relationship with my former community. I am, admittedly, proud of them. I have known women of vision, compassion, practicality. The last has been particularly attractive for me. A bit of wisdom I have carried with me since that time lies in other words from the lips of that wise woman who helped us make the transition from lay to religious life. "Virtue is practical." That appealed to me then, as it does now. I hear it when I hear James challenge us:

> If a brother or sister has nothing to wear and no food for the day, and you say to them, "Good-bye and good luck! Keep warm and well fed," but do not meet their bodily needs, what good is that?
>
> (James 2:15-16)

My novitiate year was less pleasant. I was expected to have developed a spirituality that I had, to a great extent, not found out about during my preoccupied postulancy. My salvation for that novitiate year was in the hours I spent in the motherhouse kitchen, cooking for hundreds under Sister Patrick's keen eye. I loved it; I guess I have always been a Jewish mother at heart!

With profession came my introduction to the real world of religious life. It wasn't awful for me, nor was it what I expected. Parts of it were wonderful — I was in a small, new house, and while we did not live in the proverbial lap of luxury, it was certainly more comfortable than the mass movement I had been accustomed to for the past two years. I had my own room! Only one who treasures privacy as I do can appreciate what that meant.

But there were things that disturbed and dismayed me. The worst was the fact that I was considered the "baby" of the house because I was youngest in religion. Yet chronologically I was older than everyone in the house, including the superior, and it was close on the charts as far as education and professional experience were concerned. I really resented every decision being made for me in the classroom as well as the house, and being treated as though I didn't have the necessary brain cells to survive. I guess, when it comes down to the bottom line, I hadn't really learned much about humility, surrender, obedience and all those good things. Though I didn't know it, the need to control my own life was deeply rooted. I had kept myself removed from the infusion of novitiate weed-killer.

But life there was relatively relaxed and comfortable. Three years later I found myself in a totally different kind of house — very large, very traditional, very strict. Now, just like the Israelites in the desert with Moses, I looked back on my former mission with fondness, with memories of the particular honeys and garlics of that easier time.

I was in that house for only one year, and I was taught, indirectly, by the other sisters there to regard the superior with great fear. I am not at all sure just how much of her reputation was deserved. She is now a woman for whom I have the greatest admiration. Perhaps she has mellowed and grown; perhaps I have. I suspect it is a little (or a lot) of both. She is truly a classy lady.

The last five years I spent in religious life were both wonderful and awful. I was missioned at a boarding school on the motherhouse campus, and close to the campus of one of our colleges. However, we were an entity to ourselves, and enjoyed pleasant, contemporary living and educational facilities. I had a lot of independence; I had a lot of fun. I was always exhausted!

It was the combination of my taste for independence, and that built-in need for it, I think, that eventually led me to my decision to leave religious life. In addition to all those adult years I had spent living on my own, I had been sent by the community to Washington for several summers in order to do graduate work at The Catholic University of America. Those summers were wonderful times. They were for the most part pre-Vatican II, but new life was stirring in Little Rome. I was responsible for myself, a responsibility I did not take lightly. I continued to live by my vows because they were important to me. But I was part of an adult world, peopled with professors and fellow students who respected my experience and my opinions. I met wonderful people, religious and lay; the city and university were cultural oases. I was as close to heaven as I could get down here.

Then I finished the degree! And I went home to my "former more austere but happier way of life." However, seeds had been sown. Eventually I discovered that I had to leave a life which I loved but could not live. I left not because I thought there was anything wrong with that life, nor with my community. I had grown into a better understanding of myself. I did not belong in community life; I needed to be my own person, to make decisions, to chart my own life.

As I said earlier, I was never unhappy. Religious life, as I had found it in my community, was good, protecting, benevolent. Though there were abrasive personalities, even abnormal personalities, in the community and its leadership, I knew from my experience in that before-life that these kinds of personalities are found everywhere, in every kind of job and social situation. A woman does not shed her nature automatically upon entering religious life. Most work hard to remove those qualities which are offensive, not suitable to the life. Not all succeed.

I was convinced then and more so now that overall *they* did the best job they could under those particular circumstances, at that particular time, with the kind of leadership training available at the time. This was the positive edge of giving my old bones to God. I had had a lot more experience with people, a greater ability to cope with difficult people, and perhaps fewer pedestals. Luck of the draw, believe me. I am no Pollyanna.

So. I was not unhappy. I was disgruntled once in a while, sometimes in a real snit. But who isn't? If my feelings of unrest were growing more frequent, it was because I had this growing need to control my own life. I had grown in a different direction.

Suddenly, early in September of 1966, at 4:45 in the afternoon, as I was putting on my veil to go to chapel, I saw myself in the mirror and had one of those "a-ha!" moments. Silly, I said to myself, you don't belong here anymore. You have to leave, that's all. And that was that. I was at complete peace.

I slept on the thought for two or three weeks, and then contacted two priests for whom I had much respect. The process began.

I was in no hurry. As I said, I was not unhappy, certainly not miserable. Further, I was in a boarding school. I decided that the sudden vanishing of a sister, with all its attendant rumors and emotions, would be disruptive for the forty-some thirteen-year old girls in my wing, and also for the older girls in my classes.

I didn't realize at the time how this eight or nine month wait would work in my favor. The details and mechanics of the leaving process are of no importance. It is important for all to know that I was lovingly supported in my decision by my community. My way was made very smooth, and all the ducks fell in a row. By mid-year I had a teaching contract for the next year in Maryland, where I wanted to settle. My family was able to give me a small loan. I had an apartment lined up, a used car coming, even a summer job. There was no way I could doubt the wisdom of my decision. I only regret that other sisters, in my own community and in others, have not been so fortunate.

So on a bright June morning, at the age of thirty-nine, I found myself in my car, packed with books and the beginnings of a wardrobe, heading, contrary to Mr. Greeley's advice, East. I had signed my papers the night before to avoid goodbyes, but the sisters with whom I lived had each found time during the evening to wish me luck, to hug me, or to shed a tear or two. One even tried on my clothes!

It was a wonderful journey, with visits along the way, with shopping, with getting used to having legs again, and to wearing shoes that were definitely not sensible! And I must confess that my first purchase was a pack of cigarettes. I had thrown my last one out of the taxi window eleven years before. Some habits (oops!) are harder to change than others. I hasten to assure you that the nicotine fixation didn't last too long. My lungs are all pink and healthy again.

I set about building a life, and it has been good. There have been upheavals along the way, but that's to be expected. I was employed for twenty-one years by an excellent school system, and I have had many opportunities to grow, to be enriched. I have been blessed with friends, and yes, I have been back to the motherhouse, welcomed, invited to be the homilist. I truly love those good sisters, and miss having more contact with them than I do. But I have never regretted either of my two big decisions — the first to enter religious life, and the second to leave it. I have gone through two distinct growth periods. Both were necessary for me to become the person I am, was meant to be.

What am I doing now? I am retired from the public schools, but I still substitute occasionally. It's nice pin money, and it keeps me in touch with friends, and with some of the realities of life. I travel a little, garden, go to the opera, and am possessed by two cats. Somehow, somewhere along the way, I have become the parish maven. I serve in many areas, but the most exciting thing that I do is coordinating and teaching the RCIA class. The people are wonderful. The freshness of their perspectives on the Church are the source of constant renewal for me. It is exciting.

However, I don't swallow the Church whole. There have been times in my life, both before and after the nun-time, when I have walked away from Rome for fairly long periods. I must confess, however, that these times were more for personal convenience than for philosophical stands.

That does not change the fact that there are still things about the institutional Church that do not make much sense to me. I live with them because the Church is, for me, the only avenue to the sacraments, and I need the sacraments. I think that it must be like living in a good marriage: one accepts the good and the bad in a sort of compromise.

I have no difficulty in teaching the Church. Each individual in my class must make a personal choice about how he or she will worship. All of them deserve as complete an information bank as I can provide. I tell them what the Church teaches. The decision is theirs.

I feel integrated, whole. The Hebrew word for integrity is *tmemos*, and it is usually translated as "walking with." I am walking with God more closely than at any other time in my life. That closeness did not happen just because of my years in religious life, nor did it come automatically upon leaving that life. That closeness is the culmination of all my life experiences, painful and joyful, sinful and Spirit-filled. Each phase, each cycle, each experience contributes to the person that I am.

I am grateful for all that I have known.

Mary Patricia Kennedy
Sisters of Charity of the Blessed Virgin Mary

Retired

Bachelor of Music Education, Clarke College, Dubuque

Additional study: DePaul; University of Minnesota; St. Norbert's in
De Pere, Wisconsin

Workshops with Fathers Gelineau and Deiss in Music and Liturgy

Community Archivist

Sister Mary Patricia may be officially retired, but her life style does not reflect
this status at all. She lives at the motherhouse, and adds to her ministry of
archivist, which involves the taping of the lives of the sisters, some housework,
a continued work in music, and service as companion and driver. She is vitally
interested in Creation Spirituality and music, and hopes to continue the
ministries in which she is so active. She enjoys "visiting our Sisters on the
missions, my relatives and former students."

Mary Patricia Kennedy

Thank You, God,
for Everything

My parents were born in the reign of Queen Victoria: my mother, in Manchester, England, to Irish parents, and my father in Montreal, Canada. His family had fled from Ireland to Paris; later his family came with the French to the New World. Mother's family found refuge in Holy Family parish in Chicago; Dad came alone to Notre Dame, the French church. That church had an all-city choir to which my mother belonged, and so they met. They were married at St. Jarleth's Church. Dad was twenty-five; mother was twenty-one.

I was born on April 25, 1911, when my brother Dudley was three years old. When I was one we moved to Ascension parish in Oak Park. I made my First Communion when I was six. Mother and I had gone to Maxwell Street for my dress. It was very pretty, prettier than anything we could have afforded elsewhere.

I started piano lessons with the nuns, but they were too strict, so Mrs. Pinkerton was engaged. I loved her, and loved my classroom teachers, too.

When I was nine my father died. Dudley grew up overnight, and has taken care of me ever since. I love it! Mother found work, first housework, and then later at the first Chicago Sears. Dud went to live with some cousins, and I lived for seven months with the Chambers, old friends of my mother. Then Mom bought a delicatessen in Oak Park so we could live together behind the store.

Two years after Dad died, John Doyle, whom Mother and Dad had known at Holy Family, heard that Mother was a widow. His wife had died, leaving him with two little boys, Donald and Eugene. When I was in sixth grade the two families were joined and all went well with the exception of my reactions. I did not want anyone to replace my father, and I was as nasty as I could be. When John bought me one of the very first "Mama" dolls for Christmas, I put it under my bed and never touched it. It took me a good while, but I mellowed, and I learned to love my step-father.

John Doyle was an Irish Chicago fireman, so we had to move to Chicago in the middle of seventh grade. Heartaches! Dud was at St. Mel's by this time and the three of us young ones attended our Lady Help of Christians. My teachers there helped me heal the wounds.

The first time I played the organ in church was there. I must have turned green while we were on the way, because my mother said, "Now, dearie, nobody in that church knows that any better than you do. Go play it." Mother said many wonderful things, but the two I remember best are: "God made you, and you are beautiful," and "He who never makes mistakes, never makes any progress." We were free to make mistakes in our home.

My step-father was hurt at the stock-yards fire; he fell three stories, breaking both arms and both legs. When he was convalescing we bought a car and made trips to the country, particularly Lake County. We camped on the Wilcox farm, on Channel Lake. The following winter the farm was subdivided and we bought the barn; we remodeled it and it became our summer home.

I graduated in 1924. I wanted to go to Trinity High School with my friends from Ascension, but the two car fares to get there prevented that. I went to St. Mary's, and though I never made friends there, the teachers were terrific. In my sophomore year I went to boarding school in Davenport. Mother thought I did not have the privacy I needed with the three boys. I hated being away from home, and the only respite was going to St. Joseph's in Rock Island for weekends. My aunt, Sister Mary Humbaline, was there. Sister Mary St. Alice made the best fudge!

During my senior year we were drilled for the Normal exams every school day at eight o'clock. My schedule started with 6:15 Mass — in seventh grade I fell in love with Jim Burke and that's when I started going to daily Mass. God has ways! I had a quick breakfast, a trolley ride, classes, home on the trolley. At Madison and Crawford, there was always a stop for ice cream.

When I graduated in 1928 I intended to go to DePaul, but Dad had been hurt going to a fire in March. Doctors told mother to get him out of the city, so she sold everything, winterized our summer place, and when Dad left the hospital in September we all went to Channel Lake. I told Mom I could get an apartment in Chicago and still go to DePaul. She said, "Oh, no you won't. You can go to Antioch High and take something you did not have at St. Mary's." I took three commercial subjects, world history and chorus.

Antioch High School was my introduction to coed education. I met a most wonderful boy, Daniel Eugene Sheehan. One day word came that Gene had been hurt in scrimmage. A crowd gathered, and then dispersed. I said to Gene, "Where is everyone?" He answered, "You're my girl now." I said, "I can't be anybody's girl. I'm going to be a nun." When I heard myself say that, there was no one more surprised than I was! I had not been thinking about that since I was five years old and I told my mother that when I grew up I was going to get all the wash done, and then be a sister.

St. Peter's Church was being built at that time. I became the first organist.

In spite of my remark to Gene we dated frequently, though not "going steady" until the third year. Gene taught me to drive in the fall of 1928, and I have been grateful all these years.

In the spring of 1931 I was twenty years old, and Gene had completed two years at Marquette. I went to talk to Sister Mary Gerontius about going to the novitiate. This was necessary because the pastor, Father Dan Frawley, was planning to send me to Mundelein Seminary for a year's study for organists. It was difficult telling my family and friends, especially Gene and his family. However, coming from the family that I did, it was quite natural to be a sister. Mother had four sisters and a cousin who were nuns; there were other relatives of hers and of Dad's. The year after I entered, the set included my second cousin. Father Dan wrote my recommendation; it is in my file now.

Entrance day was September 8, 1931. The postulant mistress had taught my aunts. That fall my cousin came to see me. I told her I was staying. She said that wasn't fair, that I had been influenced by "these nuns." "If you can tell Gene personally, I'll believe you," she said. The next visiting day she came with Gene. I did have the grace to tell him.

Reception Day arrived. I had asked God if I couldn't have Gene's last name, might I please have his first name. My prayer was answered. I received the name Sister Mary Danette.

Sister Mary Ernest, the novice mistress, was another remarkable woman, both kind and strict. I composed a musical setting for a poem that had been written about the stained glass window over the altar. Sister heard about it, and told me to destroy it, that we just didn't do things like that during our canonical year! I went to one of the music rooms and played it over and over until I was sure it was firmly in my head. Then I destroyed it. I wrote it down again after I reached the missions.

I was professed in March of 1934, and was sent to St. Dorothy's in Chicago. Sister M. Samuel had everything ready for me; it helped immeasurably. She had a book all written out with procedures learned at the Schonti Music Workshops, plus her own experience. Marvelous!

September found us opening St. Ferdinand School and Convent. The years there were wonderful but difficult. The fourth year there I almost left the community, but Sister Dormitilla understood and saved me. Perpetual vows were scheduled for 1939. My mother asked, "Are you leaving?" She knew I was having doubts. These continued during my first seventeen years. On vow days I really meant what I said, but in between there were many questions.

However, everything musical that I touched turned to gold. I think that is how the Lord kept me — that, and the friends I made in the novitiate and on the missions. During those years my Dad Doyle died. I will never forget how he cried on the day I left home. I had never seen a man cry before that day.

I returned to St. Dorothy's briefly, and then I went to Rapid City, South Dakota. Both the superior and senior teacher were most supportive, as were all the nuns in the house. I loved that place and those children and their parents and the priests. This is where I definitely decided to stay in the convent!

Summers had been spent at Mundelein and Clarke, where I earned a BME in 1950. I had also spent a few weeks every summer driving at the motherhouse.

I was sent to St. Helen's in Sioux City. I did not get along with the superior, who had written to Mother Josita about me. I wrote to my provincial, and a month later she took me to St. Ann's in Butte, Montana. It was a grade school. The superior was kindness personified. I had been scheduled to begin work at DePaul, and she said, "You will." The

Rockies were gorgeous, as was everything out there. Vacation School in Virginia City was an experience. I spent five months there, and then returned to the Sioux City diocese to teach in grade and high school. I had five very happy years. However, it was during this time that I lost my precious mother, who had attended every recital I gave in the Chicago area and who had visited me at each of my missions.

Ten years of prayers returned me to Rapid City. I was now teaching in the grades the children of the students that I had had in high school in the forties. I spent a glorious six years there, followed by a change to Boone, Iowa, where I was uncomfortable. The consensus on change was coming, and I wrote to Sister Mary Miles. In 1968 she sent me to St. Peter's in Antioch. They had engaged a secular to take the piano lessons, so there was only the sight singing for me. The nuns at Grayslake asked me to take their music, too, so I had half a week at each place for two years before deciding to stay at St. Gilbert's. There were five more splendid years.

Then I began to feel that I was not giving my students what I had been able to give in previous years. I talked to my regional, and I became the housekeeper at the motherhouse in 1975. It was different, but still wonderful. It was during those years that the third floor dorms were divided into private rooms. I suggested that we build a wall, forming an inner hallway where we could have a linen cabinet on that side of the house. So — I own a wall in the motherhouse!

I talked to my regional about returning to the missions. I had a community grant to join two sisters in Oxford, Mississippi. I had written to them on December 8; they answered on December 12, and I had received the grant on the feast of Our Lady of Lourdes. I figured she wanted me in Oxford. These were three most stimulating years, doing pastoral work and liturgical endeavors. I spent a year at St. Clare House of Prayer in Kankakee, Illinois, with the Joliet Franciscans. There were magnificent graces.

Then I was cook at Grayslake for two years before we were asked to leave after forty years of BVM presence there. Heartaches!

I have had some wonderful trips. The first time I travelled, other than going to an assigned mission, was in the late fifties. I attended a liturgical conference in Washington, D.C. with another sister, and we went a week early to see the town while staying with the Madames in

Georgetown. I returned to that city another time alone, and I attended a liturgical conference in Buffalo, New York. My principal insisted that I fly. It was my first time!

Once I flew to a liturgical conference in St. Louis. The nuns meeting me there were so relieved when I arrived. I had forgotten the hour's time difference, had napped a bit, and thought we were just about on time. They were frantic. We had been circling an hour because of a storm.

I took one bus trip through Detroit, Canada, and New York. I had a special insight in Montreal where my Dad was born.

My Golden Jubilee trip was arranged by my brothers and cousins. We left from Oxford, Mississippi, and headed West by Ameripass on the Greyhound. Dud wanted me to rent a car in Los Angeles and drive to San Francisco, but the Los Angeles nuns said that I would be busy driving and my companion would be the one to see everything. Even more, Highway One fogs up. So we took the bus to Salerno and Monterey, where we rented a car and drove to Carmel and Big Sur, thus satisfying my brother! We continued north to Seattle, and then east through Montana, and on to home.

I went to Springfield, Illinois to lobby for the ERA. I was the oldest woman in the group.

The first year that I was at Wright Hall I took three months off and traveled around visiting our sisters. When the Senate was in Denver we expanded the trip to the Tetons and Yellowstone Park. I went on a Carmelite tour of Marian shrines, and I also enjoyed a bus trip around Lake Superior. I had long dreamed of driving that way, but realized that I was too old for such an adventure. I have visited Colorado Springs, the Air Force Academy, Garden of the Gods, the Royal Gorge, and have reached the top of Pike's Peak. I have attended an Elder Hostel.

After we received permission to spend time with our families I visited with my brothers Dud and Gene and their families. I have spent some time in summers with the Kennedys at their cabin at Lake of the Woods. Gorgeous. I have often travelled to visit former students.

My Silver Jubilee was celebrated in Waterloo. The sisters did everything to make the "in convent" celebration most memorable. For my Golden Jubilee, there was no convent celebration, as I was in the process of moving. But the sisters in Oxford sent a lovely plant, and the three days at Dubuque were most satisfying. A group of us planned the

474

liturgies. I was privileged to sing a solo at Communion time, "Take and Receive," by John Foley, S.J.

My spiritual life was founded in my home, and fostered during my postulate and novitiate. I made my first directed retreat at the Cenacle, and with one exception, have made directed retreats ever since. My year at St. Clare's was refreshing. One of my former students has been sending the *Creation Spirituality* magazine for some time now. I enjoy thinking of God and praying to God as Mother as well as Father.

Are you wondering what became of Daniel Eugene Sheehan? When I entered the convent he quit Marquette, where he was on a football scholarship. Later he married and had three girls. He died in March of 1958. Heart.

And Jim Burke? He went to Quigley Prep Seminary. He was dismissed because he was caught attending a party. Jim was taken by Bishop Muldoon into the Rockford diocese. His last assignment was chaplain at the mental hospital in Dixon. He died young.

Now I am retired at the motherhouse. More time for prayer, quiet, reminiscing about the joys of teaching, writing letters, walking in this splendid setting. All our needs are met. We have good meals, nurses, medicines. Retreats are here, or we may go away if we wish. For the last four years I have had a season ticket for the Dubuque Symphony, and I take advantage of offerings at Clarke and Loras. There is time for playing the piano, so my profession goes on. There are exercises five days a week in the community room with a VCR given us by Jim Spiegel. Our administrators are exceptional.

My favorite pastime? Sitting in the chapel after supper.

Truly the hundredfold . . . and then looking forward to eternal life.

Thank you, God, for everything. It is good to be home!

Mary Ann Butkiewicz
Former Sister

Single

Home Health Care

Elementary and Special Education, College of Steubenville, Ohio

Certified Nursing Assistant,

Home Health Aide, LaMaze Child Birth

Ministry of visiting the sick, Parish discussion group

Mary Ann ties her professional skills to her ministry of visiting the sick. In addition to her work and ministry, she is concerned about children and their interests and needs. She enjoys music, especially opera, art and dancing. Her ambition is to return to college, "becoming a registered nurse, and eventually teaching nursing."

Mary Ann Butkiewicz

Religious are
Professional People

The very name of Christian means we are professional saints. Christ once lived and gained followers. Christ died, but His following continued after His death in which He took upon Himself all of our sins. Therefore Christians are professional saints. A look at past religious life leads to a better understanding of our present religious life. Shouldn't religious be specialists in sanctity, and give greater meaning to the name professional saints all Christians are meant to be?

My name is Mary Ann Butkiewicz. I was born on March 22, 1948 to two everyday Christian parents, Henry Walter and Esther Mary (Panfil) Butkiewicz. Very traditionally I was baptized on April 14, a few weeks after my birth, at our parish church in my hometown, Chicago. After completing kindergarten through eighth grade in Catholic grade school, I attended four years of Catholic high school.

Three months after my graduation I entered the novitiate of the Sisters of Our Lady of Professionalism. That September 11, 1966 could have been like any other Sunday afternoon, but instead I was embarking on a whole new page in my life. This made it a day I would never forget. My parents, my sister, our friend, and my youngest brother discussed what my name would be with the mother superior and mistress of novices. It seemed like another visit with a nun friend of our family back in Chicago. My family often visited with our friend Sister Juniper, so this scene wasn't uncomfortable.

But being told that your name had to be changed because they already had a Sister Mary Ann was uncomfortable! It really began to hit me. I had just driven some six hundred miles from Chicago to Ohio with the familiar feeling of being with my father, mother, sister, brother, and my friend; I would soon be saying good-bye to them and being introduced as Sister Esther (my mother's name) to some strangers who were in the same position I was. It was momentous. "What am I doing here?" thought I.

While reading the *Sacred Heart* magazine in the summer of my sophomore year of high school, I had come across the ad for this order of sisters who were still wearing habits. That's the first thing that attracted me to them. Oh, how naive I was, and proved to be, choosing a community by whether or not they still wore a habit! My main concern should have been with what this community could offer me that would enhance my aspirations toward this particular vocation.

It was not just a way to earn a living, but a way of life that would fulfill several life-long dreams. I wanted to live with people who were special, people who like myself had left behind self, family, friends and possessions to exhilarate their spirits with a sense of joy, peace and the love that one can only find when living and working with people in love with the same bridegroom, Christ. The life of a sister, in my heart and mind, is one of complete dedication: in community life, in prayer life, and in the apostolate that the community embraces.

The ongoing apostolate for my order was care for troubled girls and unwed mothers, but by the time the original group of sisters started their work in this small farmland town, the Bishop of the diocese asked them to take in and house the children on the streets of his river city, the diocese's home base. Since the location was also the mother house for women aspiring to be religious, its complex began to grow. An un-planned apostolate worked its way into the facility; we now housed boys and girls. Among the children entering the home were physically and mentally handicapped. No one wanted them. The schools at the time didn't have the means that are available today for helping these individuals. Families could keep them at home or send them off to school and work shops as they do today in this country. In short, they were being put in institutions. Many horror stories surrounded these overcrowded establishments, and once word got passed along that a country facility operated by nuns was available, people from all over the country brought children to be cared for by the good nuns.

My love for children kept me interested enough to continue writing to the mother superior, who was also the vocation directress. Especially appealing was the statement that these sisters promised a fourth vow above poverty, chastity, and obedience: the zeal for souls. Through

480

their work and prayers they were leading souls to heaven. Many times during my correspondence I used to think about the joy these sisters must feel in gazing upon the smiling faces of God's helpless little ones and knowing that they had helped to put that smile there. The rest of the apostolate listed in the ad may as well not have even been there.

Many of my preconceived notions about what life must be like, living in and among these professional people, were soon shattered. My childhood experiences with different orders of sisters were always favorable, and I found myself always defending any less than professional behavior as stemming from their humanity. Less important to my ideal of life in the convent was the hope that my love for choir and chorus singing would fit in well with angelic sisters' voices singing at Mass and chanting the Office together.

Wrong! This group of sisters put that notion to rest. Although a trained choir directress (one of the sisters) tried, she couldn't bring their voices nor their spirits in cooperation to fulfill this community's need. This should have been my first indication as to what was in store. Certainly these girls and women in the novitiate, all near enough in age to have experienced group singing, could strive, in my estimation, to meet the fulfillment of this task.

Because of the diversities of employment and of the people in this community, much in the way of needed training and education were overlooked or compensated for in order to have an income. Perhaps all of the original sisters teaching in some of the schools had their teaching degrees; I know of several at this time who didn't. As many of the original teachers left the order, sisters replaced them without teaching degrees or certification. The community, in an effort to become more learned and proficient in this profession, permitted the sisters to go to college, an hour's drive from the motherhouse where they lived.

The early seventies brought about a change in the practice of not permitting T.V., radio, newspapers, and magazines. Every effort to read books and magazine articles dealing with various aspects of their work was put forth by the sisters. I went to college while trying to keep up with my prayer life, community life, apostolic life, and personal life. All the resources of our intelligence, will and talents were called upon.

Faith and love gave meaning to our obedience, helping to resolve the inevitable conflicts and difficulties which come from human weakness and being stressed out. "Where God has planted you, you must blossom" was a phrase often used to conjure up the devotion necessary to ignore the weariness or annoyance caused by great demands placed on us. Often I reflected on this super nun pep talk in order to keep me striving to acquire a well-integrated personality. Making the best use of education was always my priority.

Perhaps one of my biggest disappointments upon entering the novitiate was the lack of any real structure in their formation of the girls and women wishing to be nuns. My religious vocation meant to me both a call and a response. To me, as a Christian, this call by God was to consecrate myself more intimately in union with Christ in the service of His people, and a response by which I pledged myself to live in charity through the profession of the vows. The awakening and discernment of my vocation is a responsibility which should have been felt by each member as her personal concern and the concern of the Church.

All the members share the responsibility for encouraging by prayer, witness and welcoming those who have been called. Careful selection for the admission of candidates should be the responsibility of a competent authority or a panel of competent sisters. The candidate should have spiritual maturity relative to her age, physical, psychological and moral health. Although in many communities the postulancy and novitiate are kept separate, in this one everyone in both groups were kept together for almost everything.

The heavy burden of the care of the apostolate here was shared with the postulants and novices almost as quickly as they entered. Many of the girls were sent right into the children's homes to be caregivers and baby-sitters for large groups of mentally retarded children. There was no preparation to meet their special needs. Others were even sent into classrooms to teach without certificates. Most of any formal training for the postulants and novices took a second place to the need for them to be working. Still convinced that my being there had its basis in God, I persevered, feeling that God was leading me on through all of my uneasiness.

My *Curriculum Vitae* for the time from September 11, 1966 until February 1, 1980 is as follows:

September, 1966 through January, 1967

At the motherhouse my duties were: teaching religion to children in three neighboring towns; sewing in the novitiate; child care; household work.

January 1967 through August, 1970

I served at the children's home as a cook. In 1969 I started as a part-time student at the neighboring college.

August, 1970 through July, 1977

I was stationed in the same town; I was enrolled in college. I worked in the bishop's residence as his cook and housekeeper. My other duty was teaching high school religion. For six weeks in each of the summers of 1975 and 1976, I went back to the motherhouse to take the place of the housemother of forty teenage girls and adult retarded women while she went away for summer school.

August, 1977 through June, 1978

I was stationed in a town down the river to be a teacher. I taught the second grade, and fifth and sixth grade religion. I was also a member of the women's choir.

September, 1978 to February, 1979

I moved up the river to another town as a teacher and local superior of the convent. My grade assignment was the eighth; I also taught seventh grade math and reading.

February, 1979 through January, 1980

I was brought back to the motherhouse as mistress of novices/ assistant superior/ council member. My duties included having complete authority when the superior was absent or unavailable; handling problems and complaints, religious formation of the postulants and novices, guidance and counseling, distributing health supplies, and acting as infirmarian. Additional services performed were: answering the telephone, bookkeeping, picking up supplies, driving sisters and children to and from the doctor.

No complaints have ever been made about me concerning any aspect of the performance of my duties. Changes in placement came about solely through requests for my services. Throughout the years various sisters asked me to work with them in individual houses for the children. Those on teaching missions asked me to teach at their schools. The reasons given for requesting me were that they knew me to be cooperative, sociable, and a good teacher.

The bishop recommended that we update our ceremonies for the habit reception, first profession, and final profession. I worked cooperatively on this committee. These meetings were in the chancery office. A priest was assigned to the task, also.

From the time I entered the community the consideration of the superior's age was a major concern among the sisters. In 1966 when I entered, the superior was in her 70's, but seemed to be extremely competent in her position. No preparation was being made for her successor. We were told by the superior and her assistant that since Mother was the original founder, she was a life-time superior. Therefore, she kept control of more than her share of the governing responsibilities of the community. At the same time she had charge of the finances of the children's home, located on the grounds of the motherhouse.

Many of the major decisions made by her were irrefutable. While managing all the business and governing aspects of this institution, she also took on many household tasks for the whole complex. These should have been delegated to several other sisters, or to hired help. A few of these jobs were as follows: running the large industrial size machines in the laundry, cooking for the sisters, taking care of the flowers and shrubbery, vocation directress, and fund raising.

I had basically been away from the motherhouse for nine years out of my thirteen-plus years with the community. That lack of constant contact made some of the problems less of a priority. The advantage of being able to share my personality and capabilities with others in my assigned missions seemed to make the years go by. At the same time, being away from the motherhouse didn't spare anyone from reproach. In August of 1970 I was assigned to the bishop's residence by the superior. The work there was considered unimportant by the community, and a waste of two sisters' time. The community offered no support because of this attitude. Mother superior often stated that she didn't want to keep us there, but that it was the bishop's wishes. Many times we were ridiculed for following through with our job demands. Through all this my companion and I supported each other for the full seven years that we were at the bishop's residence.

My first year teaching was another mission, but there was the same lack of support for all of us there. The distance from the motherhouse was a six-hour drive, which made fast trips back to the motherhouse impossible. The distance wasn't taken into consideration, and her criticism was great. Letters from the superior touched upon this as well, including many complaints about how overworked she was because the sisters wouldn't help her.

When I was into the second half of the school year in another mission I was called back to the motherhouse to run the novitiate because the mistress of novices left. I was required to explain my departure to the school administration. I wasn't given any orientation or training for my new role. My nine years in mission work had lessened my familiarity with all of the sisters. I was held accountable anyway, without an awareness of the sisters' needs or the problems they had with them- selves and others.

When I was appointed assistant to the superior, my duties as mistress of novices weren't dropped. According to the superior my appointment held no duties, just obedience to her. The circumstances surrounding my appointment were questionable, too. The current assistant to the superior at the time was in Rome for the Council meeting of the Order. Prior to the Rome meeting she was on mission work. Apparently she was unaware that I was assigned in her place in a permanent appoint- ment; I had been told by the superior when she appointed me that Sister knew of her discharge.

On her return from Rome the new appointment was discovered in an embarrassing incident in chapel, with many of the sisters present. All of the sisters returning from that trip to Rome took Mother into conference and demanded that she revoke my appointment to a position that was still filled by her previous appointment. They reminded her that she couldn't make this drastic move without consulting the council sisters. The superior came back to me after that private meeting to tell me that she was staying firm in her decision, chiding the council for what she considered a power-hungry attitude.

Too many times to mention I was manipulatived to the superior's advantage. When I was effective in handling what she delegated to me to do in many situations, she made accusations that I was moving in on her job, taking an authoritative role. There were many inconsistencies in what she wanted done, and she changed her mind often. Controversy began to surround every attempt to instill harmony and order. There was a definite sense of anarchy. The lack of order destroyed the essentials for community living.

Two events of physical damage to my body less than five months apart from each other may have played its part in the degeneration of my spirit. In August of 1978 I fell and broke my left ankle before the start of the school year teaching the eighth grade. In January of 1979 I slipped on the ice and shattered the top part of my humerus in my left shoulder. After finally getting over one major hurdle, I was hit with another even more intense in pain then the last. I felt overwhelmed. During many sleepless nights I met pain's loneliness, and cried out loud for it to end. The severity of this pain awakened in me a true respect and sensitivity toward anyone in pain.

Writing my request for dispensation was a long and painful process for me. So much in the way of deep hurts and sad disappointments, so much of a loss of what started for me as a call to sanctity, went into every line and page. Since I myself had spent many hours suggesting other recourses to the many finally professed who left the community before me, I tried everything suggested by the Vicar of Religious. As the departure of these friends had saddened me, so too was the mother superior saddened over my wanting to leave. She commended my past performance in the community. She expressed her great expectations for me, were I to remain.

Through the years I've dealt with the ex-nun element in my life in different ways. Many facets of my personality give the impression that I am a nun. Other people have said, "Stop acting like a nun," or, "Gee, you would never know you were once a nun!" Yet the prevailing inner calling to respond to people in need can never be hidden. An example of this happened to me in Florida where I got my first job without mentioning that I had been in the convent. This was the first time in eleven years that I had the experience of interacting with people on the basis of my own merits as an everyday person, not an ex-anybody, just me. My boss, after only one year, sensed that there was more to me than what my occupation required. I told her then of my past, and she praised my contribution to the work place.

As a nursing assistant my current work is that of a caregiver to people who need my help . What I've gained from my past is the need to have a better understanding of what will be required of me in my field. Although my certification permits me to do a lot for people, I am currently challenging myself by going for my degree as a registered nurse. This was an uphill battle with myself to gain the confidence, to challenge myself again to become a professional person.

Marie Grellinger
School Sister of Notre Dame

Manager, Catholic Charities Helping Center

Bachelor of Arts, Business and Education, Mount Mary College

Master of Science, Library School, College of St. Catherine

Hospice training,

Nursing home ombudswoman

Pastoral ministry

Marie continues to be a member in good standing with her community. For the present she lives in an apartment, and spends what little spare time she has in "mastering the intricacies of the computer" and in Bible study. She hopes to "continue working as long as I can contribute in some way." She also hopes to grow old gracefully, "though being graceful is not one of my outstanding characteristics."

Marie Grellinger

An Unfinished Tale

Fifty years ago this summer I boarded a clanking orange street car for the half hour ride to the somber Milwaukee motherhouse of the School Sisters of Notre Dame. I wore a tweed suit with a yellow blouse and brown and white spectator pumps, and carried a tennis racket and suitcase. My father had insisted that I spend a year in the "real world" before entering the convent. Working in the sales office of the Simmons Mattress Company until the Army bought all their mattresses, and then at the Catholic Social Welfare Bureau, made the year pass swiftly.

The motherhouse was a fortified city block near one of the old breweries. The buildings and brick walls enclosed an old-world garden and a new life. I had come there because I wanted to dedicate my life to God as my elementary and high school teachers had done.

There were forty young women in our group, ranging in age from sixteen to near thirty. The first thing to learn was how to manage the flowing serge skirts. Regular instructions from the candidate's mistress soon oriented us to other fine points of our new life: convent table etiquette, proper conduct in the huge dormitories, and a myriad of other do's and don'ts that quickly became routine. Personal evaluations and conferences also helped in the adjustment.

Religious exercises interspersed the day, beginning with meditation and morning prayer. Mass, noon examen, visits to the Adoration Chapel, and night prayer finished it off. I was enrolled in a full schedule of demanding college classes, but there was also time for study, recreation, and outdoor exercise. I broke several windows playing ball, and another with a typewriter when my sleeve caught a door handle and swung the carriage knob into the glass. Chores, three meals a day plus lunch, and a good night's sleep filled the schedule. The value of silence may not have been too apparent to us, but it assumed significance

491

during the day and especially in the evening when the Great Silence was to be observed as part of the Holy Rule.

Monthly visits by family members were permitted during the two years in the candidature. A young man whom I had been seeing somehow managed to see me one afternoon, bringing a special treat, a malted milk shake. Following his second visit and a brief conference with the candidates' mistress, the relationship terminated. No more milkshakes.

The length of the ceremonies for receiving the white veil of the novice guaranteed my father admission to St. Peter's heavenly gates according to his way of thinking. He also had a problem with my new name, Sister John Louis.

The strictly cloistered year in the novitiate was not the exalted experience I had been led to anticipate. Operating the mimeograph and at one point dismantling it in order to restore it to working order helped me through some anxious times. This, plus previous office experience and secretarial work for the candidate's mistress and the education councilor resulted in my becoming a high school business teacher.

The roomful of young women with hands folded in prayer stood facing me, obviously waiting for me to say or do something. It was the end of my first day of teaching. My mind was a blank. The lanky freckle-faced student standing immediately in front of me obligingly recited the closing blessing when she observed my frozen expression. June was a graduate of St. Alphonsus grade school, so she knew what I should have been doing.

I was teaching shorthand, typing, bookkeeping, English, algebra, citizenship, and religion in a self-contained classroom, even though I had not completed my first degree. The sister who taught the other first year commercial class was my partner and was charged with helping me. We had mentoring down to an art. I was meticulously instructed in the intricacies of day books, tests, record keeping, and grading. I was patiently initiated into the routine, schedule, and policies. I was encouraged and advised, listened to and assisted in solving problems.

Every weekend we planned out the week's work, and every night after recreation, perhaps a rousing game of Five Hundred, we prepared

492

the next day's lessons and checked papers. Teaching had its difficulties, but I loved it and enjoyed my students.

Summertime meant summer school. Then came the dreaded period waiting for the next year's assignments. After nine years in Chicago I received an unusual one.

I was sent to a forgotten copper mining town on a craggy peninsula on Michigan's Upper Peninsula. A standard high school curriculum was maintained despite an enrollment of only eighty-eight students. I had a full schedule of classes but only remember the delightful poetry in freshman English, the three excellent students in shorthand, and bookkeeping. I had been slated to teach plane geometry, but the superior assigned that class to an older sister who did not appreciate the task. Although this caused a strained relationship, that year in snow country was possibly my happiest as a Sister of Notre Dame.

After only a year and a half, a middle of the year transfer to Indiana found me walking into a junior homeroom in a high school of over fifteen hundred students. It was staffed by another order except for five Sisters of Notre Dame and one other sister who was in the office. Paper checking became a treadmill since I had over fifty typists in a class and two typing classes. Teaching shorthand was especially stressful because of the inability of the less gifted to reach the levels of proficiency required.

Bookkeeping continued to be my favorite class. "You ought to be in television," commented one of the students following my dramatization of some business transaction and its consequences. Another student in that class thought I was tricking him one day. It annoyed me that teachers were known by their room numbers rather than their names, so I strongly suggested that they fill my name in correctly on the proper line in a standardized bookkeeping test they were taking. "What is your name?" whispered an intent, frowning senior. "John Louis," I answered, only deepening his frown. "Sure, sure, I'm Harry Truman," was his rejoinder.

The chancellor of the diocese gave a series of marriage instructions in the junior homerooms. During his first session he said to the class in my presence that if what he said differed from what I taught, I was right.

Even though it was a large school, there was a feeling of unity among the staff and a sense of accomplishment in the students.

Because my assignment in Michigan had included acting as librarian, I had been enrolled in a master's degree program in library science. When I completed the requirements during summers, I was ready to put my newly acquired knowledge to work. I began an eleven-year stay in a dynamic parochial high school in a small Fox River valley town. That is Green Bay Packer territory where, when someone dies, the question is not "Who gets the money?", but "Who gets the season tickets?"

Catholic Central High School in Marinette, Wisconsin, had a strong athletic program with all the accompanying appurtenances such as cheerleaders, pompon girls, pep rallies, homecoming, dances, parades, and float- making. The drama club put on three plays a year. The music department achieved remarkable success in their performance of classical programs. Student Council, the yearbook, the newspaper staff, the library club also clamored for attention and student involvement. Add to that the Junior-Senior Banquet and all the time consumed in producing the glamorous ambiance of the Prom. It seemed like a battle between school work and extracurricular activities, with classes on the losing team.

I arrived in Marinette as a young sister in the long multi-layered black serge with flowing sleeves, the stiffly starched wimple and veil, with no hair evident. I left as a middle-aged sister in a blue polyester double knit suit with my hair showing from under a skimpy black veil.

Middle age brought on its questions, but the uncertainty as to whether I was making a difference in anyone's life had a two-word answer, Milwaukee Spectrum. Three of us dreamed, planned and brought into being Spectrum, an alternative high school for girls, truants and dropouts, who wanted a second chance at obtaining a high school education.

After trying unsuccessfully for several years to obtain government funding, we decided to appeal against it, we would forget it. The provincial superior was not in favor of it, but when a chapter sister voiced her support and gave us our first donation, the other chapter members wholeheartedly followed. We were on our way.

Used books, supplies, furniture, mountains of school necessities were dug out of attics or closets and sent to us. Old typewriters, sewing machines, kitchen equipment, boxes and boxes of materials piled up. Bake sales and other fund raising efforts, contributions large and small from friends and relatives, and their friends and relatives helped us almost to meet the goal of $10,000. The provincial superior not only backed us at that point but made up the balance needed.

We began with seventeen students in two classrooms of a former parish elementary school. Most of our students were minorities from the inner city. "Self-respect and respect for others are integral to the program," was the opening statement in the official student-parent interview; it set the tone and basic philosophy for the very new, very tiny school. Small classes, ten to fifteen students, provided for meeting individual needs. Close cooperation with the home was insisted upon. If an absent student did not have a parent call the school, we called that morning.

Report card interviews with both student and parent and all of the staff became one of our best tools. By stressing improvement and discussing problems in a positive way, we helped students see a high school diploma becoming a reality. "I'm the first one in my family to graduate from high school," was a frequent comment heard during commencement.

The three of us on the original staff had a really great working relationship besides being complementary to each other in subject areas. Sister Shannon Marie taught reading, probably the most important subject for our students, plus social studies. Sister Joyce had a science and math background with sewing thrown in as a bonus. I taught English and business subjects. We had an arrangement with one of our high schools for proper accreditation.

Our noon hour program, which helped make the day more endurable for the students, was quite a challenge to the staff. Every third week my fourth period class planned the menu, went on a shopping expedition to the local supermarket, and then prepared and served the meals for students and staff the following week. Sisters Shannon and Joyce did the same thing.

Each student took a turn washing pots and pans, peeling potatoes, baking cakes, trying new recipes. Chicken, pizza, chili, spaghetti, greens, salads, vegetables, desserts — great variety appeared, necessarily including the basic food groups and fulfilling government requirements, but also appealing to the students. With a time crunch of one hour to get the meal ready, students learned how to cooperate and organize as well as prepare nutritious appealing food. The other two groups washed the dishes and cleaned up after the meal. Besides being a really practical learning experience, it was often the only real meal that day for many of our students.

It was always a challenge to find money to meet the rapidly increasing budget needs. Our budget jumped from $10,000 to $40,000. Writing grants, attending organizational meetings, and arranging fund raisers drained energy that was needed for teaching. Then there was a traumatic brush with the IRS over back taxes despite our tax exempt status, and a threatened lawsuit for child abuse. But as time went on our enrollment increased and stabilized, our credibility became established, and even some government funding came our way. I left Spectrum after seven years, tired of raising money, but extremely pleased with what had been accomplished.

At the ten year anniversary celebration one of my bookkeeping students related that her current job stemmed from that particular course. Another day I received a picture of a charming young mother and her son. It brought back memories of the wild tales of her escapades in the public school which resulted in her expulsion. At Spectrum she had been a determined achiever. She graduated, married, and moved to Texas. She now holds a responsible position and has a lovely family.

For me the most meaningful feedback from those years of struggling, laughing, cleaning, questioning, counseling, comforting, disciplining, record keeping, and money raising was from a graduate who was dying of AIDS. She told a nurse that the only people who really loved her were the nuns at Spectrum and Angie, a friend she had made there. That statement was worth all the struggle and heart aches involved.

Moving along now in the 60's — my 60's, that is — I spent three years in Kenya, East Africa. I was not impressed with the British system of education and its rigid discipline, nor with the lack of books.

Nevertheless it was an extremely enlightening experience. In a speech on some important occasion, the President stated with pride that no Kenyan was more than 1.8 kilometers (roughly a mile) from a source of water. We were fortunate to be in the green, mountainous thirteen percent of the country that is arable and had some water in our storage tanks. I still thankfully enjoy having plenty of water to rinse my toothbrush rather than using a limited supply from a small bottle. Fortunately the rains came before we reached the end of our water supply.

Daily life took a different rhythm in Nyabururu, East Africa. Buying freshly killed beef hanging in an open air market meant that a great deal of time had to be spent scraping away the grass and other oddments clinging to the carcass, plus the newsprint in which it had been wrapped. Water had to be boiled and filtered. The filter had to be carefully sterilized periodically. Fresh vegetables and fruits had to be treated in chlorinated water. Laundry was done in a bucket.

The most unpleasant aspects of my stay in Kenya were my attacks of malaria and my bouts with amoeba. I lost thirty pounds as a result of the latter.

Although we were almost on the equator the climate was very pleasant because of the altitude. The Kenyans' craving for education and the selfless outreach of the extended family helping each other greatly impressed me. It was fascinating to compare the Africans with the students of Spectrum and see similarities.

I never did resolve the question of whether Westernization really benefited the Africans. Failed international projects left Kenya millions in debt. There were shameful sentinels of huge unused factory buildings in Kisumu and Turkana. On the other hand, groups like the Medical Missionary Sisters were teaching simple means of hygiene and infant care. Blindness is prevented merely by having mothers wipe the eyes of babies with a clean cloth using water stored in a small gourd. Other basic needs vital to the welfare of the people are being met.

Lack of medical supplies in the hospitals was mind-boggling. In some hospitals patients were required to bring their own copy book to record medical data. Needles were used repeatedly. Even well-reputed mission hospitals had two patients in one bed.

Now in Indian Territory in eastern Oklahoma my days are quite a contrast to convent life when I was a young sister. Instead of one among forty, I live alone in an apartment, the only Sister of Notre Dame in the diocese, and one of ten sisters outside of Tulsa. Rather than being swathed in yards of serge and starched linens, with a large crucifix on a rosary looped at my side, I often wear blue jeans. When I forward my paycheck to the Milwaukee motherhouse, I make a request for my needs for the following month based on my yearly budget. I drive a car as one of the perks of my job managing Sallisaw's Catholic Charities Helping Center. What I do during my morning hour of prayer is my personal choice. I miss daily weekday Mass but experience it more deeply on the occasions when our young pastor celebrates in a tiny chapel with only two or three present.

I have never lived in an area with so few Catholics or felt as much community involvement as I do here. Catholics make up less than three percent of the population in this part of the Tulsa diocese, yet their support of the Center's food and clothing bank continues to grow. Being the one to reach out in the name of the Catholic community, giving food and clothing to families in desperate need I consider a privilege.

There are other, more significant changes. For many years I had felt like a nameless number despite efforts to involve everyone in the renewal following Vatican II. Living alone has finally enabled me to realize that I am nothing more — or less — than one person among a large group of valiant women trying to advance the Kingdom of God one day at a time in insignificant but worthwhile ways. Professing chastity in a pro-choice media-centered society is obviously counter-cultural. Facing old age with unanticipated insecurity is a different kind of hundredfold, but join the crowd. Obedience has evolved from a mother-daughter relationship into an adult state with more responsibility devolving upon me as an individual. I love it this way. Formerly a manuscript such as this would have had to be approved by a superior. Serving on the Marble City Council for several years was also my decision.

There are disadvantages to this freedom. Having to find one's own job when long past middle age is traumatic after having been moved about like a chess piece for many years.

I miss my friends and associates who have left. During our wait to begin Spectrum when I worked at local business colleges, I am sure friends and family wondered about my leaving, but I had said forever and it isn't forever yet.

Life as a Sister of Notre Dame has been full, exciting, and most rewarding. My one regret is that I haven't taken a more active role in influencing the direction of the order and of the Church, so I will conclude with a seemingly unrelated parting shot. I believe there will be women ordained as priests in the Catholic Church, not as a matter of right or equality but because of the essence of the priesthood.

Mary
Former Religious

Single

Finance Department, Law firm

Bachelor of Science in Elementary Education

Bachelor of Science, Kutztown University

Aid for Friends (a food ministry)

Conference for Catholic Lesbians

Mary, the author of this piece, was a member of a large community of teaching sisters for several years. Since she left the community she has worked as an administrator in the business sector. She is still drawn to religious life, and in the future would like to incorporate another try at living religious life with work among lesbians and gay Catholics and people with AIDS.

Words Burned into My Heart

I entered the community on September 8, 1982. There were nine other women in my band. In some ways it was like being back in college and living again in the dorm, but individual rooms had now been replaced by cubicles, and Thursday night keg parties were replaced with feast day celebrations. Those first years were fun, I do admit. There was a great feeling of camaraderie among the members of my band. We all wanted to be there; we wanted to be nuns, we wanted to be good nuns. It was easy to put up with the nonsense because we were in it together.

Looking back, we had to do some pretty outrageous things during formation. It's hard to believe that some of the things in *The Nun's Story* were quite similar to my own convent experiences some forty years later. So much for Vatican II. Anyway, all was done for the love of God in our hope of growing in simplicity and humility.

We eagerly awaited daily conferences given by our directress, and a new batch of brainwashing material on which to meditate. Each morning, for the first few months, we washed our underwear in the bathroom sink, put it in trash bags and put it out on the line to dry. Before Vesper we gathered our sometimes frozen bras to thaw for wearing the next day. We learned strict adherence to the bell calling us to prayers and meals. Each of us had the responsibility of ringing the bell for several days; at the end of that period we asked permission to pass the bell to the next sister in rank. Basically, we asked permission to do everything. One never assumed permission even for the most logical or charitable actions.

We were expected to keep night silence, which began after the closing prayer at the end of recreation and lasted until breakfast the next morning. Anyone who broke night silence had to confess this to the directress. After Mass each morning our directress would stand in the hall outside of chapel for anyone who could not live with the guilt of having broken night silence. If you could live with your own guilt, fine, but you had to worry about the sister with whom you had spoken telling on herself.

Incoming mail was opened and read; so were our weekly letters to our parents. Several of my letters were withheld and had to be re-written. Obviously, I had written something which might have alarmed my parents. Something like, "I am tired." I could understand my letter not being sent if I had written, "I am tired of this psychological torture," but not simply for having written, "I am tired." Each letter we wrote was signed, "In Mary's Immaculate Heart, I am your loving daughter, Sister ...".

We were not permitted to speak to the novices or professed sisters other than at formal gatherings. The term "particular friendships" was never used, but we understood its meaning. Family visiting was once a month. Weather permitting we set up our circles of chairs on the lawn, otherwise in the gym or community room. We did not speak to our families about our lives or our struggles. Gifts received from family or friends had to be presented to the directress; at that time we asked permission to keep only the necessary items. All gifts for which permission was denied were sent to the candy closet.

Girdles were to be worn. Occasional smacks on the butt served as a check and a reminder. I thought my leg would someday be amputated by that girdle! The use of tampons was not encouraged. Therefore, none were provided. We were not permitted to have money, not even a quarter to sneak a phone call to an old friend while at the college for a class. Obviously, we were not permitted to use the phone.

We scrubbed and buffed every part of the motherhouse. We'd line up on the sanctuary floor in chapel with buckets and rags and, on our hands and knees, methodically scrub the black and white marble. We oiled each pew in chapel several times a year. Lemon oil does wonders for dry hands — especially after a day in the laundry at the mangler. Shake, mangle and fold! Working hard all day usually provided a good reason for a party. We perpetually planned parties with elaborate decorations, skits, plays and games. God, we had a good time together! I never laughed (or cried) so much as during those years in formation.

All partying, working and studying was done in the holy habit. If we weren't wearing our habits, we were in our pajamas. We had no other clothing for playing softball or gardening or cleaning. Our bonnet (veils) were especially cumbersome. They were made of plastic and covered in polyester. I thought our congregation coined the phrase the "greenhouse effect" because of them. By the end of a sweltering day, I wondered what I might find growing under that thing.

But I thought our habit was beautiful and I was proud to wear it. Each morning, while dressing, prayers were said. For example, while donning the habit we said: " O God, my loving Father, may this habit be a sign to all men of my total dedication to You, and may its Marian character aid my perseverance." Other prayers were said as we put on the cincture, scapular, crucifix and the veil. At this last, we said: "This veil, my Lord, is symbol of my vowed consecration to You, a total self-gift with undivided heart."

It was as a senior novice that my life began to change. Prior to entering the community I thought I had my life together. I thought I had a good understanding of my sexuality and my ability to integrate it into a life of celibacy. Things changed when I realized I didn't have it all together, and that I did not know how to unite these two major parts of my life. I received little help in these areas from daily conferences or classes on the vowed life. Visiting priests who came to the motherhouse to hear confessions were sometimes helpful, and I read every book I could find on sexuality and celibacy. As stated in our rule book, "By her vow of chastity, a sister commits herself to a life of consecrated celibacy together with the obligation to abstain from any external and internal act opposed to chastity." These words were burned into my heart, for I struggled over them daily. I spent many hours in chapel gazing at the large marble crucifix above the tabernacle, questioning God and begging for understanding.

My struggle intensified as I grew in my awareness of my attraction to a postulant named Ellen. I was not permitted to speak with her and was reminded of this many times. Ellen was also attracted to me. We often planned to meet in some out of the way place — the "pit", which was below the chapel on the terrace floor, or in the stacks of the library. We'd meet just to talk for a few moments alone, hoping we would not be discovered. I knew Ellen was struggling with her religious vocation. I knew she wasn't happy; I thought I could do something to help. There was nothing I could do or say to convince her to stay. I should have simply said, "Stay for me." That is how I felt.

We grew very close in a short time. One night, a week before she left the community, she came into my cubicle, sat on my bed and stayed for hours just stroking my hair and gently touching my face. I had never experienced such warmth in the touch of a hand. I was falling in love with her. For the next week we spent every night together in bed just talking softly and holding each other. Little did I realize, if discovered, we would have both been thrown out. It wouldn't have mattered to me. I was in love and, needless to say, I was heartbroken when she left.

We had very little contact over the next year. I had not forgotten her nor had she forgotten me. We kept a journal to each other which we managed to pass back and forth through the kindness of an understanding friend. Once in a while I would see Ellen at a concert or play at the college. We would exchange a few words and deep heart-piercing glances. Ellen was considered a threat to my vocation by my directress. She was, I suppose.

First vows. Somehow I believed that making my vows and leaving the confines of the motherhouse and the scrutiny of my directress, would somehow miraculously provide me with the freedom necessary to develop a healthy friendship with Ellen. It didn't happen. I found myself longing for more and more time with her. My prayer life was a mishmash of fantasy and reality where I found little comfort. My inner struggle sapped most of my energy, leaving little for my community of sisters or my students. I was so confused about love and religious life, and how the two could possibly fit together. My guilt grew over loving, deeply, another woman. In my heart I was not chaste or celibate and I had broken my vows, not only of chastity but of obedience. I was living a lie. I wanted to be with Ellen.

I knew I needed help. I could not make a peace-filled decision without sharing openly my anguish. I spoke with my superior, who set up an appointment for me to speak with the directress of junior sisters. It was she who arranged for me to see a community appointed psychiatrist. Too bad I couldn't have made my own choice at such a critical point in my religious life.

Anyway, I met with the psychiatrist once a week for several months. During that time it became obvious to me that lesbian tendencies and religious life were not compatible. After dredging up family experiences and the typical domineering mother analysis, the thrust of each session became Mary — yes, the Blessed Mother — and my need to develop a deeper, loving, trusting relationship with her. This psychiatrist would write on a notepaper points for meditation on Mary for me to use during the week. Somehow this new relationship with Mary was to heal the broken child inside, end my same-sex attractions, and save my religious vocation. I became more distraught after these sessions.

Thank God, that at the same time I was seeing *this* psychiatrist, I was also talking with a wonderful priest, Father John. He helped me sort things out and reassured me that this shrink wasn't all right. Father John met with me and Ellen several times and compassionately listened to our stories. He was a man close to God, one who had a beautiful understanding of the human heart and its capacity for love. I am grateful for his presence at such a difficult time; it was because of his guidance that I had the courage to change my life.

I finished the school year and left the community the day after school ended. My superior drove me to my parents' home. The community provided me with $300 to begin a new life. How generous!

Ellen and I lived together for four years. The first year was filled with excitement at the newness of setting up house and a life together. The years after — slowly and painfully we began to understand that our commitment as partners was only temporary, a stepping stone to greater things for both of us.

Ellen is now happily married to a wonderful man. I am seriously considering religious life again. I move toward this with a greater awareness of God's continual presence in my life in all the experiences of heart, mind, body and soul. I believe God loves me wildly and unconditionally for all that I am and am not. This time around, I do hope to have a better understanding of the giftedness of my sexuality, or intimacy, emotional, physical and spiritual, and the ways in which these can be joyfully integrated into a celibate commitment. It will be a challenge, I am certain. In accepting my lesbianism and recognizing my own homophobia, I am compelled, as an equal member of the Body of Christ, to work for justice on behalf of all those who are discriminated against, especially my lesbian sisters and gay brothers. Our Church is less than Christian in its treatment of homosexual persons. Our society silently supports the violence and persecution we face each day, all because we have chosen to love another person.

In closing, I'd like to answer the question, "Whatever happened to the good sisters? My response. . . Many of us who have lived or are living religious life have realized that we are what all people are. We are no better, no worse. Among us are theologians and alcoholics and social workers and drug addicts and scholars and lesbians, all longing to find God, the God who dwells within.

Pat U.
Sisters of St. Joseph

Religious Staff Chaplain

A.B., Regis College, Weston, Massachusetts

Master of Education, English, University of Massachusetts

Special Training: Rutgers Summer School of Alcohol Training; University of Massachusetts Alcohol Studies

Job-related ministries

Although Pat lives in an apartment a thousand miles from her community she stays in touch through a community newsletter, and by letters and phone calls. She has recently had to relocate because her job was abolished, and her work and living situations are significantly different. Her work in the hospital involves acute care as well as a day a week in an Alcohol/Chemical Dependency Unit. She loves reading, listening to music, walking on the beach, and sitting on "my rock." Pat says that she continues to work through her grief process, and that she is "trying to stay in the present moment and not make any projections."

Pat U.

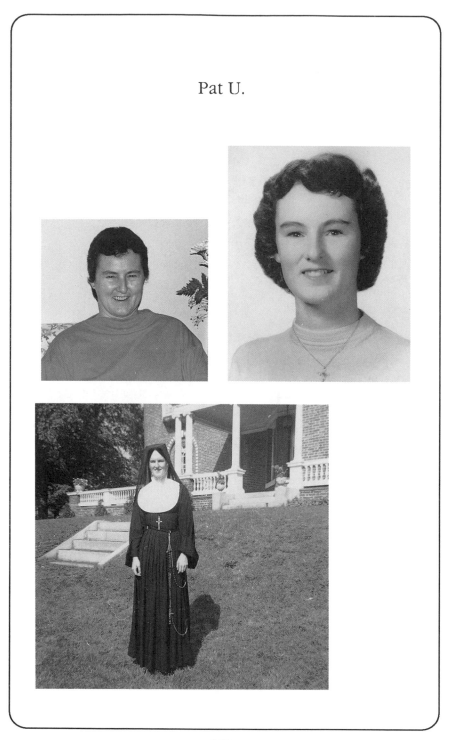

If It Hadn't Happened

Sitting at an A.A. meeting the other night, I couldn't help but wonder how my life would be today if I weren't an alcoholic.

Growing up as the oldest of seven children, I had a lot of responsibility and didn't realize how I resented it. Self-control and will power were paramount in my family, so I could usually maintain some modicum of control over my anger, but it would periodically erupt and I would lose my temper. This sometimes meant I would calmly dangle one of my siblings by the ankles over the third floor bannister. This consistently merited a strapping with a thick Mexican belt brought home by Dad on one of his frequent business trips. We moved from state to state because of his work, leaving friends every year or two, but strappings were a constant that knew no geography.

One day when I was nine years old, I unemotionally picked up my brother by the throat till he turned purple. Instead of a strapping, my mom sat me down and quietly told me that if I continued to lose my temper, I would land in a women's penitentiary (which in my child's mind, I interpreted as a mental hospital). Reverse psychology worked and I remember thinking to myself as she said this, "I will never, ever let anyone know how I feel." This solemn vow to myself has proved to be the most emotionally devastating decision I've ever made. Unfortunately, I was successful. I became a rigid, controlled, uptight person, wearing a frozen smile that said I came from a "Leave It To Beaver" family, that everything for me and my family was just fine.

By the time I entered the Sisters of St. Joseph after high school, I was a full-blown workaholic who wouldn't have known a feeling if I fell over one. I had not a clue that I came from an alcoholic home, that I was co-dependent to the max, that I was an alcoholic waiting to happen (like instant mashed potatoes waiting for the liquid to be added). I went from

511

one closed, protected environment to another in community. I had known this was where God wanted me from the last two years of high school and I embraced this new way of life after graduation with gusto and enthusiasm, self-sacrifice, dedication and my customary workaholism.

What I did made me worthwhile. How sad! Even if it had been said, I wouldn't have been able to hear anything that contradicted this fallacy. I admired and loved the sisters who taught me. I wanted to be like them: close to God, happy, a teacher who could help others. If I left home and entered community for security and protection from reality, I didn't know it then. Several of my closest high school friends also entered various religious communities at the same time and we had a lot in common.

I missed my family horribly. My youngest sister Terry was only two years old when I entered. More than anything I feared she would forget me, her surrogate mom since birth. I begged my mother to show my picture to Terry every night so she would recognize me on visiting days.

There were eighty-six of us postulants entering that novitiate building in September 1958. Pre-Vatican II theology and a 300-year-old community tradition from France combined to help mold me into the perfect sister who always did what she was told, worked hard, studied hard, not feeling anything negative and flagellating myself physically, mentally, emotionally and spiritually in my efforts to be Christ-like.

Our mistress of novices warned us repeatedly about particular friendships. It never dawned on me what she was getting at. Something told me it was O.K. to have friends, but this particular friendship stuff meant that if I were a good sister, I couldn't spend too much time with the same people and I couldn't get too close. I was too naive to have the slightest clue what was meant by all this. Looking back now, I didn't know how to feel, to trust, to be vulnerable and to risk sharing who I was rather than what I did. I was devastated as one after another of my closest friends got sent home along the route from reception to final vows.

That pain paled in comparison to my two closest friends choosing to leave community: one after ten years, and one after fifteen years. Today, I know that what I experienced after each of these departures was clinical depression. I felt my safe world had fallen apart. What I most shared with my two friends was no longer part of their life's journey. I felt they personally rejected me in walking away from what I perceived as the eternally stable life style we shared. The winds of Vatican II had been blowing through community; my friends were numbered among the rebels. I found it hard to believe they didn't have a vocation anymore. I was a follower, not a leader. Many of those sisters I liked most were avant-garde and I tried hard to keep up with their intellectualism, their philosophical debates and radical theology. Everything in my world seemed to be crumbling as my friends/mentors/leaders grazed in other pastures.

Looking back now, I realize that shame and fear were Higher Powers for most of my life. Though I prayed the Office, attended daily Mass, prayed and meditated each day with my local community, I couldn't believe that God really loved me (or that anyone else could love me either). I had to believe that if I continued to *do* the right things, somehow I would be a good sister.

My religious congregation began some experimental living in apartments in the late 60's. A sister with whom I'd lived earlier asked me to join the fifth such self-supporting group. Five of us lived in a newly-formed parish where we were actively involved with the priests as a team in collegial decision-making, as good neighbors and as active parishioners while daily commuting to various teaching positions in surrounding communities. I loved it. The other four sisters with whom I lived were very much into expressing their feelings, building a new kind of community of the future, paying bills for the first time, touching the people of God on a daily basis. I felt they had more academic degrees than I did, and in order to feel good about myself, I started a master's degree program part-time as I continued to teach junior high school full-time.

At the end of two years, I was asked to leave the group. I hadn't a clue why. They said I wasn't in touch with my feelings, that I was superficial, that I must start therapy — only then I could stay. I didn't want to start therapy (whatever that was!), but I did want to stay with the group. So, I made an appointment and went for my first counseling session. When I returned home that day I was told that they wanted me to leave anyway. The bottom of my world fell through. I had no choice but to go. I pleaded with them (again!) to explain *what* I needed to do in order to stay. No dice!

My worst fears of rejection and abandonment were realized. I couldn't fathom that what they were asking of me was what I was not capable of at that time, that it had less to do with what I could *do* to change, than who I *was* as a vulnerable human being with feelings and needs. I moved to a traditional convent on the other side of the city, commuting to the same junior high where the school year was already well underway. Now I had even more proof that I was a failure.

While I was living in the apartment, the congregation rules had relaxed enough to allow me to visit my family who now lived outside the diocese. I found that my dad's drinking was causing hushed-up problems in the family. There was plenty of booze around and I remember my first drink so well. Sitting on my parents' living room couch, tense and uptight after a long bus ride, I put the glass to my lips and had a spiritual experience! I remember saying to my new friend, "Where have you been all my life?!" For the first time in thirty years I felt comfortable in my own skin.

Depressed at being kicked out of a place and parish that I loved, I poured alcohol into me at every available opportunity. I made great sacrifices of time and money to get the bus up to New Hampshire to visit my parents, who were in ill health. As the oldest in the family, the perpetual caretaker, I told myself that it was my duty to find out how Mom and Dad were, and to keep my brother and five sisters informed since I lived only one state away, and the others had moved further away (California, East Africa, New York, South Carolina). Today I can be honest and say I went to New Hampshire to drink.

At the close of that school year, I made a conscious, deliberate, well-planned attempt on my life. That summer the sisters I lived with were in and out on retreat, vacation, volunteer assignments. I went to New Hampshire for a mini-family reunion and returned to my convent in Boston unbeknown to anyone. As I snuck up the back stairs, making sure no one knew I had returned, I got undressed and as I stood next to the sink, I prayed, "God, I know You can't want me to be in this much pain and I don't believe any of that garbage about going to hell if I commit suicide. Everyone will be better off. Please help me do this right."

I had purposely tanked up on wine and vodka before leaving New Hampshire because I knew this would take all the courage I could

514

muster. I then swallowed my cache of 150 carefully-stored Mellaril. I don't remember anything else. Four days later one of the sisters came looking for me. Mom had called and wanted to tell me something. Despite the portress's insistence that I was still in New Hampshire, my mother finally convinced her that I had returned to Boston four days earlier. No one knew exactly what happened, and I sure didn't tell them. I didn't go to the hospital; I didn't have my stomach pumped; I was sick and needed to be left alone. They did as I asked. Years later when I saw the movie *The End* with Burt Reynolds and Dom De Luis, I really identified with Burt's rage at finding himself alive after committing suicide.

This was the *beginning* of my alcoholism. It could only get worse. On the outside my workaholism covered for the lack of control I progressively experienced with my drinking and abuse of prescription drugs. After a weekend of drinking at my parents' home, I would often wake up on Monday morning with what I know today was a terrific hangover. About to face a couple hundred junior high kids, I'd take a few Fiorinal for the migraine I was sure to get. I had no idea I was "chewing my booze", taking the morning drink in pill form.

I had been raised with good values like honesty, like care and respect for others. But how could I be honest with anyone else when I lived with the self-delusion that alcohol and prescription drugs were not a problem for me. I lied to myself and others about what I drank, how much I drank, when I drank. When a generous parishioner gave our convent a Christmas gift of a case of twelve quarts of coffee brandy, I snuck one bottle up to my room each night, and drank it, sitting on the side of my bed with a paper cup. After five or six days, the sister who cleaned that first floor closet noticed that half the case was empty bottles. I remember standing with a group of sisters outside the closet being appropriately horrified at her discovery and saying, "Maybe the janitor has a problem ... "

I hated myself for what I'd become: a liar, a cheat, ruining this man's reputation. The shame and humiliation suffocated me. And I hadn't a clue that any of this had anything to do with my alcoholism. As my disease progressed, the shame and fear were unbearable. They made so many of my decisions for me! And how could I love my students and the sisters I lived with when I hated myself so much. Alcoholism/chemical dependency ground me up and pulverized me till I had no self-worth or dignity left. I knew that if the sisters I lived with knew how I felt inside, they would institutionalize me. This fear, coupled with my perfectionism, had me staying up every night in the community room doing lesson plans perfectly, and correcting papers till the wee hours.

One month before I hit my bottom, the principal told me she was concerned about how much I was drinking at faculty parties, that I might need to get help. Because her term of office was over, she was leaving for another assignment and had nothing to gain personally from taking this risk with me. She was the only sister who cared enough to confront me lovingly instead of putting on blinders and enabling me to continue the downward slide into the emotional hell so impossible to describe.

It was also about this time that I broke out in the one and only case of eczema I ever had. As I was having the prescription filled, I asked the pharmacist what caused eczema. He said, "Psychological trauma." I never made the connection with alcoholism. It was indeed the grace of God that enabled me to pick up the phone and call AA. In hushed tones I threatened I wouldn't go to a meeting if they sent anyone from the parish. I could taste the shame and humiliation. I gave up trying to be the perfect sister, at least temporarily.

In fact, no one I lived with knew where I was going every night. I'd wait at the window in the back laundry room till someone from AA picked me up for a meeting. Alcoholism was such a moral issue for me that I would duck down in the car as we drove through my neighborhood enroute to a meeting! Tension in the convent increased as the nights rolled by and the sisters saw me get into one strange car after the other. But no one said a word to me about their growing alarm. I finally could stand the tension no longer. One night at a house meeting, I mustered all the courage I could and said, "I'm having some problems that necessitate my going out every night. I just want you to know that I'm not dating, and I'm not leaving the community."

Looking back I know today that my community was as sick as my dysfunctional family of origin. The rules in both were: don't talk; don't trust; don't feel. Secrets were rampant; it was all I knew. It was very important to look perfect. So much time and energy went into looking good on the outside so I wouldn't need to feel the shame, fear, confusion, anxiety, anger and resentment on the inside. The booze kept me anesthesized.

The very first person I ever really trusted was my AA sponsor. Her daughter was a nun. My sponsor helped me to see that alcoholism was an equal opportunity disease, that the booze didn't know as it went down my throat that I'd taken vows of poverty, celibacy, and obedience. She helped me realize that it wasn't what I drank, or how much I drank, or where I drank that mattered; it was important to know what booze did to me when I drank.

I stayed sober out of fear. Though I claimed I had never had a blackout, I drove an elderly sister home from visiting our respective families and never remembered the one and one half hour conversation on the way back. When she mentioned it the next day, I got panicky. At that point I had been going to AA meetings for thirty days trying to control my drinking, saying, "Of course not," when people asked if I had ever had a blackout.

I remember ruminating that if AA was right about blackouts, then maybe they were right about other stuff, too. So out of fear I didn't drink, went to meetings, got a sponsor, got active in my home group. Yet I still had the obsession to drink on a daily basis because I refused to surrender to my powerlessness over alcohol and other drugs; I refused to do Step One. I had to surrender in order to win, and I hated the thoughts of it. I fought and fought with my usual will power. My false pride and denial resulted in white-knuckled sobriety with no serenity.

After two years of not drinking, going to meetings daily, following suggestions, God did for me what I couldn't do for myself. He helped me to surrender to my powerlessness over alcohol and other drugs. He/She helped me see that I never had been, never would be a social drinker. The pickle could not go back to being a cucumber.

The Twelve Steps of Alcoholics Anonymous are a spiritual way of life that has literally saved my life! The best of what I'd learned in a religious home and in my religious community began to make sense. God didn't die and leave me in charge. I didn't need to control anyone or anything. I can relax and be a human being who makes mistakes: no better than anyone else; no worse than anyone else. Such relief! It's been slow going; healing takes time. I'd gotten sick spiritually (loss of values), then gotten sick mentally and emotionally, and finally physically. In recovery I began to get well. First physically, then emotionally and mentally, and finally spiritually. I never thought the day would come when I could say, "I like Pat" — but it's here more days than not.

I was nine years sober and had been teaching junior high for about twenty-five years; I finally accepted the fact that I was burnt out. A bad case of esophogitis and erosive gastritis was one clue! With encouragement from my sponsors (in the community and in AA), I approached higher administration in the congregation to get some other training in order to work in the alcoholism and chemical dependency field. I was one of ten educators awarded a Prudential scholarship to the 1986 Rutgers Summer School of Alcohol Studies in New Jersey.

Being with five hundred adult students from many disciplines and many different countries was such a broadening experience! We were there because we wanted to learn and grow personally and professionally. One of my teachers was Janet Woititz, the best-selling author of *Adult Children of Alcoholics.* Each day I left her class in tears, identifying all over the place, but in deep denial that I, too, came from an alcoholic home. Wouldn't you think that with all the struggle/denial of my own disease, it would have been easier to admit that my dad was an alcoholic? It wasn't easy for me to let go of that "Leave It To Beaver" image I had of my family. For so long I needed that in order to feel worthwhile. My first ACOA meetings were at Rutgers. What if anyone saw me going to those meetings? That shame and fear again.

Healing takes time. Several sisters from various communities suggested I take some Clinical Pastoral Education (CPE) to help me in my transition from teaching. Not having a clue as to the intensity of CPE, I took an extended basic CPE unit while at the same time doing the University of Massachusetts Alcohol Studies Program (five courses the first semester and a three hundred hour practicum the second semester). My CPE supervisor had no mercy when I fell asleep in group after studying half the night for my psychopharmacology exams! Needless to say, I got confronted in group about my workaholism and lack of self-care!

Through the influence of a priest friend in AA, I took another full-time CPE quarter to qualify for consideration in Hazelden's Clergy Training Program in Minnesota. While waiting to go there I worked per diem as a counselor for two months in a thirty-day court-ordered alcoholism treatment center for women.

In November 1987 I loaded the Dodge Omni and headed for five more CPE units at Hazelden Foundation in the middle of God's country. This was an experience that would change my life.

Living alone in an apartment was a learning experience for me. Financial responsibilities were only one of many growth-filled experiences ahead of me. Training outside of parochial Boston was an adventure. I learned to enjoy the three lakes I passed daily enroute to Hazelden without griping how much I missed the ocean and "my rock" at Rye Beach. I learned that by and large the sisters I met from the Midwest were more open and accustomed to change, to women in ministry, to dealing with males in the church who weren't necessarily chauvinists, patriarchal, or demigods. The broadening experience of training at Hazelden with people from all over the world was a breath of fresh air. The gentleness and humor of both supervisors and peers enabled me to learn so much more quickly than I ever had. Personal and professional growth issues were presented in a caring confrontation that spoke to me of unconditional love.

With these people and in this atmosphere, I blossomed. I learned to respect and love myself to a degree that I never thought was possible. I finally believed in my gut that God truly loved me as I am. For me Hazelden was the closest thing to a womb experience that I'll ever hope to have. Daily journaling, sharing that with my supervisors, living alone, helped me be more honest with myself and others, to laugh at myself, to share my feelings as I never shared before. Yes, it was tough — but feeling loved and cared for made all the difference.

Just before leaving Hazelden I attended an intensive two and one half day Sexual Attitude Reassessment weekend sponsored by the University of Minnesota Medical School and Family Practice. This desensitized me as nothing else. Having already gotten permission from my congregation and from Hazelden to do an extra CPE quarter, I faced the fact that I needed to leave the nest, return East and find a job. And so, with Joyce Rupp's *Praying Your Goodbyes* under my arm, I left the womb.

Twice during that fifteen and one half months at Hazelden, I'd tried to quit smoking. The physical withdrawal symptoms from nicotine were far worse for me than what I'd experienced withdrawing from alcohol

519

and other drugs. I started smoking at the onset of my drinking. While getting sober and going to AA meetings I began drinking coffee and promptly got addicted to caffeine. I now know that the need to anesthetize my feelings causes me to substitute one addiction for another. Withdrawal from nicotine was by far the worse for me.

Each time I relapsed, I shamed myself so badly that I couldn't look in the mirror or even make eye contact with others. I felt like the woman in Luke's Gospel who for eighteen years had been possessed by a spirit which "drained her strength . . . badly stooped . . . quite incapable of standing erect ..." Each time I pray this passage I picture Jesus needing to get down on all fours in order to look up and make eye contact with this stooped woman. It wasn't till August of 1990 that I drove from Iowa to Minnesota to visit one of my peers from Hazelden. She and her husband helped me begin my journey as a non-smoker.

Following a suggestion to do something nice for myself with the money I saved from not smoking, I began a series of body massages to help me deal with the stress. Learning to trust the massage process was difficult for me. But touch is so healing! Barb told me that she had never worked on someone whose muscles were as knotted up and tense as mine were. I began finally to feel how my mental, emotional, spiritual state was reflected in my body.

The holistic approach of the massage therapist helped me deal with the bottomless pit of rage that surfaced when I stopped smoking. I'd known for a long time that nicotine and I had an unhealthy relationship that was killing me one puff at a time. It boggles my mind that so many times a day I dealt with my feelings of anger, resentment, hurt, frustration, loneliness and sadness by smoking. A lot of sisters I lived with over the years hated my smoking and their reactions and remarks fueled my fears of rejection and abandonment. During my drinking and during those times that others misunderstood me, it seemed that nicotine comforted me, calmed my nerves, soothed my sensitivities, and let me know repeatedly that I wasn't alone. I grieved the loss of " friend".

Six months after leaving Hazelden, I was driving to the Midwest again — this time as staff chaplain at Mercy Hospital Medical Center in Des Moines, Iowa. I was hired specifically to work full-time in their Alcohol and Drug Recovery Program.

Vespers

I made it a point each day to get down to the Pastoral Care department in between appointments with patients, but it was hit or miss as to whether any of them would be there when I went down. I was the only chaplain considered to be a member of two departments. Most of my friends in Des Moines were other recovering women in AA, a couple of whom worked with me. After almost two years the hospital decided to relocate the alcohol and drug unit outside the hospital, to downsize it, and abolish ten jobs in the process, including mine.

After relocating 1500 miles for that job, I was in a state of shock the day we found out. It was at least a month before I could mobilize my inner resources enough to restart the resumes and interviewing process all over again. I am still grieving the loss of that job I loved so much and the wonderful friends in Des Moines who remain a part of me.

Fear and shame periodically become Higher Powers for me again. One more time I've relocated far from home, leaving a place where I felt there was a niche for me with people I love, support groups I've become a part of, my family of origin and my families of choice. It's hard. Somehow in all this, God has a plan for me, another lesson to be learned — about myself, about others, and about a loving God in my life Who continues to heal me.

When I got my present job as staff chaplain at St. John's Health Care Corporation, in Anderson, Indiana, I was lucky enough to be hired not only for acute care chaplaincy in the general part of the hospital, but also to work one day a week in their Anderson Center, a beautiful building across the street which houses their chemical dependency and mental health unit. After the hectic, crisis-ridden, emotionally draining schedule of full-time Chemical Dependency ministry, I thought acute care ministry would be so-o-o boring. But then, as an ACOA, I'm used to living from crisis to crisis; I'm now finding that it's O.K. to have a few breathers in my day.

I still love living alone. The space I never had growing up with six siblings is much appreciated at the end of a busy day.

Some miracles lately have increased my gratitude. After my dad's eighth heart attack last year, his doctor asked me to sit in with him as he spoke with Dad about getting alcoholism treatment. Mom and five of us have been going to Al-Anon for the last couple years. I've watched my seventy-seven-year-old mother change and grow as she works the Twelve Steps of recovery in her life. The miracle of it all is that so many of us, affected by Dad's alcoholism, could find healing and serenity for ourselves in our own recovery programs.

I also attend ACOA and CODA meetings for the same reasons. Dad did go into treatment. Last week he celebrated his first sobriety birthday! At seventy-seven he's lucky to be alive. Thanksgiving morning the two of us went to an AA Gratitude meeting. I finally saw just how much of an effort it is for him to leave the house. His many terminal illnesses have kept him house-bound since then; he has the aid of Hospice, a blessing for my family. Our going to that meeting on Thanksgiving Day is a special gift I'll always be grateful for.

I've made my peace with Dad. I'm not angry with him anymore. I don't blame him for my being an alcoholic as I did early in sobriety. The fears I've had for so long that Dad would die before I was able to resolve my feelings for him are gone. I can and do tell him that I love him. It's real. God has effected so much healing.

In July 1990 I made a "Once in a Lifetime" retreat given by and for our sisters. I felt so connected to my community roots as we prayed, reflected and shared together those stories only we can tell: our own story. I had shared much of mine over the years in therapy, in AA (especially with my sponsors), in CPE, and spiritual direction. I've had growth-filled advantages that some sisters only dream of. Many of the sisters on that "Once in a Lifetime" retreat were not accustomed to sharing secrets/feelings from their pain-filled life experiences. They told me repeatedly how much they appreciated my honesty and I realized anew that God must have known how much I needed each addiction I've wrestled with, each stage in recovery that has helped me get in touch with my feelings and give me the courage to share those feelings with others and with my God.

I've needed every bit of the therapy, spiritual direction, AA, Al-Anon, ACOA, CODA meetings and seven quarters of CPE. God has spoken to me/loved me through so many wonderful people in my life.

It was on this retreat that I shared the hurt in being put out of the apartment and lives of the other four sisters I'd cast my lot with. I shared the attempt I made on my life, the story of my active addiction to alcohol and prescription medication, my recovery through the Twelve Steps of

AA, the rejection and hurt I'd experienced at the hands of another sister I lived with, one who scapegoated me with so much of the rage she felt after a family member's death from the effects of addiction. Pain was expressed and healing took place in a way I hadn't ever experienced on a community retreat with my own sisters. I felt at one with God and with my community.

Last summer (1991) I made a retreat in the Midwest for sisters from all communities who are living a Twelve Step spirituality in their lives on a daily basis. There were sisters there in AA, Al-Anon, OA, ACOA, Survivors of Sexual Abuse. So much sharing of the pain-filled, resurrection journeys we've traveled, so much joy and gratitude at the marvelous ways God has worked through our powerlessness and the unmanageability of our lives due to addiction — to a trust and dependence on Him/Her that we never would have had otherwise.

It seems lately with all the adjustments in my life to a new state, work ministry, support groups, apartment that my community members in Boston seem awfully far away. On those days when I'm feeling that normal, human loneliness and angst, I can't help wondering, "Do they think of me? Pray for me?"

What's happening with so many of the sisters I've lived with over the years, especially the ones I've lived with since my move from the apartment in 1971? One of those sisters died last May, the day before I found out that my job in Iowa was abolished. Another sister with whom I've always had a special bond has been at our hospital these last few months, mentally deteriorating to a point she doesn't know any of us. I miss them.

As I continue to let go of one unhealthy coping mechanism at a time, I'm learning I don't need old patterns in order to deal with my feelings. Those unhealthy patterns have ceased to work for me and in letting them go, I'm becoming more sane, sober, and happy.

Editor's note: Pat's father has died since this writing.

Barbara Mae
Exclaustrated Franciscan

Publisher's librarian

Master of Arts, Library Science, Rosary College, Illinois

Special training: Public Relations, Addiction Counseling

Minister of Communion, St. Irenaeus Parish

Barbara Mae enjoys discovering the unusual while visiting boutiques, malls, art fairs and museums. She likes good music, and is delighted with Grant Park concerts, with the Taste of Chicago, and spur of the moment explorations. She loves finding a good bargain in Field's or Bloomingdale's. "I have a millionaire's taste and an empty pocketbook." Barbara Mae is now in her second year of exclaustration, and is making herself available to the Lord before making her final decision. "Only He knows what that will be."

Barbara Mae

God Changed My Lot

As I neared the separation of Interstate 90/94 near Tomah, Wisconsin, I decided to head toward LaCrosse instead of Eau Claire. It was around noon. I could make it for lunch at the Hot Fish Shop in Winona.

I was on my way to the Minneapolis area to spend a long weekend with my mother and my brother.

When I crossed the Mississippi River into Minnesota from LaCrosse I felt the familiar thrill that no other place gives me. The car seemed to be heading right into the side of the hills that bank the river. As I turned north on Highway 61, I looked up the river and gave thanks. I've seen it high and low, in fog, rain, and brilliant sunshine. That day it was brilliant sunshine. The thirty-five mile road between LaCrosse and Winona is curving, hugging the hills that reach over 500 feet high above the river. On a clear day one can see the hills on the Wisconsin side and up the river ten or twenty miles. Often there are tugboats pushing as many as nine barges up or down this mighty waterway. Along the highway there are seemingly abandoned cars. Their owners are down on the river fishing, probably for sunfish.

About twenty-five miles along, I spotted the silver dome of St. Stanislaus, the church of my baptism as well as that of my grandmother, my parents and my brother. The white tower of the home office of the J.R. Watkins Company also gleamed in the sunlight.

A few more bends and more familiar landmarks and I was at the foot of Sugar Loaf Mountain and in the town of my birth and early childhood.

On that day I had a more than usual sense of being home in nurturing and comforting surroundings. Winona, Minnesota, has embedded itself deep in my psyche, my memory, my personality.

My family roots are there for four generations on my mother's side, three on my father's. Some day I may learn how my great-grandparents and grandparents came to settle among the Polish immigrants in that lumbering and flour milling railroad river town. But in the first nine years of my life, Winona meant safety and love and freedom to grow and strength of survival.

For the last four years of those nine, my brother and I lived with our maternal grandparents. We had the carefree life of school, homework, and play — lots of play. Some of those friends are mine yet.

I never questioned why we were living by Grandma's. Or why my mother was working in Minneapolis. Or where or who my father was. The latter issue was settled very firmly one day when some playmates, in Grandma's hearing, asked me about my father; before I could respond that I did not know, I was emphatically called into the house. And that was that. It was a very early lesson in the rule of "Don't talk, don't ask." I never dreamed to ask questions. I accepted what life was giving me. At that time I was enjoying it all.

The reality was that my mother put my father out because of his drinking; she returned to work as a power machine operator. When the company moved to Minneapolis she went along, and my brother and I were cared for by my grandmother. I was always proud of my mother and proud to wear the clothes she made for me. At one time she made me a fur coat (Lambkin lamb), hat and muff set which I grew into and out of.

But in time, when I was nine and my brother seven, my parents got back together in St. Paul, Minnesota, and my brother and I were taken to live with them. For two years I went to St. Agnes School where I made my First Communion in fourth grade. At liturgically progressive St. Agnes I was out of sync since my classmates made their Communion in third grade. Confirmation was in fifth grade.

I was not aware of the developing alcoholism of my father. I never asked questions, just accepted what life gave me.

My parents selected a house to buy, but at the critical time my father was hospitalized for what I now suspect was alcohol-related problems. Again, I never asked questions.

We then moved and changed schools where I met the sisters of the community I subsequently entered.

My father's alcoholism progressed rapidly. I became aware of his physical abuse of my mother; I became terrified of his rage. It could be triggered from the least incident, even the kind of bread he was served. I became aware of the lack of money in the house and the stretching of food. I liked to bake, but always substituted water for half of the milk called for.

Mom was working again, this time as a sample maker for the Winter Olympic teams. I took on more responsibility for the house. But I found plenty of time to help the sisters at school and in the sacristy. We lived only a half block away, so Sister often sent someone to get me. Yet at that time I had no desire to enter the convent.

As grade school graduation approached I joined the junior sodality, a strong spiritual force for the girls in our parish. I advanced to Senior Sodalist when I became sixteen, and remained active until I entered the convent. Shortly after grade school I began working. From that time on I supported myself in clothes, books, school supplies, and entertainment. And I kept my mouth shut about my father's physical abuse of my mother and about his drinking.

In spite of the fireworks when he got home, of short money, of not knowing how or whether to talk to Dad, we managed to do things that are precious memories today: Sunday rides, short excursions into the country and to local parks, visiting with friends. And, for me, playing the piano — classical music only, please.

When I was in eighth grade, I got a piano for my birthday and I began taking lessons. This was the fulfillment of a lifetime dream and continues to give me pleasure today.

When it came time for high school, I surprised my parents by asking to go to the local public high school. I developed into a good student. I wanted to have many friends and to be popular. I was too intense in pursuing those two goals and found myself with precious little of either. At the second half of my sophomore year something clicked with study and I began to enjoy it for itself and the sense of discovery it offered me.

Between my sophomore and junior years I sat upright in bed one night and decided that my place was in the convent, that my focus was really on the Lord. When I awoke the next morning my life was directed toward that goal. But I said nothing to anyone, seeking help only in prayer.

After looking at three communities that ministered in St. Paul at that time, I found myself attracted most to the Felicians. They seemed the most simple, most down to earth people. I seriously considered the St. Joseph Sisters, but at a critical moment, I could not stand the large stiff collar they wore! Years later, this "sign" was the topic of much laughter with the many friends I have in that community.

Finally, I had to discuss this with my parents. It was more of an announcement than a discussion. My dad went to his very religious mother and asked her what he could do to stop me. She told him to leave me alone. He did not talk to me for three years, and forbade my mother to write to me after I entered. By the time I made my first profession of vows he came for the ceremony and began bragging to everybody that his daughter was a nun. My mother had said she could not sign any papers agreeing to my entering something she did not believe in. I waited until I didn't need her signature.

So I worked a year after high school until I passed my eighteenth birthday. When I was a senior, my English teacher recommended me for a job at the James Jerome Hill Reference Library in St. Paul. There began my love affair with librarianship. I worked as a page, shelf reader, filer of catalog cards. Did you ever file a thousand cards beginning with the word "water" into fifty card catalog drawers? After that task, I could not spell "water." Later I was transferred to the acquisitions department. Then I checked in periodicals and prepared them for binding. Here I got introduced to the Commerce Clearing House Loose Leaf services when I had to take care of the updating subscriptions by replacing the outdated pages with the newer ones. CCH became an important part of my life many years later.

All the while my father's alcoholism was progressing on its downward journey. We dealt with it by avoiding encounters with him and living our lives independently of him. He was a bartender and generally slept during the day and worked at night. The only bad part of that was that when he was sleeping we had to be more quiet than if a baby were napping. Unfortunately, my piano was in the room just below his bedroom. My mother continued to work; I continued to enjoy my friends. After I stopped wanting to become popular, I found myself surrounded with friends. These, too, remain close to me today. My mother and I began to do many fun things together: shopping, going for outings to parks, visiting friends, making the novena in honor of our Lady of the Miraculous Medal, and attending plays at the Edith Bush

Memorial Theater. I loved my piano, but was cautious about playing when Dad was home.

On July 2, 1948, a former Felician who later returned to the community and died a Felician, rode the Zephyr with me to Chicago for my entrance into the postulancy of the Felician Sisters. That began a period of my life that was to last forty-two years.

Here, too, I quickly learned to accept what life had to offer me and to keep my mouth shut. I often was assigned to practice the piano while other postulants were washing dishes. I felt the isolation, but that did not matter. I was determined that I would make this work for me.

The novitiate classes and retreats at that time were conducted in the Polish language, a language that I did not know and that I never mastered. So I again became my own counsel, reading whatever material I could get my hands on. I had some good directors: Edward Leen, Abbot Marmion, Thomas Merton, Father Raymond, to name a few. This all helped to deepen a theological and spiritual grounding that enriched my life more than I can ever relate. I learned to judge matters more by their harmony with the loving God I met in scripture rather than the vengeful punishing God of the visionaries and the current theological and spiritual focus.

This got me in trouble, too. I quickly decided not to buy into the negative, authoritarian spirituality that was everywhere around me. During my novitiate I had a deep sense that I did not belong in that environment; this was the temptation of all novices. If only I observed everything perfectly, things would be better. So, I thought to myself, "When you observe everything perfectly, when you do all your spiritual reading and meditations, and still feel you do not belong, then you can leave." It took forty-two years to realize that that was not the issue.

I set out on a spiritual journey that has brought me to a deep sense of God's presence in myself, in the world and in the people around me. The Spirit was doing his own thing while I was squirming and seeking. He carried me. He walked beside me, in front of me, behind me. Periodically through the years the gnawing sense that community life was not nurturing, but rather, stifling me, returned with varying degrees of intensity.

At the same time, I threw myself into a professional life with vigor. For the first four years after profession, I taught children in the middle grades in schools in Chicago and Cudahy, Wisconsin. I was transferred to Cudahy so that I could take courses in librarianship at Cardinal Stritch College in Milwaukee. This launched my long career in a field I found enriching, satisfying, and supportive. The purpose of the Felicians sending me for these courses was that I had been selected to become the Head Librarian for Felician College, then a two-year liberal arts college for the education of the young sisters. This was during the Sister Formation Movement. I held that position for twenty-eight years and was part of the growth of the college to a co-educational institution carrying North Central Accreditation.

After finishing my bachelor's degree at De Paul University in Chicago, I applied for, and obtained the Andrew Bowhuis Scholarship from the Catholic Library Association, and attended Rosary College. It didn't take long before I was an active member of professional associations, serving as officers and in committee positions. But that is a whole other story. At the college, the library program was a vibrant one, integrated with classroom activities.

In the mid-1970's, I took on the responsibilities of Director of Development and Public Relations in addition to that of Head Librarian, relinquishing the Library position in 1982. It was then that I began to work with the executives at CCH whose home office was across the street from the college.

This professional life meant many meetings and many conventions where I got to enjoy the world of social drinking. I drank a lot, but did not think I was in trouble. I credited my father's alcoholism with the talent I had to hold my liquor. It took about twenty years of drinking before I noticed any problem. But, as is the scenario for this disease, I denied it and soon became dependent on alcohol. In the meantime I celebrated my silver jubilee as a Felician after two years of debating with myself whether I belonged in the convent. One friend said after the event, "Well, you made it."

But I didn't. My struggle to find my place expressed itself in the drinking and in my increasing loneliness, frustration with myself, and inability to accept the support of those around me.

Around 1983 I felt I was falling apart and did not know where to turn. Prayer wasn't doing it. Retreats weren't doing it. I could not identify with the many friends I had who cared. I made a private retreat during which a priest told me to put aside all books except Scriptures. He said I needed to learn how to affirm *myself* or else anyone else's affirmation would not mean anything. How right he was on that one. He also gave me Philomena Agudo's *Affirming the Human and the Holy*. This book helped me understand that much in my life was not my fault and that I did not have to fix everything in the world. This was the first time I could recognize and accept that fact. I count that retreat as the beginning of conscious healing. Two years later I made a holistic retreat. For the first time I allowed myself to recognize that I had a problem with alcohol. I began the road to self-understanding and self-acceptance, though I had a terrible time with affirmations.

The following year I was to make the holistic retreat again. Just before I was due to go on that retreat I was hospitalized with a gastric problem. I knew well that it was alcohol-related, but I kept my mouth shut. I went into the retreat late and gained much from it. In the next few months, I seriously considered asking for help, but I did not know how or whom to ask.

By the time I wrote a nasty note to our new president I was ready for surrender. She called me to her office and told me I had a problem and needed help. I said, "Yes." I called a treatment center, got an appointment for assessment that same day and was admitted into the outpatient program. I was on my way to a life of recovery. The date: September 2, 1986.

Since then my life has never been the same. I embraced the treatment program willingly, thankful that I no longer had to work things out by myself. I began going to AA meetings five times a week. The desire for alcohol left me and I enjoyed being free of it.

My job did not last, though. In December I left the college wondering what I would do. After a month's vacation with my mother I was asked to serve as secretary to the provincial administration. The job gave me time to work my program freely, going to meetings and continuing psychotherapy.

Of course, recovery is not only abstinence. I knew that there were many issues I would have to face, that there were unresolved matters that I would have to deal with, my lifestyle included. Soon in my recovery the second step became a meaningful and a guidance for my life; I "Came to believe that a power greater than ourselves could restore us to sanity." Although I did not know what sanity was, God did and God would lead me in his way, in his time. It was my business just to let God work. And work He did.

Attendance at AA meetings taught me to listen. I said my bit and then listened to others. I learned to accept others as they accepted me. I found personal psychotherapy valuable in discovering and understanding myself in working through the myriad issues I carried with me.

And, yes, the subject of whether I belonged in the convent resurfaced, but this time I did not push it away. I looked at it and found that the doubts I had forty years previously were not just temptation, but nudges which I rejected. But now there was another more frightening prospect. I was sixty years old; I knew I could expect no pension from the convent if I left. I doubted that I could get a job, qualified though I was. Too qualified, in fact. As I pondered this question in agony and fear, the Lord found ways to show me how he would take care of me if I would but let Him.

One day I was meditating in the chapel praying the eleventh step, "Lord, tell me what your will is for me and give me the power to carry it out." I was always afraid to pray that prayer that way because I was afraid of what the answer would be. I sensed a loving arm around my shoulder and understood the promise, "Don't worry. I will take care of you." The words of Jeremiah took on new meaning, "For I know the plans I have in mind for you, plans for your good, not your woe ... When you pray to me I will listen and I will change your lot." This was scary stuff.

Through a whole series of events and people that were put in my life, I gradually got the confidence to trust that I could make it. At least I had to give it a try or else look forward to ending my life in bitterness and regret, attitudes that would be dangerous for anyone, especially an alcoholic. So I started looking for work. Eventually I was offered a job as a cataloger with Baker & Taylor Books.

Cataloging was one of the aspects of librarianship I enjoyed very much. I am good at it. Baker & Taylor Books was a company with which I did much business when I was a librarian. In April I shared my decision with my provincial superior; again it was more of an announcement than a discussion. She and her council were supportive, at least

534

emotionally. I got help in the form of furniture, a car, and some money to get started.

On May 1, 1992, I took possession of my own apartment and moved. The following Monday I began my job. There have been adjustments, there have been fears, but the Lord God is with me and I do not want. There is much uncertainty about the future but I cannot forget that promise, "I will take care of you." I know that is true and I am grateful. What the future holds, I do not know, but what gives me comfort is that I do know who holds that future. And that is all that matters.

Caressed by Love
It's my waterfall,
A bank of boulders
At a drop in the creek bed.
Water, silvery, smooth, and quiet
Flows onward.
Then
Cascades, bounces, plays
As it drops
Over smoothed boulders,
Running in crevices
Foaming at the bottom
And jumping up
Before skipping on its way
Until it
Continues silvery, smooth, and quiet
Flowing onward.

I sit, mermaid perched
On my boulder. Am I rocks?
Am I water?
I sit
Letting life
Letting God
Letting Spirit
Flow and rush
Over me

Shaping, forming
Smoothing rough edges
I'm rock.

I move
Peaceful, smooth, cascading
Affecting who I touch,
Taking some particles
Then falling
And bouncing
And continuing on life's journey
Agitated for a while
Then calming and
Going peacefully on
Dropping what I no longer need,
Picking up new
As I flow along.

I'm water.
I'm rock
Letting water form me.
I'm water
Moving, peaceful, agitated.
I'm the loved one
Caressed by Love.

8
COMPLINE

Behold how good and how pleasant it is,
For brethren to dwell together in unity.
Behold, now bless ye the Lord,
All ye servants of the Lord;
Who stand in the house of the Lord,
In the courts of the house of God.

Joanne Rooney
Former Benedictine Sister of Charity

Married

Six "acquired" children: Patrick, Daniel, Michael, David, Kathleen, Jeanne

Elementary School Principal

Bachelor of Arts, Mundelein College, Chicago

Master of Education, University of Chicago

Active parish member

Joanne is still actively involved in education on a professional level and on an interest level. Beyond sharing in the raising of the six children who became hers in marriage, other interests include camping, swimming, and writing. She plans to continue writing, and to "pursue an independent career after retirement."

Joanne Rooney

Images and Observations

Many Catholic young women entered convents in the fifties. Some of the best and the brightest of graduating high school girls felt the call to a religious vocation. The role model represented in teachers who were nuns and the sense of dedication exemplified in religious life spurred many to hear "Come, follow me" as a personal call. I was one of many who responded.

What in my background prompted an energetic, intelligent, normal eighteen-year-old girl to join a semi-cloistered convent? Many forces coalesced to draw me to the conclusion that this was the life meant for me by God. Not the least of these was my devout Irish Catholic father.

Dad had devoted seven years to the pursuit of a religious vocation and had been well on his way to ordination before he, or perhaps someone else, decided the priesthood was not for him. He spun stories about those years and hinted at some deep sorrow about leaving them. No doubt he sincerely hoped that one of his own children would complete the vocation he had once begun.

Mom stood in sharp contrast to my father. Her conversion to Catholicism thinly covered her less than religious but deeply embedded Jewish background. The differences between my parents were acute and frequently erupted in loud and painful arguments. Long, hurt silences followed these disagreements and our home was less than comfortable much of the time.

The resolution to become one of God's chosen may have come out of a great desire to please my dad. It may have come equally from some subconscious wish to hurt my mother. My entrance into a semi-cloistered Benedictine community after one year of college accomplished both.

The date set for entry was September 14. My friends had a shower different from any I have attended since. Its memory still brings back the unique humor of being Catholic and nineteen-years-old in the early 1950's.

The trunk was the big item. It was to contain everything I needed in convent life including six sets of union suits. This one piece monstrosity even sported the back seat opening which in my case had been sewn shut by my comical friends. Notes were tucked between bars of soap, toothpaste, black cotton hose, and the Wizard of Oz witches' shoes which were general issue for all nuns.

We told jokes that evening. We drank beer. We sang to our high school memories and saluted friendship longer lasting than impregnable convent walls. Our goodbyes were final. I knew instinctively that the bond we experienced throughout adolescence and young adulthood was to be replaced by a sisterhood much more demanding and adult. We laughed. Then we wept for the passing of our childhood.

On September 14, I appeared at 10:30 a.m. on the steps of the convent. My father, toting a big black trunk, followed me up the concrete steps leading to the convent doors. My mother followed dolefully behind. I was paralyzed with fear. My last cigarette had not calmed my nerves. The thought of the single deprivation of living a smokeless life blocked out the many others that I was about to undertake.

The mistress of novices led me upstairs for my first glimpse of the world behind convent walls. There on a chair was the outfit I would wear as a Benedictine postulant. It was ghastly. As I donned the black cotton stockings, long black wool skirt, black cotton blouse and cape the reality of my decision became more apparent. A gauzy black veil finished the grotesque vision.

I returned to say good-bye to my parents. Mom burst into uncontrollable weeping at the sight of her beloved daughter throwing away her life. Dad was equally supportive. He assured me that if only I stayed a few days, I would learn many worthwhile things. With that kind of encouragement my adolescent determination became firmer than ever.

Our initiation began immediately. We were led to our cells, the spot of room in which we would sleep. Although we were not alone in the huge dormitory, each space containing a bed and small nightstand, was surrounded by bleached white curtains. Our small closets would contain an alternate set of clothing identical to that which we wore. This second set was for Sunday. Several duplicates of our underwear, black long-sleeved blouses and another pair of the black, stocky-heeled shoes for Sunday completed our wardrobe. Though very small, our closets were amazingly void of our accustomed array of clothing.

Essential toilet articles were permitted. One of many subsequent shocks came when the razors we had all brought were collected. There would be no need to shave our legs. The thick black cotton stockings, part of our permanent costume, would hide whatever was visibly left of our legs beneath the three quarter length black pleated skirts.

Silence, we learned in our first convent lesson, was critical to our success as candidates to religious life. We were confused. It seemed there were all kinds of silences.

Talking, in general, was rarely allowed. When it was time to talk, it was still not permitted in most areas. Corridors were sacred: no talking, ever, unless absolutely essential to health and safety. Our novitiate room was silent except when we were allowed to talk. Washrooms and stairways were always silent and one was never, ever to talk in the dormitory. Meals were eaten in silence, accompanied by reading to edify and educate unless talking was allowed for special occasions.

The Grand Silence prohibited all conversation. From night prayers through breakfast the Grand Silence reigned. Our minds were to turn to God. Our eyes, downcast, would keep us from distraction. God was paramount. Discipline was the path to holiness. Silence was the language of contemplation.

As a result of these many and seemingly conflicting rules and regulations, we talked everywhere. No place was sacred. We giggled in the hallways and whispered in the dorm. We consoled each other's homesickness and questioned the strange convent customs in the bathrooms. During Grand Silence we wrapped ourselves in black bathrobes and bedroom slippers and convened in the shower rooms to gossip.

Not for long. Our novice mistress, a nun twenty years our senior, got us into shape quickly. We learned to keep quiet, if not silent, most of the time in most of the designated areas and during most of those times allotted to holy silence.

We also learned to laugh uproariously during our recreation time; to spill out our new life's culture in a humor which alleviated the intense stress we all suffered as we made the first noble efforts to become good nuns.

After a year of novitiate training we were deemed ready for formal reception into the religious community. The ceremony was elaborate and symbolized our becoming brides of Christ. When completed we would be official nuns, wearing the habit of the religious community and being called new names. It was the first giant step.

The processional into the chapel consisted of four young women, dressed in bridal gowns (one size fits all!), marching solemnly toward the altar. The liturgy began. Toward the middle each of us individually was called by the celebrant to kneel in front of the altar. Prayers were said.

The congregation strained to see as the presiding priest ritually snipped a lock of hair from each of our heads. The giving of our new names followed. In a loud voice he proclaimed: "Miss Joanne, your name in religion will be..." I held my breath.

Sister Mary Richard. There it was. Richard—a man's name. It sounded strong. I liked that. It was softened by Mary. I liked that, too. It was the name I had requested, knowing full well it was probably the one I would get. Because a recently deceased and much loved chaplain of the convent was named Richard, someone was bound to carry his name.

The big moment now arrived. We all left the chapel. Friends and family remained for the few minutes it took us to don our religious habits and return to the chapel.

The most often-asked question about religious life? The "did you or didn't you?" question. The answer is yes, we did!

The evening of our reception we gathered in silence for our first convent hair cut. It took only a few minutes. Between the nervous giggles we looked furtively at the heads of our confreres slowly losing their youthful hair. Our crowning glory became a mass of tangled tresses around the bathroom floor.

It was later in the evening, as I sat in a warm tub and saw the shadow of my new hairdo on the wall, that I realized that rounded reflection was my head.

As with so much other things in convent life, those outside of it made much more of an issue of its vagaries then did those of us within it. Our monthly hair cuts became routine. The folds and layers we wore over our bare heads adequately kept us warm though some chose to delay haircuts in winter. I found, as did most of my friends, that the "buzz" was the best. It was efficient and clean.

Nuns prayed. We prayed frequently. Some of our prayers were short; others seemed endless. Much of what we prayed was in Latin, which was difficult. Although we had studied a year or two of high school Latin it was never enough to truly understand what we prayed each day. But pray we did. Our day was punctuated with the Divine Office as well as many other public calls for God's intervention in our lives.

The prayer of the Divine Office, which constituted a good three hours of each day, was filled with rituals. Standing, sitting, reading, bowing kept us alert a good part of the time. Although the total meaning of the prayer was vague because of our inability to understand the language, the reverence of the ceremony had a comforting and prayerful effect. We were, indeed, lifting our minds and hearts to God.

The motto of the Benedictine order is *Ora et Labora*—Pray and Work. As noted above, we indeed prayed often and long. We worked equally often, equally long and extraordinarily hard. Manual labor was honored. Eradicating dirt became a way of life.

Spring cleaning was accomplished weekly in the convent. Although Roman Catholics do not theologically claim that cleanliness is next to godliness, one would have thought in those early days of convent living that dirt was the devil and God smelled much like furniture polish. Our house was clean.

The first and most energetic target was, of course, the chapel. Exorcising God's house of dirt was, indeed, a daily ritual. Corners were first wiped clean with oily rags, followed by a firm sweeping of all soot. The final mopping picked up the few specks left from our previous attack.

Dusting was equally vigorous. With skirts hiked up and wrapped in aprons we prevented the enemy, dust, from invading our personal clothing. Our leader led the way, timing the operation. Forty minutes and we were history. The smell of mops and oily rags remained, fusing with the residual smell of incense.

We needed no aerobic workouts. The three quarters of an hour spent on hands and knees, bending, sweeping and mopping was equal to it. Our work day had begun.

Common rooms were no exception. Everything in its place and a place for everything was burned in our minds. Nothing was without a shelf, drawer or specified area. The spirit of poverty prohibited the collecting of "stuff" even in a world where there was so little "stuff" to collect. Even the few things left carelessly about common rooms were returned to their proper places.

"Wallmopping" was customary. Neither before nor since my convent years have I heard the expression "wallmopping". Each Saturday, however, with specially designated mops, we attacked walls from ceiling to floor. Our stretching out was accomplished by reaching to the ten foot high institutional ceilings down to the floors so that we freed each inch of wall from any imperceptible fleck of dust.

Taking turns at dishwashing was also part of our routine. Although our community, at its highest number totaled less than two hundred nuns, doing dishes was a major chore.

And pots and pans, done in huge sinks, were even less fun. We were reminded often that it took the cooks much more time to dirty the dishes than it took us to clean them. Now, on quiet Sunday afternoons I often recall the hours spent on past Sundays, scrubbing pots and pans that had held the roast beef and mashed potatoes for one hundred or so hungry women.

"A good appetite is the sign of a vocation" was echoed throughout the first years of novitiate training. Eating was a pleasure — one of the few available — and we took full advantage of it. Meals punctuated our routine of work and prayer.

Breakfast was early and simple. Crisp white-aproned sisters served fruit, a choice of hot or cold cereal and, almost daily, freshly baked bread or rolls. Our baker sisters were German women whose godly task was to prepare the most succulent bakery goods possible.

At about ten each morning, between cleaning the chapel and class, we ate our first "lunch". The breads from breakfast, with jellies and butter, re-appeared in our novitiate room to renew our strength. About 3:00 p.m. we lunched a second time with almost with the same of menu. Frequently, at this afternoon snack, Sister Ilsa, the baker, would share her freshly baked cookies with us.

Sister Ilsa's cookies were only one treat this German born, magnanimous woman baked. By 4:00 a.m. each morning the ovens were warming; the heavy trays of newly kneaded breads rotated evenly in her always spotlessly clean oven. Rarely was a breakfast served to the hundred or so sleepy religious at 6:30 a.m. without still-warm crescent rolls or freshly frosted cinnamon rolls.

The main meal was eaten at noon. After the routine prayer thanking God for food, Benedictine peace and serenity, we dug into Sister Blanche's soup, meat, potatoes, vegetables and salad, all served twice, on the outside chance that we had missed something the first time around. Accompanying these was the usual array of home-made breads. No noon meal was complete without dessert, also a product of Sister Ilsa's baked nurturing.

The sister cooks were Irish. Sister Kathleen, Sister Margaret, and Sister Mary Bridget never lost either their brogue or their Irish humor. The warmth they possessed, expressed in never-ending work in the kitchen, produced meals which were a daily wonder. Their service of God produced tangible results in the three meals a day prepared for the community.

Suppers were simple. Cereal. Yes. Cereal was always served as a staple in the evening. Older sisters, soon to retire for the evening, were not able to digest heavy food so we all ate cereal. One more starch by that time made little difference.

Following was the nightly repast, a light meal of fresh, homemade bread, cold cuts, leftovers from dinner and fresh fruit or bakery goods concluded our last and "light" meal.

However, our evening recreation was most often celebrated with a treat of Fannie Mae candy, homemade fudge or some special treat sent by someone's family or friend.

To this day, when a two pound box of that very special treat is opened before my eyes, I can identify each caramel, nougat, coconut, creme or fruit.

Did we gain weight? Yes. A lot. My normal not at all light body usually weighed in at 140 before convent days. By the time I was ready to receive the habit six months after my joining the convent, I weighed in at a hefty 185.

As nuns were not vain, nor conscious of their bodies, soon to be formerly dedicated with their souls to God, weight was not an issue. For the only time in my life, pre- or post-convent, I ate all I could without guilt. Because we had no mirrors to reflect our growth it made little difference.

My mother sobbed. Weight, to her, was a battle to be fought and won. She was already convinced that only fat girls entered convents. Now her beloved daughter who had always fought the noble fight against weight had succumbed to the final enemy, *fat*. If I had to be a nun, Mom would have much preferred a thin, beautiful one!

College for most is a four year experience. Perhaps, with luck, young people can stretch a fifth year out of their parents' generosity. Ours was a bit longer.

I completed a full year of college before entering the convent. Graduation came nine years later. Endless Saturdays and summer vacations were spent in college classrooms for those long years. We always went to school. Because Catholic school teachers at that time did not need state certification, we taught without it. As an aside, however, we pursued our degrees and certification.

When, indeed, graduation occurred, we immediately enrolled in more courses, either beginning our Masters' degrees or pursuing further study in some aspect of theology, Scripture or education. School was a way of life. Reading was compulsory.

Occasionally we had the privilege of attending a summer seminar or workshop on a university campus. This was a rare treat and resembled a vacation. Although we were expected to maintain the same rigorous prayer life, we found we could sleep past 7:00 a.m., talk without restraints, take long relaxing walks and other nuns from different communities and with whom we could share our thoughts and aspirations. These learning experiences, not recorded on any formal transcripts, enriched our ongoing education.

As I look at my transcript which now resides in the public school files where I am employed, I am assured it is unique. Who, for example, has three college credits in "Community Living?" And is there another who received an "A" in "Personal Holiness"? My credentials have both!

Despite the fragmented sequences of college courses we became well educated women. The humanities were the meat and potatoes of our curriculum. Because we had few distractions we were able to study, discuss, and in every way digest what we were learning. While I do not recommend that anyone duplicate my fragmented education, I never feel it necessary to apologize for it, either.

Laughter was the best medicine we found to ease the stressful, work-filled life we led. The short formal recreation we shared lasted a full thirty minutes on weekdays and a generous hour an Sundays. Some of these brief minutes were spent uproariously. All decorum was set aside and we became kids again.

Our discussions ranged from immature attempts at intellectualism to preparing funny skits we might perform for the next big feast day. The sisterhood was genuine. We cared for each other and looked to relieve the stress most felt as the schedule of convent living pressed down on our physical and psychological strength. We counted on each other. From the early days of novitiate training we knew we needed each other.

However, personal friendships were actively discouraged. Never was the word homosexual mentioned. It, like any discussion of sex, was simply not alluded to. The fear of it, however, was tangible. "PF's," as particular friendships came to be known, were not to be formed. We loved all the sisters in community equally. Of course we liked some more than others, but this was never to be visible in our conduct.

Physical contact was not, however, completely discouraged. No greater enthusiasm could be exhibited than the bear hug called the Benedictine Pax or Peace shared on feast days. Love was all over the place. Unaffected, genuine caring was the earmark of a good religious and one could feel it in the large community.

As I matured in religious life I discovered that not all loved. Some tragically, had locked up all affection in a tightly sealed, mean and destructive righteousness that choked their own humanity and seared all those around them. Fortunately, the majority of women were somehow, miraculously, able to be celibate, chaste and, in my experience, magnificently caring.

Friendships formed despite warnings against them. Secrets were shared. Concerns about tenuous vocations, loss of faith, inability to make sense out of the whole way of life were discussed in all the places and at all the times allotted to silence. The need to be in touch at a deep level with a good friend could not be barred by convent walls. And it never was.

The presence of overt sexual behavior is another case in point. I am sure, to this day, that some of the women with whom I lived were involved in sexual relations. I am certain that many of the attractions felt between women were sexually driven. As much, however, as popular literature would want us to believe differently, this was minimal.

We did not associate friendship with sex. Human relations were our mainstay. We believed we served God through our love of our fellow man. The admonition regarding particular friendships was neither taken seriously nor taught vigorously.

Novitiate lasted two years. Our formal training on how to be good sisters was curtailed as we were needed in the missions. Unlike popular understanding of mission, our "missions" were local parochial schools staffed by our community and much in need of new, fresh teachers.

This was the 50's. Catholic schools were popular as was a faith that encouraged parents to produce large numbers of children to fill the rows of desks. A black habit, white-coifed face and a class of forty-eight children somehow made us automatic teachers. And teach we did.

The summer before I was assigned to a large, wealthy parish to teach, I received my introduction to teaching skills in two three-hour courses in methods of math and methods of teaching social studies. Two weeks before school opened I found my assignment was second grade. Ordinarily a self-assured young woman, the thought of a room stuffed with seven-year-old children sent me into panic.

I was a few months short of being twenty-one years old, and had completed all of one year of college. I had absolutely no idea how to teach. I studied teacher manuals. I talked to the sisters I lived with. Some of their advice still rings in my ears. A long-time second grade teacher was appointed to help me. Taking out my lesson plan book, she explained concisely:

"See all those boxes? Fill them up. Make sure you don't leave any blanks. That's all she (meaning our principal) checks. It doesn't matter what they say. She doesn't ever read them. Just fill them up."

I filled them up. I decided on the traditional three reading groups. I learned the difference between a blend and a digraph. I made charts with words that ended in "at" and "it" and "en". My own learning to read had been natural and spontaneous. Books had always been my best friends. I remembered none of the gymnastics of phonics that I was called upon to teach.

Math was easier. The workbooks gave me some idea of what to cover over the year and therefore where to begin and end. Religion instruction was mapped out, lesson by lesson, and the directions needed only to be read and implemented.

At the end of my first day of teaching, I was exhausted, discouraged, disorganized and dismayed. I felt like I was starting on a very long boat trip and would suffer chronic and nauseating seasickness throughout the journey. Sending the children home, however, did not complete my day.

Catholic schools are and always have been short on funds. In order to save custodial salaries, the next function of the teaching nun was cleaning the room. This, I found, I was much better prepared to do.

Up went the long black skirt. Out came the long black apron. Moving desks to one side of the classroom I methodically swept the clear side of the room and double-checked its cleanliness with an oil soaked mop. The other half of the room came next.

Once the room was back in order and ready for the next school day I hurried back to the convent to meet the 4:00 p.m. deadline that had been set for us. I rushed to my room. The first day of the Catholic school was "pay day". Each child came to the classroom with an envelope of money for the following: book fees, lunch money, bus money, uniform costs, and/or tuition. My job now, before the 5:00 p.m. bell rang for evening prayers, was to sort out the jumble of checks, bills and coins.

It was long past my 9:00 p.m. prescribed bed time when the columns balanced and each child had proper credit for the envelope of monies brought to Sister.

My whole first semester of teaching differed little from that first disastrous day.

But the kids learned to read. We both learned vowels, short and long, digraphs and diphthongs. They mastered carrying and borrowing in math. I read every word in the manual. I filled every box on every page in the plan book. I studied. I asked for help from everyone. I worked late after official lights out. I learned that children could love school, learn much and still live within limits set by the teacher.

Saturdays were spent in school. In order to finish our college degrees we hopped on a bus bright and early and hurried off to the local Catholic women's college to be educated. Most of the day was spent in class or going and coming to and from it. The rest of Saturday was spent in weekly spring cleaning.

Sundays were a relief. We started with a "late sleep". This meant the clanging morning wake up call came a half hour later. Aside from school planning for the week, studying for our own course work, a regular prayer schedule plus early Mass followed by the children's Mass, we were free! No cleaning. A specially prepared meal and a full hour of recreation in the evening celebrated the Lord's day. On Monday, the week began again.

And we were tired. We were tired all of the time. From the thirty-three strokes of the morning bell (which were to remind us of the thirty-three years of Jesus' life) at 4:55 a.m. each day to the ending of the day, frequently very late at night, we were tired.

I learned to sleep everywhere. To sit down meant to sleep. Buses were made for napping. Prayers turned to dreams. Long sermons became respites of slumber. Blurred lines connected otherwise coherent college notes. Our bodies and minds were pervasively fatigued.

Sleeping everywhere can be dangerous. Luckily, we were not allowed to drive cars. Sleeping everywhere can also be very funny. We developed some extremely creative ways of sleeping.

The veils which we wore as part of our habit were long. The "tails" came well down below our waists. These were pinned by a series of black-headed straight pins to a variety of caps worn on our heads.

If we sat very straight it was possible to tuck the tips of our veils under our seats. In this position our heads were held erect no matter how soundly we slept. It was not possible to bob or slouch; our sleep was imperceptible.

The monsignor who was pastor of the first parish in which I taught was a righteous, arrogant Irish priest. He prided himself on the tough approach he had with his parishioners. The good nuns worked for the Lord and he was going to be certain that the Lord got his money's worth!

He preached most Sundays at the Mass we attended. Seating was by rank, meaning the youngest (and most exhausted) of the group sat closest to the front of the church. We were immediately in view of Monsignor's piercing eyes. We had learned to time the end of his sermon.

When the sermon began we would tuck our veils firmly under our bodies, look straight ahead and fall fast asleep. Our heads never moved. When Monsignor finished his usual tirade against the sins of the world, the flesh and the devil, he would loudly pronounce the sign of the cross. At the words, "In the name of the Father, and of the Son and of the Holy Ghost" (Spirit had not yet taken the place of the old "ghost") we would wake, sign ourselves and stand up.

It worked every time but once.

The Sunday celebration was the feast of the Ascension. In this New Testament story, Jesus stands on the mountain before ascending to heaven and gives his apostles their final mission. Monsignor was waxing eloquently about midway in the sermon as he quoted the Lord saying: "Going therefore, preach the Gospel to all nations, baptizing them *in the name of the Father, and of the Son and of the Holy Ghost*."

He had pronounced the key words. Six of the younger sisters responded like Pavlov's dog. We blessed ourselves carefully and stood for the next part of the service.

He was not at all pleased. The redness on his face matched the monsignor-red trim of his vestments. We knew immediately that we had seriously jeopardized our shaky relationship with both the pastor and our local sister-superior who ruled the local community with an iron hand.

As a result we did not sleep through sermons for at least a week. Fortunately our exhaustion overcame our fear and by the time the Holy Ghost descended (ten days after the Ascension) we were again fast asleep, veils tucked tightly under our bottoms, waiting for the signal to stand and get on with the service.

Meditation was part of each day's routine. Our first period of meditation was at 5:30 a.m., one half hour after being awakened by the aforementioned thirty-three rings of the bell.

Getting dressed was a chore that took all of those thirty minutes. Our costume, or habit, was simple enough. A long black, multi-pleated serge dress belted by a black leather girdle was easy to put on and not uncomfortable to wear, hot weather excepted. The headgear was ludicrous.

A small white cap stretched over our foreheads and tied in the back. The white coif, ironed in tight, tiny starched pleats draped over the cap and down around our necks. Many pins connected the two coverings. Following the coif was a stiffly starched band that fit, boxlike, over our foreheads, That, too, tied tightly behind our heads. Two veils, one shoulder length and one longer were pinned, somewhat precariously, onto the coif.

Only a mechanical engineer could have understood how everything went together. All of us knew, however, that to be secure for the entire day, many and careful pins were needed. That took time. When we got to meditation we were wide awake. It took about sixty seconds to fall back to sleep

Luckily meditation ended with a light tinkle of the superior's little bell. This was meant to call us from the heights and/or depths of contemplation. For the majority of us, it did call us back — from a short but restful nap, the first of many throughout the day.

The 50's ended. Vatican II, the spontaneous reformation efforts of Pope John XXIII accompanied the social upheavals of the now famous 1960's and 1970's. Even convent walls were not impervious to the attacks of this era.

Reform literature began to filter into our daily reading. Because religious life embodied so many of the Roman Catholic traditions in their pristine purity it was uniquely vulnerable to criticism. Values held absolute began to be questioned. The cracks in our traditions, imperceptible at first, grew so large and so deep that the whole structures which held religious life together began to crumble.

554

The religious habit, the symbol of a life dedicated to poverty, chastity and obedience, came under question. Should these outdated, uncomfortable costumes be changed to practical, simple dresses? Or should they, perhaps, be abandoned completely?

Some thought we should charge ahead. Change everything! Go from the traditional garb to "lay" clothes in one fell shot. Arguments went from the theological to the urbane.

Some contested that to "look like lay people" left religious without symbolic value. The habit had a message of its own; it spoke to the world that women were dedicated, celibate Christians in a society whose values were quite contrary.

A sister, known as the community curmudgeon, appropriated the microphone during one of our many meetings discussing the changes impacting our lives.

Change, she protested, was essential. We could wait no longer. The Church was calling religious women to a new era. Sister called us to move forward to become the marines of the church: the first on the beaches, the risk-takers and leaders of the new Church.

The senior members of the community scowled their most devout disapproval. One could almost imagine them physically hanging on to the flowing robes and neatly pressed veils.

I can still see our beautiful and brilliant community treasurer suggesting that we retain a simple black and white veil. She reached out to the older women with a plea for an understanding of the new Church, of the future of Benedictine women in the decades to come.

"Change", she said, "is like a sail boat. It needs a strong wind to move it forward. The sail, in its resistance to the wind, controls and directs the forward motion. Without the winds of change we would not move. Without the restraints of the sail, the ship would move swiftly but without direction."

We left that historic meeting unbelieving and dazed. I knew, as did most of my confreres, that my life would experience explosive changes. Intuitively we realized that we had bound our identity to long black skirts, white wimpled coifs and long black veils.

Not only would our witches' shoes be replaced with modest pumps, the very essence of our womanliness would be shaken out of the mothballs in which it had been stored since late adolescence. Adapting to regular clothes for the first time in decades was not without its own kind of humor.

The debate on whether to change and if so, how much, had been heated. The practical questions, as simple as "What size did we wear?" brought experiences both of embarrassment and hilarity.

I remember my first shopping trip.

I was thirty-five years old. The last time I had dressed in normal clothes was before my nineteenth birthday. I wore a size nine or twelve as best I could remember. That was before Sister Ilsa's baking, Sister Kathleen's cooking and sixteen years of being covered with flowing folds of fat-hiding black habits.

Sister Joyce was best suited for my shopping companion. We were good friends. She was a free spirit; I was much more conventional. She was also a beautiful woman who humorously contended that she was an immediate descendant of an Egyptian princess. People literally stopped on the street in wonder.

We got off the Chicago subway at the old basement entrance to Wieboldts and headed for the sale rack. The forty dollars allotted for a complete wardrobe wasn't a whole lot of cash, even in 1967! A maze of clothing seemed to engulf us.

We aimed at the size eighteen for openers. These would fit for sure.

Neither of us imagined ourselves in any kind of form-fitting skirts though we had the good sense to have worn our best bras and underwear.

As good fortune would have it, the proverbial friendly salesperson approached us gingerly. "Umm, Good morning, Sisters. May I...that is, is there anything..."

I interrupted, thankful for her intrusion and anxious to have all of us at ease. We dumped our story. We were shopping for real clothes. No, we were not running away from the order. Yes, we were going to still be nuns. Yes, truly, only forty dollars. None of the clothes on the rack were within our budget. We just wanted to find our correct size. We were also in need of some friendly advice.

After listening to the usual "I went to Catholic school and never had nuns like you" story, we were escorted into changing rooms with an array of sizes and shapes of contemporary women's clothes. We found that size eighteen was a high estimate! I was indeed happy to find out that even a size twelve hung relatively loose around my maturing body.

Our next move, on the advice of the Catholic-schooled saleslady, was to find a second-hand store on Rush Street. Off we went in our long black habits, bundled in black shawls and hanging on to our flowing veils for the last time in our lives.

I arrived home that evening toting a blue plastic bag in which a two-tone fine wool suit and white blouse securely hung. Black shoes and "real stockings" finished the very conservative outfit. My short black veil had already become part of my new wardrobe. I was ready. The next day was Sunday. Now for the courage to appear in public as the new Sister Joanne. Sleep was scarce that Saturday evening.

The first realization as I walked out of the front door on Sunday morning was that there was a cold breeze on my legs. Except for the inch between the end of my long skirt and the beginning of my black shoes, no part of my legs had been exposed to air for over fifteen years. The cold winter wind was a sharp reminder of this.

I was soon to find out that the looks of many of the Catholics congregated for Sunday Mass were no warmer! Modern nuns were threats to a religion that was unquestioned. Many were affronted at our appearance that Sunday morning.

Others were delightful! Their support rescued us from embarrassment and uncertainty.

Clothes only symbolized the depth of change taking place. Work, for example, had always been one of obedience. On August 15th each sister would receive a sealed envelope in her assigned seat in the chapel. After the offertory of the Mass, each of us opened the envelope anxiously and with not a little apprehension.

One never questioned the will of God as received through the superior. No matter how ill-prepared we were nor how distasteful the work might be, good sisters did not complain.

Suddenly, we were allowed to request assignments. We formed a personnel board which examined the needs of the community and tried valiantly to match general needs with the expressed wishes of each individual sister. Many opted to remain in traditional roles. We were trained school teachers and committed to Catholic education.

Others disillusioned with the teaching profession, or simply in need of a new way of life, chose alternate careers. Some were employed outside the community schools; others returned to full time school as students. This radical departure from "the ways things had always been done" had extensive impact on the Catholic schools all of us had served without question or salary. It had equal effect on our sense of community, which had been grounded in common work.

Clothes changed. Work diversified. Latin prayers were translated and prayed in English. The Vatican Council, which revolutionized the Catholic Church in the 60's, took firm hold of the great oak of religious life and shook it so hard that many of its trappings loosened and fell crashing to the ground.

The next changes were inevitable.

Vows were meant for life. Like the commitment made in marriage, our promises of poverty, chastity and obedience were meant to be lifelong. We clearly expected to live and die in the communities in which we were professed. Even this, the most profound aspect of religious life, developed cracks which soon brought many women back to the world from which they had come.

I had recently requested a transfer from the parochial school where I had been happily employed as principal for four years. My new assignment was that of assistant principal of the community high school. Although I knew little of secondary education, I was determined to give the job a try even though I had done some exploration into other positions outside the traditional community framework.

I brought my suitcases to the convent connected to the high school. My wardrobe had expanded a bit and at the bottom of one bag was a trendy two-piece bathing suit I had purchased during a trip to California. Tucked neatly between other articles of clothing were several packs of Virginia Slims. My years as a non-smoker had ended. Returning to that habit had been natural and I had been quick to begin smoking again at the first opportunity.

My new room was similar to the small chunk of space I had once occupied as a new member of the community. The curtains were still clean and stark white. The closet was now much too small to hold my modest but expanded wardrobe. The privacy to which I had become accustomed had vanished. The small family-like group with whom I had lived was replaced with a large and more impersonal group of women.

My decision to leave the convent was made in a moment. The seed had been planted and nurtured for several years. I no longer could live the life of a dedicated religious. In fact, now that I faced the inevitable, I realized that much of my religious life of the last two years had been, at best, superficial. I had questioned everything from the very existence of the God I had vowed to serve to my own ability to remain celibate for the rest of my life.

The time had come. The realization was overwhelming. The immediate rush of excitement competed with a profound sense of sadness and loss.

My request to leave the community was of no great surprise to superiors or confreres. The writing on the wall had been more obvious to them than to me. The sadness I felt was expressed by the major superior of the community. She embraced me. We wept together.

I left religious life in 1971, nineteen years after that first day of farewells to my family and friends. I still knew and loved my sisters, now married with large families. My brother and I had maintained periodic contact.

Because I, like other religious women, was well educated and effectively prepared in our profession, finding a job and beginning a new life was not as difficult as one might assume. After several weeks of searching, I accepted a position in education comparable to the one I had left as principal.

The finding of a place to live, purchase of an automobile and the initial creation of a new life made the first weeks of the real world exciting and memorable.

Family and friends trickled back. Old relationships were re-established; new friendships formed quickly. For many weeks a kind of euphoria engulfed my life. It was all new and exciting. I was ready. My first real paycheck confirmed the realization that I was "out" and truly launched into my new life.

It was only two short years after that I met and married a man that I care for deeply. Pat was a widower. My life with him and our shared raising of his six children (now ours) is another story. That chapter in my life is equally as poignant and as memorable as my convent story. The theme of our wedding summarizes for me the way life happens for most of us: "When one door closes, another opens".

The door to my religious life closed in August 1971. Behind that door are memories of a way of life that for the most part have passed into history. The sharing of the story told in these few pages needs to be done, lest that whole chapter of Roman Catholicism be lost to history. Or worse, the journey of religious women in contemporary history might be written by those who have not had the opportunity to walk in those shoes themselves.

We all know that patent leather shoes do not reflect up. We know much more. The women behind those legendary wimples and flowing robes were real people, invested in a great love of God, the Church and the people they dedicated their lives to serve.

Their memory deserves much more than a good belly laugh. The history of the Catholic Church in America was built on the hard work and devotion of thousands of Benedictines, Dominicans, BVMs, Franciscans, Sisters of Charity, Sisters of St. Joseph, to mention only a few of the major communities in the United States.

Feminists may write of their theories; the Church continues to seek for equity for women in ministry; glass ceilings may crack and women may, some day, play an equitable role in American society.

Behind those scenes, hard at work and at prayer, stand American religious women. Tall and firm.

Carmen T. Moya Czajka
Former Franciscan

Married

Homemaker

Webster College

Lector, Eucharistic Minister, Care Giver

While Carmen hopes to "get a job" she would also like to travel and become even more involved in her new parish. She enjoys singing and sewing, cooking and reading, hiking and bicycling, and dancing!

Carmen T. Moya Czajka

Counting Stars

My name is Carmen T. Czajka. I was born in Alamogordo, New Mexico on April 29, 1942. I have resided in South Chicago Heights, Illinois for about twenty-two years.

Both of my parents have been deceased for about nineteen years. I am the twelfth of thirteen children.

In 1947 Jesus let me know that I had a holy vocation to be a sister. I was then five years old. It was one hot evening when my father and I were sitting out on the front porch looking at many stars in the sky. My father asked me why I was looking at the stars for so long a time. I said, "I am trying very hard to count the stars, but some seem to go out and I lose my place." Dad replied, "Carmela, you are not able to count the stars. Only God can do that, because He made them."

At that moment my father thought it necessary to tell me about my twin brother who was still-born. Up to that time I was not aware that I had been a twin. My heart did a big flip, and my whole being became so very happy to hear such great news about my twin brother. I do not know my brother's name because my parents did not give him a name. Although my brother was dead, my thoughts were that I would see him again, since my dad had just told me about him. Not to be so! My dad told me that when a person dies that person is gone forever. My brother had gone to heaven, and I would not be able to see him until I would die. I was happy for my brother, but very sad for me.

It was at this very time that my father went into a beautiful discussion of God, His Son, and His Son's mom, Mary. That night I was determined to put a cross on my brother's grave. His grave was outside the front window of our house. My brother was so small my parents buried him in a shoe box outside our front window. Next morning a small home-made stick cross was put on my brother's grave by my father and me.

563

It was a beautiful moment for me, and I experienced a great feeling of closeness with my brother.

The same night that my father told me about my brother I had a very strange and wonderful dream. I dreamed that my brother came to my bed and woke me up to take me to play with him in a beautiful place near heaven. We played in a pretty meadow with green grass and all kinds of beautiful flowers. He talked to me of God and heaven. He also expressed how happy he was to be there. We then went back to play in the meadow until he said he must leave me to go back to God. My reaction was, "I want to go with you!" My brother then told me that I was to come later, and that he would pray and wait for me. This good news has been with me all these years of my life. At this very moment I chose to be as good as possible, so that I can be prepared to see God, too!

In 1955 in September of the school year my desire grew stronger to enter a convent. I begged my mother and father to let me enter the postulate in St. Louis after I graduated from the eighth grade. My mother told me if my desire was still strong after completing four years of public high school, she might consider discussing the subject of my entering a convent.

About this time my life became so very peaceful. Nothing mattered except loving God and being very good. I started little by little to give my clothes away to the poor and stayed at home to do simple household tasks before and after school. Today I still follow this simple way of living. In those four years my everyday routine was as follows: attend daily Mass and receive Communion; read many spiritual books; recite the rosary daily even though people would accuse me of being a religious fanatic; practice corporal works of mercy; finish my twelve years of religious education; correspond with Bishop Fulton J. Sheen. The Franciscan sisters of our home parish educated me in many spiritual matters and taught me how to teach religious education to young adults.

Time moved on until one day the Franciscan sisters invited me to come to visit them in their convent. I asked my mother for permission, and it was granted. When the day arrived I was so very excited and happy inside myself. The sisters made me welcome in their house and gave me good refreshments. They confided in me their opinion that they believed that I had a holy vocation and suggested that I tell my mother and father all that they had discussed with me that afternoon.

When I left the good sisters, I told my parents the good news, but they became sad. As the days went by my visits to the sisters in their convent became quite frequent. They even picked me up in their car every morning to take me to church. The church was seven blocks from my house and they thought that I should ride with them instead of having to walk all that distance. I was very grateful to them for everything.

In 1959 my senior year came to be a reality to me. My desire to enter a convent became more intense. My desire was to enter the convent where the sisters had an orphanage with their convent in a town called Tularosa, New Mexico. It was twelve miles from my former residence. My mother used to give clothes to the orphans living there with the sisters. My mother would take me with her on these journeys, and I learned to like to go and play with the orphans while my mother took care of the clothes with the sisters. Once I asked my mother if I could live there, not knowing any better. The mother general in charge of the sisters told my mother that one day her daughter would be back with her. My mother didn't say a word, but only smiled.

In the latter part of 1959, my parents took me to Tularosa to find the sisters that had the orphanage which I remembered from earlier years. To our great surprise the site had been sold, and a grocery store had been built in its place. We inquired about the sisters' new location. The news was that two or three sisters entered different orders. Either they entered an order or they would have to disband. The people did not know where the sisters had disappeared.

In the month of May of 1960, the Franciscan sisters accepted me into their postulate. I was to enter on August 12th, which was their entrance date.

My mother told me if I did not go with the sisters of our parish when they left for the summer on June 12, I would not be permitted to go into the convent.

Because of the fact that my parents had very much tried to discourage me from entering the convent, I was unprepared to go so early. For one important thing, the order I was entering required $200 for a dowry before entrance into their community. I was in no position to pay any amount at the time. In my mind I knew that God had given me (undeserved on my part) this vocation. The next week was spent on planning how I was to get $200.

My first impulse was to ask or beg my parish priest, Father Hyatt, to lend me the money. I was very scared of him, because he was so very crabby and strict with young people. He would holler at you for any reason. My opinion was that he didn't like young people. Well, I ventured on to the rectory despite my parents' objection.

The secretary of the rectory led me into Father Hyatt's office. It was dark and gloomy in there. Father sat at his desk and asked, "Why do you want to see me?" I answered, "I want you to please write me a check for $200. It is to be used for my dowry to enter the Franciscan sisters". Every nerve in my body at this moment was shaking and I wanted, very fast, to go and hide somewhere so that I would not have to hear Father's reply. Father came back with some questions that very definitely needed to be answered. What is your name? Why do you want to enter a convent? Why did you come to me? My response was as follows: "My name is Carmen Torres Moya; I want to become a saint. The convent is the only place that I can live the spiritual life that I am so earnestly seeking. You, my good parish priest, are the only one that can possibly help me."

Father then reached for his pen and with a big smile on his face gave me a big blessing with a check written out to me for the amount of $200. My departing remark was "Thank you, Father. My brother will pay the money back to you in installments."

As soon as I was led out of the rectory I ran home and told my parents, sisters and brothers what had taken place in Father's office. They were all surprised! By the end of that week my mother and brother went with me into town to purchase a big trunk, convent clothes, and other required convent needs.

As the days went by swiftly, my mother would cry almost every day, especially when she would see me getting my things ready to leave for the convent. She would plead for me not to go because she needed me at home. I knew my mother would miss me not only because she loved me, but because the chores at home were mostly done by me. Sometimes I would do my sister's, too. My allowance amounted to one dollar; sometimes I would give fifty cents to my mom or sister and the other fifty cents would be sent to Bishop Fulton J. Sheen for the Propagation of the Faith. My attitude of sharing began at a very early age in my life, thanks to God and my parents.

It was May and high school graduation was here. My parents took all the family by car to Disneyland in California. We enjoyed the trip together very much. We stayed about one week.

A few weeks before I left to go to the convent my father got employment doing some work in the mountains. My mother, sisters and I helped my dad clean the little two-room adobe house which was to be his week-end residence at certain times. When we finished cleaning the house one afternoon, my father and my three brothers went rabbit hunting in the mountains. It got dark and they got lost. My mother and sisters were worried. I suggested praying the rosary for their safe return home. As I said the rosary my prayer was to ask the Blessed Mary to appear to my dad and brothers in a form of a tree with two limbs pointing the way home.

Early in the morning my father and brothers arrived. They entered the house very quietly and pale in the face. My mother said, "It looks as if you have seen a ghost." My brothers told the story to us of a bright light on the road where a lady was standing. When they came closer it was a tree with a limb pointing to a road which they took all the way home. I spoke up and told them what I had asked the Blessed Mother to do for us as a sign for me to know if I truly was to enter the convent. No one knew of this until that moment when my brothers told their story. We all took time out and thanked God.

On June 12 my family gave me their blessings and I left to enter the convent. I took the train with the four Franciscan sisters of our parish I had chosen their order.

When I was dressed as a postulant my soul was so very happy. On July 4 we had a big picnic with all the sisters of the motherhouse. Sisters from all over St. Louis were there to celebrate, too. It was on this day that I had my first glimpse of the Franciscan sister who took care of the orphans in Tularosa. My body was numb. WOW! Could this be a big miracle? I ran to Little Mother and embraced her. She was overjoyed when she heard my story about the time I looked for her in Tularosa.

She told me that God had really wanted me to be a religious. Sister said that the Franciscan order had lovingly taken her and her three sisters in religion into their order. Sister was told by the reverend mother general that she could keep her title Mother, but sister most humbly asked to be put back as a postulant, not sparing her anything in chores and the like.

My impression of her was that she was a very holy and devout religious. When I met her she was a perpetually professed religious in the order. We got to be very good friends, and we would spend recreation together when occasions presented themselves.

Years went by, and I became a novice named Sister Mary Margarita. I was missioned to teach first grade during my second year as a novice.

When I became a senior novice Little Mother was called to heaven. I told reverend mother my secret story and she permitted me to be Little Mother's pallbearer at the funeral. When the sisters in the congregation saw one novice with all the perpetually professed sisters carrying the coffin, they were in awe. Novices weren't permitted to do such things! That particular day was one of the greatest honors of my life.

My novitiate was spent with such great joy for me and for all my sisters. My life was very spiritual and so very much filled with true Franciscan joy. I was always so happy and cheerful that I was chosen to play St. Francis of Assisi in a play called *Little Flowers of St. Francis.* I also belonged to a choir, and I thought it was just a beautiful way to express my joy in song to God. Constantly the sister superior would ask me to lead the sisters in Vespers. Also I would read the daily morning and evening meditation. At times with the sister superior's permission, she would permit me to chant the Holy Office at one of our sisters' funeral. All these honors were treasured in my heart.

Over a period of three years my temporary vows were pronounced. In 1966 my perpetual vows were pronounced. Most of my missions were two-person missions, teaching four grades at once with fifty-six to fifty-eight students. It was extremely difficult, but I was very, very prayerful, and was helped most generously by God.

All these years up to now were so joyful and spiritually rewarding. God gave me the gift of being an exemplary sister, thus becoming a good teacher. I loved everyone and everything. Nothing negative ever entered my mind. My favorite vow was obedience, because if this vow was cherished and practiced, the vow of poverty and chastity were surely a joy to keep. Every day was a great thanksgiving for me. My convent time was exciting and beautiful. The sisters were helpful to me in getting my spiritual life in order. God bless them!

In 1968 reverend mother sent me to go to a mission with a few sisters. My joy was overwhelming. One week before departure reverend mother missioned me instead to teach in Chicago Heights, Illinois. My trunk and belongings were at my first assignment. The reason for the sudden change to Chicago was because the school needed a bilingual sister. I spoke Spanish fluently.

My will was not to go, but I had learned to accept cheerfully the will of God as seen by Him.

In the month of September I found myself with about five sisters in an Illinois convent. The first Sunday the children's Mass was at 9:00 am. My duty was to be a participant at the Mass, and to be mindful of the children's behavior.

During the Mass my glance went to a couple with five children about four benches before me. The mother had a beautiful operatic voice. This family was very active and well respected in the parish. The children went to public school and they attended CCD every week. The oldest boy of ten years was with the altar boys that I taught in the parish. I also taught him in religious education every week. My only regret was that I did not get the opportunity to meet the mother of these nice children.

That same Sunday afternoon the family was hit by a young drunken driver in a head-on collision. We heard of the accident on our way back from visiting sisters at another convent, who had invited us for an all afternoon get-together. We immediately said prayers for the poor family.

That particular night I had a dream that a marriage was to take place with Joe Czajka and myself, and that I would suffer very much with my first child. I woke up in the middle of the night and I became very much concerned about this dream. My life had always been centered around my dreams. This time it just didn't make sense to me. I confided this dream to one of my sisters the following day. We both decided to dismiss it from our minds and pray about it.

The next day we heard all the details about the accident of the Czajka family. The father had a broken arm and teeth; the mother had internal injuries and broken teeth; the oldest girl had a big dent on her forehead and a leg injury; the second oldest girl was in a coma that lasted for eight days; the third oldest girl had a bad injury on her forehead and a leg injury; the fourth oldest girl had a broken collar bone; the oldest son was spared from any injury.

All injured were hospitalized, and within fifteen days the mother went to heaven. The children were told of their mother's death by their dad. It was a very emotional time for everyone. The family was dismissed from the hospital and they all attended the mother's funeral. The two girls with very bad head injuries were bald and had hats on. The dad had his right arm and right leg in casts. The oldest boy was a server at the funeral. My duty at that time was in the classroom and I was not able to participate at this sad event.

That year was hard for all the family. The parishioners took turns cleaning their house and bringing them food until they could manage on their own. Every Sunday I would see the father of the Czajka children come by the sacristy to talk to the priest. I was the sister sacristan at that time.

My contact with Mr. Czajka was on business affairs only. I took care of his children when he had Holy Name meetings after Sunday Mass. I also dealt with him at altar boys meetings.

The days went by and the children were coping better with life. Father Jack, our pastor, and other people asked Joe when he was getting a new mother for his children. He was concerned, but he would answer, "Not yet."

Summer came and sister superior had left me with the duties of the parish: sacristan, church laundry, cleaning the church and sacristy, servers. Sister would be going to the hospital and would have time to recuperate.

By this time my spiritual director knew about my wanting to leave this convent and enter an contemplative order. Mother general instructed me on what I was to do to get a proper dispensation of my perpetual vows. I wrote to the pope for a dispensation of my vows. He responded, permitting me to take a leave of absence for one year. After one year I was to return back to the order. It didn't happen.

In June of 1969 I left the convent. My parents welcomed me with warmness in every way. My home was to be with them.

In August my employment was as kindergarten teacher in the Catholic school in my town, Alamogordo, New Mexico. My teaching career lasted about five months because I got a dispensation and got married to Joe Czajka in December 27, 1969. We moved back into Chicago Heights, into Joe's house.

Of all of Joe's children, only the oldest boy accepted me without any conditions. He has to this day kept his affection for me.

The children were raised with a good spiritual and physical background. It was an extremely hard time for me raising these five instant children.

In 1971 Joe and I had a baby boy; in 1972 another baby boy; 1974 a baby girl. Now we have mine, his, and ours, eight wonderful children.

Now in 1992 I am raising my last child who is seventeen years old. She will graduate this year and go on to college.

Even though I am in the married state, my striving for spiritual perfection is stronger than ever before.

Years before our parish, St. Joseph, closed, my duties there were as follows: CCD coordinator; marriage counselor; Altar and Rosary ladies organization member; starting the first choir in our parish; teaching one year in our Catholic school; cantor or lector on Sundays; Eucharistic minister; teacher of boy servers; cleaning the rectory and church; serving the youth organization; acting as lay representative of our parish for the diocese of Chicago; teaching religious education to people wishing to teach CCD classes; being a prayer group member and a Bible group member; teaching adult education when necessary.

Today my husband and I belong to a new parish and I am currently serving as lector and Eucharistic minister. My involvement might be more as the time of adaptation to this new parish takes form.

Through the school years of all my children I was very active in school with them as follows: PTA; room mother; president of the high school girls' chorus; seamstress for the eighth grade band girls for two years. Lastly, I was a chaperone for dances and field trips.

In the 1970's. some of the village people and I formed a Concerned Citizens political group in South Chicago Heights for the betterment of the village. It lasted about three years, then disbanded.

My closing statements about my religious life are as follows:

1. I left the convent because my life would be lived more religiously out of the convent than in the convent. My giving of myself totally to God could only be done in the life I am living now. I have no regrets about leaving, but thankfulness in my heart.

2. I do miss the sisters to some extent. In fact, on some occasions I have visited them and do write to them when possible.

3. My role as a wife, mother, and grandmother has not in the least interfered with my spiritual life at home. My day starts at 8:00 a.m. with daily mass, Holy Communion, and reading of the Holy Word. At 10:00 a.m. my prayer time starts with meditation, rosary, Bible reading and spiritual reading. This might take one or two hours. At times I visit the sick, the needy, and bring them Holy Communion.

Thank you for letting me share my thoughts with you.
    God love you!

Ellen F. Dunn
Dominican

Director of Human Resources, Dominican Congregation

Bachelor of Arts, Ohio Dominican College

Master of Arts in Education, University of Notre Dame

Master of Theological Studies, Weston School of Theology

Special Training: Spiritual Direction

Job related ministry

Ellen has lived in an apartment for the past five years, and has worked for her community for four of those years. Since that community ministers in twenty-four states and five countries, her friendships are widely spread through several geographical areas. She enjoys teaching theology, and pastoring in general. Golf is an enjoyable activity, as is reading feminist literature, especially religious feminist literature. She sees herself "working in the Church of the World." If the present patriarchal structure is dying, she refuses to catch "the terminal illness."

Ellen F. Dunn

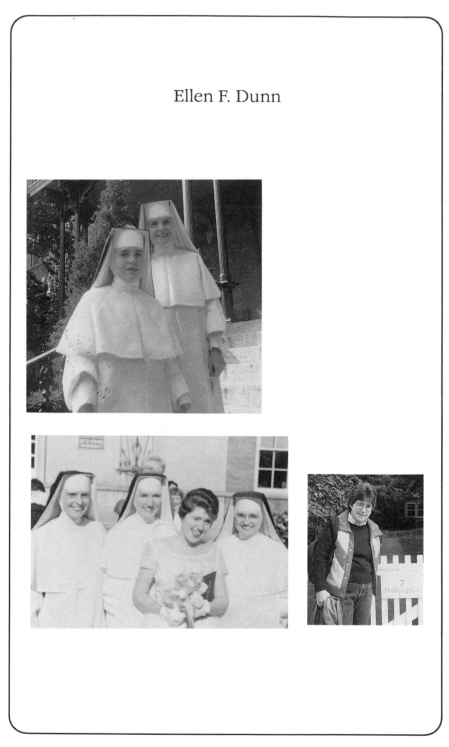

The Good Sisters
are Still Around

As of April 29, 1992

This question evokes the best and the worst of responses in me simultaneously! On the one hand, I want to say: "The good sisters are right here, still serving the Church of the '90's." But on the other hand, I believe that the categoric and legendary "good sisters" are gone for sure and gone for good!

I attended Catholic grade and high schools like my peers in the neighborhood. My high school was a private academy for girls, and I chose to enter the convent the fall after I graduated. I knew from the time I was in the eighth grade that I wanted to be a nun, but it was a carefully kept secret — except that my older brother and I would talk about it late at night. My parents thought that I was too young, but somehow were afraid to stand in the way of God's will as it was viewed at the time. I learned years later that my younger brother — a freshman in high school when I left home — was really concerned that I was leaving home. He said to my mother, "What are we going to do without Ellen?" We still laugh about it today; he still denies having said it.

Although I was a fairly mature eighteen-year-old when I entered the Dominicans, I had much growing up to do as I progressed in religious life. There were thirty-three in my group and two thirds of us were right out of high school. Most of what we did was done in groups, and in silence. I can remember being confused about who I was. Nevertheless there were several significant experiences which stand out for me as formative for my young adult self.

During novitiate we were allowed to go swimming for the first time! We were at a lake at a nearby Catholic institution, and one of the professed sisters who had sponsored my entering the community was with us as a lifeguard. She got my attention as soon as we got into the lake, and whispered to me to swim out into the deep water so we could talk. I remember her expressing concern that I had grown too serious and did not seem like my usual fun-loving self. She encouraged me, at all cost, to *be myself.* I was relieved and grateful and began to be more centered in myself as a person.

I remember always having a mind of my own and doing things which were not allowed, if I thought they were all right. The earliest convent rule I broke was when I went to the attic (very scary, because of the bats!) and retrieved the pretty aqua two-piece suit I had worn on entrance day. Somehow I smuggled it out to my mother on visiting Sunday that month. She had always loved this particular outfit and we wore the same size. I think it was a way of her having a little bit of me back home again. I knew if *they* sent me home, *they* would have to find something for me to wear.

Later on, after teaching high school for only seven years, I came to a crisis of meaning inside myself. I was twenty-eight at the time. I knew I did not want to teach French verbs to disinterested adolescents for the rest of my days. Something much richer would have to happen to keep me in the convent. So I made an appointment with the major superior and told her I wanted to study theology and get into the field of religious education. Although this kind of request was simply not made by a young sister in those days, this woman of vision did allow me to make the change. The story was not quite that simple, of course; there was a lot of struggle and pain. But within a few months, I was launched on a new path as a parish Director of Religious Education. It was the new beginning I needed at that moment.

Today I am often asked why I don't leave the convent or why it is I remain a religious woman in this patriarchal-based Church. The truth is that I do not feel called to leave for anyone or anything else. Religious life is not problematic for me at this time. I have struggled with the departure question at specific moments during the past thirty-five years. But, frankly, today I find myself thinking first about leaving the Church. Or I wonder if I will die a Catholic.

I clearly entered religious life in the era of the good sisters. It was the late 50's and religious vocations were abounding. We could hear the sounds of the steam shovels breaking the ground for new buildings to house all of us. I even think that, in those early years, I was one of the good sisters. Then Vatican Council II happened and everything began to change, myself included. And I was ready and willing.

It's not that we good sisters stopped being good, but rather that we who had long been grouped into this category (for centuries, really!) began to become real, live, individual persons with real personalities and, *mirabile dictu*, with real live ideas of our own. Then, with the rule of silence lifted, we began to talk to one another and to express our ideas, hopes, fears and dreams among ourselves and with others beyond the convent walls (with seculars!). This was new behavior. It resulted from the wave of renewal in the universal Church, especially in the American Church. And it definitely contributed to the disappearance of the good sisters.

When the *good sisters* changed and became just plain good sisters, problems began to arise for us on many fronts. The general Catholic populace was not eager for us to change in any significant ways. We were their symbols of stability: if we stayed the same, like good sisters after all, then all would be well. But change we did! We changed our names and expected people to learn them and remember them; we changed our clothes; we changed our convents into home. In doing so, we stepped out into the crossfire of criticism and challenge. Those years were simultaneously wonderful and terrible; they brought hope for the future and much conflict and pain. But all new life is born of pain and struggle.

It was by then the early 70's, when the exodus of the once good sisters became obvious. Where did they all go? Well, some stayed in and some went out, but most of us had very similar experiences in the process of integrating massive doses of change. Today we realize that we were the shock troops of that earthquake-like event we now fondly call Vatican II.

A number of us simply woke up and realized that this life was not for us after all, that we had lived by someone else's rules for too long. Some set off in search of our true selves — wherever that search would take us. Some found desired companions in friendship or marriage for the ongoing walk of faith. Many of us decided to express our gifts in different careers than teaching or nursing. We returned to family members left behind, or to parents older and in need of care. Some travelled afar and found God in distant places and faces. Others left the safe womb of the Catholic Church and joined other denominations. Some went back to school to continue learning; many went to theology school to rediscover the God of our understanding . Some became ill and died; some suffered personal tragedies and sought help to survive. In or out, these women are alive and well; many have a new identity as women in the Church.

In my own experience with so many departures of close friends, I found that the boundaries of inside and outside religious life became blurred. The idea that some former members are now out of the community came to have little meaning because, in some cases, those relationships had grown stronger than before. And frequently, these women now outside the formal legal structures of religious institutes are still working directly in mainline Church ministries. Their motivation and dedication have a new perspective, no doubt, and we remain in a definite sisterhood in service of our Church.

During the decade of the 1980's I was a member of a small base community of nine women in my congregation. If I describe this group it will help to put faces on the descriptions given above. This was a group that chose to meet regularly in order to be of support to one another in our diverse ministries. We were living in four different cities, but managed to meet two or three times a year for the entire ten years. The group called itself the Chicago Cluster because three members were studying there. I remember it fondly as energizing and fun. We gave those gatherings priority in our calendars and in our hearts. I can see from where I sit today that in that one circle of women there is a real sampling of the diversity of responses to that initial query: Whatever happened to the good sisters?

In 1980, there were nine members in the Chicago Cluster. One never really committed herself to the group. She wasn't able to identify with such a radical fringe group within the congregation, and she dropped out after two years. The oldest and most revered member died of cancer and overwork in 1986; she was a prominent, internationally known prophetic woman, someone who had been in trouble with the Vatican and with the U.S. Government. Another member married a Jesuit co-worker and remained an active member of the group. Another woman, in a significant leadership role in Catholic higher education, left the religious life but not the cluster group. Still another individual married

578

a former Episcopal priest and continued with the cluster; she is currently studying for ordination in the Episcopal Church. And a seventh person finally left the convent to pursue her dreams in theology and education. Two other sisters and myself remain as active religious today. The group members are still in touch, but the official base community died of natural causes in 1990. In many ways we were a significant sampling of what became of the good sisters.

It was precisely our good sister characteristics which got us into the situation we face today. That is, we obeyed the Pope and the Council decrees. We studied the Church documents and rewrote our constitutions and rule books. And this very process brought us to a new identity as women of the Church of the twenty-first Century. We find ourselves today — some thirty years after Vatican II — at a very challenging and demanding moment in history as religious women. We stand on that mountain top today, peering into the unknown future. It's a kind of flashpoint between the lightning and the thunder clap. Action of some sort will no doubt be required of us soon.

I was asked recently to give a talk for an annual lunch for Directors of Religious Education in our diocese. The occasion caused me to become reflective about my own years as a DRE in the late 60's. The parish was, as I have stated, middle-size and middle income. I was fresh out of theology school and ready for the challenge. A new pastor had come; the one who pushed the parish council to hire me had gone. My office was in the basement of the rectory — highly symbolic of my role then in things pastoral. But I had two good years of learning there and still enjoy friendships with some of my first catechists.

In preparing to address this highly particular group in the Church today, I found myself focusing on several basic issues which come up almost daily in my human resource work for my congregation. The issues I highlighted for the DREs were visibility, inclusivity, and accountability. These were problematic for me in 1969; they remain so for DREs in the parishes today.

The weekly *National Catholic Reporter* carries any number of openings for DRE and Youth Ministry positions in parishes around the country. There is no real change in those impossible job descriptions! But what has changed is that neither the good sisters nor the laity are clamoring for these jobs anymore. We all want to be part of the pastoral team, working collaboratively with the clergy at these and other tasks of parish life. We want to be included in planning, decision-making, and ministering. We want to receive just compensation and benefits. We want to have our gifts recognized and utilized.

My own experience as a woman in full time ministry in the Church over the past thirty years offers me some good insights today. I am currently the Human Resource Director for my community and have been in this job for four years. Dramatic changes are taking place for the now nuns; the job market in the church is drying up. Fewer openings come each year from parishes and diocesan organizations. The reasons cited are the economy, the need to trim the budget, and the high cost of salaries for religious. It is a fact that in our mid-western state the good sisters are seeking a wage that is in parity with the laity. The now nuns and the ex-nuns are in the same situation, along with the devoted laity in the face of the clergy church who are our employers.

This shrinking job market in the church is a curious phenomenon at a time when the clergy are aging and ill, declining in numbers, and generally overworked. Everyone knows that there is no vocation shortage, just a shortage of creative imagination and an unwillingness to recognize the gifts and competence of women and men in our midst. I would like to exercise my demonstrated leadership gifts as a parish administrator in the near future, but there is no openness to this in my home diocese. Today, I choose to use my gifts in other arenas rather than to squander them where they are not acknowledged. I wish to work *with* others in ministry, not *for* them. Collaboration in the work of building God's kingdom is a requirement for many of us today. Accountability in a situation of mutuality and equality is also essential. We will not accept less.

The good sisters are still around. We are primarily involved in the task of shaping a new identity for women persons, one which will be descriptive of every human person. And I am comforted in knowing from the writings of contemporary theologians like Rosemary Radford Ruether and Johannes B. Metz that this shaping of a new identity is the critical work of politics and culture today. It is at the heart of peacemaking; it is the Gospel work demanded of us as citizens of the first world.

As church people, we must begin to acknowledge that women and laity are the poor and marginated, the Third World component of the church today. We religious women are dedicated to just this: to claim a freedom of personhood and an autonomy that is appropriate to full humanity; to achieve a new relationship with ourselves and with others which is not exploitative or dominative.

When this is accomplished, there will be no need to wonder about the plight of the good sisters of the past or the present.

John Kenneth Scott
Sister of St. Joseph

Part-time staff nurse

Diploma in Nursing, Providence Hospital, Detroit

Bachelor of Science, Nursing Education, Marquette University

Master of Science, Nursing Education and Administration, CUA

Executive Development in Long Term Care Administration, St. Louis University.

Job-related ministry

Sister John Kenneth lives in a community of seven at her motherhouse. Five other small communities share the facility. She is the youngest member of the community there. She has a special interest in bioethics and impending health care rationing. She pursues her interests in wildlife preservations and the environment, and for relaxation enjoys using her mind by following and playing *Jeopardy*. Retirement? She would like to "do something less physically strenuous than staff nursing."

John Kenneth Scott

Reflections of a Now Nun

I renewed my vows this morning after thirty-five years as a Sister of St. Joseph. I spent some time before Mass re-reading the notes I made during the retreat prior to receiving the religious habit on March 19, 1957. They reflect well the tenor of religious life prior to Vatican II:

"Poverty is an instrument of perfection — at the basis of the vows."

"Chastity empties us to all that is not God."

"Obedience — the vow of religious life. Do what I am told because I am told."

"A Masterpiece of Holiness — The Catholic Nun."

So, where am I now after thirty-five years in the religious life? But perhaps I am getting ahead of myself. I should start from the beginning, which is some thirty years prior to becoming a religious.

I lived in a small town in the Midwest and attended public school except for one year at "sister school" when I was in the third grade. I have an older sister and a younger brother. I was always a great reader, visiting the public library often, even when in the second grade. During high school I read almost everything in our school library. This included *Anthony Adverse, Gone With the Wind,* and a series of books on the Civil War.

I grew up during the depression. I knew we were poor but I never felt myself deprived. My mother inspired me to go to college. My dad was a truck driver-philosopher who remarked in the sixties: "There was no poverty in America until we got television!" I understand better what he meant when I hear of violence among young people over who has designer jeans or the "proper" brand of sneakers!

I had always been a rather religious person; raised to attend Mass every day during Lent, to say the rosary in October, attend Mother of Perpetual Help Devotions and do all the other things a Catholic girl

585

might have done in the pre-Vatican II era. I was atypical in one respect: my dad was a convert. The Bible we had in our house was a copy of the King James version. I didn't know until I was in the novitiate that it was a "sin" to read that version!

While in high school I worked during the summers in a restaurant, a hospital, and during my senior year with the help of my mother, I wrote the local town news for a newspaper. My dad taught me to drive a truck with a stick shift, shoot a rifle, and build a log cabin. All these experiences helped me when I later had to work as a nurse to pay for three and a half years of undergraduate education. I could do what I had to do.

After high school in 1944 I joined the U.S. Army Cadet Nurse Corps and attended a Catholic school of nursing in Detroit. During the 1940's a diploma school of nursing was run much like a boot camp in the Army. This helped me to later accept the things I lived through in the novitiate. I graduated in 1947 as a fairly competent nurse. I then worked in a number of different positions: staff nurse in a hospital and obstetric clinic, office nurse, camp nurse (Girl Scouts) and dormitory nurse while in college. During this time I continued to read widely: *The Prophet* by Gibran, *Seven Story Mountain* by Merton and the *Imitation of Christ* by Thomas a Kempis.

The thought of entering the religious life had crossed my mind during my teens and early twenties, but only as an option *not* to be taken. I did not have many positive experiences with religious women even though I attended a Catholic school of nursing and worked with sisters in a Catholic hospital. My main feeling about sisters at that time was that they were either too distant or too little-girl-like for me. I felt sisters lived a sheltered life and I probably had not a great deal of respect for them until I met sisters who were truly professional women as well as religious. This happened when I studied with some Sisters of St. Joseph while doing undergraduate work in Nursing Education Administration at Marquette University in 1951-1952. I had chosen to go to school for a degree rather than accept a commission in the Army Nurse Corps for which I had applied in 1950 during the Korean affair. After college I taught with some of the same Sisters of St. Joseph at a small diploma school of nursing for four years. I learned to admire and respect them. During this time I had my own apartment which I shared with my younger brother who was attending college. I owned a new car and looked forward to a career in Nursing Education Administration.

Then, all of a sudden, I knew with great certainty (I call it a special grace) in the space of a couple days that God was calling me to the religious life. In the fall of 1956 shortly following my thirtieth birthday I entered the novitiate of the Sisters of St. Joseph.

My novitiate was, I suppose, much like that of most other religious congregations in 1956. We were separated from the world by a daily horarium and by customs, also by stone walls. I will always recall the first time I saw the novitiate building. It looked more like a prison than a convent. However, this did not daunt me. I came to love the place, though the adjustment was not easy. Most of my group were eighteen-year-old girls. Some of them reacted more, I think, as they might have in boarding school. It was always deadly serious with me. I learned to appreciate the silence and rules we followed: they provided the space I needed in order to survive among the younger people in my group and in order to fit in as best I could with older sisters.

Still, life was much different. We wore a postulant garb which I felt looked a little silly on me; people felt free to call me by my first name (which no one had done since I left home); we did everything as a group, so individuality was discouraged. With all, I loved the religious life. I felt proud to be a Sister of St. Joseph. I received my religious name when I received the habit. I have never felt called upon to go back to my baptismal name. I believe "He called me by name" and it was my religious name.

In respects other than age I was also atypical. I was not very playful in those days. This term "playful" is my way of describing a change in attitude that overtook me in the 1980's. Others might describe me as "irreverent"; I think I am a prophetic voice. I cannot say with certainty that the open windows of Vatican II caused this or if it was just an unrelated factor. Perhaps, just growing older would have produced the same changes. However, since we are all products of our environment, I think the changes in the Church and religious life had much to do with it.

In any event, I began to take myself less seriously. The previous rigidity in religious life, "a place for everything and everything in its place," had fit me well. During the novitiate I was able to make a reasoned commitment to whatever was taught or required, since this would lead me to union with God in the most direct fashion. I did not require any rationale other than that to accept all the little rules and regulations (some seeming so strange today, and then too!) that made up a novice's life. I believed that they would help me to know God as nothing else. They did. I was blessed with experiential prayer and a degree of contemplation during my novitiate years. In this I was most fortunate to have a wise novice mistress. She always seemed able to keep a perspective and to distinguish means from ends. Even with her help I left the novitiate with a pretty rigid life style, professional as well as religious.

It was said in 1957 that one could enter any house of the Congregation at 5:00 p.m. and join in the same prayers and feel right at home. This might not have been literally true in all respects; this example indicates the uniformity that characterized our lives prior to 1965. I remember being at our motherhouse one day during the novitiate. We were all standing there: dressed alike, acting alike, and presumably, thinking alike. The superior general came out to talk to us. I felt such a common bond! So much a part of things! All in all, the habit did a great deal for me in those years. You could always identify another Sister of St. Joseph. I was proud of the similarities.

After the novitiate I returned to the same diploma school at which I had taught before entering. I imagine my life for the next eleven to twelve years was much like any other member of a religious community. I observed the rule, made an annual retreat, tried to be faithful to prayer and to do my work in a loving manner.

However, in some respects it was different. Until the last few years I had never held a position which was not one of some authority. Being a health care sister and working with many men also made a difference. I never felt intimidated by the clergy. Neither did I ever have much conflict with them because I was usually superior to them in the administrative line. Other than that our paths seldom crossed.

I never went around with only bus fare in my purse. I did some other things younger members of the community might not have done, especially during years under final vows. I went to see the movie *The Nun's Story* in 1959. I asked my superior if I could go. She told me to ask the advice of my former novice mistress. I asked the mistress if she thought I should go. She did; I went. Later I thought the film should have been required viewing in all novitiates for men and women religious. It seemed to me to be a good example of distortion of the vow of obedience. I don't believe I ever heard of it being shown anywhere.

I applied the same methods to religious life as to professional life: learn all you can about your field, use the best techniques coupled with highest concentration, and you will achieve success. This has happened to me.

I have achieved the goals that I set out to achieve in my profession. I also feel I have progressed in the spiritual and religious life. To do this, just as in the professional field, I had to be ready to keep up with the new. I read widely in religious literature, engaged in much dialogue with others in religious life and functioned on committees, assemblies and chapters in my religious community.

Later I became Director of the School of Nursing, was appointed to the State Board of Nursing, served as chairperson of the Board for one year, acted as a consultant to a local college in setting up a degree program in nursing and generally functioned as a professional nurse-educator. I earned my master's degree in Nursing Education Administration in 1965.

During the fourth decade in my life came changes in my health and a lessening of my drive because I had achieved the professional goals I had set for myself; there also came the changes in religious life and the Church. I died a sort of death during those years. I came out a more gentle, less rigid, more compassionate human being. I think the suffering connected with what might be called a breakdown in tried and true rules in religious life, as well as in other circles, caused me to get down to essentials: faith in the Father's love and Jesus' commitment to me. Now things were more serene and I no longer felt the stress and strain of earlier years.

This is not to say that the social climate of the novitiate and to some degree, later community life, were not designed to produce a specific mind set. They were. Many of the same techniques used in the military, mental hospitals, and prisons were used in religious life to form one into an acceptable member. I was somewhat aware of this during the novitiate and speculated on these characteristics later in 1964 when I read Goffman's book *Asylums*. The ability to do this seemed to help me to stand back and observe my own behavior as changes occurred.

As a result I was able to undertake to change such behavior when the new social climate of religious life demanded such change. Though there were many hard times, I feel I was usually able to distinguish means from ends and was not so unnerved as some. Although I sympathize with her, I find it hard to understand the person who believes the novitiate or religious life ruined her or caused her to develop thought patterns and habits that made it impossible for her to deal with change. In the back of my mind is always the belief that these people really thought some or many of the *means* were really the *ends*.

Change became catastrophic. This new freedom, which was essentially a new way of being responsible for oneself, was very difficult for some to handle. It was as though all the structures which we had built up to serve as the scaffold on which to construct our building (community and religious life) were suddenly discarded. Some found that they had much more invested in the scaffold than in the building.

As a result, when the scaffold fell apart, they discovered very little remaining. Fortunately, this did not happen to me. I was able to make the distinction between the essential and the accidental, at first through intellectual conviction, then more completely and with more emotional strength during those uneasy years from 1965 to 1978. I was able to look beyond the rules, regulations, customs—the structure—and discovered the meaning behind them, developing new ways of expressing the same values.

One sign of the very real change in my values and behavior following Vatican II can be described by an incident that took place in Chicago in the late sixties. We had come from Union Station to attend Mass at the Old St. Mary's chapel before continuing on. We found that the time of Mass would allow us to eat and still have one hour to fast prior to receiving Holy Communion. However, when we arrived at the chapel we found Mass in progress and realized that if we were to allow the sixty minutes for the fast we would not be able to receive Communion. I quickly came to a decision to do what I thought Christ would want, and I went ahead and received. I remember feeling very free in doing what seemed to be the right thing even though technically we were not following a law of the Church.

This seems like such a minor item today, but it was not when we consider the legalistic society in which we were brought up in the community as well as in our childhood. It had now become necessary for me to try to discover what the mind of Christ would be in a given situation. There came to be fewer rules as such; fewer prescriptions of superiors; fewer concrete guidelines. Instead, it became necessary to consider a given situation and arrive at appropriate action more or less on one's own. Superiors were there to discuss the situation, but only rarely did they tell you what to do. Just as we had more latitude in deciding, so also did we come to realize that the outcome of our actions was heavier on our own shoulders.

I think all of us were forced to examine deeply our identity as religious persons and our understanding of structure and reasons for acting/reacting as we did. I went through stress with each new thing.

This usually occurred in three stages: At first I was resistive and considered those who changed early as somewhat frivolous and not sufficiently interested in the more important things. Later, I came to tolerate differences to some degree and I spent time working out a justifying rationale in my mind. Finally, I have come to the point where I take pride in the very existence of difference in our community, as long as a deeper unity remains. I feel this deeper unity in myself these past years, though it is not always easy to articulate.

Looking back now I can recognize in my experiences some of the stages one passes through in the dying process: anger, denial, bargaining, and then, acceptance.

I believe the emphasis on our early charism has helped me to see that our unity must rest on the mutual support we give one another as we all journey to the Father. We are truly called to be a faith community whose unity rests on our charism of unity and reconciliation and not on similar dress, work, or daily horarium.

But over the years this deeper unity was expressed through these externals. By means of them our values and understandings were passed on from older to younger sisters to preserve our traditions. Otherwise, our community would not have survived these many years.

The more leisurely society of fifty to one hundred years ago permitted time for learned behavior to be transmitted to a new generation through example given by the older members to the younger. Parents passed on values to their children. In a similar way customs, traditions and values were transmitted in community. However, with the beginning of the nuclear age, change in society began to occur so rapidly and in such radically different ways that parents no longer could call on experience to guide their children in many areas. Knowledge is said to be doubling each seven years now instead of in a generation.

With such rapid change it became difficult, or impossible, to measure the effect of change when decisions were made. Thirty years ago none of us really anticipated the problems of disposing of nuclear waste. The same thing happened in religious life. Two examples seem most relevant to me.

The first was the change in the habit. I am not sure we adequately thought through the changes in behavior that would accompany such a move. We thought of how the laity would view us; the inability to give an outward witness to those who did not know us; the extra cost of clothing. What was not always so clearly foreseen was the resulting change in self-concept. In effect, we were no longer on duty twenty-four hours a day. We could move more freely in places I doubt many of us would have frequented in the traditional habit. I thought of this when I crossed the picket line to attend the film *The Last Temptation of Christ.* In a very real sense we had a freedom to do and act in ways probably not possible in our community since its earliest years when a habit as such was not worn.

The second example is the ability to drive automobiles. This has produced a radical change in community life, work, and even spiritual development. I don't think this was ever anticipated. At first it seemed a convenience to be able to drive and no longer need to depend on lay people for transportation. Then gradually it became apparent that having increased mobility made it possible for one to work apart from community-sponsored institutions or to pray, to recreate away from the local community. It no longer was necessary to do things as a group. In addition the drivers tended to be younger people so the actual power flowing from mobility and a more subtle power of no longer being dependent on the group, passed from older, more senior sisters to younger sisters.

In past years privilege in one respect or another was somewhat dependent on rank. Younger sisters did more housework and deferred to their elders in matters of opinion, since the elders were presumed to be more experienced. Now younger sisters either live or work apart, or if they do live in a convent, are involved in so many diverse occupations outside the experience of most older sisters that age seems to have lost its venerated position. I don't think this is true, but it does seem that the younger are looking less today for intellectual or professional leadership from their elders than they are for wisdom to help them determine the meaning of things and for a deeper stability in spiritual matters to which they can cling.

A change in our lives that was particularly difficult for me to accept was the change in our work relationships. When I entered the community our work or service was seen as the secondary end of our congregation and was the means to attain the primary end which was the salvation of one's soul and the soul of one's neighbor. As a result, everything should be directed toward excellence in one's work. Community life became, for me, primarily a means to support my service. Almost all of us worked in community-sponsored institutions which we controlled and used for ends as we determined. In a very real sense we controlled the system in those days and were able to use our institutions to accomplish change in health care. We were able to influence to some extent the disposition of federal funds and local civic activities if we so chose and were professionally capable.

Everyone used the same outward expressions of prayer in 1956. We attended community-sponsored, preached retreats. Then change began.

Discussion-centered retreats came into vogue. This was in accord with the move in the community for participation. At other times we had liturgy preparation sessions. The point seemed to be to get sisters talking to each other about God and matters of faith. This was most difficult. I recall writing a remark for a senior sister and then nudging her at an appropriate time during the discussion so she could participate by making her comment!

The guided retreat, or directed retreat, became popular as change progressed. I made my first directed retreat in 1985. From that time on, I have made only one preached retreat (not my first choice) and usually feel no desire to make another. In 1978 I made a month-long contemplative retreat in Canada that was coordinated by lay people. This represented about as wide a departure from traditional thinking as one could get. Prior to 1960 too much contact with seculars was seen as a sure way to lose one's vocation. Now I found myself accepting spiritual direction from a group of lay persons.

At present I live with a group of sisters, most of whom have never made anything except a preached retreat. It seems they are still looking for someone (a priest?) to tell them what to think and do. Perhaps this is the wrong interpretation: they may have arrived at the place in spiritual growth where intellectual dissertations are no longer all that relevant. Could this be real holiness?

This whole matter of prayer forms has been a real problem in community. If six sisters live in a house, there are potentially six different methods of prayer. I am not sure that meaningful methods of prayer are always arrived at in local community. A great deal of give and take is necessary. Too many seem to think that what they don't understand cannot be accepted.

Some older sisters seem to think the younger sisters who like records, lighted candles, and spontaneous prayer are somewhat superficial in their approach. Those who favor a more open sharing of faith and prayer experience find it hard to understand those who are unable or unwilling to talk about or share such experience. I have always felt it most unfortunate that sisters in religious life so many years are not able to give more direct evidence to others of their experience of God. I have always believed more older sisters should offer this service to the community.

My perception is that the great majority seem unable to do so. We need wisdom in our community, a relish for the things of God. The older can no longer offer increased knowledge or experience to the young. They, we, must concentrate on wisdom or run the risk of being taken less than seriously by younger sisters.

But during the past year I have become one of these older sisters; I am now sixty-five years of age. Can I offer wisdom to those younger? It is difficult to know. Most of the real insights I have had during the past years are really not easy to describe. I know what it means that all things are held in being by God, yet God is not limited by all things; I know that all people are the resurrected Jesus. How does one explain these concepts when they are learned not through intellect but, through a special grace. I know the place and time when I received this grace. The practical outcome of all this is that I can share any kind of prayer or no kind. It is enough for me to believe that the people with whom I live are prayerful.

I still read widely the *National Catholic Reporter* to know what the "radical fringe" is thinking; *America* for middle of the road thinking and opinions; the diocese newspaper, especially the editorials, to find out what I don't agree with. I believe films can still prompt much reflective thinking. Some years ago I attended *The Name of the Rose*. As I recall, the setting was a monastery in the fourteenth century. A meeting between representatives of the Vatican and an order of religious men was being held. I remember one question had to do with the extent to which all knowledge of God had been revealed by that time. Another question was, "Did Jesus laugh?" Apparently some theologians thought it a heresy to believe so. I thought the film should have been shown at a general session of the U.S. bishops who were meeting at the time in Washington, D.C.!

I really don't have any problems with the leadership of the Church, but neither do I take verbatim some of the positions held by some church leaders on questions of human sexuality and prolongation of life of the terminally ill. I do not, however, support abortion or euthanasia. I believe strongly in the Eucharistic liturgy and do not understand those who refuse to go to Mass if celebrated by a man. The humanity of Jesus is found in the Eucharist in a special manner not duplicated elsewhere. I am not ready to forego any means of meeting and knowing the Lord, so I go to daily Mass. I do, however, try to be supportive of non-Eucharistic liturgies when held at community gatherings.

Increasingly, during the latter part of the last decade, I became aware that things were changing in a much more significant way than during the twenty years following Vatican II. If some mistakenly believed the scaffold to be the building, others now realize that the absence of a scaffold today does not indicate freedom from constraints but rather a lack of vision about the shape of the building. One can hardly erect a satisfactory scaffold for a building not clearly envisioned.

I see myself during the last few years increasingly distressed because of the difficulty of articulating a focus in my congregation. Something I call the "Ferris Wheel Syndrome" takes place when we have a community meeting to discuss goals and the future: we have a wonderful ride, a beautiful view, but when all is said and done we are still at the same place when we get off as we were when the ride began! This is not to say we have not tried to move forward with defining a building for the twenty-first century. Nor is this to suggest a return to the methods used in the past to produce a closed society, but rather to highlight the need for rituals that can be used to pass on new understandings and traditions for the future. The real problem is the inability to precisely label these understandings, this focus, as we were able to do in the past.

In the 70's I worked in a community agency for the aging and as an assistant hospital administrator at one of our own institutions. Early in the 80's I became a licensed nursing home administrator and spent seven years as administrator of our sisters' retirement home. I also did general institutional administration for a Congregation on the West Coast for one year.

I am now employed as a part-time nurse in long-term care at a local hospital sponsored by a community of men. There is no doubt what these religious are about: care of the sick, elderly, and those most likely to need special consideration: AIDS victims. Sometimes I seem to resonate with their philosophy more than I do with that of my own congregation. I think this is because it is so similar to our own charism during the last 150 years!

During the last five years my community has developed a mission statement that identifies our charism as loving unity reflected in all our activities. To the extent that we encourage such unity, our work becomes ministry. Given the widespread alienation and extreme individualism in our society, this is an appropriate charism. It is just so difficult to pin down as the focus of my community when it seems appropriate for all Christians. However, I know when my work becomes ministry; I am not nearly so sure how or if I can pass the charism on to others. In any event I think of myself these days as a *religious woman* rather than a *woman religious*.

A significant change that is taking place in my community is the gradual trend toward moving out of traditional convents to live in apartments. Some of this is the result of smaller numbers and fewer sisters involved in institutional ministry such as health care in hospitals or teaching in parish schools. Some desire to live with persons who share the same intellectual bent, prayer style, recreational interests. This is a departure from the community I entered. I still live in a convent with a group of sisters with whom I share support and love. This is the same convent where I spent my novitiate. Commonality of interests is not basic to our sisterly relationship. I don't think I am convinced my life style is necessarily better than others; I have lived in apartments and find them more confining than my present home. It remains to be seen what this trend will eventually produce.

Another area where change is occurring is in our understanding of leadership. I am not sure how many of my sisters still believe in the charism of the superior: the grace of office. We now have team leadership. There seems to be a reluctance to admit to having ideas or trying to influence the community to provide leadership in the commonly understood meaning of the term. Maybe they, the superiors, are in the same boat I am in: unable to articulate clearly the focus of our community. I recall at a Chapter some years ago someone describing the leadership as "A group of nomads wondering around the desert looking for a watering hole."

In relation to the vow of poverty, I find even greater changes and differences in understanding as well as reluctance to discuss basic issues. Some see incongruity between "preferential option for the poor" and ignorance of basic economic issues. Whether we like it or not we live in a capitalistic society. It becomes difficult to be countercultural if we are not sure what it is we are counter to. In regard to my own personal life , I have never worried about money since I entered the community thirty-five years ago. I know I am more apt to see the financial implications of decisions because of having been in administration so many years. I think about these things, but I do not worry.

I don't have the answers! However, I think I do see some of the questions. Persons much more able than I have discussed the questions in books such as Mary Jo Leddy's *Reweaving Religious Life* and Patricia Wittberg's *Creating a Future for Religious Life*. Perhaps, given another ten years to live through the present uneasy climate in religious life, I will be better able to analyze the changes that are occurring now in focus of ministry, life style, and living of the vows. I realize we cannot turn back, so I go forward with hope.

Since I began with an expression of the vows suitable to the 50's, I will close with my newer understanding of them for the 90's and the twenty-first century:

Celibacy: a profound sense of sisterliness. Obedience: acceptance of responsibility for one's own actions and the actions of the community. Poverty: acceptance of the burdens of ministering in a global economic society.

Finally, a prayer for myself and for a successful meeting of my sisters in religion during the near future to work on articulating our vision.

> *O Life-giving Spirit, you inspired countless sisters before us to move to new places and assume new roles. Plant deep within us wisdom to recognize our call, courage to move beyond our fears. Nurture in us the conviction that we can bring to birth the life you have given us. We make this prayer in trust, because you dwell among us. Amen.*

A Remembrance
Loretta Cosgrove
Sister of Notre Dame de Namur

Deceased

This memory portrait has been lovingly written by Isabell Beyer, whose life was blessed by many years of friendship with Sister Loretta. Isabell's sketch is augmented by the community memorial at the time of her death. Sister Loretta's life was one of kindness and great, genuine love. We are proud to share this story with our readers.

Loretta Cosgrove

In Remembrance of
Sister Loretta Cosgrove

by Isabell Beyer

I became acquainted with Sister Loretta when she came to work at my parish, St. Ferdinand Church, with the Ministry of Care program, bringing Communion to the sick and home-bound, and to others who were hospitalized.

Sister Loretta touched the lives of so many people through the years she ministered to them here from 1979 to 1987. One of her shut-ins was my dear husband. Little did I realize at that time that our relationship would culminate into a loving and caring friendship. Sister Loretta ministered to my husband for the five years of his illness, bringing him communion and praying with us.

Sister Loretta was a woman of rare qualities. She was a woman of prayer, courage, deep faith; she was a woman who made a difference wherever she went. She was an example of love and kindness to others. Her love and concern for other people were outstanding examples of Christian charity. She taught me to find love and good in all people. Sister Loretta and I grew together in love and faith. She was not only a very special friend, but she also became a part of my family.

At the time of my husband's death on November 5, 1981, Sister Loretta was a great comfort to me and my family. She prayed with us, gave us love and courage, opened her heart and love to all of us in our sorrow. She was a gentle woman of deep faith. She was my rock of support. She lifted me up when I was down; she was always there for me.

We prayed together on the phone, we prayed together at the chapel at Notre Dame Convent. We became the very best of friends. We traveled and dined together, we participated in special Masses and various church and community functions.

I recall being in the car with Sister Loretta many times. We would always begin our journey, even one of short distance, with a prayer to the Blessed Virgin Mary and with intercessions for a safe trip. She would pray and bless all the people we saw walking as we traveled. Her love and concern was always for other people.

Sister Loretta and I shared many special occasions. I recall in 1980 that Sister Loretta celebrated her golden jubilee as a Sister of Notre Dame . St. Ferdinand priests, parishioners and community Sisters of Notre Dame honored Sister Loretta at a special Mass with a reception following.

I also recall another special event given by my children. It was the celebration of my special birthday and also that of Sister Loretta. Our birthdays were one week apart in July. It was a lovely garden party, with the fragrance of flowers surrounding us, amid the laughter of love of our beautiful family, friends and neighbors. This day I will always remember in gratitude and praise.

Sister Loretta loved to sing; she would always call me on my birthday and sing "Happy Birthday" to me. She enjoyed people, loved children, and was especially fond of my grandchildren. She always found time for leisurely visits with my daughter, who is a Notre Dame alumna, and my son with his golden retriever.

Sister Loretta was unique; her countenance was one of beauty and radiance, always with a smile on her face. She was witty, had a great sense of humor and was a joy to be with. She often spoke of her early years growing up on the farmland of Illinois. One of her treasured memories was of her brother John who was a Jesuit missionary in India.

Sister Loretta had a gift for generating warm and lasting friendship, and keeping in touch through the years.

After ministering for eleven years to the shut-ins of the St. Ferdinand community, Sister Loretta received a notice that she was transferred to the motherhouse in Reading, Ohio.

Once again Sister Loretta was honored by a special Mass, with a reception following. The large attendance of parishioners, community sisters of Notre Dame, parish priests and former priests, some of whom came from a distance, was overwhelming.

It was a sad farewell for me. I knew my life would be different without her, and, needless to say, I would miss her very much.

We kept in touch by correspondence and on the phone. Even from Cincinnati we would pray together on that phone. Sister Loretta brightened the lives of ill and aging sisters. She took over the Apostolate of St. Julie; she would answer prayer requests by the phone or by mail, and thanked people for their letters of gratitude for favors received through the intercession of St. Julie.

I recall one of the letters she wrote me saying that she was grateful to God. One day after the death of my brother I was down and feeling sad. Suddenly the phone rang and it was Sister Loretta calling from Cincinnati. We prayed together, and once again she lifted me in faith with her love and kindness. She was always there for me.

Sister Loretta came back to Chicago for brief weekend visits. We were so happy to spend time together. We continued to keep in touch. In the latter part of July I received a call from her, thanking me for the cards, letters and gifts she had received; she had just celebrated her seventy-ninth birthday. She was happy, she said, and grateful for the goodness of God.

Again we prayed, thanking God for our loving friendship, but little did we know that it would be our last conversation. A few days later I was notified that Sister Loretta suffered a brain aneurysm. Needless to say, I was deeply saddened; my prayers and concerns were all for her, but it was God's will to take her to a happy dwelling place.

Sister Loretta passed away on August 19, 1991. For her, life closed quickly and unexpectedly. We shall remember her as we saw her last, smiling and greeting us at all hours of the day as she passed.

I pray that some day, if it is God's will, that I will be inspired to serve my family and my community with the same love and concern and deep faith that Sister Loretta did while ministering to the community at St. Ferdinand.

Sister Loretta will be remembered for her gift of reaching out to others. As a typical mark of her generosity, she had donated her body to medical research so that others could have a better life. She said, in a letter addressed to her community and friends:

> Why did I give my body to science? It was not a light decision, but I feel a just one. If the only part of me to be used is my skin for "burn victims" whose recovery will help them to glorify God, then I'm satisfied. Remember I'm right here but you can't see me. I love each of you. May God heal you of any hurt

I have caused. Please continue living joyfully for Him and singing Alleluia!

Sister Loretta Cosgrove, September 1, 1989

A memorial Mass was said for her at Mount Notre Dame and also at St. Ferdinand Church. The following is taken from a memorial delivered by Sister Mary Evelyn Jegen at St. Julie Chapel:

My first memories of Sister Loretta Cosgrove, then Sister Loyola of the Sacred Heart, go back to 1948. She was a young teacher then, here in Reading. Our meetings were in the kitchen, loading our respective carts from the food warmers, hers for the professed refectory, ours for the novitiate. Those were the days of Sister Ann Loretta in the kitchen, Sister Monica Louise in the laundry, Sister Rose Veronica in the sacristy, Sister Louise Patricia in charge of bedding, butter and candy, and Sisters Irene Marie and Emma in the clothes rooms. These were the sisters we novices talked to; with Sister Loyola of the Sacred Heart it was a different kind of communication that did not, happily, depend on words (though if truth were told, a few words were sometimes used!). Somehow, we knew from her lively eyes her deep interest in the novices. She gave me an impression that lasts to this day, of the joy of being an SND and a teacher.

It was many years later that Loretta and I lived together for more than ten years at Notre Dame High School, Chicago. How many evenings after supper I saw her in a tiny telephone booth on the second floor, making phone calls to her dear shut-ins, arranging to bring them Holy Communion the following day. Her ministry to the sick and elderly of St. Ferdinand Parish was marked by extraordinary kindness and sensitivity to each individual.

I was in Chicago when I heard that Loretta was dying. I went to tell a Jesuit friend, Father Bob Harvanek, who had been John's provincial, and who had also been in community with John when he died. Father Harvanek told me that he had met Loretta only a few times, but that he remembered her as a very lovely and gracious Sister. Loretta was exactly that, with a love and graciousness that were the fruits of the Holy Spirit, to whom she had a very special devotion. St. Paul enumerates those fruits for us, in his Letter to the Galatians. They read like a very careful description of Loretta: love, joy, peace, patience, kindness, goodness, trustfulness, gentleness, and self-control.

Loretta had a wonderful capacity for human relationships radiant with faith. She shared with all she met simply by her presence, her deep personal love of Our Lord, her devotion to his Sacred Heart, and to His and the Father's Holy Spirit. I think that is why I liked to be around Loretta, and why my family, who came to know Loretta, liked to be around her, too. She made faith and love visible and tangible. Many evenings we danced together in chapel, to the Pachelbel Canon. It was not really a dance, by contemporary standards, but a few simple steps from an 18th century French folk dance, one that St. Julie might have known and actually stepped to, before she became crippled. We had the chapel to ourselves, content to be like two children playing before the Lord.

Loretta dear, are you not dancing for joy now, united in a more immediate and intimate way with the God with whom you were and are so deeply in love?

How good it is for you to be with your dear parents and other members of your family, and especially with that one who held such a special place in your affection, John, the Jesuit missionary in India. His missionary vocation rubbed off on you, and through you, on how many others? How many of the young people you taught through forty-two years caught something of the fire of the Gospel through you? Discovering the answer to this question may well be one of the particular joys of heaven for you.

How happy we are tonight, Loretta, to know you as a member of our family, for some, as the Cosgrove family, and for all of us as the Notre Dame family. We will miss you in a hundred very particular ways, but even through our tears we rejoice with you. You have not even left us your body for burial. We know, Loretta, that for you, this gift of your body was one more opportunity to express your love.

Sister Loretta came into my life at a time when I thought I could not go on living any more.

My husband's long, intense illness of five years was getting me down; my strength and my patience were running out. Then came Sister Loretta. God must have known how much I needed her. She changed my life with her love and concern for me.

I am a stronger person now. I am closer to God in love and faith. I thank God for bringing her into my life. She made a difference.

God bless you, Sister Loretta. Pray for us as we pray for you.

Publisher's Note:

With the publication of *Whatever Happened to the Good Sisters?*, Whales' Tale Press has begun a series of healing books called *Finding Our Voice*. Using the model of the Big Book of Alcohol Anonymous, we are inviting writers, published and unpublished, skilled and unskilled, to find their voice and tell their story, thus continuing the delicate process of healing for both the writer and the reader. While you may not have experienced these issues directly, if someone you love has been affected, you have also been affected. And your story is important, too. We need to add that these stories, while beginning in pain, are stories of the *victory* of the *human spirit* over *secrecy, shame* and *misunderstanding*.

We are asking for manuscripts for the following topics:

- Recovery from Codependency/Adult Children issues
- Recovery from Depression (bipolar/unipolar) stories
- Recovery from Eating Diseases (bulimia, anorexia, over-eating) stories
- Recovery from Divorce (adults, children) stories
- Recovery from Alcoholism, Drug Addiction stories
- Recovery from Family/Friend Suicide stories
- Recovery from Sexual Abuse stories
- Priest (ex and now) stories
- Gay/Lesbian (children, parents, mates, etc.) stories

To receive general guidelines for submission of a manuscript, please send a self-addressed, stamped envelope to:

Whales' Tale Press • 160 Wildwood • Lake Forest, IL 60045
Attention: Joan Hall

If you have any other ideas for this series, please share them with us.

New from Whales' Tale

The Good Sisters

Whales' Tale Press is proud to announce the first *paperback* publication of the 1983 novel, *The Good Sisters* by Kathleen W. FitzGerald, Ph.D.

If you enjoyed *Whatever Happened to the Good Sisters?*, you will not want to miss reading the book that came before!

Publication Date: November 15, 1992; $12.95 USA, $14.95 Canada

THE GOOD SISTERS

A Novel

KATHLEEN W. FITZGERALD, PH.D.

"Kathleen FitzGerald has spoken the words I have never been able to form. She has released the angst in my heart. I want my family, I want my friends to read this. I don't have to be alone anymore."
　　　　　　　　　　　　—Joan Ebbitt, Former Nun

"The nuns of two decades ago move through the pages of this semi-tough, bittersweet novel most authentically."　　　　— *Publishers Weekly*

"*THE GOOD SISTERS* is full of humor and surprises . . . From the first pages I had absolute confidence in the author — in the accuracy of her observations, the honesty of her feelings, and her ability to find the right words for both."　　　— Bette Howland, author of *BLUE IN CHICAGO*

"FitzGerald spent 13 years at a convent, and there's a roistering authenticity here."　　　　　　　　　— *The Kirkus Reviews*

"*THE GOOD SISTERS* authentically portrays convent life as I lived it for twenty years before the Renewal."
　　　　　　　　　— Sister Margaret Ellen Traxler, S.S.N.D.
　　　　　　　Founder of the National Coalition of American Nuns

Sacred Trust:

Adoption Stories

Publication Date: January 24, 1993; $14.95 USA, $16.95 Canada

Shamed No More:

A New Look at Alcoholism

by Kathleen W. FitzGerald, Ph.D.

Publication Date: December 10, 1992; $14.95 USA, $16.95 Canada

Formerly published as *Alcoholism: The Genetic Inheritance* (Doubleday, 1988). 17,000 hard cover books sold.

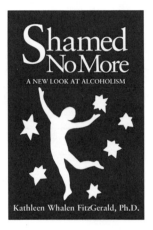

"For over thirty years the AMA has recognized alcoholism as a *disease* with identifiable and progressive symptoms that, if untreated, lead to mental damage, physical incapacity, and early death. Yet we still do not treat alcoholism as a disease, but as a sin, a social stigma, a moral aberration."

FitzGerald traces the roots of this disease to the alcoholic's unique and unusual body chemistry, laying to rest arguments for weakness of will or "alcoholic personality." *Jellinek's disease* is used as a synonym for alcoholism.

This sound and sensitive book addresses the very real pain that those who love an alcoholic must bear.

With compassion and honesty, the author speaks to these other victims — the family and friends — and gives voice to its silent victims — the children. Moving stories illustrate the universal suffering that everyone whose life is touched by alcoholism knows so well, inviting them out of isolation into their own recovery.

Rarely does a book on alcoholism focus its attention on the family and friends of an alcoholic; this one does, and it does so with depth and understanding. It translates the cold, scientific pathology of alcoholism into meaningful human terms.

No matter how alcoholism has touched your life, this is the one source book that offers you complete understanding, sound medical facts, and, most important, realistic help.

This revised paperback edition includes new chapters on Codependency, ACOA issues and other addictions.

Order Form

TITLE	PRICE	QTY	TOTAL
The Good Sisters (Novel)	$12.95		
Whatever Happened to the Good Sisters?	$14.95		
Shamed No More: A New Look at Alcoholism	$14.95		
Sacred Trust: Adoption Stories	$14.95		

Subtotal _____

$3.00 shipping and handling _____

Illinois residents add 6.5% sales tax _____

TOTAL _____

Ship To:

_____
Name

_____
Street Address

_____
City/State/Zip

_____
Phone

PHONE ORDERS:
(708) 295-2350

Or Call our **24-HOUR ORDER TOLL FREE NUMBER**
1-800-428-9507
(Toll-Free number is for orders only)
When ordering by phone please specify *Good Sisters* as the novel.

FAX ORDERS ARE WELCOME
(708) 295-2349

Payment: ____Check /Money Order in the amount of _____
____Visa ____Master Card

Card #_____Exp. Date_____

Signature_____

Clip and mail this form to:
Whales' Tale Press • 160 Wildwood • Lake Forest, Illinois 60045